THEORETICAL DIMENSIONS OF EDUCATIONAL ADMINISTRATION

Theoretical Dimensions
of
Educational
Administration

WILLIAM G. MONAHAN

West Virginia University

MACMILLAN PUBLISHING CO., INC.

NEW YORK

COPYRIGHT © 1975, WILLIAM G. MONAHAN

PRINTED IN THE UNITED STATES OF AMERICA

MACMILLAN PUBLISHING CO., INC.
866 Third Avenue, New York, New York 10022
COLLIER-MACMILLAN CANADA, LTD.

Library of Congress Cataloging in Publication Data

Monahan, William G
    Theoretical dimensions of educational administration.

    Includes bibliographical references and index.
    1. School management and organization.   I. Title.
LB2805.M635   371.2   74-11749
ISBN 0-02-381940-5

Printing: 2 3 4 5 6 7 8   Year: 6 7 8 9 0

77-2160

I am particularly grateful to R. Jean Hills, whose three papers represent a very substantial contribution to this book; to James Anderson of Purdue University, Thomas Wiggins of the University of Oklahoma, and Fred Ignatovich of Michigan State University, who also prepared papers especially for this volume; and to my co-authors in another venture, Bill Lane and Ron Corwin, for permission to include a revision of a chapter previously appearing in *Foundations of Educational Administration: A Behavioral Analysis,* also with Macmillan.

I am especially grateful to Andrew Halpin for his paper on "Change: The Mythology," and to *Theory Into Practice* for permission to include it. It is a most appropriate way of ending a book on theoretical dimensions of educational administration.

Finally, I am indebted to Ms. Donna Moore, who struggled through so much of my penmanship and entirely obscure transpositions, which were a result of a typing machine that occasionally operated much slower than I could tolerate.

W. G. M.

CONTENTS

PART III
DEVELOPMENTAL RATIONALISM

PART IV
EDUCATIONAL ADMINISTRATION,
BEHAVIORAL SCIENCE, AND CHANGE:
AN INTROSPECTION

I

OVERVIEW

THERE is a distinction between "administration" and "management." Perhaps the distinction is no longer very clear nor very important; but administration is, if nothing else, much older than management since by definition administration refers more appropriately to the conduct of public rather than private activities. Management derives from the rise of corporate bureaucracy and as a "set" of activities, its genesis is more directly traceable to the primacy of economics and secondarily to social process and to cultural phenomena. Administration, on the other hand, is more historically associated with the "public business" and its primacy is rooted more in the sociocultural fabric of peoples and secondarily in economics.

As a general statement this does not suggest that administration has not been used for the most bizarre kinds of inhuman behaviors nor does it suggest that administration has not been obsessed at one time and another with economic power and plain ordinary—or even on not a few occasions, extraordinary—greed. Nor does the general statement imply that management has not been intimately concerned with its social responsibilities and with energetic attempts to humanize private enterprise. Moreover, as suggested, the two "sets" of activities have long ago recognized a common attachment and a common function—the actualization and the operationalization of authority within complex organizational systems for the pursuit of particular objectives. In large measure, even the goals themselves are more similar with the passage of time, yet a fundamental difference still remains at the goal level; management is primarily oriented to the use of capital to accumulate capital whereas administration is oriented to the use of capital to meet socially mandated needs. One may argue ad nauseum about the nature of this difference, but it is there and because it is there, it has significant implications for administration in capitalistic societies. Inevitably administration in such systems will be influenced by the practices of management moreso than the practices of management will be influenced by administration.

THE RATIONALE OF THE BOOK

All of the foregoing is by the way of introducing the rationale for this book, since much of the material included is as applicable to administration as it is to management. When one deals with relatively abstract and analytical treatment of organizational phenomena, the content should

1

certainly be of general applicability. It is largely the responsibility of the instructor to draw the unique applicable differences. And yet, this book is concerned mainly with educational administration. Therefore, I have tried to use that frame of reference throughout and have emphasized the institution of education and of educational organizations in introducing the material and in commenting upon it. In the majority of cases, that frame of reference is built into the major content itself.

It is important for the reader to understand the overall design of this text, for hopefully that understanding will aid in its use. This book is not designed for the sophisticated behavioral scientist-turned-professor of educational administration. Some of that audience will find that there are gaps in the content and that certain particularly provocative material is not to be found in the way they might prefer. There is not very much of what Merton calls "middle-range theory" in this book. Some will also say that some of the material is elementary; much of it is. Moreover, there is little empirical work included; there are no reviews of the literature dealing with micronistic interests simply because that material is more accessible in journals, graduate reading lists, and in other sources.

The book is designed for the beginning graduate student who, in educational administration, very naturally brings to the study of this area limited previous academic experience with the intimate interaction of social system, culture, and personality. It follows a very successful course that I taught for seven years at the University of Iowa, and the material included must surely be supplemented by assigned reading in other related areas.

What was found in teaching about the conceptualization of administrative behavior and activity was, among other factors, that students needed to understand the philosophical and historical antecedents of educational administration. In a sense, this is a part of what Merton referred to by "general orientations to substantive material."[1]

The environment that spawned the bulk of the political, social, and economic conditions of contemporary life was that of the French and industrial revolutions. Included early in this book is Robert Nisbet's excellent treatment of that period. Similarly, the rise of a rather new conceptualization of *authority*—with which we are still dealing—is also traceable to that period in human history that saw the passing of medieval community and the progressive emergence of the modern state. Again, Nisbet provides us with the best description of the particular variables, contentions, and philosophical, as well as sociological, events that altogether provide operational definition of that pervasive concept.

In my own general introductory article, I attempt to provide a broad statement of a variety of antecedents and events that give perspective

[1] Robert Merton, *Social Theory and Social Structure* (New York: The Free Press, 1957), p. 87.

to the study of administration and, hopefully, marks the way for much of the material that follows. Since theory must involve theoretical structure, Part I also includes a statement about the nature of theory and about the methodology of science with reference to it. In the latter work, R. Jean Hills demonstrates that a vocabulary and grammatical structure are necessary to the development of both theory and science. If theory is generally concerned with ways of making sense of the world, then science is concerned with rigorously defining and describing the relevant ways we go about experiencing it. Kaplan has observed that, "To engage in theorizing means not just to learn by experience but to take thought about what is there to be learned."[2]

The general concern in Part II is with the pervading aspects of organizational life and of educational administration in particular. The concepts of authority, power, influence, social system, alienation, and cultural structure constitute the major emphases. There is substantial treatment of Parsons' "model" as applied to educational organizations and treatment of a major problem confronting all types of organizations—that of integrating the individual and the organization. These are all prime issues in the study of the administration of educational systems.

Part III is a brief treatment of aspects of what I have called "developmental theory." It is generally concerned with a discussion of systematic approaches to the solution of particular problems. The article by Guba treats this issue both conceptually and methodologically, whereas the Ignatovich article takes a particular methodological interest—that of alternative futures—and presents an unusual approach. Finally, in my own article in that section, I have attempted to raise some issues with reference to the utilization of quantitative techniques in administrative decision-making to point out that in such systems, wherein cultural patterns are never far removed, the problem of values is more immediate than in organizations that operate somewhat more removed from sentiment and tradition.

Part IV is somewhat introspective. In a field in which anything resembling rigorous theoretical interest is of recent origin, dating back little more than fifteen years, it is not only appropriate but essential to engage in some "navel contemplation." It should be remembered that among those who claimed particular identification with the field of educational administration, Elwood Cubberly was surely among the first, and he received his doctorate from Teachers College, Columbia University in 1905. The "academic" field is, itself, thus rather youthful, encompassing a single lifetime. About three thousand persons, who are reasonably identifiable, are at present teaching educational administration in American colleges and universities. The field has grown much in seventy years.

---

[2] Abraham Kaplan, *The Conduct of Inquiry* (San Francisco: Chandler Publishing Co., 1964), p. 295.

THE THEORY MOVEMENT

The so-called "theory-movement" as Roald Campbell referred to it, originated in work associated with the National Conference of Professors of Educational Administration (NCPEA), which counts at least as many members from nondoctoral-granting institutions as it does from those that grant that degree. The facts seem plain, however, that the "movement" centered in several major institutions with a strong research tradition and an already existing relationship with behavioral science faculty in other units of such institutions. To some extent, as well, these efforts were additionally motivated by the now defunct Kellogg-funded CPEA (Cooperative Programs in Educational Administration). The CPEA programs, situated in eight different universities, primarily directed their attention and research to truly practical problems ranging from the inadequacy of teacher competence brought about by the World War II years, to the reorganization of school districts. Yet, that program brought together a variety of people with different kinds of expertise and from different disciplines, and in the process spawned an interest in more rigorous analysis of, and methodologies concerned with, administrative activity.

Not long after the NCPEA became interested in more analytical treatment of educational administrative phenomena, the University Council for Educational Administration (UCEA) came into being. And the UCEA, especially in its early years, nurtured the "theory movement" and encouraged professors in its member institutions to deal more conceptually and exploratively with all manner of phenomena related to administration.

Yet with all that promise, the movement was perceived somehow to have slowed; especially, I think it seemed to slow with reference to the effect that it had upon the broad pattern of practice in administration, and there is some empirical basis for concluding that it may have slowed as well within the academic environment. Andrew Halpin, one of the early "mainstays" who "came over" from the behavioral sciences, has stated that the whole movement sort of fizzled out. I remember receiving a mimeographed paper from Halpin sometime in 1967 or 1968 in which he most eloquently talked about this "fizzling out" business.[3] I disagree, as is presently shown.[*] Halpin felt as though the great promise of those exciting years in the late 1950's and the early 1960's had fallen like stones in a mill pond. R. Jean Hills, who includes several articles in this work, also examined aspects of this issue in the mid-1960's by raising questions as to whether the emphasis on theory (and, as must be assumed thereby,

[3] See e.g., Andrew Halpin, "Administrative Theory: The Fumbled Torch," in *Issues in American Education,* ed. by Arthur M. Kroll (New York: Oxford University Press, 1970), pp. 156–183.
[*] These issues are further discussed in my introduction to Part IV of this volume—"Educational Administration and Social Science: One More Time."

on research) was really as widespread as some of those of us who were somewhat carried away by all of it were leading ourselves to believe. Although Hills dealt with a relatively small sample, his findings were somewhat melancholy—to wit, that not much was really happening as a result. The emphasis on research was more "myth than reality" and although there was much interest in theory, there wasn't much happening other than in a few places. But Hills said something else that intrigued me; he concluded that perhaps an important reason was the lack of familiarity with the literature about theory.[4] Interestingly, much of that "literature" was not in the general pattern of educational administration. The bulk of it was in the sociology of organizations and the social-psychology of group phenomena. Hills's title for his paper in EAQ belied the empirical findings of his own small study—apparently the field wasn't *nearly* so much in transition as a relatively small coterie of theory aficionados had led themselves to believe.

As with any emerging area within a field there was nevertheless much being written that had a theoretical flavor. A good deal of the work appearing in the new journal *Educational Administration Quarterly,* although not always or even very often *specifically* theoretical by title was, all the same, within the broad norm of "theoretical stuff." The audience for much of this was relatively small; (EAQ never has numbered more than one thousand six hundred among its subscribers). With a few notable exceptions, the bulk of really interested theory-oriented professors filled a singularly small meeting room at a Chicago lakefront hotel in 1961 at a career development seminar hosted by the University of Chicago and jointly sponsored by UCEA. I and a colleague at the University of Oklahoma drove most of the night through recurring spring thunderstorms just to get there. We thought we were in the vanguard of "the new movement." Perhaps we may have been little more than the proverbial "interest group." Even today within the family of institutions that number themselves among the fifty-nine UCEA member universities, there are still interesting contentions between those who favor a highly pragmatic approach to the preparation of administrators and those who believe that theoretical content has something to offer. A recent and pivotal study of professors of educational administration by Campbell and Newell suggests that there is still a fairly proportional three-way split among professors. Those who have a bent toward research and theory; those who favor providing prospective administrators with "real world" skills; and those who lean toward field-oriented activities, i.e., professors who are "out there" working to help administrators solve problems. The numbers of such "types" in any one of these categories are difficult to determine since the factor analytic procedure used apparently dealt with item variables (R-technique) rather than with

---

4 See R. Jean Hills, "Educational Administration: A Field in Transition," *Educational Administration Quarterly,* 1 (Winter 1965), 58–66.

persons per se (Q-technique). But, interestingly, about two-fifths of the almost two thousand participants in the study did not fit any of these three factors. Rigorous analysis of the factor analytic data suggested to the researchers that these almost eight hundred professors were either loaded on at least two of the identifiable factors ("transactionals") or were "indifferent" to any of the major orientations that were postulated.[5]

This is unquestionably a landmark study in the analysis of the teacher of educational administration. Interestingly, its findings are, at first reading, not particularly surprising for in total the study tends to support some of the earlier work of Hills that was based on a much less rigorous and systematic sample, to wit: that among the broad category of persons engaged in the preparation of educational administrators, the number of those generally concerned with theoretical orientations is smaller than might have been assumed.[5a]

But this work also lends support to some exploratory investigation that I pursued while at the University of Iowa. The results of this investigation are more optimistic about theory. I, like all UCEA member university's "plenary-session-representatives" received periodically a packet of duplicated materials describing the upcoming doctoral graduates of those institutions who had expressed interest in professorial appointments. A content analysis of that "data" revealed that in more than 85 *per cent* of the cases, the primary interest (first and second "Role" choices) for teaching and research was in "theory" or in some closely

---

[5] R. F. Campbell and L. J. Newell, *A Study of Professors of Educational Administration* (Problems and Prospects of an Applied Academic Field) (Columbus, Ohio: University Council for Educational Administration, 1973). See especially, Chap. 5, "What Are the Role Orientations of the Professors?" pp. 93–112.

[5a] Concern with "theory" was a small aspect of the Campbell and Newell study, which was a very extensive analysis. I will refer to "UCEA" and to "non-UCEA" institutions several times simply because the very important study by Campbell and Newell—and for excellent reasons—categorized institutions in that fashion. It should be explicitly stated that in the more than fifteen years that I have been associated with institutions affiliated with UCEA, I have never felt, nor perceived others I knew to feel, that these were "elitist" institutions or that there was any lack of recognition that a far greater number of other institutions were not only also in the "business" of preparing educational administrators but were doing it quite well. At the same time, there is absolutely no question that the stimulation, the professional relationships, the opportunities for dialogue, and the analytical environment that UCEA was able to generate or reinforce has had immeasurable impact upon the entire field of academic educational administration. Whether UCEA shall continue to exert that vital force is a moot question, I suppose; but in any case, its contribution has been notable and all institutions, members and nonmembers, have benefited from UCEA's thrusts. And although the "theory movement"—as Roald Campbell labeled it—was truly an outgrowth of the educational administration profession itself rather than of any single organization within it, UCEA nurtured it through its affiliate institutions and the career development seminars it jointly sponsored. Hopefully, this book will crystallize it a bit.

related area. Now clearly, this analysis was in the style of what came to be known to my students at Iowa as "quick-and-dirty," which simply means that it was not concerned with the *testing* of hypotheses as much as with the kind of exploratory activity aimed at satisfying inquiry and curiosity. The rigor notwithstanding, it became reasonably suspect that the great majority of those prospective Ph.D.'s who took the trouble to complete the UCEA forms were very interested in what I have felicitously referred to as "theoretical stuff."

The Campbell and Newell study, which categorized respondents in terms of UCEA and non-UCEA institutions, clearly reflects that interest and does it in a much more disciplined and systematic way. Those authors also deal with some of the reasons for it; the greater likelihood of interdisciplinary preparation, a greater emphasis on systematic research orientations, and perhaps most important, a high likelihood that professors in such institutions are engaged full-time in educational administration.

Consequently, even in academic educational administration there is reason to recognize the truth that times are changing. In 1965, when I first offered a course within the educational administration curriculum at Iowa in "Theories in Administration," a random selection of major university catalogues indicated that less than ten per cent of these schools included such a course (or an equivalent) in their listings; in 1972, a replication of that analysis, and of the same institutions, indicated that *all* of them offered such a course or its equivalent. Recognizing the incredible difficulty of getting a new course approved in major universities there is no way of knowing how many additional institutions are offering such work under the proverbial cover of darkness and the shade of the academic trees.

Moreover, in the Campbell and Newell study, it was found that theory courses were taught by 176 professors in their sample at least three times in the last three years, and that these courses were offered almost *twice* as often in non-UCEA institutions as in those that held membership in that organization.[6]

Diffusion is a curious process. If one examines the listing of the twenty "prestige" universities in the field of educational administration according to the work of Sims,[7] and then notes that of the more than 1,300 professors included in the Campbell and Newell study, 645, or 48.5 per cent earned their doctorates in those "prestige" institutions; (yet at the time of the study, 44 per cent of the 645 were professors in non-UCEA institutions) one might speculate that a theory course is likely

6 Ibid., p. 52.

7 Paul D. Sims, *Assessment of the Quality of Graduate Departments of Educational Administration.* Unpublished doctoral thesis, University of Wisconsin, 1970. Cited in Campbell and Newell, op. cit., p. 30.

to be offered (though it might very well have some other title) by a large number of *both* groups.[8] If that is a little hard to follow, recall that "quick-and-dirty" inquiry that I made and mentioned previously with reference to how many UCEA prospective professor aspirants indicated a strong interest in theory. Granted that not all of them secured positions where the pursuit of that special interest was possible, still a statement to the effect that the literature of educational administration "should be theory-based" in the Campbell and Newell study, ". . . elicited wide support. . . ."[9]

There is simply no question that the "new movement" is no longer very new, but at the same time, there seems reasonable assurance that what was begun is even more vital today. There is also no question that it will continue to blossom.

THE BACKGROUND OF THIS BOOK

I began work on the present volume long before the Campbell and Newell study was conceived. The fundamental rationale was a simple one and Hills's observation about the lack of familiarity with theory literature was an important input into the rationale. I was convinced that there was no book available that attempted to provide an anchoring frame-of-reference for a great number of professors in both large and small institutions that could function as a *basic* focus for dealing with this broad and obviously diverse content. There are excellent basic texts and books of readings that deal with important aspects of this area, but there was no singularly comprehensive work. I am sure that following this one there will be others with differing points of view.

In the early days of the "movement" I, too, fantasized about *a* theory of administration. I am not yet willing to give up that notion but I am convinced that it cannot come about until we have learned to "walk a bit" in these complex areas. We cannot learn to do otherwise as a practicing profession until we have examined the avenues by which those skills must be generated.

Moreover, it seems to me vital that we need not be self-conscious about our apparent inability to unveil *a priori*, a full-blown theory with all its attendant postulates and derivations; our business is not behavioral science but *applied* behavioral science, and until all institutions dealing with the preparation of educational administrators can bring their potential to bear on the problems we confront, theory will continue to be "theoretical" rather than "practical." In another place, I, and others, have emphasized that theory and practice are really one—that theory is the first cousin of common sense, and that there is nothing in all of

---

8 Campbell and Newell, op. cit., p. 31, Table 27.
9 Ibid., p. 86.

should. Such activity is a kind of mélange; a complex mixture of individual and social phenomena that are frequently incongruous and frustrating. Much of the time administrative work is concerned with confronting a variety of crises by virtue of which a man decides *not* whether a crisis exists but rather which crisis shall have priority over the others. In any case, there is precious little time for contemplating the orderly pursuit of effective organizational purposes. Sir Richard Livingston, who was a vice-chancellor of Oxford, once described administrative work by suggesting that it

consists of being pushed by events, finding immediate answers to immediate questions, and the difficulty (being) behind their urgency, to remain aware of anything ultimate, to avoid mortgaging the future.[2]

Why then do men of apparently normal inclinations pursue administrative careers? Probably for the same reasons men pursue any career —sometimes because they have found themselves by accident and circumstance "moved" into such channels; in some cases, because they have a talent for management; possibly because they have internalized normative standards that prescribe ambition; perhaps because some men enjoy power, others need conflict, and certainly because not a few of such men believe that it is vitally important work. Unquestionably, administration is important activity. Every major problem confronting modern societies is, in the final analysis, an administrative problem whether it is extricating a nation from entangling and unpopular foreign policies, or polluting the environment, dealing with criminal deviance, healing the sick, industrializing the economy, or educating the young. Every societal problem ultimately seeks its solution through some manner of administrative function.

What is administration? Academic definitions are perhaps unnecessary but such activity has an impressive history. In a work of notable effort, Bertram Gross suggests that:

When we look for recorded administrative thought in the more general sense, we find that in most cases it is part of a rich tapestry of philosophic (or even religious) commentary on man and his relations to fellowman, state, and society.[3]

Gross traces such commentaries through widely differing sources: Confucius, Liu Shao, Plato, Aristotle, Kautilya, Nizam Al-Mulik, Machiavelli, and more recently, Henry Taylor among many others. Gross concluded

---

[2] Lucien Price, *Dialogues of Alfred North Whitehead* (Boston: Little, Brown, and Co., 1954), p. 305.

[3] Bertram Gross, *The Managing of Organizations*, Vol. 1 (New York: Macmillan Publishing Co., Inc., 1964), p. 91.

from his careful analysis of such divergent content that administrators are variously admonished to be wise, good, bold, willing to compromise, unscrupulous, and well-advised.[4] Style notwithstanding, it is obvious at least that whenever organizations come into existence, regardless of their purposes or their unique structure, in order to survive over time, they must be managed; those who provide this function are administrators.

General Development of Organizational Analysis

Apart from commentaries about the kinds of persons that administrators should hopefully be, which in a classical sense suggests a concern with morals and ethics, and in a utilitarian sense represents a concern only with the very important variable of leadership, interest in the broader concept or organization also has a notable history. Malinowski has pointed toward the pervasiveness of organizational vitality with the observation that, "The essential fact of culture as we live it, as we observe it scientifically, is the organization of human beings into permanent groups."[5] He is even more explicit when he asserts that, as a general principle, ". . . the science of human behavior begins with organization."[6]

Thus, there has been interest and curiosity about organization as a generic concept for perhaps as long as there has been need for such a function; as long as people have lived together in any form of communal relationship. Specific concern with the structure and function of organizations probably grew up most notably with early military systems and with the increasing stabilization and bureaucratization of religious institutions. In his analysis of the development of the military staff, Hittle credits Phillip of Macedonia with an advanced organizational vehicle; Phillip initiated commissaries, transportation organizations, hospitals, and developed a staff position closely paralleling that of the modern provost marshall for the regulation and administration of encampments.[7]

Scholarly interest in organizations as uniquely distinct social phenomena received significant early impetus about the time of the French Revolution. This interest was coordinated with sociological beginnings. As Gouldner has stated:

Both sociology and organizational analysis were early formulated in the work of Henri Saint-Simon. Saint-Simon was probably the first to note the rise of

4 Ibid., pp. 93–106.

5 Bronislaw Malinowski, *A Scientific Theory of Culture and Other Essays* (New York: Galaxy-Oxford University Press, 1960), p. 43.

6 Ibid., p. 46.

7 J. D. Hittle, *The Military Staff* (Harrisburg: Military Service Publishing Co., 1949), p. 20.

modern organizational patterns, identify some of their distinctive features, and insist upon their prime significance for emerging society.[8]

Saint-Simon saw the emergence of new forms of human interrelationships in the form of organizations as a hopeful sign for man. He said:

(Men) shall henceforth do consciously, and with better directed and useful effort, what they have hitherto done unconsciously . . . and too ineffectively.[9]

Although it is somewhat difficult to characterize Saint-Simon's interest in organization as specifically rationalistic, the essential implications he foresaw with reference to authority based on skill and knowledge rather than upon hereditary privilege or wealth is definitely a rational view.

The Rational and the Natural Systems Models

Although it remained for Max Weber to rigorously develop the explicit nature of organizations in highly rationalistic terms through the concept of bureaucracy, Saint-Simon deserves the credit, at least, for his incisive early observations regarding the value of "consciously directed" organizational activities and, without question, Weber was influenced by these views. Saint-Simon's protégé, Auguste Comte, took rather an opposite view: Perhaps exhibiting an early manifestation of the generation gap, Comte was much more an advocate of organizational growth in terms of natural, spontaneous evolution. Comte, who is conceded as the real father of modern sociology, held the view that natural evolution was a much preferable organizational dynamic. He did not totally reject the processes of rational organization, but preferred that such processes only be instituted in the face of truly serious threats to the natural social order. Gouldner has suggested that the term *spontaneous* was, "The most eulogistic term in Comte's vocabulary. . . ."[10]

Thus in Saint-Simon and Comte, we have the genesis of two relatively different approaches to organizational analysis, both of which are decidedly sociocultural but functionally disparate in nature even though based on similar philosophical foundation. Both were philosophical *positivists;* Saint-Simon, for example, considered the medieval period to be most effectively organized as a system, but since that period passed into the abyss of oblivion he saw nothing of similar orderliness replacing it. Rather, he viewed the emerging world in which he lived as chaotic and nihilistic. The solution was the establishment of a new order and he strongly felt that such an order demanded a foundation in science—

[8] A. W. Gouldner, "Organizational Analysis," in R. K. Merton, L. Broom, and L. S. Cottrell, Jr., *Sociology Today* (New York: Basic Books, Inc., 1959), p. 400.
[9] Henri Saint-Simon, *Selected Writings,* ed. by F. M. H. Markham (New York: Macmillan Publishing Co., Inc., 1952), p. 70.
[10] Gouldner, op. cit., p. 400.

positive science; that is, on a science that was progressively more systematized. For Saint-Simon, a science achieved systematization when it no longer appealed to or was relatively well confined to conjecture. Alchemy is not a positive science but chemistry is. In the work of Saint-Simon are the seeds of socialism as a political, ethical, and social system, but there are only seeds; it remained for others to cultivate what he had sown.

Comte also looked toward a future social order with its base in empirical science generating a special kind of effective brotherhood. But Comte went much further than Saint-Simon, by formulating an entire philosophy and, from it, the science of sociology itself. Where Saint-Simon was rationalistic, Comte was systematic. Comte felt that a new social order could not be brought into existence in one fell-swoop, but rather had to develop over time. Comte's "law of three stages"— a central concept in his philosophy—conceives civilization passing from a theological stage through a metaphysical stage and into a positive stage, and in each of these stages definite kinds of social systems are prevalent. In Comte's *Positive Polity*, which is subtitled in terms of sociology, he deals with the positivistic world as he conceives it primarily in terms of the "science of order" (social statics) and the "science of progress" (social dynamics). Nisbet discusses this dualism in more detail in his chapter "The Two Revolutions," which follows; here it is useful merely to explicate the method of Comte's thought with reference to this differentiation. Harald Hoffding states:

Comte works out the relation between statics and dynamics in all the different scientific spheres. The world is considered statically in geometry, dynamically in mechanics. In physics and chemistry forces are considered partly in equilibrium, partly in activity. In the organic sphere, statics is represented by anatomy, which investigates organisms; dynamically by physiology, which investigates functions. Sociology includes both a social static, which studies the constant conditions of society, and a social dynamic, which inquires into the laws of the progressive development of society; the fundamental idea of the former is order, of the latter, progress. Statics and dynamics are closely related to one another—a fact which both the reactionary and the revolutionary school failed to grasp.[11]

The concept of community is of immense significance in the study of organizations but it has not occupied as explicit a place in the more familiar organizational literature as it probably should. Perhaps this is due to the fact that of the two emergent views of organizational analysis —rational and natural—the rationalistic view received almost immediate reinforcement. The eighteenth and early nineteenth centuries saw an almost scholarly obsession with the rule of reason. That historical en-

[11] Harald Hoffding, *A History of Modern Philosophy*, Vol. 2. (New York: Dover Publications, Inc.), p. 345.

vironment dictated this interest by virtue not only of the ascendency of science itself but also by those events that altogether comprise the Industrial Revolution. Concomitant with this was the development of democratic nationalism and its emphasis upon self-determination, both for individuals and nations, which is historically associated with the French and American revolutions.

Yet, the essence of the naturalistic model of organizational development is apparent in Comte's sociology for, as Nisbet suggests, progress for Comte is defined merely as the achievement of order. Nisbet elsewhere provides further insight into Comte's concern for the spontaneous development of order when he points out that:

Comte's sociological interest in community was born from the same circumstances that produced conservatism: the breakdown or disorganization of traditional forms of association. This point must be emphasized, for it is often said that the rise of sociology was a direct response to, or reflection of, the proliferation of *new* forms of associative life in Western Europe, forms that industrialism and social democracy brought with them. Comte was interested in these . . . but it is not difficult to show that what led to his earliest sociological reflections was not perception of the new but, rather, an anguished sense of the breakdown of the old, and of "the anarchy which day by day envelopes society," as a consequence. The ghost of traditional community hovers over all his sociology, as it does—though less obviously—over the work of Toqueville, Le Play, and their successors.[12]

The Cognitive and the Affective

It is thus perhaps of some explicatory value to briefly examine the rationalistic and the naturalistic approaches to the study of organizations in the context of a relatively familiar dualism in pedagogical theory: Most educators are now well familiar with the terms *cognitive* and *affective* as domains, which are generally associated with the work of Bloom and his associates in the development of taxonomies of educational objectives.[13]

These two concepts provide a useful dichotomy for conceptualizing both philosophical and sociocultural interest in organizational society beyond their application to the methodological pursuit of educational outcomes in the modern sense. In a way, the "rational" and "natural" approaches to organizational analysis are but particular examples of

[12] Robert Nisbet, *The Sociological Tradition* (New York: Basic Books, Inc., 1966), p. 56.

[13] See for example: B. S. Bloom, ed., *Taxonomy of Educational Objectives: Handbook I: Cognitive Domain* (New York: McKay Co., Inc., 1956); and D. R. Krathwald, B. S. Bloom, and B. B. Masia, eds. *Taxonomy of Educational Objectives, Handbook II: Affective Domain.* (New York: David McKay Co., 1964).

cognitive and affective orientations to interpersonal relationships in organizational life. This becomes more plausible when one begins to examine major sociological perspectives in the thought of the nineteenth century. If, by cognitive, we can accept (admittedly oversimplified) the idea of *reason,* and by affective, the idea of *feeling,* or emotion, then Ferdinand Tönnies' monumental work, *Gemeinschaft und Gesellschaft* (Community and Society), is, in essence, an analysis of the fundamental concept of community in the contexts of the affective and cognitive orientations. For Tönnies, Gemeinschaft was characterized by highly personal, familiar, almost intuitive conditions (feelings?) of solidarity, whereas Gesellschaft is characterized by increasing impersonality, rationalism, and bureaucracy. Moreover, these were not necessarily startlingly new ideas, although Tönnies gave them a shape and substance that was imaginative and synthesized. Nisbet states:

If we examine Tönnies' work . . . we find it to be in very considerable part a fusion, within his own distinctive typology of community, of the basic themes of von Gierke, Maine, and Fustel de Coulanges: (1) the transition of Western polity from the corporate and communal to the individualistic and the rational; (2) of Western social organization from one of ascribed status to contract; and (3) of Western ideas from the sacred-communal to the secular-associational. Tönnies gave these three themes theoretical articulation, and although his materials are drawn from the Western European transition from medievalism to modernism, his typological use of these materials permits universalized application.[14]

The "transition from medievalism to modernism" is, in a sense, a transition from emphasis on the affective to the cognitive. Moreover, this dualistic conceptualization is also useful in delineating the major strain between the conservatives and radicals in nineteenth century thought and to a large extent is equally useful in our time for providing a similar distinction between the political left and right. Nisbet suggests that, "In the works of all of the conservatives rediscovery of the traditional community and its virtues is central."[15] As one example of that kind of concern, he cites Disraeli's statement in *Sybil:*

There is no community in England; there is aggregation, but aggregation under circumstances which make it rather a dissociating than a uniting principle . . . a community of purposes . . . constitutes society. . . . Without that, men may be drawn into contiguity but they still continue virtually isolated. Christianity teaches us to love our neighbor as ourself; modern society acknowledges no neighbor.[16]

[14] R. Nisbet, op. cit., p. 73.   [15] Ibid., p. 51.
[16] Ibid., p. 52. Cited from Raymond Williams. *Culture and Society: 1780–1950.* (Garden City: Doubleday Anchor Books, 1960), p. 106.

This same kind of concern, although more analytical and less personally wistful, is apparent in the work of Georg Simmel. Simmel seemed not so much concerned with the effect of the changes that were precipitated by the industrial and political revolutions on his own philosophical values as he was in their implications for a science of social relationships. Medieval society constituted a kind of model of a special, stabilized order for Simmel and he frequently referred to this model to illustrate and illuminate the contrasts that characterized his explanations of intergroup relationships. Consider the following:

> In the Middle Ages affiliation with a group absorbed the whole man. It served not only a momentary purpose, which was defined objectively. It was rather an association of all who had combined for the sake of that purpose while the association absorbed the whole life of each of them. If the urge to form associations persisted, then it was accompanied by having whole associations combined in confederations of a higher order. This form which enables the single individual to participate in a number of groups without alienating him from his affiliation with his original locality, may appear simple today, but it was in fact a great social invention.[17]

The Institutionalization of Charisma

Nowhere is the evolution of the traditional society into the modern —from Gemeinschaft to Gesellschaft—more apparent than in an analysis of the process by which the charismatic personality is bureaucratically transformed. This process is, in fact, a fairly explicit example of the transition from affective organizational phenomena to rational.

One of the many notable contributions of Max Weber to the development of a science of organizational analysis was his painstaking treatment of the process by which the impact of charisma becomes traditionalized or, in his terminology, "routinized."[18]

In a sense, it may be said that when a charismatic personality happens upon the scene, the charismatic qualities of the personality are not measured so much by their intrinsic power as they are by the nature and intensity of the devotion that some special "following" attributes to them. In the early stages of such a "movement" and especially while the personality lives and promotes it, the following is emotional, affective, expressive. As Weber has stated, "The corporate group which is subject

---

[17] Georg Simmel, *Conflict* and *The Web of Group-Affiliations*, trans., respectively, by Kurt Wolff and Reinhard Bendix (New York: The Free Press, 1955), p. 149.

[18] The progression from charisma to bureaucracy is complicated, and Weber alludes to it explicitly and by implication in different works. See *The Sociology of Religion; The Protestant Ethic and the Spirit of Capitalism; The Theory of Social and Economic Organization;* and *Economy and Society.* It is also treated in Julien Freund's *The Sociology of Max Weber* (New York: Pantheon Books, Inc., 1968), and in H. H. Gerth and C. W. Mills, *From Max Weber: Essays in Sociology* (New York: Oxford University Press, 1946).

to charismatic authority is based on an emotional form of communal relationship."[19]

Charismatic authority is clearly an exceptional form of power and although relatively rare in the large measure it is perhaps more significant because it is particularly upsetting; it is antitraditional, a revolutionary force. Weber borrowed the term, according to Freund, from Rudolph Sohm, a Strasbourg church jurist and historian.[20] The term means literally, "gift of grace." Our interest in charisma is not so much in terms of the concept itself as in the importance of its application to an understanding of formal organizations by virtue of the processes by which this kind of authority and its effects are progressively rationalized. In a sense, charisma belongs, categorically, to that kind of spasmodic administrative concern that has historically waxed and waned and can generally be labeled the "great man theory" of leadership. Gross suggests that this notion is to historical explanation in leadership terminology what the "Robinson Crusoe" theory is to economic behavior. He further comments:

At their worst, these theories purport to explain human behavior in terms of pure individualism. At their best, they regard all other factors as "exogenous" or as part of a *ceteris paribus,* to be examined by someone else; they then proceed to concentrate on a thin and artificial segment of human behavior.[21]

It should be clearly understood, however, that the concept of charisma as it has been given theoretical function by Weber is considerably more substantive than the "great man" idea even though there is, in it, the genesis of that notion. The charismatic phenomenon, which, in fact, is much more transcendental, is defined by Weber in the following manner:

(that) quality of an individual personality by virtue of which he is set apart from ordinary men and treated as endowed with supernatural, superhuman, or at least specifically exceptional powers or qualities. These are such as are not accessible to the ordinary person, but are regarded as of divine origin or as exemplary, and on the basis of them the individual concerned is treated as leader.[22]

The idea of charisma is also "value-free"; that is, it is as equally applicable to the "bad" guy as to the "good" guy; a Christ or a Hitler. Moreover, as an objective kind of measure of the possession of this quality in an individual, we are dependent more upon the nature and commit-

[19] Max Weber, *The Theory of Social and Economic Organization,* trans. A. M. Henderson and Talcott Parsons, ed. by T. Parsons (New York: Oxford University Press, 1945), p. 360.

[20] Freund, op. cit., p. 232.

[21] Gross, op. cit., pp. 331–332.

[22] Weber, op. cit., p. 358.

ment of the followers—the "ites" for its "ism"—rather than specifically upon the personality itself. In this regard, Nisbet points out: "We identify the charisma of Jesus or Caesar not by the substantive character of what either said or did but by the supra-rational, supra-utilitarian attachment of followers to each.[23] It should not be assumed, however, that such a personality depends upon followers for his charismatic qualities, but merely that without disciples and devotion of masses, the charismatic phenomenon can only persist in the moments of its existence. Under such circumstances, it has little chance of surviving into an institution and can have little relevance for history. These aspects of the charismatic phenomenon and the processes involved in the transition from *affective,* personal, and expressive conditions of legitimization to *cognitive,* rationalistic, impersonal, and bureaucratic are treated in greater detail in Part II. Suffice it here to consider this process as one more illustration of the disparate nature of the rationalistic and natural-systems views of organizations but, at the same time, this process suggests a continuity—from affective to cognitive; Gemeinschaft to Gesellschaft—of these two views rather than a true dichotomy.

The Cognitive and the Affective in Contemporary Theory

Although the scope of contemporary scholarly interest in organizational analysis is quite broad and the range of empirical concern is both macronistic as well as detailed, there are still in contemporary views theoretical manifestations of the same kinds of categorical orientations that have herein been characterized as the cognitive and the affective.

Principally, this is notable in the work of Talcott Parsons and particularly in what he has called the "pattern variables." In Parsons' conceptualization, there are five major sets of variables that govern the pattern of both orientation toward, and categorization of, social objects. Although his work is treated in some detail by Hills in this volume, it is useful as a reinforcement to the present discussion as well as a basis for Hills' contributions to mention this component of his general theory.

Working for many years toward the articulation of a "general theory of action" in sociology, Parsons has frequently employed the terms *instrumental* and *expressive* as modes of categorizing social objects and ways of relating to them. In this context, *instrumental* is seen as conceptually paralleling, if not being clearly synonymous with the term *cognitive;* and *expressive* is similarly related to *affective.* But Parsons makes the relationship still more explicit with the pattern-variables. There are five sets of these categories that Parsons sees as the basis for classifying, ". . . the components of action." For Parsons, "Action is

23 Nisbet, op. cit., p. 253.

thus viewed as a process occurring between two structural parts of a system—actor and situation."[24] And further, he explains:

In carrying out analysis at any level of the total action system the concept "actor" is extended to define not only individual personalities in roles but other types of acting units—collectivities, behavioral organisms, and cultural systems.[25]

The five sets of pattern variables are:

Affectivity/Neutrality
Quality/Performance
Universalism/Particularism
Diffuseness/Specificity
Self/Collectivity

As an example of the point, consider the variable "quality/performance." In essence, what Parsons is suggesting is that in relating to social objects, one's response may either be in terms of certain *qualitative* aspects of the other person, or it may be couched in terms of the other person's performance—his achievement. Thus, one might speculate as to whether or not a teacher in a small town high school—characterized by much familiarity—awards marks on the basis of what pupils accomplish or in terms of who they happen to be. In the former case, we might assume that the teacher behaves rationalistically (cognitively), whereas in the latter case, he behaves affectively. Except for the self/collectivity variable, the same distinction can be drawn with reference to the other three; in each case, if one looks at one side of the pattern, one evokes cognitive considerations whereas the other half of the dichotomy tends to evoke affectivity. The self/collectivity pattern variable is clearly distinctive from the other four. Parsons holds that it

(becomes) increasingly clear that this variable (has) to do with relations between systems rather than with the internal constitution of a system itself. . . . What it does is to formulate the difference between two modes of integration of a subsystem in a superordinate system. The collectivity-oriented case is that in which a role or function in the superordinate system is directly constitutive of the goals of the subsystem.[26]

For example, if one is acting in terms of his role in the family and behaves in some manner that can be interpreted as being in his own

[24] Talcott Parsons, *Sociological Theory and Modern Society* (New York: The Free Press, 1968), p. 194.

[25] Ibid., p. 194.

[26] Talcott Parsons and Robert F. Bales, *Family, Socialization and Interaction Process* (New York: The Free Press, 1960), p. 142.

best interests rather than in that of the family's, he is acting in terms of the "self" dimension of the variable. Still, at a somewhat higher level of integration, however, say in terms of his neighborhood, if he acts in terms of what is in the best interests of his family when that action may be viewed as being detrimental to the neighborhood, again, he is acting in terms of the "self" dimension of the variable. But in either case, his behavior in these situations may be categorized simultaneously by other actors in those situations in terms either of who he is (quality) or in terms of what he does (performance). Moreover, it might also be characterized in terms of whether it is universalistic/particularistic, diffuse/specific, affective, or neutral. Additional discussion of these concepts with particular emphasis upon the school as an organization is provided in some detail by R. Jean Hills in Chapter 8. Here, again, the point is made that contemporary theory may be viewed in terms of the affective and cognitive orientations.

Cultural Lag and the Transition to Mass Society

Also, concerning the relationship between the so-called rational and natural systems views of organizations and the notion of transition from affective to cognitive orientation in those terms, there is some relevance of the concept of *cultural lag*.

The term *cultural lag* was introduced into the literature of sociology by William F. Ogburn in 1922. This condition is descriptive of much of the social dissonance characterizing present-day circumstances, and according to Phillip Hauser, confronts us with an anachronistic and "chaotic" society. Writes Hauser:

> It is my contention that the confusion and disorder of contemporary life may be better understood and dealt with as frictions in the *transition still underway from the little community to the mass society;* and that the chaos of contemporary society in large part, is the product of dissonance and conflict among the strata of culture which make up our social heritage.[27]

Hauser suggests that virtually all of our present urban dilemmas are the result of such frictions: As a number of manifestations of such cultural lag, Hauser cites the fact that although in 1960, there were thirty-nine states in which urban populations were in the majority, none of these states were controlled at the legislative level by such people. That the cliché "that government is best that governs least" has not made any real sense since about 1800—asks Hauser, "Can you visualize a United States today without a Social Security system, without public health

---

27 Phillip Hauser, "The Chaotic Society: Product of the Social Morphological Revolution," *American Sociological Review,* **34,** No. (1) (1969), p. 8. (This author's italics.)

purposes and interests, held out as legitimate objectives for all . . . (and) cultural structures (which) define, regulate, and control acceptable modes for reaching out for these goals."[39] This, in effect, defines the situation of anomie as it was originally conceived by Durkheim. Durkheim introduced the concept of anomie with almost incidental definition in his classic analysis of suicide. Among the different kinds (motivations) of suicide that he considered, Durkheim stated:

Anomy,* therefore, is a regular and specific factor in suicide in our modern societies; one of the springs from which the annual contingent feeds. So we have here a new type to distinguish from the others. It differs from them in its dependence, not on the way in which individuals are attached to society, but on how it regulates them. Egoistic suicide results from man's no longer finding a basis for existence in life; altruistic suicide, because this basis for existence appears to man situated beyond life itself. The third sort of suicide, the existence of which has just been shown, results from man's activity's lacking regulation and his consequent sufferings. By virtue of its origin we shall assign this last variety the name of anomic suicide.[40]

Anomie is most generally associated with a state of normlessness, as is implicit in this statement. Merton has variously interpreted this phenomenon as ". . . a climate of reciprocal distrust . . . in which common values have been submerged in the welter of private interests."[41] And, ". . . a breakdown in the cultural structure occurring particularly when there is an acute disjunction between the cultural norms and goals and the socially structured capacities of members of the group to act in accord with them."[42] Merton takes pains to point out that in his view, Durkheim's original use of the term (which he evidently revived from a still earlier usage—about the sixteenth century)[43] referred to a condition or "property of the social and cultural structure"[44] rather than a property of individuals as the term was applied by MacIver and also by Riesman. These latter scholars limited the concept to apply rather particularly to individual psychological behavior.[45] MacIver states:

Anomy signifies the state of mind of one who has been pulled up by his moral roots, who has no longer any standards but only disconnected urges,

---

39 Robert Merton, *Social Theory and Social Structure* (New York: The Free Press, 1957), pp. 132–133.
   * This way of spelling has now become obsolete.
40 Emile Durkheim, *Suicide: A Study in Sociology*, trans. J. A. Spaulding and George Simpson (New York: The Free Press, 1951), p. 258.
   41 R. K. Merton, op. cit., p. 109.
   42 Ibid., p. 162.
   43 Ibid., p. 135.
   44 Ibid., p. 161.
   45 Loc. cit., p. 161.

who has no longer any sense of continuity, of folk, of obligation. The anomic man has become spiritually sterile, responsive only to himself, responsible to no one.[46]

In this context, MacIver seems much closer to the conditions of alienation that Durkheim discussed in relation to his theoretical conceptualization of egoistic tendencies toward suicide that Durkheim saw as "springing from excessive individualism." Durkheim stated:

society cannot disintegrate without the individual simultaneously detaching himself from social life, without his own goals becoming preponderant over those of the community, in a word without his personality tending to surmount the collective personality.[47]

Durkheim also discusses these conditions of egoism as contributing to relatively unique forms of alienation that are different from anomic strains by still further emphasizing the relationship of personality to social system when he asserts:

Life is said to be intolerable unless some reason for existing is involved, some purpose justifying life's trials. The individual alone is not a sufficient end for his activity. He is too little. He is not only hemmed in spatially; he is also strictly limited temporally. When, therefore, we have no other object but ourselves we cannot avoid the thought that our efforts will finally end in nothingness, since we ourselves disappear.[48]

Individual psychology may, of course, be treated and dealt with in terms of the concrete individual, but personality is inseparable from both culture and social system. The extent to which interpersonal orientations are significant dimensions of personality and of behavior is no longer subject to dispute in the general sense. Thus, in organizational analysis and in dealing with administrative theory, all three of these systematic phenomena—personality, social system, and culture—must be taken into account.

The rationale is essentially straightforward; since personality, social system, and culture all function as determinants of behavior (whether within or outside formal organizations), it is useful to examine personality in terms of its actualization in social relationships. Anomie is concerned with motivations and responses of persons when goals are internalized but means are blocked; moreover, work by those interested in the "human relations" views of management emphasized interpersonal

46 R. M. MacIver, *The Ramparts We Guard*, quoted in R. K. Merton, et al., pp. 161–162.

47 Emile Durkheim, "Types of Suicide," reprinted in Talcott Parsons, et al., *Theories of Society* (New York: The Free Press, 1961), pp. 213.

48 Ibid., p. 214.

relationships in terms of the kinds of needs and expressions that persons have vis-à-vis each other. Both conceptualizations are anchored in social and cultural dimensions of organizational life, whether primitive or modern, formal or informal, and repeating Malinowski, as stated early in this chapter, organizations are all pervasive.[49] Chapter 10 examines these conceptualizations.

The Division of Labor and Efficiency: The Rational Model

Saint-Simon's *On the Reorganization of European Society* was published in 1814. Just prior to the end of the eighteenth century, Adam Smith's *An Inquiry into the Nature and Causes of the Wealth of Nations* was published in 1776, in which Smith observed:

As soon as land becomes private property, the landlord demands a share of almost all the produce which the labourer can either raise, or collect from it. His rent makes the first deduction from the produce of the labour which is employed upon land. . . . The produce of almost all other labour is liable to the like deduction of profit. In all arts and manufactures the greater part of the workmen stand in need of a master to advance them the materials of their work, and their wages and maintenance till it be completed. He shares in the produce of their labour. or in the value which it adds to the materials upon which it is bestowed; and in this share consists his profit.[50]

Following a century of intensive development of this relationship between the master and the laborer, Weber was more explicit in his definition of the sociological implications of industrial rationalism: He stated:

Every type of social action in a group which is oriented to economic considerations and every associative relationship of economic significance involves to some degree a particular mode of division and organization of human services in the interest of production. A mere glance at the facts of economic action reveals that different persons perform different types of work and that these are combined in the service of common ends, with each other and with the non-human means of production, in the most varied ways.[51]

Thus is defined the modern concept of the *division of labor.* In that context, division of labor is treated as primarily an economic phenomenon defined in the utilitarian tradition of Locke and Smith, but it was Comte first and later Durkheim, more extensively, who held that the division

---

49 See p. 15.

50 Adam Smith, *The Wealth of Nations,* cited in T. Parsons, et al., *Theories of Society,* op. cit., p. 412.

51 Max Weber, *The Theory of Social and Economic Organization,* trans. A. M. Henderson and Talcott Parsons, ed. by Talcott Parsons (New York: The Free Press, 1947), p. 218.

of labor had ramifications extending beyond economic considerations.[52] Some discussion of the implications of this analysis is given elsewhere in this volume. At this point, the rationalistic economic consideration occupies our main interest since this view dominated management theory throughout the late nineteenth and early twentieth centuries, at least until the late 1920's. This more rationalistic orientation to division of labor led to the kind of specifically mechanical treatment of work that characterized the contributions of F. W. Taylor and that is familiarly known as *scientific management.*

The Evangelists of Routinization

Bertram Gross has stated:

All the ancestors of administrative thought operated on the explicit premise that by the exercise of reason men could devise feasible and consistent means for attaining desirable ends. It was on this basis that they offered advice to rulers, concerned themselves with administrative education and studied formal organization.[53]

Although Frederick W. Taylor is the name most notably associated with the "efficiency movement," there were others whose contributions were equally significant: Henry Fayol, Luther Gulick, and Lyndall Urwick are three who deserve mention.

All of these were dedicated to the principles of rationalistic management although Taylor, much more than any other, was chiefly concerned with the worker himself. Although Taylor extended his principles of scientism to management, it remained for Fayol, and more systematically, Gulick and Urwick, to emphasize rational administration.

Taylor had acquired a liberal education in European and American schools, but finding himself idle during the economic depression in the early 1870's, he applied for training as a machinist and subsequently secured a job with a Pennsylvania steel firm. In 1884, he was promoted to the position of chief engineer of a plant. During his years in the steel industry, Taylor was preoccupied with problems of increasing productivity. He soon focused his attention on the improvement of machinery (and is credited with a surprising number of developments, such as high-speed cutting steel), but more and more his attention was drawn to the productivity of the worker. The series of experiments that most effectively characterized Taylor's work involved the differential

52 For an excellent treatment of this Durkheimian analysis in terms of "organic" and "mechanical" solidarity, see Talcott Parsons, "Durkheim's Contributions to the Theory of Integration of Social Systems," *Emile Durkheim; 1858–1917: A Collection of Essays with Translations and a Bibliography,* Kurt Wolff, ed. (Columbus: The Ohio State University Press, 1960).

53 Gross, op. cit., p. 117.

efficiencies of coal shovelers in the Bethlehem Steel works. He found during these observations that the average shovel load of coal varied from about sixteen to thirty-eight pounds, and that efficient shovelers would be much more productive if the shovels were designed to handle a load of about twenty-one pounds. In all, depending upon the material to be shoveled, Taylor determined that about fifteen different types of shovels were required. (Even today, grain shovels are, therefore, much larger and differently shaped than dirt shovels.) Moreover, Taylor's methods disclosed that if one wanted "good" shovelers, he would be well-advised to seek out short, stout men rather than tall, lanky ones since the former wasted less motion and, being constructed "closer to the ground" were clearly more efficient for that type of work.

Taylor's implements in the pursuit of his "theories" were the stop-watch and the tape measure. The simple fact that his methods were pragmatic and produced startling results (plus the fact that after a time his "principles" received wide publicity) insured immense success. Taylor referred to his system as "the task system" but later, Louis Brandeis, who represented shipping concerns in litigation designed to block the Interstate Commerce Commission from increasing railroad rates, emphasized the term "scientific management."[54] Brandeis's premise was that through the application of more efficient methodology in management and labor practices, the railroads could do quite nicely on what they were currently charging.

A "cult of efficiency" was aborning; by the time of World War I, scientific management was applicable (and being applied) to almost every aspect of societal life; to churches, families, and—of course—to schools.[55]

Fayol, born fifteen years earlier than Taylor and surviving him by ten years as well, was also by training an engineer. But unlike Taylor, Fayol was principally concerned almost from the beginning with management and administration. From a position in the engineering section of a mining company he was promoted to general manager and found himself faced with an almost bankrupt organization. Fayol applied a special kind of rationalism to management and it worked. He conceived of administration as being dependent upon the successful prosecution of a series of functions: forecasting, planning, organizing, commanding, coordinating, and controling. Although he practiced his special "kind"

---

[54] Taylor had also used this term but it was Brandeis who popularized it. cf Milton Nadworny, *Scientific Management and the Trade Unions* (Cambridge, Mass.: Harvard University Press, 1955), p. 35.

[55] A well-documented account of the application of scientific management to schools is contained in Raymond Callahan's *Education and the Cult of Efficiency* (Chicago: University of Chicago Press, 1962). See also: W. R. Lane, R. G. Corwin, and W. G. Monahan, *Foundations of Educational Administration: A Behavioral Analysis,* (New York: Macmillan Publishing Co., Inc., 1967), Chap. 1.

of management for many years, it wasn't until the late 1920's that Fayol's *Administration Industrielle et Generale* was translated into English. (It was originally published in France in 1916 in a minerals industry bulletin, *Bulletin: Societé de l'Industrie Minerale*.) Fayol contributed terms such as the "scalar chain," "unity of command," and "esprit de corps." Moreover, Fayol was among the first to recognize both the need for administrative theory as well as for the inclusion of the teaching of administration in the academic programs of engineering. He was, in a very real sense, one of the original founders of the "profession" of management. In addition, even though Fayol was clearly rationalistic and mechanistic in his orientation to administrative function, he was much more kindly disposed and incisively aware of human resources in the plant than was the negativistic Taylor. For Taylor, workers were basically lazy, resisted work, required discipline (and surveillance), and produced fundamentally on the basis of incentives. Fayol held, on the contrary, that effective productivity from workers demanded, in addition to supervision, "kindliness and justice."

By the end of World War I, efficiency had become an American business ethic. Ideas such as cost accounting, span of control, unity of command, line and staff, incentive pay, time and motion study, traffic structure, and expenditure per unit of production—all of these and countless others had become an integral part of the language of industrial management and institutional administration.

Providing a kind of synthesis to this creed were Gulick and Urwick. The former contributed the acronym PODSCORB as the answer to the academic question: what do executives do? And Urwick contributed among other ideas the concepts "six-subordinates-per-supervisor" (span of control) and "delegation of responsibility."[56] PODSCORB is undeniably a classic verbal invention, the letters of which stand, respectively, for: Planning, Organizing, Directing, Staffing, COordinating, Reporting, and Budgeting.[57]

What Gulick and Urwick provided was a detailed and systematic treatment of the intricacies of bureaucratic stabilization. When Urwick pointed out, for example, that "No supervisor can supervise directly the

56 This is not to underrate the immense contributions of Gulick and Urwick; Gross states: "Both were indefatigable publicists, propagandists and promoters of the gospel of neutral principles directed at raising the level of organizational efficiency" (Gross, op. cit., p. 143). Indeed they exerted tremendous influence on both the teaching and the practice of business administration. The bulk of their writings—at least in terms of authoritative pronouncements—were contained in a series of papers generated as a result of Gulick's service on a Special Committee on Administrative Management commissioned by President Franklin D. Roosevelt in the 1930's. (See next citation.)

57 Luther Gulick and Lyndall Urwick, "Note on the Theory of Organizations," in *Papers on the Science of Administration* (New York: Institute on Public Administration, 1937).

work of more than five or at the most six subordinates whose work interlocks," he was making even more specifically routine, the Weberian bureaucratic principle of hierarchical structure. Thus, through such explicit "memoranda" of management, these writers brought the bureaucratic system into its most exquisite explication; they dotted the i's and crossed all of the t's.

Curiously, this systematic annunciation of rationalistic formal organization was articulated almost exactly ten years after the occurrence of events that spelled its decline. One is reminded of Whitehead's observation (the context of his remarks related to the magnificent Yankee clipper ships): "As I remember," said the philosopher, "perfection just precedes a change, and signifies the approaching end of an epoch."[58]

Human Relations—"People Without Organizations": The Natural View

Warren Bennis has observed that, in a sense, the scientific management period could be characterized as one in which there were organizations without people, whereas the human relations period could be characterized as one in which there were people without organizations.

Perhaps it deserves to be emphasized that what Bennis implies with that analogy is not *reality* so much as *generality;* in other words, the record that is traced in these pages and that is obviously marked by an emphasis on a kind of management that held economy and efficiency as high order values is characterized by a *modal* mentality. Therefore, it should not be assumed that there were not a great many industrial leaders who behaved kindly and benevolently toward their employees. Nor does the characteristically rational emphasis exclude interest by many people in other premises upon which management philosophy and procedure could be established. As a matter of fact, as is typically the case, reaction toward such an emphasis generated concerns about its shortcomings and led to new conceptualizations. But these, in turn, had to mature in an intellectual soil in which other serendipitous ideas were also being seeded.

Two factors related to this historical condition deserve mention. First, with reference to theory, it is the nature of theoretical evolution that, particularly in times of accelerated activity, effective theory tends to be self-destructive merely by virtue of the fact that it generally has a high propensity for producing new developments. Second, there is always an overlapping of events in all fields with the result that even as there is a tendency for some movements to overshadow emerging ideas, the latter will presently occupy the center of attention. Thus events occurring at one time do not so much determine those that shall follow but rather

58 Price, op. cit., p. 55.

make them possible. (Not what God hath wrought but what He hath ordained.)

We deal with the modalities—the generalities, if you will—because they were popular, widespread, influential, and because it is a convenient way to attempt to discuss process. Now clearly, process is a most difficult concept to deal with and historical process especially so because it seduces us with the illusion of sequentiality. It should be remembered that within the infinite linearity of time there is an equally infinite breadth of human space within which events may occur. The order of events has relevance only in terms of their relatedness.[59]

The "People" Champions

In light of this discussion, I haven't the remotest idea who deserves to be credited as the first bona fide industrial psychologist. Arguments may abound; his identity is probably obscured by the shadows of history and by the reputations of those who followed after (among whom were some giants).

But certainly one who manifested early psychological insight about industrial conditions was Sir William Mather, one of the principals of an English manufacturing firm, who in 1893 experimented with reducing the work week from fifty-four to forty-eight hours. When this was done, Mather noted that production markedly increased. Although such a magnanimous gesture was still within the essential context of worker efficiency, the fact remained that it was a decision against the tenets of the time. The incident is reported in a series of documents concerned with worker fatigue, which was of considerable interest during the heavy industrial retooling necessitated by World War I.[60] Mayo states that as a result of a series of established institutes of various types that came into existence during World War I there was increased concern with health, fatigue of workers, and so forth. Interest in industrial research along such lines led to the establishment, in 1921, of the National Institute of Industrial Psychology in England, founded by C. S. Myers who resigned as director of the psychological laboratory at Cambridge to assume the new post.

But regardless of the early interest in industrial psychology, there can be little doubt that in the United States Harvard University became the center of such activity during the late 1920's and dominated the field for some time thereafter. And just as Taylor's "scientific management"

[59] Nisbet suggests in a discussion of Comte's *Social Statics* (order) and *Social Dynamics* (progress) that the former occupied a more important place in Comte's thinking (op. cit., p. 56).

[60] Report No. 27, Industrial Fatigue Research Board, cited in Elton Mayo, *Human Problems of an Industrial Civilization* (New York: Macmillan Publishing Co., Inc., 1933), p. 2.

can be conceived as a kind of engineering application of Weber's bureaucracy, it is convenient to conceive of that period in management, generally characterized as the "human relations period," as being similarly generated by industrial psychology.

Fatigue and Fun

The period in the development of scholarly interest in management that is frequently labeled "human relations" is badly distorted in the hortatory and vulgarized literature about "good human relations." Even though such sermonizing was (and is) largely derived from much of the more substantial work that preceded it, the earlier work constitutes a remarkable and impressive chapter in management theory and, notwithstanding the great amount of overgeneralizing that was based on it (for which many of the early workers were not to blame), the fact remains that much of the research was rigorous and exciting.

Although numerous investigations and papers were authored by a variety of people during the human relations "movement," the entire period is most closely and intimately associated with the Hawthorne studies. A brief description of these episodes is a useful way of characterizing the period.

In essence, the whole series of experiments can, in retrospect, be viewed as a curious combination of interest in fatigue and "fun." As has been indicated, there was considerable interest among industrialists and statesmen in worker fatigue that began in earnest during World War I. Following that, the interest in worker fatigue and the empirical record accelerated. Among the concerns that were pursued, a number were concerned with boredom and monotony and their relationship to fatigue. Hence, my facetious reference to "fun." If somehow, work was more enjoyable, it would be less monotonous, and thereby, less fatiguing. Concomitant with the work on fatigue that was going on in England was a similar line of inquiry in the United States. Yet Mayo maintains that "at no time during the early development of the inquiries (was there) any relation between the investigators here and in England."[61]

In 1923, Mayo and some of his associates at Harvard were asked to undertake certain inquiries into working conditions in the mule-spinning division of a textile plant in Philadelphia. The essential problem was an abnormally high annual worker turnover (reported as 250 per cent!). In order to keep forty people continuously working, the plant had to take on about one hundred new people each year, and the turnover seemed greatest at peak activity periods. Mayo describes the working conditions in the plant as follows:

[61] Elton Mayo, *Human Problems of an Industrial Civilization* (New York: Macmillan Publishing Co., Inc., 1933), p. 42.

On first inspection, conditions . . . did not seem noticeably inferior to the conditions of work elsewhere in the plant. The spinners, like the others, worked only five days in the week; on Saturday and Sunday the factory was closed down. The working day was ten hours in length, five hours in the morning and five hours in the afternoon, with an interval of forty-five minutes for lunch. The work was done in long "alleys" on either side of which a machine head was operating spinning frames. The number of spinning frames operated by each machine head varied from ten to fourteen; all these frames required close watching by the "head-tender" and the "piecers" in charge. The number of piecers in an alley varied according to the type of yarn that was being spun; as a general rule there were two or three. The distance between the terminal frames was approximately thirty-five yards. The work was repetitive; the piecer walked up and down the alley twisting together broken threads. When there was a "run" of inferior yarn the work demanded vigilance and constant movement. The only variation in work was that which occurred when the machine head was stopped in order to "doff" or to replace a spool. Machine breakdowns of a minor character were fairly frequent.[62]

One need never have stepped foot into a textile mill to realize from Mayo's description of this operation that it was an insidiously monotonous form of work. Clearly boredom will be a factor in any kind of endeavor when the activity is seldom varied, when there is no extra compensation for increased productivity, and when tasks are not only self-contained but are interminably the same. Moreover, the nature of this kind of work did not lend itself to *group* activity; that is, each worker did his own thing.

Mayo and his associates were able to institute a variety of experiments that were mainly concerned with rest periods and production incentives. After a series of such experiments, a program of periodic rest was instituted as was a financial "bonus" incentive based on an experimentally generated measure of optimum productivity. Needless to say, under the conditions existing at the time, these innovations were indeed effective. Over the twelve-month period in which the studies were conducted, there was no labor turnover in addition to minor dislocations for reasons other than dissatisfaction with the work.

The Hawthorne Studies. Beginning at about the same time that Mayo and his people went into the Philadelphia textile mill, the Western Electric Company collaborating with the National Research Council launched some research that was primarily concerned with attempts to assess the effect of illumination upon worker efficiency. These activities culminated in 1926. One of the interesting findings of this study was that when groups of workers were separated and lighting conditions in *one* of the rooms was experimentally varied, there was no significant difference in worker output. This, added to the already considerable contemporary interest in fatigue and monotony, was cause for initiating

[62] Ibid., pp. 43–44.

additional research. The names associated with the "relay assembly test room" at Western Electric include some of the significant pioneers of the human relations period—Mayo; W. J. Dickson; Fritz Roethlisberger; T. North Whitehead; and many others.

Mayo gave the following detailed description of the experimental situation.

The operation selected was that of assembling telephone relays. This consists in "putting together a coil, armature, contact spring, and insulators in a fixture and securing the parts in position by means of four machine screws"; each assembly takes about one minute, when work is going well. The operation ranks as repetitive; it is performed by women. A standard assembly bench with places for five workers and the appropriate equipment were put into one of the experimental rooms. This room was separated from the main assembly department by a ten foot high wooden partition. The bench was well illuminated; arrangements were made for observation of temperature and humidity changes. An attempt was made to provide for the observations of other changes and especially of unanticipated changes as well as those experimentally introduced. . . . Thus constituted, presumably for a relatively short period of observation, the experimental room actually ran on from April, 1927, to the middle of 1932, a period of over five years. And the increasing interest of the experiment justified its continuance until the economic depression made further development impossible.[63]

Roethlisberger was intimately associated with these studies almost throughout their duration. His comments are equally instructive:

records were kept, such as the temperature and humidity in the room, the number of hours each girl slept at night, the kind and amount of food she ate for breakfast, lunch, and dinner. Output was carefully measured. . . . Literally tons of material were collected. Probably nowhere in the world has so much material been collected about a small group of workers for so long a period of time.

But what were the results? They can be stated very briefly. When all is said and done, they amount to this: a skillful statistician spent several years trying to relate variations . . . in physical circumstances to variations in output (and the attempt) resulted in not a single correlation of enough statistical significance to be recognized by any competent statistician as having any meaning.[64]

The *essential* results of these important studies, of course, culminated in a "new" management ideology. Through these investigations, a variety of now familiar concepts began to emerge both more visibly and more intensely; it is not as if "social structure"—"informal organization"— "internal equilibrium"—"morale"—(and more) were new terms. They were not, but these experiments gave them a new conceptual basis.

[63] Ibid., pp. 57–58.
[64] F. J. Roethlisberger, *Management and Morale* (Cambridge, Mass.: Harvard University Press, 1955), p. 12.

educational administration. Called the Cooperative Program in Educational Administration (CPEA), the contribution, influence, and general significance of this activity cannot be overstated. It provided the vehicle necessary for bringing scholars and practitioners together; helped them to learn from each other, to be less suspicious of each other, and generated inquiry, more rigorous methodology, new practices, and higher levels of competence both within the universities as well as in the field.

It was through the efforts of the CPEA program that interest in more vigorous analysis of educational administrative phenomena was generated. This interest led first to dialogue and later to collaboration between students of educational administration and students of the behavioral sciences.

Yet in the intervening years since those immediately following World War II and the Korean War, we have seen an educational revolution. Many things have changed. We have seen a much more significant role in education assumed by the federal government, as well as an increasingly sophisticated technology of education being applied both at managerial and instructional levels. In addition, we have seen the effective development and function of a new kind of social consciousness with all of the attendant painful manifestations that any revolution can have when people perceive that both their leadership and their policies are incongruent with grass roots definitions of national purpose.

In all of these events and developments, education has been central. And even in the most complacent of times, the status and tenure of the educational administrator is fragile. Such is the peculiar nature of the historic conditions that define those roles. The difficulties of these administrative tasks in the past two decades have been enormous and the need for a continued analysis of the social, cultural, political, and psychological dimensions of this activity is axiomatic. As I stated in the "Overview," the "new movement," as it was characterized by Roald Campbell, former dean of the School of Education at the University of Chicago (and more recently, Fawcett professor of educational administration at the Ohio State University), is no longer especially "new." But the movement is all the more essential and it is with the hope that it can be still moved a little further along the way that this book was conceived.

3

COMMENTARY

THERE is absolutely no question that one who aspires either to be a successful theorist or one successful in applying theory, must certainly be keenly interested in immediate events. But by the same token, one must also understand the nature of events that have transpired that have significance for what currently might be happening.

With reference to these concerns, R. Freeman Butts has recently reminded us that:

> The almost incomprehensibly rapid changes of the last quarter century (are) basically the result of the application of knowledge, of science, of technology, and of social organization to practical affairs by the highly trained products of Western-type educational systems. The changes are so momentous that thoughtful analysts and predictors are beginning to say that we are moving into a form of society which they variously call postindustrial (Daniel Bell and Bertram Gross), postmodern (Peter F. Drucker and Amitai Etzioni), tecnetronic (Zbigniew Brezinski), or postcivilizational (Kenneth Bouding).[1]

One cannot help but wonder what these thoughtful scholars might have noted about the world of nineteenth-century Europe had they been its observers. Just about all of what we are or have become had its most significant developmental beginnings in those turbulent years. Not only are the germs of ideational social concerns that led to the rationale of "education for citizenship" and, therefore, to the American design to be found in this period, but also the sources of understanding about conditions that mold science into effective practice and the development of modern organizational thought. Here then is a historic period in which to begin looking at the antecedents of administrative theory. Associated very vitally with that is, of course, the obvious necessity that anyone aspiring to roles in educational administration must be firmly grounded not only in the specialized content germane to the day-to-day decision-making, which constitutes technical management, but to a sensitive recognition of the traditional meaning and function of public education in American culture.

Accordingly, it is instructive to remember that Whitehead once observed that:

> It is no accident that an age of science has developed into an age of organisation. Organised thought is the basis of organised action (and) organisation is the adjustment of diverse elements so that their mutual relations may exhibit some predetermined quality.[2]

[1] R. Freeman Butts, *The Education of the West* (New York: McGraw-Hill Book Co., 1973), p. 563.

[2] A. N. Whitehead, *The Aims of Education* (New York: The Free Press, 1967), p. 103.

The conditions that led science into an age of organization are nowhere more clearly and interestingly traced than in Robert Nisbet's The Sociological Tradition[3] *from which the following chapter is reprinted. In this chapter,*'"The Two Revolutions," *he focuses upon the two most significant movements that changed forever the stability of human social order. Although that may seem overstated there are few who would really argue with this statement. The French Revolution ushered in a completely new systematic process of polity whereas the Industrial Revolution made bureaucracy appropriate and effective, initiating thereby a completely new process for systematizing work. In essence, as Nisbet demonstrates, the political and Industrial Revolutions were in historical perspective one set of events rather than two. Yet they must be treated somewhat separately if for no other reason than these two revolutions were experienced differently by the people who lived them; moreover, their impact was differentially assessed by social theorists and political philosophers during their occurrence.*

The "themes of industrialism" that Nisbet discusses are fundamentally the same general themes that pervade modern organizations and to which they owe their genesis. In a way, such themes when examined in concert with the intensification of individual freedom and nationalism manifested in the political activities that accompanied and complemented them constitute the conditions that predetermined the modern complex organization and, unquestionably, the American mass public schooling idea traces directly to that combination. For this reason alone, Nisbet's essay provides a vital focus for any analysis of the theoretical dimensions of organizational behavior and of educational organizations in particular. What is clarified is the nature of the general orientation that is vital to the development of a theoretical perspective —a historical perspective; but one quite distinct from the more familiar historical perspective in education.

THE TWO REVOLUTIONS

Robert A. Nisbet

The Breakup of the Old Order

THE FUNDAMENTAL ideas of European sociology are best understood as responses to the problem of order created at the beginning of the nineteenth century by the collapse of the old regime under the blows of industrialism and revolutionary democracy. This is the only conclusion one can reach when he looks at the character of the ideas, the nature of the works in which they appeared, and the relation of

[3] Robert Nisbet, *The Sociological Tradition* (New York: Basic Books, Inc., 1966).

idea and work to age. The intellectual elements of sociology are re-fractions of exactly the same forces and tensions that also produced the outlines of modern liberalism, conservatism, and radicalism.

The breakup of the old order in Europe—an order that had rested on kinship, land, social class, religion, local community, and monarchy—set free, as it were, the varied elements of power, wealth, and status that had been consolidated, however precariously, ever since the Middle Ages. Dislocated by revolution, scrambled by industrialism and the forces of democracy, these elements can be seen tumbling across the po-litical landscape of Europe throughout the nineteenth century in search of new and more viable contexts.

In the same way that the history of nineteenth-century politics is about the *practical* efforts of men to reconsolidate these elements, the history of social thought is about *theoretical* efforts to reconsolidate them: that is, put them in perspectives having philosophic and scientific relevance to the new age. The nature of community, the location of power, the stratification of wealth and privilege, the role of the individual in emerging mass society, the reconciliation of sacred values with politi-cal and economic realities, the direction of Western society—all of these are rich themes in the nineteenth-century science of man. They are equally rich as issues in market place, legislative chamber, and, not infrequently, on the barricades.

Two forces, monumental in their significance, gave urgency to these themes: the Industrial Revolution and the French Revolution. It would be hard to find any area of thought and writing in the century that was not affected by one or both of these events. The cataclysmic nature of each is plain enough if we look at the responses of those who lived through the revolutions and their immediate consequences. Today it is only too easy to submerge the identity of each revolution in long-term processes of change; we are prone to emphasize continuity rather than discontinuity, evolution rather than revolution. But to intellectuals of that age, radical and conservative alike, the changes were of almost millennial abruptness. Contrast between present and past seemed stark—terrifyingly or intoxicatingly, depending upon one's relation to the old order and to the forces at work on it.

We shall be concerned in this chapter less with the events and changes of the two revolutions than with the images and reflections that are to be found in the social thought of the nineteenth century. What either the Industrial or the French Revolution was in its historical actual-ity, in its concrete relation to what preceded and what followed, is not a matter for assessment here. Our interest is in ideas, and the relation between events and ideas is never direct; it is always mediated by *con-ceptions* of the events. The role of moral evaluation, of political ideology, is therefore crucial.

The Industrial Revolution, the power of the bourgeoisie, and the rise of the proletariat may or may not have been all that Marx thought them to be, but the fact remains that apart from his *conception* of them there is no way of accounting for perhaps the major intellectual and social movement in the subsequent history of the West. The same is true of the French Revolution. Alfred Cobban has recently referred to "the myth" of the French Revolultion, by which he seems to mean that not only the suddenness but the significance of the Revolution have been exaggerated. But from the viewpoints of some of the founders of sociol-ogy—Comte, Tocqueville, Le Play—the French Revolution was myth in quite another sense, one rather that Sorel was to give to this word. To these minds—and to many others—the French Revolution appeared al-most as an act of God in its cataclysmic immensity. With the possible exception of the Bolshevik Revolution in the twentieth century, no event since the fall of the city of Rome in the fifth century has aroused emo-tion so intense, thought so preoccupied, nor been the basis of as many dogmas and perspectives regarding man and his future.

Words, as E. J. Hobsbawm has written recently, are witnesses which often speak louder than documents. The period comprised by the last quarter of the eighteenth and the first half of the nineteenth century is, from the point of view of social thought, one of the richest periods of word-formation in history. Consider the following which were either invented during this period or—which is the same thing—modified to their present meanings: *industry, industrialist, democracy, class, middle class, ideology, intellectual, rationalism, humanitarian, atomistic, masses, commercialism, proletariat, collectivism, equalitarian, liberal, conserva-tive, scientist, utilitarian, bureaucracy, capitalism, crisis.*[1] There were others, but these are the crucial ones for what we shall be concerned with in this chapter.

Plainly these words were not simple counters in a game of abstract reflection on society and its changes. One and all these words were saturated with moral interest and partisan identification. This was as true at the end of the nineteenth century as at the beginning, when the words first made their appearance. To say this is not to deny or cast shadow on their later efficacy in the objective study of society. All major ages of thought in the history of culture are characterized by the pro-liferation of new words and new meanings of words. How else can the bonds of intellectual conventionality be cut through except by the sharp edges of new words that alone can express new values and new forces struggling for expression? It is only too easy at the time of their first appearance to fling the epithets "jargon" and "linguistic barbarism" at the words—some of which indeed deserve the epithets and receive the just punishment of later oblivion—but the history of thought makes

---

[1] *The Age of Revolution* (New York: Mentor Books, 1964), 17 f. See also Ray-mond Williams, op. cit., xi–xviii.

plain that few if any of the key words in the humanistic study of man and society do not begin as neologisms born of moral passion and ideological interest.

THE THEMES OF INDUSTRIALISM

Nowhere is this more plainly to be seen than in the impact of the Industrial Revolution on nineteenth-century thought. Although it is English thought and writing—literary as well as scholarly—that most plainly reveals the force of the Industrial Revolution, if only because this revolution is as distinctively English as the political revolution beginning in 1789 is French, the implications of industrialism were not lost upon French and German thinkers. The wide reading which Adam Smith's *Wealth of Nations,* published in 1776, had received throughout Europe gave even the most cloistered of scholars a forewarning of what the issues of the Industrial Revolution would be. Well before the phrase "Industrial Revolution" gained currency, the words, "English System" were used by German and French writers to describe the combined forces of legal individualism and economism which were transforming English society. As we shall repeatedly see in the chapters that follow, problems of community, status, and authority were dealt with by sociologists, from Comte to Weber, in the almost invariable contexts of the changes wrought on European society by the forces of division of labor, industrial capital, and the new roles of businessman and worker.

What were the aspects of the Industrial Revolution that were to prove most evocative of sociological response, most directive in the formation of sociological problem and concept? Five, we may judge, were crucial: the *condition of labor,* the *transformation of property,* the *industrial city, technology,* and the *factory system.* A great deal of sociology can be seen as response to the challenge of these conditions, its concepts as subtilizations of their impact upon the minds of such men as Tocqueville, Marx, and Weber.

Beyond question, the most striking and widely treated of these aspects was the condition of the working class. For the first time in the history of European thought, the working class (I distinguish "working class" from the poor, the downtrodden, the humble, which, of course, form timeless themes) becomes, in the nineteenth century, the subject of both moral and analytical concern. Some recent scholarship has suggested that the condition of the working class under even the first stages of industrialism was better than that which had prevailed for a couple of centuries before. This may be true. But it was rarely the view of independent observers in the early nineteenth century. For radical and conservative alike, it was the undoubted degradation of labor, the wrenching of work from the protective contexts of guild, village, and family, that was the most fundamental, and shocking, characteristic of the new order. The decline of the status of the common laborer, not to mention the skilled craftsman, is as much the subject of conservative indictment as it is of radical. On the Continent, both Bonald and Hegel referred with distaste to "the English system," noting the general instability to society that would be the necessary consequence of man's loss of the roots of his labor in family, parish, and community. In England, as early as 1807, Robert Southey based his criticism of the new manufacturing system in large part on its impoverishment of ever larger segments of the population. Nine years later, in his *Colloquies,* he wrote: "[A] people may be too rich; because it is the tendency of the commercial, and more especially of the manufacturing system, to collect wealth rather than to diffuse it . . . great capitalists become like pikes in a fish-pond, who devour the weaker fish; and it is but too certain that the poverty of one part of the people seems to increase in the same ratio as the riches of another."[2] The contrast between his own age and earlier times is stressed by Southey, as it is to be throughout the century. "Bad as feudal times were," Southey has his central spokesman Sir Thomas More say in the *Colloquies,* "they were less injurious than these commercial ones to the kindly and generous feelings of human nature."[3]

Turn now to the writings of the ablest of the English radicals in the same period, William Cobbett, hated and persecuted relentlessly by the forces in power. The basis of his criticism of the new economy is not very different from Southey's; it is precisely what he believes to be the dismal decline of the worker's status. The new system "has almost entirely extinguished the race of small farmers; from one end of England to the other, the houses which formerly contained little farmers and their happy families, are now seen sinking into ruins, all the windows except one or two stopped up, leaving just light enough for some labourer, whose father was, perhaps, the small farmer, to look back upon his half-naked and half-famished children. . . ."[4]

"I wish to see," Cobbett wrote, "the poor men of England what the poor men of England were when I was born; and from endeavouring to accomplish this wish, nothing but the want of means shall make me desist." All around him Cobbett could see traditional, security-giving relationships being ground into dust, craftsmen and farmers transformed into "hands," subject now to "Seigneurs of the Twist, sovereigns of the Spinning Jenny, great Yeomen of the Yarn . . . When *master* and *man* were the terms, everyone was in his place, and all were free. Now, in fact, it is an affair of *masters* and *slaves.*"[5]

The likeness between the conservative Southey and the radical Cobbett here is reflective of a certain affinity between conservatism and

2 Cited by Williams, op. cit., 25.
3 Williams, 26.
4 Williams, 15.
5 Williams, 16.

radicalism that was to last throughout the century. (I am referring, of course, to the evaluation of industrialism and its by-products. There was little if any affinity when it came to political matters.) What conservatives such as Tocqueville, Taine, and the American Hawthorne were to write in horrified reaction to the scene presented in Manchester and other cities of the Midlands in England did not differ in descriptive character or emotional intensity from what Engels was to write. It was Manchester that became the "ideal type," so to speak, of conservative and radical reactions to the new industry and to the displacement of working class from rural confine.

Even Marx, whose distaste for ruralism was as boundless as his hatred of the past, found himself, in the *Communist Manifesto,* contrasting the "feudal, patriarchal, idyllic relations" of the past with those which have left no other "nexus between man and man than naked self-interest, than callous 'cash payment.'" Industrialism has drowned the "most heavenly ecstasies of religious fervor, of chivalrous enthusiasm, of philistine sentimentalism, in the icy waters of egotistical value."[6] To be sure, Marx took a cynical view of the patriarchalism of the past, seeing in it but a veil that hid real exploitation. But his terminology could have been accepted without demur by many a conservative of the time. Reference to "cash-nexus" is owing first, apparently, not to the radicals or liberals, but to Carlyle, whose *Signs of the Times,* written in 1829, dealt eloquently and passionately with the commercialism that Carlyle felt was despoiling European culture.[7] In France the conservative Balzac would write: "There is no kin but the thousand-franc note." And before him Bonald, in an essay on the rural and urban family, made commercialism the prime attribute of all that he hated about modernism.

This is why the indictment of capitalism that comes from the conservatives in the nineteenth century is often more severe than that of the socialists. Whereas the latter accepted capitalism at least to the point of regarding it as a necessary step from past to future, the traditionalists tended to reject it outright, seeing any development of its mass industrial nature—either within capitalism or a future socialism—as but a continued falling away from the superior virtues of Christian-feudal society. It was what the socialists *accepted* in capitalism—its technology, modes of organization, and urbanism—that the conservatives most despised. They saw in these forces causes of the distintegration of what Burke called the "inns and resting places" of the human spirit, Bonald, "les liens sociales," and Southey, "the bond of attachment."

6 *Manifesto of the Communist Party* in Lewis S. Feuer ed., *Marx and Engels: Basic Writings on Politics and Philosophy* (Garden City: Doubleday Anchor Books, 1959), 9.

7 See Asa Briggs "The Language of 'Class' in Early Nineteenth Century England" in *Essays in Labour History,* Asa Briggs and John Saville, eds. (London: Collier Macmillan, Ltd., 1960), 47.

The second of the themes to emerge from the Industrial Revolution has to do with property and its influence in the social order. As we shall note below, nothing in the French Revolution so outraged conservatives as its confiscation of property and its weakening of the institutional supports of property. Property, and its desired role in society, goes further than any other single symbol to separate conservative from radical in the nineteenth century. For conservatives, property was the indispensable basis of family, church, state, and all other major groups in society. For radicals, increasingly, the abolition of property, save as a vague collective sentiment, became the prime goal of their aspirations.

And yet there is here, as in the condition of the working class, a curious affinity between radical and conservative. In part it was interpretative. Marx and Le Play were perfectly agreed upon the unvarying economic basis of the family in history, and both could have agreed with some highly illuminating words that a twentieth-century conservative, Sir Lewis Namier, was to write: "The relations of groups of men to plots of land, of organized communities to units of territory, form the basic content of political history; social stratifications and convulsions, primarily arising from the relationship of men to land, make the greater, not always fully conscious, part of the domestic history of nations—and even under urban and industrial conditions ownership of land counts for far more than is usually supposed."[8] No conservative could have doubted the truth of these words; no more could a radical, though liberals might.

But the affinity between conservative and radical went further. It extended to hatred of a certain type of property: large-scale industrial property, but more especially the abstract and impersonal type of property that was represented by shares bought and sold on the market. The speculator, who best exemplified the new economic order in conservative eyes, is the special object of Burke's condemnation. The malign ascendancy of what Burke called "the new dealers"—speculators in land and property, buyers and sellers of shares of stock—figures prominently in his pages. Burke is forthright about the matter. It is the transfer of political power from the land to new forms of capital that he fears. But beyond this was Burke's deep-seated conviction that the whole order that he was so passionately committed to rested, at bottom, on landed property. In the new economic order he could see the fragmentation, the atomization, of property and its conversion into impersonal shares that would never inspire allegiance or lead to stability. And Burke was, of course, right. It was still another twentieth-century conservative, the economist Joseph Schumpeter, who made this point the very thesis of *Capitalism, Socialism, and Democracy*, concluding with the observation that a people in whom hard property has softened to possession of im-

8 Lewis Namier, *England in the Age of the American Revolution* (2nd ed.; New York: St Martin's Press, 1961), preface.

personal shares of stock will never even notice the transition, when it comes, from capitalism to socialism.

In the nineteenth-century conservative and radical alike distrusted industrial and finance capital. But whereas radicals tended more and more, after Marx, to see this mode of property an essential step in the evolution toward socialism and its capitalistic evils subject to the cure of revolutionary liquidation of the privateness of its ownership, conservatives thought that it was the very nature of such capital to create instability and alienation in a population, and that this was quite unaffected by the mere matter of public or private ownership. All that had made landed property the subject of entail and primogeniture in almost every country at one time or other—had led its peasantry and aristocracy alike for centuries to make preservation and continuity of property sovereign over all but religious values, to make it the object of boundless ambition, covetousness, and protectiveness—now made land the pillar of conservative ideology.

A third theme to emerge from the Industrial Revolution was urbanism. In the same way that the social condition of the working class became for the first time the subject of ideological passion, so did the social character of the city. Prior to the early nineteenth century the city, insofar as it was dealt with at all in humanistic writing, was seen as the repository of civilized graces and virtues. Now and then, as in Montaigne's *Essays* or Rousseau's *Confessions*, expressions of distaste might be found, but these were directed less at the nature of the city (even less at the poverty and squalor that might be found) than at the distractions its wealth and more active intellectual life sometimes caused. But actual revulsion for the city, fear of it as a force in culture, and forebodings with respect to the psychological conditions attending it—these are states of mind hardly known before the nineteenth century. It is, as we shall repeatedly see, the city that forms the context of most sociological propositions relating to disorganization, alienation, and mental isolation —all stigmata of loss of community and membership. There was, to be sure, much to shore up presentiments of evil. To take Manchester again: between 1801 and about 1850 the population shot up from some seventy thousand to slightly more than three hundred thousand. Accompanying the raw growth in numbers went, of course, increase in squalor—"illth," as Ruskin was to term it—beyond anything that European man's experience had prepared him for. Here, as in the two other themes we have noted, contrast was inevitable: contrast between the relatively simple, stable, and *walled* towns that could be seen in hundreds of extant prints of medieval urban life and the sprawling, planless, and unbounded aggregates that eyesight revealed in the new cities of the Midlands. English cities may have presented the worst of the spectacles of urbanism—so regarded by French and German as well as English humanists—but, as the novels of Balzac, Victor Hugo, and, later, Zola make plain, the phenomenon of Paris was sufficiently arresting to the imagination.

In the beginning, radicals and conservatives were largely united in their distaste for urbanism. There is as much nostalgia for the rural past in Cobbett as there is in Burke. But as the century progresses, one cannot but be struck by the increasingly "urban" character of radicalism. I mean by this not only the demographic roots in the city of almost all nineteenth-century radical movements but also the urban flavor of radicalism, the characteristically urban ordering of values that we see in radical thought.

Marx regarded the onset of urbanism as one of the blessings of capitalism, something to be spread even further in the future socialist order. The essentially "urban" character of modern radical thought (and therefore its theoretical and tactical unpreparedness for the twentieth-century role of peasant populations) derives largely from Marx and a view that made ruralism a recessive trait. Engels, it is interesting to note, whose study of the English working classes has more of the spirit of uplift in it, generally, than of strict Marxism, was, on the other hand, anguished by creeping urbanism. "We know well enough," he wrote, "that [the] isolation of the individual . . . is everywhere the fundamental principle of modern society. But nowhere is this selfish egotism so blatantly evident as in the frantic bustle of the great city."[9] His words can be set alongside these of Tocqueville, written after a visit to Manchester: "From this foul drain the greatest stream of human industry flows out to fertilize the whole world. From this filthy sewer pure gold flows. Here humanity attains its most complete development and its most brutish, here civilization works its miracles and civilized man is turned almost into a savage."[10] The conservatives emphasized the degree to which European culture—from its moral and spiritual ideals, to its crafts and songs and literature—was based on the rhythms of the countryside, the succession of seasons, the alternation of natural elements, and the deep relation between man and soil. Only rootlessness and alienation could be expected from a separation of man from these rhythms and his exposure to the artificial pressures of the city. If modern radicalism is urban in its mentality, conservatism is largely rural.

Two final themes, equally alive, equally freighted with ideological passion in nineteenth-century thought, must be mentioned: technology and the factory system. Under the impact of the former and within the confines of the latter, conservatives and radicals alike could see changes occurring that affected the historic relation between man and woman, that threatened (or promised) to make the traditional family obsolete,

9 Cited by Briggs, op. cit., 48.

10 Alexis de Tocqueville, *Journeys to England and Ireland,* George Lawrence and K. P. Mayer, trans., K. P. Mayer, ed. (New Haven: Yale University Press, 1958), 107 f.

required, and these the Revolution had in abundance. It was the Revolution that contributed to Western Europe states of mind about political good and evil that had previously been reserved to religion and demonology.

The whole character of politics and of the intellectual's role in politics changed with the structure of the state and its relation to social and economic interests. Politics now became an intellectual and moral way of life, one not unlike that which Rousseau had described in his *Confessions.* "I had come to see that everything was radically connected with politics, and that however one proceeded, no people would be other than the nature of his government made it."[18]

In his *Discourse on Political Economy,* Rousseau wrote: "If it is good to know how to deal with men as they are, it is much better to make them what there is need they should be. The most absolute authority is that which penetrates into a man's inmost being, and concerns itself no less with his will than with his actions . . . If you would have the General Will accomplished, bring all the particular wills into conformity with it; in other words, as virtue is nothing more than this conformity of the particular wills with the General Will, establish the reign of virtue."[19]

Rousseau's relation to the Revolution is an interesting one. To think of him as one of the "causes" of the Revolution is, of course, absurd. He was too little read, too little respected in France during the years that preceded the Revolution. Even in 1789, when the Revolution broke out, there is little evidence that his ideas mattered very much. But by 1791, thirteen years after his death, he had become the Gray Eminence of the Revolution: the most admired, most quoted, and most influential of all the *philosophes.* His exciting combination of individualistic equalitarianism (so vivid in the discourses on the arts and sciences and on the origin of inequality) and of a General Will that gave legitimacy to absolute political power (expounded in the *Discourse on Political Economy* and in *The Social Contract*) was made to order for revolutionary aspirations.

There was, to begin with, the majestic Declaration of the Rights of Man which clearly specified that "the source of all sovereignty is essentially in the nation; no body, no individual can exercise any authority that does not proceed from it in plain terms." And further, "Law is the expression of the general will. All citizens have the right to take part, personally or by their representatives, in its formation. It must be the same for all whether it protects or punishes. All citizens, being equal in its eyes, are equally eligible to all public dignities, places and employments, according to their capacities, and without other distinctions than those of their virtues and talents."

[18] *Confessions of Jean Jacques Rousseau* (Boston: The Bibliophilist Society, 1933), II, 141.

[19] *The Social Contract and Discourses,* G. D. H. Cole, trans. and ed. (New York: E. P. Dutton & Company, 1950), 297 f.

Much of the specific legislation of the Revolution can be seen in these terms.[20] In a law of March 2–17, 1791, the hated guilds and trade corporations were abolished for once and all, inaugurating freedom of occupation (*liberté du travail*). The law was followed three months later by a more rigorous measure, the famous *Loi Le Chapelier* of June 14–17, which not only confirmed abolition of the guilds but forbade the establishment of any analogous form of new association. "There is no longer any corporation within the state; there is but the particular interest of each individual and the general interest. . . ." At a stroke, democratic assemblies were thus able to present a magnitude of power that had eluded the efforts of supposedly absolute kings. Rousseau's dislike of "partial associations" within the state was now converted into legislative action. "Citizens of certain trades must not be permitted to assemble for their pretended interests." A state that is "truly free," one of the legislators said, "ought not to suffer within its bosom any corporation, not even such as, being dedicated to public instruction, have merited well of the country." Benevolent societies and mutual-aid associations were made illegal or at least suspect. "It is the business of the nation," Le Chapelier declared in an address before the Assembly, "it is the business of the public officers in the name of the nation, to furnish employment to those who need it and assistance to the infirm." If old corporations were unacceptable, on the ground of their corruption of general will, why should new ones be allowed? "Whereas the abolition of all kinds of corporations of citizens of the same estate trade is one of the fundamental bases of the French constitution, it is prohibited to re-establish them *de facto* under any pretext of form whatsoever."

Napoleon's later edicts respecting associations were but extensions and reinforcements of what the Revolution, in its democratic-liberal phase, had already begun, a fact sometimes overlooked by historians who stress Napoleon's "reactionary" relation to the Revolution. Admittedly his laws were more encompassing, and he had a police system for their enforcement that was lacking in 1791. But he did not originate them; he merely extended and systematized them. Thus, in 1810 new

[20] An excellent recent treatment of the social aspects of the Revolution is Norman Hampson, *A Social History of the French Revolution* (London: Routledge and Kegan Paul, 1963). See also Franklin F. Ford's distinguished article "The Revolutionary-Napoleonic Era: How Much of a Watershed?" *American Historical Review* (October 1963), 18–29. Professor Ford writes: "The most important change of all occurred in the social structure and, equally important, in the way men conceived of social structure." For the detailed institutional histories of the Revolution (which contain the real essence of its impact upon the old order), it is still necessary to go back to the remarkable group of works done in France at the turn of the century, only a few of which can be mentioned in the following pages. On the laws which destroyed the *corporations* and *communautes*, the best of all studies remain Étienne Martin Saint-Léon, *Histoire des corporations de métiers* (Paris: 1898) and Roger Saleilles, *De la Personalité juridique* (Paris: 1910).

articles were appended to existing laws which forbade associations numbering more than twenty persons. Although popular protest led to a moderation of these restrictions in 1812, it was not until nearly the end of the nineteenth century that three generations of bitter political controversy on associations were terminated by final repeal of the laws forbidding or limiting them. We will find that Comte, Le Play, and Tocqueville, to name but three sociologists, were deeply concerned with the implications to society of restriction of the freedom of associations.

The family also underwent profound change in law during the Revolution.[21] Like the *philosophes*, the Revolutionary legislators found patriarchal customs and the indissolubility of the marriage tie "against nature and contrary to reason." In a law of 1792 marriage was designated a civil contract and several grounds for divorce were made available. The arguments for such measures invariably rested on natural law with frequent citation of philosophy. That the relaxation was not unwelcome in some quarters may be inferred from the fact that in the sixth year of the Republic the number of divorces in Paris exceeded the number of marriages. But there was more to follow in reform of the family. Strict limitations were placed upon the paternal power, and in all cases the authority of the father ceased when the children reached legal age. In 1793 the age of majority was fixed at twenty-one, and in the same year the government decreed the inclusion of illegitimate children in matters concerning family inheritance. The attitude of the legislators was plainly hostile to the customs governing the solidarity of the old family. Such men as Lepelletier and Robespierre, specifically appealing to the precepts of Rousseau (in his *Discourse on Political Economy*), insisted that the state should have primacy of claim upon the existence of the young. The legislators held that within the family, as elsewhere, the ideals of equality and individual rights must prevail. The family was conceived as a small republic (*une petite république*), and the father prevented from exercising "monarchical" authority. Relations between the family and its domestic dependents, such as servants, were put upon a contractual basis. The patriarchal unity of the family was thus dissolved, in law at least, in line with general policy toward all groups.

Property was no less thoroughly modified by the Revolutionary legislators.[22] Before the Revolution, custom and law had encouraged a system of inheritance under which estates, both large and small, tended to be preserved intact, and were passed on from generation to generation in the same families. It now became difficult for family property to perpetuate itself in the aggregate. The government, taking the view that property belongs to the individual members of the family, proclaimed the *partage*

[21] The best study of the impact of the Revolution on kinship in France remains Marcel Rouquet, *Evolution du droit de famille vers l'individualisme* (Paris: 1909).

[22] See Philippe Sagnac, *La Législation civile de la Révolution Française* (Paris: 1898).

forcé, whereby the father was legally obliged to will to his children equal amounts of property. By limiting the testamentary freedom of the father and forcing an equal division of property, the economic solidarity of the family was weakened. This, as we shall note, above anything else the Revolution did, obsessed Le Play, leading indeed to a vast study of family and property.

As one more expression of its dedication to the liberation of individuals from ancient authorities, the government, in 1793, took from the family the control of education.[23] Previously, primary education had been the joint concern of family and church. Universities in France were semi-autonomous ecclesiastical institutions. The successive governments of the Revolution, believing with Danton that "after bread, education is the chief need of the people," passed numerous measures designed to centralize and broaden education simultaneously, making it not merely the right but the political duty of all citizens. This legislative design for centralization of education was given powerful effect by Napoleon, who avowedly regarded education as a machinery for the production of efficient subjects. "In the establishment of a teaching body," he remarked, "my principal aim is to have a means of directing political and moral opinions; for so long as people are not taught from their childhood whether they are to be Republicans or Monarchists, Catholics or free-thinkers, the State will not form a nation."[24] Omitting the matter of motivation, the words could have come from either Rousseau or one of the Jacobins.

Religion also was deeply affected, and here the link between Enlightenment and Revolution is perhaps clearest of all. The Abbé Raynal, whose anti-ecclesiastical writings had earned him censure by the church, achieved belated revenge during the Convention, when his words were read aloud enthusiastically. "The state is not made for religion; religion is made for the state. The state is supreme in all things; any distinction between temporal power and spiritual power is a palpable absurdity, and there cannot be more than a sole and single jurisdiction throughout in matters where public utility has to be provided for or defended."[25] At the outbreak of the Revolution there was no manifest wish to abolish Christianity, but there was plainly desire to regulate it completely. If there was to be a church, it must reflect the character of the new political order. In the name of *liberté,* the Assembly suppressed all perpetual monastic vows and all religious orders. Educational and charitable functions held by the church and its various orders were transferred to the

[23] Antonin Debidour, *Histoire des rapports de l'église et de l'état.* 2nd ed. (Paris: 1911).

[24] G. Lowes Dickinson, *Revolution and Reaction in Modern France* (London: 1892), 54.

[25] Cited in Charles Guignebert, *A Short History of the French People,* F. Richmond, trans. (New York: 1930), II, 265.

state. Bishops and parish priests were to be elected like ordinary officials. It was ruled that clerics must accept their living from the state, and in such capacity must take an oath of fidelity to the state. Those who refused to swear fidelity were declared enemies of the people.

But the most severe blow fell when the property belonging to the church was confiscated by the state. From the point of view of the nature of social groups and associations under the law, the chief interest of this act lies in the discussions which were precipitated concerning the corporate nature of the church. The question was raised by more than one member of the Assembly whether the church, by its corporate being, should not be indemnified for the expropriation. Older corporate ideas of jurisprudence still found expression, even in that body. But they were drowned out by the overwhelming flood of natural-law arguments that persons other than natural persons (that is, individuals) do not in fact exist, and any rights which the church might claim disappear before the sovereign rights of the state. Thouret declared, in a legislative address: "Individuals and corporations differ in their rights. Individuals exist before the law, and they hold rights drawn from nature that are imprescriptible, such as the right of property; all corporations, on the other hand, only exist by law, and their rights are dependent on the law."[26] He concluded with the pregnant observation: "The destruction of a corporate body is not a homicide."

In countless ways, then, the Revolution must be seen in fact for what it was in image to generations of intellectuals afterward: the combined work of liberation, of equality, and of rationalism. Tocqueville was to write that equalitarianism quickly became, after libertarianism's first excitement had waned, the compelling moral ethos of the Revolution. But we should not overlook its rationalism and the appeal that this rationalism had for all those who, following Plato, believed in the rational foundations of the just state. A passion for geometrical unity and symmetry in the minds of the Revolutionary legislators drove them beyond such relatively minor matters as reform of the currency system and standardization of weights and measures to the more exciting task of rationalization of the units of space and time within which men lived. The ancient provinces were to be abolished, to be replaced by geometrically perfect units and sub-units of political administration, all oriented ultimately toward their center, Paris. The calendar was reformed, with new names for the days and months in order to remind the people constantly of their separation from the old regime. For, if a people are to be both free and wise, they must be liberated from old memories and the prejudices embedded in traditional associations and symbols. Traditional centers of education having been abolished, new centers must be

---

26 Cited by Paul Janet, "La Propriété pendant la Revolution Française," *Revue des Deux Mondes* (1877), 328.

established, an office of propaganda formed, in order that the people might be emancipated, in Rousseau's words, from the "prejudices of their fathers."

The Revolution was also the work of power; not power simply in the mechanical sense of force applied to a people by external government in the pursuit of its own objectives, but power regarded as arising from the people, transmuted by libertarian, equalitarian, and rationalist ends so that it becomes, in effect, not power but only the exercise of the people's own will. This was Rousseau's dream and it was the dream of a great many during the Revolution.

What gave the Revolution epochal significance in the minds of its leaders and, even more, in the minds of nineteenth-century revolutionaries for whom the Revolution became an obsessive model, was its unique blend of power and freedom, of power and equality, of power and fraternity, and of power and reason. From a purely intellectual point of view these affinities come close to representing the successive phases of the development of the Revolution. How else than by the massed power of the people, represented first by Assembly and Convention, then by Committee, and finally by one man alone, could the freedom of the millions of suffering and oppressed be achieved from the hated authorities of church, aristocracy, guild, and monarchy? From power conceived as liberation it was but a short step to power conceived as equality, for if each citizen of France was by definition a participant in the new political order, did this not bring with it equality of power; the most basic form of equality? And in the structure of the nation, which had from the beginning been declared the only legitimate source of authority in the Republic, lay a form of fraternity that made all older forms seem obsolete and discriminatory. Finally, how else could the political, social, and economic confusion that was the legacy of feudalism be exterminated, and a new system of society inaugurated, save by the exercise of a power that would be as rational as it was limitless?

"The transition of an oppressed nation to democracy," the Committee of Public Safety declared, "is like the effort by which nature arose from nothingness to existence. You must entirely refashion a people whom you wish to make free, destroy its prejudices, alter its habits, limit its necessities, root up its vices, purify its desires."[27]

Nor can one miss in the Revolution the rising note of political moralism, sometimes total moralism, that is added to the themes of liberation, equality, reason, and power. Rousseau had shown the way in his *Discourse on Political Economy* and in *The Social Contract*. Power without morality is tyranny; morality without power is sterile. Hence, as the Revolution progressed, the increasing appeal to virtue in support of the most extreme measures taken by the government. With moralism went,

[27] Cited by John Morley in his biography of Rousseau (London: 1915), II, 132.

inevitably, a new manifestation of religious consciousness. "How are you to know a Republican?" asked Barère de Vieuzac. His answer might have been taken directly from Rousseau's chapter on the civil religion in *The Social Contract*. You will know him, Barère declared, when he speaks of his country with "religious sentiment" and of the sovereign people with "religious devotion." With reason have historians of nationalism traced its modern origins directly to the Revolution. Political sentiment became a flame, melting all social relationships and symbols that stood between the citizen and the goal of France *une et indivisible*.

It was Jacobinism that came to appear, in later decades, most expressive of the Revolution's unique fusion of rationalism, moralism and absolute power. No matter what recent research has revealed of the middle-class origins, the merely economic objectives, and the debating-club techniques of a majority of the members of the Jacobin clubs, the image of Jacobinism that was ever after to inspire the radical and to torment the conservative was of something much closer to the reality of twentieth-century revolutionary politics than of anything to be found in liberal, bourgeois, nineteenth-century society. The historian, Robert Palmer, has suggested something of this in the following words on the Jacobins:

"Their democratic Republic was to be unitary, solid, total, with the individual fused into society and the citizen into the nation. National sovereignty was to check individual rights, the general will prevail over private wishes. In the interest of the people the state was to be interventionist, offering social services; it was to plan and guide the institutions of the country, using legislation to lift up the common man. It was to resemble more closely the states of the twentieth century than those of the nineteenth . . . 'The function of government,' Robespierre had said on 5 Nivôse, 'is to direct the moral and physical forces of the nation.' "[28]

From power to terror is the final step. In a revolution worthy of the name this step must be taken. For, as Robespierre declared: "If the basis of popular government in time of peace is virtue, the basis of popular government in time of revolution is virtue and terror: virtue without which terror is murderous, terror without which virtue is powerless."[29] No doubt some of the fascination and sense of self-justification which Christian onlookers found in the burnings of religious non-believers and heretics during the Inquisition were found by Revolutionary onlookers of the guillotinings of political counter-revolutionaries and traitors in Paris in 1794. It was in the context of the Terror that the peculiarly modern connotations of treason and subversion had their origin: each connotation is as inseparable from the character of modern mass democ-

[28] Robert R. Palmer, *Twelve Who Ruled* (Princeton: Princeton University Press, 1941), 311.
[29] Cited by Palmer, op. cit., 276.

racy as heresy is from the character of the medieval church. To a Saint-Just, inspired by the spiritualized, disciplined ferocity of a medieval inquisitor, terror could take on the properties of a cauterizing agent: indispensable, however painful, to the extermination of political infection. It was in these terms that nineteenth-century revolutionists, such as Bakunin, could justify the use of terror. It is a justification that continues in the twentieth century—in the works of Lenin and Trotsky, of Stalin, Hitler, and Mao. There is, to be sure, a vast difference between the reality of the French Revolution and the reality of twentieth-century totalitarianism, but there is, as such present-day scholars as J. L. Talmon and Hannah Arendt have stressed, following insights of Tocqueville, Burckhardt, and Taine, vital continuity nonetheless.

Individualization, Abstraction, Generalization

If one looks at the two revolutions from the point of view of the most fundamental and widespread processes they embodied in common, three are especially striking. I shall call them *individualization, abstraction,* and *generalization.* Together these terms convey a great deal of what revolutionary change meant to philosophers and social scientists of the nineteenth century. And the relevance of each has lasted well into the twentieth century.

Individualization. Everywhere in the modern world, the clear direction of history seemed to be toward the separation of individuals from communal or corporate structures: from guild, village community, historic chruch, caste or estate, and from patriarchal ties in general. Some, perhaps most, people saw this separation in the progressive terms of liberation, of emancipation from tradition grown oppressive. Others took a more somber view of the separation, seeing the rise of a new type of a society, one in which moral egoism and social atomism were the dominant qualities. But whether from the over-all point of view of progress or decline, there was a unanimity of recognition that covered philosophers as different as Bentham, Coleridge, Tocqueville, Marx, Spencer, and Taine. Not the group but the *individual* was the heir of historical development; not the guild but the *entrepreneur;* not class or estate but the *citizen;* not corporate or liturgical tradition but *individual reason.* More and more, society could be seen as a vast, impersonal, almost mechanical, aggregate of discrete voters, tradesmen, sellers, buyers, workers, worshipers: as, in short, separated units of a population rather than as parts of an organic system. To be sure there were those such as Marx who saw, along with the decomposition of old hierarchy and authority, the formation of a new type—that of the industrial system —but this did not prevent Marx from seeing the individual as nonetheless the beneficiary of the process and, when once separated from the tyranny of private ownership of industry, the recipient of final salvation.

Abstraction.   This is related to individualization, but refers primarily to moral values. What struck a great many minds in the century was not merely the tendency of historic values to become ever more secular, ever more utilitarian, but increasingly separated from the concrete and particular roots which for many centuries had given them both symbolic distinctness and means of realization. Honor—as Tocqueville was to show in a masterly chapter of *Democracy in America*—and loyalty and friendship and decorum had all begun, as values, in the highly particular contexts of locality and rank. Now, without their appeal as words, as symbols, becoming in any way lessened, the contexts through which their meaning and direction had for centuries been communicated to human thought and behavior were undergoing profound alteration. Many of these values had depended for their effect on man's direct experiencing of nature: of its rhythms and cycles of growth and decay, of cold and warmth, of light and dark. Now a technological system of thought and behavior was coming between man and the directness of natural habitat. Still other values had depended on the ties of patriarchalism, of close and primary association, and of a sense of the sacred that had rested upon a religious or enchanted view of the world. Now these values were becoming—through processes of technology, science, and political democracy—abstract; removed from the particular and the concrete. Here, again, this could represent progress to many, cultural decline to others.

Generalization.   The nation and even the international sphere come to be seen more and more as essential areas of man's thought and allegiance. From family and local community to nation, to democracy, to visions of international order: this is the course of thought in the age. Loyalties become broadened, along with interests and functions. So do perceptions. Men saw their fellows less as particular individuals and more as members of a general aggregate or class. As Ostrogorski has written: "In decomposing the concrete, the logic of facts as well as that of ideas, opened the door to the general. Here, as elsewhere, industrialism gave the first impulse. In the eyes of the manufacturer the mass of human beings who toiled in the factory were only *workmen,* and the workman associated with the factory-owner only the idea of *capitalist* or *master.* Not being brought into immediate contact, they formed a conception of each other by mentally eliminating the special characteristics of the individual and retaining only what he had in common with the other members of his class."[30] What the Industrial Revolution accomplished in the economic sphere, revolutionary democracy did in the political. In each instance the particularism of the old order—the tendency to think in terms of the concrete, *identifiable* rich or powerful, poor or helpless—disappeared along with its localism. The same tendency to think now increasingly in terms of "the working class," "the poor,"

[30] *Democracy and the Organization of Political Parties* (London: 1902), I, 48.

"the capitalists" expressed itself with equal force in the tendency to think in terms of "voters," "bureaucracy," the "citizenry," and so on.

In his *Reflections on the Revolution in France* Burke wrote: "Many parts of Europe are in open disorder. In many others there is a hollow murmuring underground; a confused movement is felt, that threatens a general earthquake in the political world."[31]

But not even Burke's prescience could have told him how general, how limitless, was the earthquake that began in Western Europe, spread to the rest of Europe and the Western hemisphere in the nineteenth century, and goes on unabatedly in the twentieth century in Far East, Middle East, Latin America, and Africa.

[31] *The Works of Edmund Burke* (New York: Harper and Brothers, 1837), I, 524 f.

4

COMMENTARY

THE *objective in the previous two essays was to establish a frame of reference for a theoretical perspective in educational administration. In the following essay, this attempt is continued by providing a discussion of theory itself. The discussion deals with what theory is, what it isn't, and some of the essential concepts and conditions with which theory is concerned.*

It may seem an altogether abrupt switch to move from a general historical and philosophical point of view to an abstract and rather structural one, yet when Nisbet suggests that the breaking up of the old order in Europe gave way, or freed elements such as power, wealth, and status, he is dealing with some of the fundamental concepts in organizational analysis. In order to fit these concepts into appropriate operational definitions that have practical application for educational executives, it is necessary to move the discussion away from the importance and meaning of events to the meaning and imimportance of process. In order to do this with a reasonable expectation that certain theoretical dimensions of administrative activity can be brought into practical application, it is useful to examine certain aspects of theory itself.

In providing such a process view, the reader will find that this essay not only attempts to deal with elements of theory but deals as well with some of the particular concepts that are appropriate to the functions of the educational administrator in the context of theoretical treatment. In approaching this task, it is clearly assumed that the educational executive—any organizational leader for that matter—must confront a bold and overarching interpenetration of three suprasystems: culture, personality, and social. If one were able to conceptualize these phenomena such that each interacts with, acts upon, and interrelates with the others, he would have some notion of what a relatively total and general system controlling human behavior is like. Of course, that would only be a rather vague notion of the total system. In order to really come to grips with even a small number of the variables of such a suprasystem, one would have to come to grips as well with a great variety of concepts and structures and functions and effects of such variables.

Clearly recognizing that an introductory treatment of the nature of theory can only present the outlines of such a task, this first chapter dealing specifically with theory attempts just that. We follow it with a trail that leads us to consider certain, more specific aspects of this conceptualization in a somewhat more intensive fashion, particularly the importance of language and concepts in theory and scientific activity. This latter discussion is presented in the context of a particular theoretical point of view: that of Talcott Parsons.

in the organization, and whether value prescriptions, lists of functions and tasks, and endless lists of other concepts are essential subjects of investigation. Social scientists are also still arguing over a general orientation and are not even agreed on types of variables that ought to be accounted for (some are still debating whether a social science is possible). One theorist, for example, proposes that a theory of administration must include such variables as value patterns, situational patterns, aptitudes, skill and knowledge, personality, physical energy, and capacity of the administrator in addition to individual and organizational performance.[12] This is indeed a comprehensive list, but admittedly too abstract to be meaningful until these types of variables are refined under more specific situations. The crucial question is *which* variables are important? One primary move in this direction is being made by Haas and others who are studying the possibility of an empirically derived typology of organization using ninety-nine variables.[13] No one project could possibly consider all relevant variables and their specific applications; there must, therefore, be a conscientious selectivity at this stage of the theory construction. Because of the elementary level of theory construction in the field, this book will have achieved its purpose if it does little more than suggest guidelines for an orientation to administrative theory by illustrating the types of variables that promise to be important.

Concepts. Language provides a perspective. Concepts sensitize the observer. Concepts point to important aspects of the situation to observe and implicitly determine what is not to be observed. Therefore, conceptual development is a crucial phase of theory construction.

It is difficult to define a concept because it is normally used to stand for the very words one must rely on to describe it. A concept is a kind of "bucket term"—and it is useful because, analogously, it is easier to carry the bucket than what is in it. Theory is, of course, a particularistic form of conceptualization; the theorist must deal first of all, therefore, with concept construction and must exercise both care and precision in such construction. It is to this task that the theorist applies operational definitions. Such definitions not only provide a measure of logical precision to the particular theorist's constructs but they also protect him from others' meanings (which might be quite different) for the concepts he is using. Bass has characterized this quality of operational definitions as follows:

The operational definitions and their meaning are critical for empirical verification of the adequacy of the theoretical model developed to account for the phenomena under study. But their meaningfulness to the public has nothing

---

[12] C. L. Shartle, "A Theoretical Framework for the Study of Behavior in Organizations," in *Administrative Theory in Education*, op. cit.

[13] J. E. Haas, "Toward an Empirically Derived Taxonomy of Organizations," unpublished manuscript.

to do with the validity of the deductive proofs of the relations between the constructs defined by the operations.[14]

Thus, if a reader understands that morale in an organization means *esprit de corps*, then whatever principles or theorems relating to morale that a particular theory produces will be applied, in that reader's case, to *esprit de corps*.

Post Factum Interpretations. The term *post factum* refers to interpretations of observations after they have been made, as opposed to empirical testing of predesigned hypotheses. Explanations construed in this way after the facts are in can be extremely consistent, and hence convincing; but precisely because they are convincing, they may obscure alternative explanations. Moreover, since new explanations can always be constructed to account for the exceptions, this type of explanation is not subject to disconfirmation. Yet, despite these inadequacies *post factum* interpretations are extremely useful as plausible starting points during the creative stages of theory construction. There is no mistaking that school administration had been in this creative stage at least until about 1960.

Empirical Generalizations. Establishing empirical generalizations constitutes one of the main theoretical tasks. These generalizations are sometimes mistaken for theory. For instance, the discovery of a correlation between the level of administrative success and amount of scientific training might be construed as a "theory." This is not precisely theory, although it is true that empirical generalizations are important elements of theory.

Before a generalization may be considered appropriate, several conditions must be fulfilled. First, there must be more evidence that confirms the statement than disconfirms it. This seems obvious enough, but untested hypotheses are easily mistaken for generalizations. Complete confirmation would require a systematic search for evidence to modify or refute the hypothesis, but sometimes all that one investigator is able to do is provide examples that *support* the hypothesis. In this sense, initial investigations take the form of a "grand jury investigation to determine whether there is a "case," or in other words, whether there is reason to explore the hypothesis further.

Second, the *conditions* under which the generalization is valid must be specified. So long as the prediction occurs under the stated conditions, the statement is true regardless of the infrequency with which these conditions might occur. For instance, it may be found that Catholic school administrators are less geographically mobile than Protestant administrators, but the generalization is limited to the South and not in the North. Any such limitation does not destroy the statement's validity and theoretical utility. The point is that generalizations need not be "uni-

[14] Bass, op. cit., p. 27.

versal"—that is, applicable to all situations (even the law of gravity is limited by vacuums). At the early stages of theory formulation, exact limits often remain unknown, and the theorist must content himself with establishing whether or not certain relationships occur at all and must postpone more refined analyses of the limiting conditions for further research.

Finally, precision of generalization is increased as the exact form of the relationship is discovered. Crude hypotheses are usually only first approximations that assume a simple linear relationship. For example, it may be hypothesized that the level of ambition progressively declines with age; it could be true up to a point, but a more refined analysis might reveal that near the age of retirement it rises again. Increased precision in stating the nature of the relationship is essential at the later stages of theory construction, but cannot be demanded during the initial stages.

Codified Knowledge. Although theory consists of generalizations, one generalization does not equal a theory; nor does a body of generalizations in themselves constitute a theory. For theory to exist, the empirical generalizations must be related logically. This logical component is an essential feature of full-blown theory. The test of theory, in turn, is whether other generalizations can be derived from it. For example, codified knowledge might take this form:

(*Law 1:* Ambition to achieve economic success is greater for minority groups than for the general population.
Observation: Jews are a minority group.
Derivation: Jews have greater ambition than the general population.

To be tenable such a postulate rests partially on the confirmation of the derived statements. If true it would apply to other minority groups as well. If it does not apply to blacks, Italians, and Puerto Ricans, the initial premise must be modified. This is, of course, a simplified illustration, but it is also useful for noting another dimension of codified postulates—that the larger "systems" (values, mores, cultural conditions) from which such postulates are themselves logically derived must be relatively stable over time. With reference to this simple example, achievement of economic success as a cultural thrust is itself diminishing in importance as we learn still more about some of the conditions that the social order imposes upon certain classes.

There are two common misunderstandings about theory: (1) that it is speculation, and (2) that its goal is only to predict. The tendency to distinguish between "theory" and empirical fact is a false understanding of the term. Correctly understood, an empirical theory *is* fact—that is, an organized body of empirical generalizations (and the assumptions on which they are based). The other misunderstanding is that the goal of theory is only to predict. If theory is a logical set of laws, then the goal is not to predict, but to derive other laws.[15] Once such a logical relationship is established, prediction more easily follows. Although prediction is, of course, extremely important, its importance to theory construction rests merely on its utility as a *tool* of science; it is employed to *test* the validity of theory. That is, if a derivation does not accurately predict, of course, the theory is inadequate. But the ability to predict in itself is not the distinguishing feature of theory. A set of random predictive statements does not constitute theory, no matter how practical they may be.

This point is not purely academic, because a search for predictive statements often proceeds differently from a search for theory. For example, if it were learned that body build is related to administrative success, the person who visualizes prediction as his goal would be satisfied, but the theorist would be puzzled. Although prediction may have great utility and although it may be a point of merging interest between practitioner and theorist, it is not a substitute for the scientific goal of theoretical explanation. So long as school administrators demand of social science only that it solve their practical problems of management, they are not, no matter how great their faith in social science, directly contributing to the development of explanatory theory. Of course, practical research may bear some theoretical implications, by accident if not by design, but zeal for practical solutions may actually divert investigations that otherwise would have been more directly focused on explanatory work.

The whole question of the relevance of theory to daily problems partially involves the question of what is practical. It is not entirely clear that solving the daily problems is more practical than developing more fundamental understandings about them. It is not by accident that the most advanced of the applied sciences—notably medicine and engineering—are grounded in such theoretical disciplines as physiology and physics. In the words of Walton, "It is perhaps because of impatience with theorizing and because of eagerness to get at practical applications of our knowledge that we overlook the essential practicality of sound theory, out of which sound practice can be developed."[16] Yet, at this point even many of the sympathetic administrators who otherwise express a fondness for "theory" tend to retreat under the daily pressures of

15 R. G. Francis, "Prediction and Science," *Midwest Sociologist*, 1956, pp. 7 ff.

16 Walton, op. cit., p. 172. This disdain of "theory" in the study of administration is imbedded in a long tradition, one spokesman for which was Frank Spaulding, who believed the purpose of the course was to meet the present needs of administrators; he proposed that "It should be intensely practical, not at all academic; doing, not mere knowing, should form the goal and the atmosphere of all the work" (F. E. Spaulding, *The Aims, Scope, and Methods of a University Course in Public School Administration*, Iowa City, University of Iowa, 1910, p. 11).

work to what seems for the moment the more practical affairs of administration.

EXPLANATION

The overarching function of theory is to *explain*. In ordinary conversation we talk about this concept of explanation in a variety of ways, but essentially, the issue in explanation is to make ourselves "clear" to another and thereby to help him better understand whatever it is that compels us to explain in the first place. But although that may seem a terribly simple purpose, its achievement is immensely complex. Still, clarity is at the heart of theory; the early advocate of *pragmatism* as a philosophical system, Charles Peirce, pointed out the vital importance of ideational clarity when he observed: "A clear idea is defined as one which is so apprehended that it will be recognized wherever it is met with, and so that no other will be mistaken for it. If it fails of this clearness, it is said to be obscure."[17]

With reference to clarity, explanation involves at the very least, two quite different dimensions of validation. In one situation an explanation may be meaningful because it concerns something that one has experienced and it does not matter whether anyone else ever experienced it the same way or at all—the *experience* is itself real for the one who had it and telling of it (the explanation) is equally valid. Again, Charles Pierce provides some insight into this important distinction; he reminds us that,

There are . . . phenomena within our own minds, dependent upon our thought, which are at the same time real in the sense that we really think them. But though their characters depend upon how we think, they do not depend upon what we think those characters to be. Thus a dream has a real existence as a mental phenomenon, if somebody has really dreamt it; that he dreamt such and so does not depend on what anybody thinks was dreamt, but is completely independent of all opinion on the subject.[18]

Thus, it seems reasonable to follow Peirce's notion that what is *real* is whatever might be substantially independent of whatever anybody might think it happens to be. Unfortunately, as Peirce himself suggests, this does not help us very much to distinguish *true* reality from *fictional* reality. What, in fact, is at issue is essential in theory—and that is *relatively useful meaning*. In other words, we apply (as much as is humanly possible) an objective and almost clinical belief in objectivity to the observations that confront us in the hope that what we ultimately obtain is a *reasoned* definition of reality. Thus theory is a kind of exalted

[17] Charles Peirce, "How to Make Our Ideas Clear," in W. Barrett and H. D. Aiken, *Philosophy in The Twentieth Century*, Vol. 1, New York: Random House, Inc., 1962, p. 106.
[18] Ibid., p. 118.

common sense; it attempts to deal with what is relevant and probably should not bother too much with what (by any cautious analysis) is not. Said Peirce:

(I must confess that) it makes very little difference whether we say that a stone at the bottom of the ocean in complete darkness, is brilliant or not— that is to say, that it *probably* makes no difference, remembering always that that stone *may* be fished up tomorrow. But that there are gems at the bottom of the sea, flowers in the untravelled desert, etc., are propositions which, like that about a diamond being hard when it is not pressed, concern much more the arrangement of our language than they do the meaning of our ideas.[19]

Implications. Empirical theory, then, may be defined as a logically coherent body of confirmed generalizations that have in common certain assumptions and concepts that can be specified with a degree of precision. *Theory develops, when it does, as a result of a series of modest attempts to imaginatively think through problems in conjunction with rather close and systematic observations.* Despite some claims, there is no formula for achieving this success. In order to evaluate the current state of progress intelligently, it is imperative to first identify the particular stage of theory construction that the field has achieved. A realistic appraisal of the current state of administrative theory reveals that social science is still wrestling with problems of the elementary stages of orientation and conceptualization. Criticism must fall within the range of reason set by this current level of theory. The contemporary theorist cannot properly be criticized for failing to provide a full-blown theory before its basis has been established. Such criticism often reflects the disappointment of persons who are zealously interested in achieving the more advanced stages of theory without bothering with the preliminary turmoil. We are aware—and comforted by that awareness—that theory is, above all else, heuristic—that is, theory begets theory. And perhaps at this point, we are back to common sense. There is startling scientific clarity in the adage that one must crawl before he walks.

Perhaps it is also well to remind ourselves that in the field of administration rigorous and systematic study of organizational process must candidly recognize the difficulties imposed by the bifurcation of practice and science. Halpin states this dilemma incisively:

Our problems . . . are exacerbated because administration may be approached from the point of view of a normative discipline as well as from that of descriptive science. Both approaches are important, but the researcher must keep the two realms straight and must know at all times which approach is being used. Administration as a normative discipline deals with how an administrator ought to behave and is predicated on an ideal situation in which time is theoretically infinite and choices are not coercive. In studying admin-

[19] Ibid., p. 121.

istration as social scientists, our concern is with how administrators actually behave in a real world where time is limited and choices must be made. . . . Research in administration has been severely impeded because the language of these two realms has been confused.[20]

Underlying Assumptions of Theory

Theory construction probably best begins with an exposure of critical underlying assumptions.

It is impossible to think about assumptions apart from relations. (In this context, we *assume* that the expression, "*a* and *b*," is a relation, and by the same token that, given the expression "*ab*," we can *deduce* that "*b*" is derived from "*ab*," and that this is also a statement of relations.) In a very real sense, then, theoretical explanation is largely dependent upon the ability to discover and understand the interconnections between elements in a situation. To move even dimly in this direction demands the articulation of assumptions. "Sets" of assumptions in a very real sense can be seen as synonymous with "models." Assumptions, therefore, make it logically feasible to generate working hypotheses that, in turn, constitute particularistic consequences of the assumptions that underlie any inquiry. If a *test* hypothesis is confirmed, we might then refer to it as a fact and, upon it, we may subsequently develop other assumptions. Underlying assumptions may thus involve not only relations among phenomena but also the nature of derivations from them. The consequences of certain assumptions lead us to the formulation of working hypotheses and these, in turn, to test hypotheses, and, ultimately from these, to the formulation of certain "laws" upon which we can depend.[21]

Suppose, as a fanciful example, we confront a problem within the personnel component of a particular school; we have some fundamental observations (perhaps themselves subject to much "reality-doubt") to the effect that there is some kind of relationship between the school principal and a second grade teacher that is "dysfunctional." We proceed by making certain assumptions about the relationship between principals and teachers that might be either highly propitious to "function" or to "dysfunction." For example, we might assume that the relationship between principals and teachers ought to be thus and so, and to be otherwise creates dysfunctional consequences for the system. Such

---

[20] A. W. Halpin, *Theory and Research in Administration.* New York: Macmillan Publishing Co., Inc., 1966, p. 71.

[21] See R. C. Collingwood. *The Idea of History* (New York: Oxford University Press, 1946.); H. Frudenthal, *The Concept and the Role of the Model in Mathematics, and the Natural and Social Sciences.* Holland: Dordrecht, 1961; R. B. Braithwaithe, *Scientific Explanation,* Cambridge: Cambridge University Press, 1955; and an excellent more recent work is A. Kaplan's *The Conduct of Inquiry,* San Francisco: Chandler Publishing Co., Inc., 1964, chap. 7.

assumptions would apply regardless of the personalities involved in any particular situation and would hold for all persons in such roles.

The form of such a common-sense assumption might hold that "familiarity breeds contempt." (A more sophisticated and esoteric formulation might go as follows: Given that the relationship between differential roles in the social system of a school must be founded on neutrality rather than affectivity, when a principal responds to an attractive, young, second-grade teacher in other than professional role-expectations, the consequences might prove disruptive to the general pattern of personnel relationships that are essential for the maintenance of balance over time.) The inquiry might proceed as any other scientific investigation; that is, data will be collected, analyzed, and interpreted, and additional hypotheses might be formulated along the way.

Surely it is a fanciful example, but the inclusion of the more precise and formalized language is not accidental. It is vital in the journey from theory to research that assumptions, assertions, suppositions, and so forth be as carefully formulated as possible so that the meaning intended is as close as possible to the meaning communicated. This is a necessary condition of theoretical activity and, in a sense, was what we referred to when we discussed the importance of concepts and operational definitions in theory-building.

But suppose that, with reference to the problem of the principal and the attractive teacher, we discovered that there was *no* dysfunctional relationship, or that there *was* a relationship but it apparently was *not* dysfunctional, or still possible that there was no relationship in the "real" sense, but that the *assumption* of the relationship (when in fact there was none) was as dysfunctional as a real relationship might have been. All of these possibilities could be the case but in none of them is there reason to reject the original assumption as generally applicable. On the contrary, there is some reason to affirm the assumption from at least two of the possible situations. What, then, are some of the kinds of assumptions that might be useful in the development of theoretical notions related to educational administration? The following are presented as examples of underlying assumptions that have some bearing. In many instances, similar assumptions have guided recent research in educational administration upon ways of explaining aspects of the behavior of school administrators.

1. There are certain administrative problems that are shared by all types of organizations. Educational administration does have much in common with other administrative fields from which insights can be drawn.

2. The nature of administrative problems and effective principles are more a function of the *organizational* structure in which the administrator works than of his line of work. That is, the nature of administration is as much determined by such conditions as the size of the organiza-

tion, and whether it is privately or publicly controlled and whether it is complex or simple, than whether it is educational, business, or political. (This does not mean that the administrator can function in ignorance of his particular institution; on the contrary, in order to exert leadership in any area he must appreciate its basic values and goals. However, given a school administrator and businessman each of whom understands his respective field, the similarities and differences in the problems they face will be greatly influenced by whether or not they work in the same size of organization, and so on.)

3. The administrator works with organized *groups* rather than directly with individuals themselves. The problems of administrators are better understood from the perspective of social organization rather than from the psychology of individuals.

4. The educational leader is not a "manager" aloof from the organization, but a *part* of it. Therefore, administration is best understood as a *relationship* between persons and groups rather than techniques and rules of administration. Accordingly, the factors of subordination, cooperation, are the primary tools that administrators must understand. With regard to relationships, administration must be understood from the standpoint of the subordinates—that is, the teachers' as well as the superior's standpoint. This will mean that "school administration" is not an exclusively executive function, but that it is distributed throughout the organization in terms of these interrelationships between teachers and supervisors.

5. Modern organization is characterized by internal contradictions among the various principles on which they are organized. These contradictions, often produced by environmental pressures, are a source of internal conflicts "built" into the organization itself. The administrator and his employees "inherit" problems from the situation.

6. The important supervisory and leadership decisions concern the regulation of these internal contradictions and environmental pressures. The operating decisions often inadvertently lead to organizational "drifts" between social policy and practice.

7. The significance of these contradictions within organizations has been insufficiently stressed in the past, and much of formal theory, consequently, amounts to little more than assertions of myths about organization. A theory of organizational process as well as structure is needed.

8. Validated knowledge ought not be confused with the process of theory development; codified theory cannot be achieved without beginning systematic analysis at less ambitious levels. Synthesis of abstract hypotheses with illustrative material and concrete examples is a convenient point of departure.

Sometimes assumptions are most clearly exposed by the model of society that the investigator imagines. Attention is now turned to a review of some of the available models of the nature and function of models.

Models and Theory-Building

If one wants to demonstrate the new styles in women's fashion, or sell toothpaste over television, he seeks a "model" for the purpose. Models in either that sense or in the theoretical sense are pretty much in demand in our time. Playing on the definition, one could say with some sense of certainty that models are very fashionable!

For that reason, the term *model* in theory and research is getting a lot of popular attention and, as is usually the case when a term is so widely employed, it begins almost to mean anything, everything, and—therefore—practically nothing. Yet, a model—the *idea* of model—is of immense importance in disciplined inquiry and theoretical activity. So, let us attempt to deal with the concept in what we hope is an appropriate context.

There are a number of excellent guides to a sophisticated explanation of the structure, function, and creation of theoretical models. One can talk about physical models, semantic models, formal models (and, I suppose implied thereby—*in*formal models), about mathematical models, and others—there seems no end to the ways in which men have devised for analogies of *x* to *y*. But most models *assume* more than analogousness, and most scholars who talk about models include considerably more in their conceptualizations than the extent to which some *x* is *isomorphic* to some *y*. The notion of isomorphism is, however, generally included as a central idea in any discussion of models-as-models and it means merely that the *x* is like the *y* even though it may be smaller or symbolically manipulable, or mathematically representative.

In general, one subject is a model for something else when the concepts of both subjects are *isomorphic*. This means that (1) there is a one-to-one correspondence between the concepts and assumptions of the model and the observed world, and (2) the relationships take the same form.[22] Isomorphism suggests hypotheses. For example, if a school system is like the human body, then the main office of the system may function like a brain, and decision processes may be likened to a nerve center. Since a disturbance in one part of the body affects all other parts, the same may be expected of the school system. However, some of the disadvantages of models should also be apparent in the same illustration: because models are seldom perfect analogies, they can be seriously misleading. Yet, sometimes they are used to the point of seeming real; they may become so sacred that the investigator is more in-

[22] M. Brodbeck, "Models, Meanings and Theories," in *Symposium on Sociological Theory*, L. Gross ed. New York: Harper & Row, Publishers, Inc., 1959.

terested in preserving the model than in interpreting reality.[23] Because of such disadvantages a model may actually obscure the actual relationships. This is especially true when models are chosen on the basis of their prestige or their success in other fields rather than any isomorphism or inherent similarities to the subject matter being studied. The prestige of physical science models may be a consideration that underlies their prevalence in the social sciences. For social science has relied heavily on physical, geological, and ecological models, and none of them are particularly relevant to *social* conduct. Models derived from cultural activities, such as the dramaturgical or even the musical model, have been ignored despite their possible relevance to everyday life.

KINDS OF MODELS

As has been pointed out, models are not the substance of theory; yet, clearly, the utilization, development, and analysis of models is intimately related to theory. Simply put, models allow us to characterize the phenomena in which we are interested in such a fashion that we can "see" most of the components, their interrelationships, and functions. The model lends itself to manipulation such that we can predict the consequences of manipulation; i.e., if we do something to component *A* we can "test" its consequences on components *B*, *C*, and so on. Let us take an oversimplified illustration. Consider the following "model:"

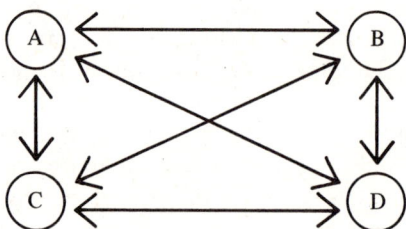

We can think of this figure as a system containing four components and the relationships among them (there may be many more than four components in some real system for which the model might be constructed). In a sense, we might think of this as an input/output model for lack of something better to call it at this point. The model suggests first of all that each of the components is *essential* to the function of the system. It does *not* suggest which—if any—of the components is more or less important than the others. It also suggests that in order for component *A* to produce whatever it produces that it must receive something from components *B*, *C*, and *D*. And the same applies for the other elements in the system. In a way, then, this model represents the

[23] See, for example, I. D. J. Bross, *Design for Decision*. New York: Macmillan Publishing Co., Inc., 1953, pp. 171–172.

the school's relationship to pupils and parents. There is usually some competition between home and school for the allegiance of children.

Third, there are explosive impediments to accurate *evaluation* of the success of schools. Policy statements tend to be so abstract that they are useless in establishing criteria of success. What is "good citizenship?" Does it include critical attitudes toward the American government or not? What are the criteria of good teaching? What is a "successful" student? Often many years are required before attitude changes effected by high schools are revealed in behavior. This ambiguity in evaluating teaching success is less apparent in some phases of business, particularly in sales, where effectiveness can be measured in terms of sales volume and effectiveness of promotion campaigns. The actual criteria of success used by teachers and administrators have been left directionless by the ambiguity of goals and standards of success, and these criteria must be hammered out in practice from the different available expectations.

Fourth, education differs from other organizations in the structure of the forces that control it. School boards represent various special interests of the community and have almost complete legal control over school policies; school administrators have almost no legal status, and their job is subject to the school board's pleasure, which greatly impairs the administrator's control over his organization. He is forced to compete for the support of various special interest groups that attempt to influence school practices, and he must often act as a mediator between them. Because these groups are inexperienced and untrained in education, the administrator may wish to resist some of their demands; but because they control his job, he may be in a poor position to do so.

Fifth, the school staff is professionally trained; many teachers have as much education as the chief administrator. Professionalization requires autonomy over work, a requirement that is often at variance with actual control by the administration. Their level and type of training, together with legal tenure provisions and the support of several professional organizations, gives the teaching faculty more legal autonomy than, for example, unskilled factory laborers. At the same time, teachers do not have as much authority over their spheres of work as do those in many of the more established professions. In fact, perhaps no other professional group, except perhaps nursing, is so completely subordinate to its administration as are teachers. The traditional authority of laymen over the schools, the ensuing professionalization of teachers, and the delegated power of administrators and school boards over teachers are basic characteristics of teaching that breed alienation between laymen, the administration, and their subordinates.

Finally, the school's physical structure and organization merit special attention. Unlike many organizations, such as the hospital, the school cannot be understood as a separate unit, for it is part of a system of units physically dispersed throughout the community and state. The fact that the superintendent's office is physically remote from the principal's office may be of some consequence for the development of unauthorized autonomy in some schools, problems of communication, and the kind of criteria used to evaluate teachers.

School administration is obviously, then, not identical to other forms of administration in all respects. The differences, however, should not be permitted to obscure the similarities; and in fact they may merely serve to highlight many of the same characteristics found in other modern organizations to which conflict models have demonstrated relevance.

The concepts that underlie models are tools of analysis. They set the perspective and point to the questions that are to be raised. Concepts have a fundamental role, therefore, in directing the investigation of organizations.

POWER AND AUTHORITY

Organization is primarily supported by two types of force, power and authority. Power is sometimes conceived as the nonlegitimate or illegitimate threat of force to achieve an end, whereas authority is the *right* to use force, which is granted either by the consensus of those over whom it is wielded, or by delegation from other authorities. Power, then, will refer to the potential of force, and authority will refer to the right to exercise that force. Power is calibrated from minor *influence* at one extreme, to complete *control* at the other. Whereas both power and authority involve the threat of force, force need not be actually applied in order to exert either power or authority.[31]

Excessive display of authority may in fact dissipate power as repeated applications use up the available alternatives.[32] Unexercised power may also lose some of its threat, of course, but the more significant fact is that power is directly proportional to the number of alternatives available and is diminished when they are used. It is, for example, evident that persons who are willing to use illegal and unethical alternatives have more power than those who feel constrained by legal and ethical principles. Similarly, within the legal and ethical limits, each application of power consumes an alternative and simultaneously commits the organization to a line of action that further restricts its alternatives in the future. For example, in March, before the annual contracts have been signed, principals have a source of power over teachers that is not available in April after they have been signed. Similarly, a principal has more power over an incompetent teacher before the disposition of her case is decided than after she has been demoted.

31 Cf. R. Bierstedt, "An Analysis of Social Power," in *American Sociological Review,* 15, Dec. 1950, pp. 730–736; and H. Goldhammer and E. A. Shils, "Types of Power and Status," in *American Journal of Sociology,* 45, 1939, pp. 171–78.

32 E. Abrahamson, H. A. Cutler, R. W. Kautz, and M. Mendelson, "Social Power and Commitment," in *American Sociological Review,* 23, 1958, pp. 15–22.

A person may have authority without actually having the power to implement it. In fact, because power is a function of the alternatives available, authority and power may be inversely related. That is, the very legitimacy of authority constrains the kinds of alternatives that an authority may use in order to exercise its power. Authority is constrained by popular expectations, values, and traditions, which necessarily bind the use of power. The restraints on power that accompany authorization are apparent in the fact that fraud and bribery are very effective kinds of power that are precluded to persons in authority. The power of the principal to fire incompetents is similarly constrained by the existing community sentiments toward the incompetent, opinions of his colleagues, and humanitarian concern about how it will affect his personal life. The number of persons who can be demoted or negatively treated by the chief executive in any one year is limited; at some point resistance will develop. Therefore, the availability of each negative alternative is diminished every time it is used. Moreover, the way that the principal handles a particular incompetent will set a precedent that in turn restricts the alternatives that are proper for dealing with incompetents in the future.

To summarize, power is based on the ability to control rewards—an action that may be seen as a threat; to be effective, it must be used occasionally. However, just as power increases as the range of alternatives increases, it diminishes as alternatives are actually consumed, for each application sets a precedent which precludes other alternatives. Authorized power is regulated by public opinion or organizational consensus. In the long run, though, there seems to be a tendency for those who exercise sheer power to gain public respect and legitimacy over a period of time. Because the greatest power is held, at least temporarily, by persons who are not constrained within the limits of legitimization in its exercise, there is a tendency for power to become separated from authority.

OFFICIAL AND INFORMAL STRUCTURES

Uses of authority and power form several distinct structures within organizations. A *structure* includes both a set of positions that prescribe broad functions and specific duties to incumbents, and a system of norms that regulate the relationship between incumbents of different positions. Official positions in organizations are referred to as *offices*. Each office constitutes a system of jobs, or roles, that prescribe the responsibilities (rights and obligations) of that office with respect to other offices in the system. Accordingly, the superintendent's office cannot be understood apart from the responsibilities of other offices in the system, including the roles of classroom teachers.

Although the term *structure* implies a stable pattern of relationships, it may be viewed as a variable; organizations can be more or less structured in several respects. The most structured system is the official authority system. The official obligation of superintendents is to provide facilities for teachers and to influence their direction; the principal is responsible for staffing and coordinating classrooms; the teacher is supposed to instill knowledge and values in pupils without showing favoritism, and soon. There are, however, contradictions even within the official system. Authority may have several bases. It may stem from traditional rights to make decisions, it may be delegated by political powers vested with legal and institutional authority, it may be assumed by mutual agreement among personnel, or it may be assumed by some individual because of a special competence. These forms of authority may be inconsistent, and rifts and power conflicts may develop among personnel within the organization who are committed to different authority systems.

Moreover, there are competing systems in the school, in addition to the official one, which create even further variability in the extent to which the overall system can be said to be "structured," or coordinated. These competing systems give rise to several different *informal* authority structures in addition to the legal and official ones. Informal leaders develop among teachers on the basis of the esteem of their colleagues. Since the authority arising from these unofficial sources is independent of the legal-official structure, it in effect constitutes a separate system of authority—the *informal authority* structure. The informal authority structure is intermediate between the official structure and the informal *power* structure. In the sense that such uses of power are not officially authorized, they technically constitute a power structure, yet, in the sense that they are authorized by group opinions, they are authority structures.

Systems of completely unauthorized power, or *power* structures, complicate the picture still further. Informal power structures exist simultaneously with, yet independently of, the informal authority structures, being unauthorized even by mutual consent of colleagues.

To summarize, there is a structural connection between authority and power and, respectively, the official and the informal organizations which they underlie. It is a crude relationship since some facets of the informal structure are authorized informally, and because competing bases of legitimization exist that are decided by power conflicts. Because authority relationships are infinitely more predictable than power relations, which by definition may exist outside the normal structure of expectancy and group control, authority is an understandably popular approach to organizational theory and planning. However, because structure is a variable and because there are a variety of structures (some based on unstable power relations), change and instability must be recognized as inherent to organizations. The notion of process must be incorporated into attempts to predict and plan organizational behavior.

The problem of predicting *events* based on unstable, semistructured power relations seems to be overwhelming at this point. The problem, however, of dealing with such dynamics as a *class* of events does not appear as forbidding. It may be necessary and useful to incorporate a set margin of error into predictions—that is, a specific measure of error to be expected from unforeseen disturbances, shifts of power, and environmental changes. In any event, attention needs to be given to the conceptualization, prediction, and explanation of power relations as distinct from authority relations.

Status and Office.[33] It is by now a truism that the official and informal structures of an organization are drastically influenced by the society in which they exist. The statement, nevertheless, is a reminder that administration cannot be viewed apart from the general status system of the society and the manner in which the status is translated into organizational practices. The concept of status refers to a position in the general *society;* it parallels the term *office,* which designates positions within a particular *organization.* The distinctiveness of organizational and societal positions, or office and status, is illustrated by Lazarsfeld and Thielens in a study of academic freedom.[34] College social science professors believed that they were ranked low in esteem by businessmen, congressmen, and college trustees. That is, they sensed that they held a low social status in the society. But the professors who had higher official and professional ranks within the educational system felt they had lower social status than the lower ranking professors. In other words, the professors felt that their official achievement was not accorded sufficient recognition by members of the broader society.

There are sometimes contradictions between what treatment a person may expect because of his status, and what the actual duties of his office are. A superintendent, for example, assumes the status of "educator," but his official duties may be more akin to those of a businessman and, in some smaller communities, of a records clerk. Conversely, different prestige statuses may be bestowed on offices with the same rank in different associations. In one study, for example, it was found that school superintendents of wealthier school systems were accorded more prestige than superintendents of the same rank in less wealthy schools.[35] It is the variations in prestige between offices of the same official rank which, of course, motivates mobility patterns within the school system.

Contradictions between status and office are also sources of dilemmas. For example, *age* has a different meaning within the status system of the broader society and the official system of the school. For, although it may be officially proclaimed that ability is the only important consid-

[33] Cf. K. Davis, *Human Society.* New York: Macmillan Publishing Co., Inc., 1949, pp. 88–89.

[34] P. Lazarfeld and W. Thielens, *The Academic Mind.* New York: The Free Press, 1958.

[35] W. S. Mason and N. Gross, "Intra-Occupational Prestige Differentiation: The School Superintendency," in *American Sociological Review,* June, 1955.

eration for promotion, within the school age *is* important. Because responsibility is supposed to be relegated to older persons, a young principal or superintendent in command of older persons can create a problem. Female high school principals who command a predominantly male staff may create a similar dilemma. Women officers occupy positions of incipient conflict because of inconsistent expectations of the subordinate place of women in our society and increasing sensitivity to discrimination against women has yet to affect this situation in a significant way.

Institution and Organization.[36] Statuses and offices comprise different "social orders." Offices constitute the fundamental element of an organization, whereas statuses are the basis of social institutions. Together, the offices constitute the responsibilities of the school system its job or its "roles," which outline rights and duties with respect to other offices. They comprise, in other words, the *organizational* structure providing the organization's regularity and stability; conflicts between offices provide its dynamic quality as well.

Organization behavior is to be understood in terms of offices rather than exclusively in terms of members' personality characteristics. Modern man lives in a "contract" society in which people react to each other often without knowledge of their personalities. Administrators do business with teachers, contractors, students, and parents, sometimes with almost no knowledge of their personal characteristics, yet with relative ease and success because people are *expected* to behave according to their status. Little insecurity is felt by school officials when they entrust the schools' monies to bank tellers who may be virtual strangers, because even though the teller may have dishonest tendencies, he will nevertheless tend to conform to the obligations of his office rather than give in to his personal inclinations. Similarly, teachers may be personally prejudiced against blacks, but strive to be equalitarian with black students in schools where discrimination is condemned, and, conversely, personally unprejudiced teachers may be forced to racially discriminate in some systems.

Although the official system is not determined primarily by the personalities of those who are in it, it is primarily affected by the institutional system that underlies it. The institutional "order" consists primarily of the statuses that compose each institution. Institutions are rules that link cultural values to specific situations. They have no official name and location as organizations do, and institutions are more abstract than organizations, being comprised of values and rules that transcend a location and specify the general organizational forms. Thus, although teachers are employed by the New York City schools, for example, and

36 Cf. E. Hughes' discussion in *An Outline of the Principles of Sociology*, R. E. Park, ed. New York: Barnes & Noble, 1939, pp. 283–88.

presumably have some allegiance to these organizations, they also are subject to the institutional values of teachers and citizens in other parts of the country, including the political, religious, economic, professional, and educational values that dominate the society. Each of these institutions is distinct in the sense that it is comprised of a network of interrelated statuses that are less related to other institutional areas. For example, politics is comprised fundamentally of relations between politicians, governors, cabinet members, the voting citizens, and so on. Education is comprised basically of relations among school board members, the citizens of the community, the state boards of education, superintendents, teachers, and pupils.

Since there is, in each institution, an element of the ideal, these statuses and expectations can be more or less compatible within a single institution. Thus, the job of "educator" is straightforward; he is to develop in children knowledge and character. But what is distinct about the institutional order is that there may be inconsistent expectations among institutions. A "good family man," for example, is expected to spend his evenings at home with his family, but the good community citizen is expected to spend his time working on community projects, and the good businessman is expected to use his evenings to work overtime and "get ahead." The point then is this: a single institution, such as education, is implemented in a number of different organizations in addition to the schools, such as the church and businesses and the military, all of which have educational programs; and a single organization, such as a particular school, is comprised of a variety of often inconsistent institutional statuses. The job of a teacher at school X is hardly described simply by her status as an educator; that job is comprised of a variety of institutions, among them business, politics, religion, and so on. In addition to teaching the children, a teacher may also be expected to keep attendance records, chaperone parties, monitor the cafeteria, encourage patriotic and religious devotion, and provide spiritual and vocational guidance. In these activities, educational values must be *compromised* with recreational, business, patriotic, religious, and other institutions in the work place. The "official" job then, comprised of a variety of institutions, is an arena of institutional conflict where compromises among political, religious, business, educational, and other value systems are carved out of the daily work routine. In the process, educational ideals are sometimes implemented, sometimes usurped, by other institutional means. This implies that the character of the public schools cannot be understood solely in terms of educational principles and philosophies, but must be understood within the context of the broader institutional order, including politics, business, religion, and other basic value systems. It also means that the official system is inherently one of conflict, the same conflict that persists in the more abstract institutional order. But the inconsistencies and conflicts are more notable and severe as the teacher experiences them on the job because it is on the job where they must be reconciled and translated into action.

Again, lest it be misinterpreted, it should be noted that such conflict is not always debilitating; on the contrary, it can be and frequently is highly productive. The school like any other organization is a dynamic system. It is by virtue of the dynamic interaction of its various components that the organization maintains what Parsons and others have called its *equilibrium,* or "steady states." When conflicts are severe enough to create imbalance in the system, they are responsible for readjustments, which in turn may result in or intensify other tensions.

Locals and Cosmopolitans. The simultaneous existence of the institutional and organizational orders poses conflicts of loyalty for employees. Loyalty to the employer, to the school—its customs and regulations, or its administration—is often a precondition of success; but, on the other hand, teachers may be more or less attached to various institutional principles that transcend the particular school. For example, if the school's policy forbids the teaching of religion, some teachers will feel guilty about ignoring it, or will teach their own brand of religion anyway. School systems differ greatly in their attitude toward the part that different institutions play in their operation. Some teachers may stress the educational aspect (that is, the transmission of knowledge) more than others, whereas other teachers may stress efficiency, or the use of business techniques, or the "politics of the game" more than others.

Institutional loyalty creates a particularly acute problem in a mobile society where the local place of employment, and particular family boundaries, no longer constrain a person's career nor exclusively define his standards of achievement. In a time when one part of the country may serve as a model for another part, it is no longer apparent that compliance with the job requisites is any assurance that the major institutional values are being fulfilled. It is possible for a teacher to be "successful" without actually contributing anything toward development of the nation's educational goals.

Members whose primary commitment is to the school's *local* community will seek to win the community's support for their school program and their place in it. This makes it more likely that the community will influence the basic character of the school. However, those members whose primary loyalty is cosmopolitan in nature (that is, committed to the broader national values) will be more influenced by national and international pressures on education that, as a matter of fact, can adversely affect the interests of a particular community or region. Thus any attempt to curtail a vocational agricultural program in a predominantly rural community would probably meet resistance despite the well-known decline of agricultural opportunities, just as zealous attempts to integrate Southern schools in the national interest will be unwelcome.

Professional and Bureaucratic Orientations. The dilemmas of employed professionals constitute a peculiar form of the local-cosmopolitan dilemma. The bureaucratic employee is expected to reserve his primary loyalty for the school where he is locally employed, particularly to its administration. The professionally oriented teacher, on the other hand, will probably be more influenced by the stands taken on issues by professional societies, by professors at influential training centers, and by colleagues across the country. Conflicts in the professional and employee orientations can become particularly acute when the issue involves racial integration, school consolidation, or relative importance of seniority and merit.

Commitment. Although exercised by individuals, power and authority describe characteristics of the organization. Commitment and involvement, however, provide a parallel set of concepts that describe the power system from the standpoint of the individuals in it. Although commitment and involvement tend to be correlated processes, they can be distinguished analytically. Considering the extremes, a person is completely "involved" when he does something solely because of personal desire without any formal obligation to do it. Although there is an element of compulsion implicit in a commitment, it arises largely from the ethical and social pressures from precedented acts rather than from threat of direct force.

These concepts are useful in analyzing the strategies by which individuals and organizational leaders handle their problems. In complex organizations, persons often must do what they dislike in order to obtain their preferences. As a result a person may commit himself to something and be involved with an entirely different matter. In other words, people exchange obligations for rights. Their life becomes a dynamic balance of commitment and involvement. Such systems of exchange are regulated by norms of *reciprocity*, which means that when a person gives up something, he can expect something in return.

The concept of commitment is also useful for the analysis of power, which, as indicated, is a function of the number of available alternatives. Every major commitment consumes one or more alternatives by binding the organization to an irrevocable line of action. Moreover every decision creates still other commitments, ones that are often unforeseen. Informal commitments usually accompany the formal ones. For example, when a school attempts to recruit a teaching staff that is entirely middle class, white, and Protestant, it is also committing itself to distinct practices, curriculum, and operating goals that, in turn, limit the school's alternatives for dealing, for example, with lower-class blacks.

These unforeseen and compulsory types of commitments create considerable *institutional drift* from long-range goals. Selznick cites two sources of these strains between actual and operating goals.[37] First, the daily minor decisions can lead the organization in directions it did not set out to travel. Old techniques of administration and teaching have a way of becoming sacred; thus, the goal of efficiency may actually be subverted by a seemingly minor decision to hire a tradition-directed accountant when planning to mechanize the records-keeping system. Second, drift is partly a consequence of a limited administrative perspective that naturally occurs because administrators tend to stress rationality and formal organizational goals. In stressing the rational formal goals, unintended outcomes of decisions on informal goals tend to be overlooked, or are considered to be irrelevant because they are *logically* irrelevant. The task of simultaneously "keeping an administrative eye on the ball" (as Selznick puts it), *and* systematically observing conditions seemingly irrelevant to the goals that arise independently of intentional acts, introduces a complexity into administration that is difficult to manage. However, both the relevant and nonrelevant conditions obviously do shape the character of organizations.

The concept of commitment, then, implies a *strategy of organization* as well as individuals. The act of commitment is potentially an act of change that may eventually affect the organization's structure and goals. There is a need for organizational theorists to study this class of strategies, for the notion of commitment as a strategy calls attention to the simultaneous structure and change that constitutes the science of administration. The view stresses the flexibility of organizational structure and helps to offset some of the traditional emphasis on structure and goals as "given" qualities. It suggests the feasibility of viewing organization as a development over time by analyzing its strategic acts. The decision-making process is a particularly important crux of such analyses.

The analysis of organizational process had been so neglected, and the need for new departures so urgent, that there is some justification for taking the opposite viewpoints—that process, strategy, and sheer "accident" are the "normal" states of organization, and structure is the "abnormal" state.[38] Pursuit of such a view would require special conceptual tools. A few of the most promising of these tools include *interplay, co-optation,* and *reciprocity. Interplay* stresses the strategic character of organizational decision-making. It is a tactical relationship wherein the action of one person depends on the unknown *outcome* of a previous act; an administrator's decision to fire or retain a teacher, for example, depends in part on anticipated community reaction. *Reciprocity* refers to the norm of exchanging favors. Persons may often engage in conduct that is not personally approved by them, but promises the fulfillment of an obliga-

37 P. Selznick, *TVA and the Grass Roots.* Berkeley: University of California Press, 1949, pp. 250–259.

38 T. Burns, "The Forms of Conduct," in *The American Journal of Sociology, 64,* 1958, pp. 137–151.

tion or the return of a favor. *Co-optation* refers to a type of compromise in which an opponent is incorporated into the leadership structure of a group in order to control him better; some control over organizational affairs is sacrificed in exchange for greater control over the opponent. These concepts describe some of the types of commitments by which organizations are guided and *compromised.* The important function they play within organizational processes also suggests another basis of the organization's cohesiveness in addition to power and consensus—that is, *constraint.* These terms are explored throughout the following chapters.

These and many other concepts reflect something of the substance of any attempt to apply organizational theory to educational administration. Our understanding of organizational life has evolved over a great many years and what might, at one point in time, represent a philosophical attitude toward community and society becomes, at another later point, the essence of a set of assumptions upon which empirical generalizations and research methodologies are based.

ception is thereby placed in a position to select rationally from among the available alternatives.

Rational selection, however, implies selection with an end in view, and this brings us back to the question that was previously left dangling; the question of the grounds on which an articulated standard might be found wanting. There may be many such grounds, but one that comes to mind readily can be identified. At a higher level in the normative hierarchy, that of norms, I might believe strongly that wives have a right, although perhaps not an obligation, to have and pursue interests beyond those that come under the heading of housewife. Clearly, the system of expectations that gives me the right to deny any request for help with housework is incompatible with that which asserts the right of my wife to pursue interests outside the home. (This assumes, of course, that we have limited resources and cannot solve the problem simply by employing maids, nurses, and so on.) The search for an alternative value on the variable—an alternative normative standard— then, is guided by our knowledge that that variable is correlated with some other variable, or condition. I have to select a standard from among the alternatives that will permit my wife to pursue her interests. It is in this sense that it seems fair to say that an individual's *generalized* capacity to achieve desired ends is enhanced by the possession of conceptual, analytical tools. "Generalized" is underscored in the preceding sentence because the same conception can facilitate the achievement of a variety of ends, not just the particular one cited in the illustrative discussion.

At this point we are in a position to identify an extremely important difference between the ordinary-language level of characterization and characterization in terms of an analytical-conceptual framework. An ordinary-language description of how I "see" my participation in my family would probably be couched in terms such as these: I provide the income for the family, hence, I'm away from home a considerable part of the time. When I am there, I take care of the yard; keep the house and appliances in a good state of repair; help teach, supervise, and discipline the children; and so forth. This list is far from complete, and perhaps not very accurate, but it will serve to make the point. What is particularly noteworthy about such a description, the more so the more complete it is, is the degree to which it is tied to a particular situation. The content of the description depends very much on the fact that it is a family that is being described, not a university department. Beyond that, it depends to a considerable extent on the circumstances that are peculiar to that family; is the home an apartment, or a single dwelling; is it rented, or is it owned; is it a fixed home, or a mobile home? Only to a limited degree would we find that the same descriptive concepts and categories used in one description also appeared in other descriptions. Thus, ordinary-language level descriptions of diverse situations require the use of diverse concepts, and any given description is tied to the particularities of a specific situation.

It is precisely this limitation that higher-order concepts overcome. Through their higher levels of abstraction, analytical concepts achieve greater generality and wider applicability across diverse situations. The result is that otherwise diverse and incomparable situations are made comparable. There is a close and useful parallel between the functions of analytical concepts in the context of information processing, on the one hand, and the functions of money in the context of economic exchange, on the other. One of the principal functions of money is to render commodities as diverse as mouse traps and mobile homes comparable on the dimension of economic value, thus permitting the rational allocation of resources (Parsons, 1961). In the absence of such a symbolic measure of value, the value of a particular commodity must be determined *ad hoc* in each particular barter-type exchange, and is thus tied inextricably to the particularities of that situation. Linguistic symbols, words and concepts, have a function similar to that of money when contrasted with prelinguistic signs. For example, if another person and I were lying in wait for deer while on a hunting trip, and I were to point in a given direction, my companion would doubtless understand the message as, "Something is coming from that direction." That particular nonlinguistic sign, however, would be tied very closely to that particular situation, or situations very much like it. It would have very little meaning if given on the street, in my home, or elsewhere. On the other hand, the linguistic message, "Something is coming" has meaning in almost any context in which the English language is spoken. It renders comparable certain features of all sorts of situations, just as the word *dog* renders comparable (and discriminable) a wide variety of four-legged animals.

These considerations, particularly the monetary analogy, suggest a further interesting parallel. The only situation in which there is a need for a monetary medium is that in which economically valuable resources have become emancipated from ascriptive ties and, hence, available for exchange. So long as property rights are transferable only through inheritance, and labor is allocated through hereditary succession, there is no need for money. Presumably, emancipation is a condition of the development of a monetary system. The parallel in the conceptual area would seem to be the necessity for elementary observational experiences to become emancipated from the objects of common sense that are held. The naïve outlook of primitive realism must be abandoned. Early men doubtless knew that the metal called lead was gray and heavy, but it never occurred to them that what they experienced directly was grayness, heaviness, and solidity and that the material object "lead" was a "construction," an inference, based on those experiences. Failing in that, they could neither take their elementary experiences and reassemble them in more useful ways, nor abstract grayness and heaviness from the objects with which they were (in their view) associated. The same kind of problem appears in current thought when we tend to view social system theory as a way of viewing organizations such as the school, rather than an entirely different conceptual organization of experience that does not speak directly to the organization of common-sense at all.

There is still another extremely important parallel between the several cases under consideration here. Consider money first. By far its most important property, from the point of view of those who possess it, is its capacity to serve as a highly generalized resource. It is tied in advance to no specific use, and hence can be used in the pursuit of a great variety of specific goals. Exactly the same thing may be said with respect to the symbolic representations of the world that we speak of as "knowledge." It too is a highly generalized resource that is capable of facilitating the attainment of a wide variety of goals. In that sense it enhances the adaptive capacity of those who possess it.

As indicated earlier, this chapter is addressed to the presentation of at least a partial conception of the scientific enterprise. That task is undertaken in the conviction that such a conception will not only help researchers to "know what they are doing" in the sense previously illustrated, but will also aid practitioners in making intelligent use of the products of researchers.

Preliminary Considerations

The view of the scientific enterprise presented here is grounded in a conception of the nature of the environment of life, on the one hand and of human life on the other. With respect to the former, the most fundamental proposition is that it is ordered, or structured both spatially (not only in the sense of physical space) and temporally. Spatiotemporal order or structure is generated by, or is a manifestation of, *constraints* that control spatiotemporal neighborhood relationships.

In the temporal domain order is . . . generated by the constraints of the "Laws of Nature" which, on the macroscopic scale of direct observation, control the chain of events. Chaos would permit transitions from any state to any other state, mountains transforming themselves into flying pink elephants, pink elephants turning into yellow goo, etc. Not only are organisms impossible in this world, for by definition, there is no law that holds the organism together; but also this world is indescribable, for description requires names, and names refer to the "invariabilia"—the constraints—in the environment. (von Foerster, 1968, p. 172)

As an example of spatial structure generated by spatial constraint, consider the familiar snow crystal. Were it not for the physical constraint on the growth of snow crystals associated with the triangular shape of the water molecule, we should perceive no such structure as the snow crystal. Hydrogen molecules are not at liberty to attach themselves to oxygen molecules in any way they please; they must approximate either a thirty degree or a sixty degree angular relation. The freedom to approximate either of these two relations allows for the nearly inexhaustible variety of snow crystals, yet the variation is sufficiently constrained to discriminate all members of this class of structures from other structures and identify them as snow crystals (von Foerster, 1968).

Thus, spatial constraints are manifested in the structures they produce, or generate, and the latter include all the objects and entities of experience. We tend, in the common-sense view, to link the concept *space* to the concept *physical,* but one may think of a variety of spaces other than physical, and, in general, structures may be viewed as patterns of relations among parts that persist through time. It is the relations among the parts that is constrained—although the parts themselves are manifestations of lower-order constraints—as in the case of the snow crystal. Another example may be seen in what is termed "social structure," but here the space involved is not physical. Perhaps it is well to speak of a "relational space." In the case of the snow crystal there are three hundred sixty conceivable whole angular relations, but natural laws constrain the growth of such crystals to approximations of only two of these. In the case of "social structure" there are numerous conceivable relations among units, but these are constrained by social laws, norms, of which the legal variety is only the most formal and explicit.

Spatial constraints, then, place limitations on the relational patterns that can hold among the elements of a structure, and temporal constraints place limitations on the kinds of events that can be neighbors to one another in time, i.e., that can follow and precede one another. Thus, given a structure such as the snow crystal—the manifestation of spatial constraints—there are limitations on the kinds of transformations it can undergo. The crystals may be transformed into water, but not into wood or stone. Constraint in the temporal sense means that given certain conditions, some events are more likely to follow than others.

If chaos permits every event to appear with equal probability, order emerges from chaos when certain transitions become more probable than others. Certainty of an event following another creates a perfect, deterministic universe, and the problem of how to survive in such a deterministic universe is reduced to finding the constraints that govern the transitions from one event to the next. Clearly, the simplest of all such deterministic universes is the one where no transitions take place, i.e., where everything is at motionless and uniform tranquility. Hence, the oceans, where temperature variations, changes in the concentration of chemicals, destructive forces, etc. are kept at a minimum, were the cradle for life. (von Foster, 1968, p. 174)

We now turn to the organism side of the organism—environment duality. As von Foerster (1968) points out, all multicellular organisms have, distributed over their surface, highly differentiated sensory receptor cells; some are sensitive to pressure, some to chemical change, and some to light distribution. The function of such cells, in von Foerster's view, is to compute environmental constraints, both spatial and temporal. It would appear that the ability of organisms to compute environmental constraints has been acquired through processes of natural selection in which organisms with neutral systems that successfully computed adaptively useful environmental constraints had a survival advantage over other organisms. We might liken the organism to a computer and speak of the program that determines what operations are performed on data inputs. Thus, from the data of light distribution, the nervous system of the frog computes certain environmental constraints that are different from those computed by the nervous system of the honey-bee. Using this analogy, we may say that infrahuman organisms, to a much greater extent than human, are genetically programmed. That is, far more of the constraints that they compute (perceive) are determined by their physiology. As one author has stated, "To build a dam, a beaver needs only an appropriate site and materials. His behavior is determined by his physiology" (Geertz, 1966, p. 7). This, of course, is an exaggeration. There is great variety among the species, and even very simple organisms undergo additional programming by the environment. That is, the behavior of infrahuman organisms do learn to compute both spatial and temporal constraints.

The great distinction between infrahuman and human organism is in the latter's capacity not only to compute a much greater variety of environmental constraints but also to create symbolic systems with which to compute. The human creates symbols that stand for, as Morse code stands for letters in the alphabet, the constraints of the environment. His language, or at least parts of it, approximates in its semantic and syntactic constraints the constraints of the environment. If his symbols are well chosen, he can manipulate them in such a way that the consequences of the symbol manipulation symbolize the consequences of the physical operations and events symbolized. Through the manipulation of symbols, the human organism can experience symbolically the consequences of physical operations without performing those operations.

The enormous advantage of organisms that are able to manipulate symbols over those who can only react to signs is that all logical operations do not have to be acted out. It is obvious that this saves considerable amounts of energy. But the really crucial point here is that errors in reasoning are not necessarily lethal. (von Foerster, 1968, p. 180)

To paraphrase Galenter and Gerstenhaber (1956, p. 219), science is neither more nor less than constructing a symbolic model or representation, of the environment, running the model faster than the environment, and predicting that the environment will behave as the model does. Once a symbolic model has been constructed it can be manipulated according to its own constraints under various hypothetical conditions. The organism is then able to observe the outcome of these manipulations and to project them onto the environment as predictions. Science, as we know it, would be impossible without symbols, both for reasons of inability to create models, and for reasons of inability to communicate in more than a rudimentary fashion with other modelers; past, present, and future.

Science and Common-Sense

If we view what we customarily speak of as producing knowledge, thinking, and reasoning as constructing, manipulating and testing symbolic models which purport to replicate in some degree in their internal and external constraints the constraints of selected aspects of the environment, then any substantive distinction between the construction and use of scientific models on the one hand, and common-sense models, on the other, immediately disappears. Both kinds of models may be regarded as symbolic representations, and any knowledge capable of transmission from one person to another must be so regarded. Whether the model originated as an outcome of a scientific research program, or as an outcome of every-day efforts to earn a livelihood is irrelevant. As a matter of fact, all sciences seem to have had their origins in the practical, everyday concerns of practical, every-day men.

From this point of view there is no fundamental difference between manipulating the symbol systems that we designate scientific theories, and those which we designate practical, common-sense knowledge. Both are symbolic representations, both are manipulated and the outcomes of the manipulations are projected on the environment. This is not to say that there are no distinctions of any kind between scientific symbolizations and those which we might designate otherwise. For the most part, the scientific symbolization may be regarded as a model *of* some aspect of the environment, while many of those spoken of under the heading of common-sense (as well as "applied science") may often be regarded as models *for* controlling some aspect of the environment. However, if one includes the actions of human manipulators, or controllers, in the events to be symbolized, then even that distinction disappears. Another possible difference of degree, although not of kind, concerns the manner in which the two kinds of representations are regarded by their users and may be seen in the tendency of a scientific community to check and recheck the goodness of fit between its symbolic representations and that which is symbolized. Still another difference is the relative tentativeness with which the symbolizations are held. More important is the deliberate effort on the part of the scientist to represent the broadest possible spectrum of environmental constraints with the least possible number of symbols. One of Newton's great contributions was the development of a single symbolic representation that did the work that had, until then, required two sets of symbols. Newton made it possible to represent the constraints of both terrestial and celestial motion within a single set of symbols. Most of the "great" contributions to science have had this characteristic. Darwin provided a symbolic system that represented the origins of both man and lower animals; Einstein represented both matter and energy within the same symbolic model. The list could be extended to include Aristotle, Hertz, Maxwell, Weber, Smith, and others.

In everyday affairs we introduce terms into our language without much regard for the question of whether or not it is necessary to do so. In a science, on the other hand, new terms are introduced somewhat more sparingly, and only when there are specific reasons for doing so. There are two major occasions on which the scientist regards the introduction of new terms into the language of science warranted. One is the occasion of the identification of a new class of phenomena, e.g., when biologists observe a previously unknown species, or when the phenomenon of magnetism was encountered. The other is when, given some phenomenon, one attempts to invent an account that explains the existence or occurrence of that phenomenon. For example, suppose we have observed that when certain kinds of metals are placed in close proximity to certain other kinds of metals, then the two pieces of metal move together with no interference on our part, and we decide to call this *magnetism*. We have, of course, only named the phenomenon. If we stop here we have explained nothing, just as we have explained nothing by saying that an animal eats because it is hungry.

But we can introduce new terms into the language and use those terms to invent an account of the mechanisms that "lie behind" the appearance. This is a perfectly legitimate scientific procedure as long as the account leads back to the realm of observable events. That is, there must be a way of coming back to new observations to test the usefulness of the invention. If we postulate an ego, an id, and a superego, but have no way of relating these to observations other than those that led us to use the terms in the first place, we have explained nothing. Suppose we say, then, that all things in the world are made up of tiny bodies called *molecules*, that these molecules are in constant heat motion, that the more heat we apply to the object, the faster the molecules move, that each of these molecules is itself a magnet with a north and south pole, and that in those pieces of metal that we observe to attract other metals, these small molecular magnets tend to be lined up so that large numbers of them have their north and south poles pointed in the same direction. In that manner, the separate attraction of each molecule supplements that of each other molecule and we have larger magnetic body. Where this is not the case, the magnetism of the several molecules cancels out.

Given such a fanciful account, one can reason as follows: "If there is anything to this account, that is, if it is 'true' that magnetic attraction occurs because of the small magnetic particles in motion lining up in certain ways, and if it is 'true' that these small particles move faster when heated, then if we heat a magnetic body its magnetic strength should be reduced, and if we cool a magnetic body we should be able to increase its magnetic strength." Here we have a way of returning to the observable world, and although we may never see a molecule, we do have a way of checking the plausibility, or the usefulness of our invention. If the invented account is compatible with the facts of the case, then we should indeed observe that heating a magnet decreases its magnetic strength. If we do not observe that, if adequate controls have been utilized, then we may conclude that the invented account is incorrect.

The introduction of new terms into the language of a science in the manner described constitutes a deliberate attempt to invent an account such that the observations we have at hand are logical consequences of that account. Given an account of which certain observations are logical consequences, one may also derive other observation statements that are also logical consequences, but for which no observations have yet been made, e.g., the observation that heating a magnet reduces its magnetic strength. If the predicted observations are made, that is, if the hypotheses are verified, then we can say that the hypothetical account is compatible with our observations. But we cannot say that it is true, in the sense that this is the way things "really" are. The symbolic model that introduces terms for which there are no corresponding observations sets up a hypothetical world, it postulates a world underlying the observable world in which there are entities having certain properties and whose behavior is regulated by certain laws. In the successful case, we demonstrate that such a world is compatible with the world of direct experience. Since there are any number of hypothetical worlds that may be compatible with our observations, we can never know that a given one is correct. We can only know, by the fact that the observations that a hypothetical world leads us to expect do not occur, that some hypothetical worlds are incorrect. We can disprove theories, but we cannot prove them.

Components of Scientific Language

The notion of two major occasions for the introduction of new terms into the language of a science leads naturally to the view of such a language as divisible into two major components. Although the division cannot be made cleanly and with finality, it seems useful to think of one component of the language of a science as linked directly with the world of percepts. For the most part, terms in this component of the language are defined in terms of observations. This is the language in terms of which we describe and state facts about the world. "The house is green," "The dog is heavy," "The cat is a four-legged animal," and "The post office is three miles northwest of my house." Without observations, and without a language in which to record those observations, there is no science. Newton's work could not have been done without the thousands and thousands of observations that were preserved in the form of descriptive statements made by the Babylonians, the Greeks, the Moors, and particularly by the Danish astronomer Tycho Brahe. In fact, the work of Ptolemy and Copernicus could not have been done without the vast amount of recorded observations provided by a great many of their predecessors.

In any science the story is the same. Invariably, the great accomplishments of the Newtons, Darwins, Daltons, Bohrs, and others have been preceded by years of painstaking observation and description. The descriptive efforts of biologists go back to the days of Aristotle and earlier, and the beginnings of chemistry are lost in the history of alchemy. This is a point that cannot be sufficiently emphasized. In these days of mathematical physics, mathematical biology, and highly advanced theoretical developments, it is easy to lose sight of the necessity for descriptive natural history materials in a scientific field. But, if it is true that there can be no science without observation and description, it is equally true that these alone do not constitute a science. A science is not an accumulation of factual descriptions. Nor is it a vast quantity of unrelated bits of information. The facts, the observations, and the descriptive materials Ptolemy and Copernicus had to work with were exactly the same. Copernicus did not have more observations to work with than did Ptolemy, nor did he have more accurate descriptions. Both Copernicus and Ptolemy had the same data to work with.

The primary datum is the observed sky. The sky cannot be touched; it can only be seen. Thus the datum is wholly visual. Let us suppose the sky is being continuously watched by an intelligent man who knows nothing whatever about astronomical theories, ancient or modern. At night he will see a blue dome speckled with shining spots. These he calls stars. Most of these spots will remain in a fixed position, but others will noticeably change their position relative to the rest and to the observer's point of view. These he calls planets. On some nights he will see a round silvery disk with shadowed markings. This he calls the moon. As he watches, the moon moves across the sky from east to west. On successive nights its shape changes, it wanes to a slender crescent; the time of its appearance becomes later. Then no moon appears. After the lapse of a few nights it appears again, a slender crescent low down in the sky. Sometimes a coppery shadow falls across the moon, blotting out the light. This he calls an eclipse of the moon. In the daytime he observes a shining yellow disk which he calls the sun. This also moves across the sky from east to west. Unlike the moon, the sun's shape does not vary, it rises, a circular disk, above the horizon every day. But its size and color vary. The movements of the moon and the sun are periodic; they follow a regular order. Sometimes, however, the light of the sun is eclipsed at different periods of the day. It would not be long before our observer would have formed definite expectations as to the appearance of the sun and the moon. But the planets would present a more puzzling problem. Their movements across the sky are irregular, continued observation would reveal a backward movement at some periods of the year.

These, then, are the facts that have to be ordered; the movements of the sun, of the moon, and of the planets; eclipses of the sun and of the moon; the changing shape of the moon. Our hypothetical observer would be in possession of these data only if he kept records of these movements over a period of many years. (Stebbing, 1961, p. 294)

Now let us imagine Copernicus and Ptolemy, each in possession of these descriptive materials. What does each do with them? Does he simply present them as a description of the way the world is? Obviously not. Each attempts to invent a hypothetical world, such that these data are logical consequences of that world, and to construct a symbolic model of the world that will enable him to deduce each and every one of the facts that he has before him. Important as they are, empirical observations are, in one sense, only grist for the scientific mill. By themselves observations are no more than an assortment of differentiated bits of information. It is only when they become logical consequences of a deductive system that they constitute a fully developed science, or an organized body of information. It is possible for data to be organized to a considerable extent in its own terms. That is, one can note relationships between the position of the moon and the eclipse of the sun, between the passage of time and the waning of the moon. One can construct such a thing as a correlational science, but it is far less economical than a deductive science, and it suggests no hypotheses.

Just as facts by themselves are an insufficient basis for a science, so are logically developed deductive systems. The scholastics of the Middle Ages were skilled logicians, but they produced no empirical science. It was only when Galileo joined together the logic of the rationalists and the observations of the empiricists that modern science came into being. Rational, logical symbol systems by themselves are empty, and observations that are not logically ordered are extremely difficult to manage and unproductive with respect to new knowledge. Science is the product of the union between observation guided by symbols and the manipulation of symbols. Both are essential to science. As Hawkins has stated:

We may construct coherent theories at the expense of empirical reliability of the concepts employed, or we may give concepts reliable empirical reference at the expense of significant generalizations about them. Either procedure may be a useful tactic in scientific research, but neither is more than that. Using the labels as names for intellectual tendencies rather than for philosophical theories, we may refer to the former procedure as rationalistic and to the latter as empiristic. Empiricism, the tendency to specify descriptive concepts primarily with reference to means and methods of observation and measurement, may lead to revised concepts, among which new theoretical relations can be conjectured and, in the end, demonstrated experimentally. Rationalism, the tendency to elaborate theoretical systems without much reference to the empirical meaning of concepts, may lead to new sorts of observations and measurement. . . . Both tendencies, interacting, are involved in successful scientific inquiry. (Hawkins, 1964, p. 98)

One of the major kinds of words in the language of science, then, is descriptive words, words having more or less reliable empirical reference. Of these Hawkins has said:

Descriptive concepts have as a function in the economy of knowledge the linkage of two universes of discourse, the concrete perceptual and the abstract conceptual. In being classified under this or that conceptual heading, any empirical object or state of affairs is not merely brought into relation with the particular abstraction that is the basis for classifying it; it is classified with some things, and apart from others, and it is involved in all the consequences resulting from the linkages, logical and factual, of this class concept with others. (Hawkins, 1964, p. 97)

A descriptive concept must be usable as a basis for classifying things and it must be linked with other concepts in a way that supports reliable inferences about the things thus classified. It must have, as it were, two kinds of reliability; that of being reliably related to other concepts in the system of knowledge, and that of reliably guiding the classification of particulars. . . . What is characteristic of common-sense concepts is that they are linked together in a rather loose, implicit system of beliefs; and, since such concepts are not sharply defined in an empirical sense, it is a considerable problem to say just how they apply in particular cases. (Hawkins, 1964, p. 98)

The ultimate objective, of course, is the development of a language with the greatest possible degree of internal consistency, and the widest possible degree of empirical applicability. The kinds of languages in which these characteristics are most prominent are mathematical, or deductive, systems, and these have a number of characteristics worth noting. Any scientific language that has matured to the level of a mathematical science contains (1) a number of undefined, or primitive terms, (2) a number of other terms defined by the primitive terms, (3) a number of unproved postulates, or assumptions, involving those terms, and (4) a number of theorems derived logically from the postulates. In geometry, the undefined terms may be "point," "line," and "plane." An example of a term defined in terms of these is "circle," the set of all points in a plane equidistant from a given point. The postulates specify

specific sentences until one has the file of specific sentences at hand. Thus, it makes no sense to write, "All mammals give live birth to their offspring," until one has a large number of sentences such as, "Whales give live birth to their offspring."

Let us examine briefly, the manner in which the early subject matter of botany might have developed. At some point in the history of man, it may have been found useful to distinguish between plants and non-plants. This kind of distinction could be made only if all those objects classed as plants were perceived to have certain likenesses that were not shared with other objects. At some subsequent time it must have been useful to make further distinctions within the category of plants, perhaps a distinction between edible and nonedible plants. This distinction, like that between plants and nonplants, could be made only if some subset within the category of plants exhibited less variability on some dimension within the subset than between the subset and the remainder of the category. We depend, then, on variability within similarity or differences within likenesses, i.e., a difference is an instance of a number of things having likeness not shared by other objects. To identify an object as a particular object is to say that it has certain likenesses with certain other objects, and at the same time is unlike a number of other objects. If one describes a plant as having X number of Y-shaped leaves in configuration Z, one identifies one likeness in identifying the object as a plant, another in speaking of leaves, another in speaking of number, yet another in speaking of shape, and still another in speaking of configuration. One proceeds by making finer and finer discriminations, by which we mean finding likenesses within likenesses, which is the same as finding differences within likenesses. But the whole point of making finer discriminations is to lay the groundwork for making broader generalizations.

From Gorn's point of view, making finer discriminations is adding more specific sentences to the file. Instead of writing sentences such as "All mammals are vertebrates," which encompasses specific sentences such as, "The dog is a vertebrate," and "Heavy bodies fall to the ground," and "Stones fall to the ground," one breaks the latter sentences down into more specific sentences such as, "All Chihuahuas are short-haired dogs," and "Lead is heavier than wood." There are, then, at least two general directions of development in the growth of a scientific language; one tending to add increasing numbers of increasingly specific sentences to the language, the other tending to take the place of increasing numbers of those specific sentences. In the long run, neither development can occur in isolation from the other.

One cannot say at just what stage in the development of a file of information it is appropriate to invent categories that permit summary sentences to be written. It is clear, however, that this can be done prematurely. For example, in the eighteenth century the theory of four humors was utilized as the basis for classifying illnesses into four extreme types. As Bronowski points out:

> The folly of the theory was that it tried to impose a system on events which had not been sufficiently observed; and in time it came to shape the observations themselves. In the eighteenth century the doctors dominated by it could think of no advances except to reduce the observations to fewer extremes than the classical four. . . . It was these large reckless theories which made a caricature of medicine and turned the doctor into a quack: bleeding, drugging, and a sawing, curing Bishop Berkely with tarwater and killing Oliver Goldsmith with fever powders, all by rules which were simply fanciful. The great advances in medicine from the end of the eighteenth century were of quite a different kind. They were scrupulous observations of complex symptoms which characterized one disease and not another. (Bronowski, 1951, p. 56)

The issue, however, seems not to be one of categorizing versus not categorizing, but one of the level at which categorizing is done. In order to make observations at all, or at least to report them in the form of descriptions, one must categorize. In order to make scrupulous observations of the complex symptoms that characterize a disease, e.g., smallpox, one must write such sentences as, "All observed cases of smallpox are accompanied by symptoms a,b,c, and d." And in order to write such sentences one must utilize nouns and verbs corresponding to perceived likenesses. Given a number of such sentences about a number of diseases, one may then look for likenesses among diseases, and, upon finding them, invent words, e.g., "infectious" and "fever," which make it possible to write more general sentences. Thus, one may be in a position to write a sentence such as, "All infectious diseases are accompanied by fever." But, one may also move in the other direction. That is, one may become interested in the specific symptom "fever" and look at a variety of situations in which that symptom occurs with the intent of finding likenesses there and writing more specific sentences about them. If one examined a number of instances of fever, one might find eventually that they could be differentiated from one another on a numerical scale of temperature. That is, some fevers are alike in that they produce a thermometer reading of 99 degrees, some a reading of 100 degrees, and some a reading of 101 degrees. From this point of view, numerical measurement is simply a highly refined way of identifying likenesses, or of categorizing. There is no intrinsic difference between classifying a given fever as a fever of 101 degrees and classifying an animal as a mammal. In both cases the object or event of interest is being placed in a class with other similar objects or events, the animal in the class of mammals, the fever in the class of 101 degrees temperature. The difference between these two examples is not that one is classification and the other is measurement; both are types of classification and measurement. The difference is rather in what can be done on the basis of the acts of classifying. *To identify an animal as a mammal means that it has certain other properties, and that it stands in certain relations to other sorts of animals in terms of evolutionary development.* On the other hand, the identification of a fever as 101 degrees means that that fever stands in all the relations to other fevers with which 101 stands to other numbers. *Given one entity identified as a mammal and another identified as a reptile, one can then say that the reptile is the evolutionary ancestor of the mammal.* And, given a fever of 101 and another fever of 100, one can say that the former is greater than the latter. One can also introduce operations and write, for example, "Mammals cannot cross breed with reptiles," and "A temperature of 101 degrees cannot be added to any other temperature, i.e., temperatures are not additive."

Another way of stating this is to say that, given a number of species of anything, say diseases, and given a sufficient number of observations concerning their symptoms (differentia), one may then look for likenesses among these symptoms with a view toward inventing new genera under which to classify the several species. Thus, smallpox may be treated, along with diphtheria, cholera, chicken pox, mumps, and the like, as species of diseases each having characteristic symptoms, and one may find it possible to identify likenesses among the several species that lead to the writing of such sentences as "Smallpox is an infectious disease in which the symptoms are. . . ." Here the term *infectious* is a new term, a genus, which may be used in more general sentences of the kind, "All infectious diseases are accompanied by fever." But, one may also move in the other direction. Instead of moving from the level of specific sentences concerning species of the more general level of sentences concerning genera, one may focus on the differentia of a given species (the symptoms of a particular disease) for the purpose of determining what subsets of likenesses may be identified within it. That is, one may set out to scrupulously observe and describe fevers in the same way that one set out to do the same with respect to diseases. If one succeeds in differentiating subclasses within the class of fevers then he may ask the further question, "What is the relation between fever differentia and, say, blood pressure differentia?" This is much the same kind of question as, "What is the relationship between mammals and reptiles?" The difference is that in one case the relations of interest are evolutionary, and in the other they are mathematical. Both mathematics and the theory of evolution are concerned with units, with relations among these units, and operations on, or events involving those units.

This provides a clue to what one is about when he engages in taxonomic studies, or at least, what tends to be the outcome of such efforts. The point can be seen very clearly in several areas of scentific investigations, particularly biology and chemistry. In the early stages of biology one classificatory system was based on toes and teeth. The English naturalist John Ray,

divided mamals into two large groups: those with toes and those with hoofs. He divided the hoofed animals into one-hoofed (horses) and two-hoofed (cattle), and three-hoofed (rhinoceros). The two-hoofed mammals he again divided into three groups: those which chewed the cud and had permanent horns (goats, etc.), those which chewed the cud and had horns that were shed annually (deer), and those which did not chew the cud (swine). (Asimov, 1964, p. 36)[*]

Ray's system did not survive, and at least one of the reasons for its demise was probably its lack of economy. As Kuhn (1963, p. 32) has noted:

After various classification systems are tried, that one is considered best which contains the largest amount of information for the purpose of the scientists. It is the most efficient system for handling the kinds of information that scientists want, or more precisely the system which permits the largest amounts of information to be deduced from a given amount of other information.

In the case of whales and porpoises, for example, it is clear that they could as easily be classed with fish as water-dwelling animals, as with men and elephants as mammals. That is an alternative way of classifying animals according to where they dwell, on land or in water.
But the two schemes are not equally efficient.

Under the existing system, if we possess a specimen of a thing called a fish, we know without looking further that we will find a particular kind of circulatory, nervous, excretory, and other systems, and that we will also find gills for the breathing of water. Suppose instead that the term fish was broadened to include whales and porpoises, because they look like them and live in water. Then even if we knew that we had a fish in front of us, this fact would not tell us whether the specimen has lungs or gills. Another well-known conspicuous example is the classification of bats as mammals instead of birds. (Kuhn, 1963 pp. 32–33)

To paraphrase Kuhn, the person who is naïve in these matters may insist that whales and porpoises *are* mammals, that we have no choice but to call them that because the names of things reflect their immutable nature. The commonness of this view should not obscure the fact that things are classified for human convenience and can be reclassified for the same reason.
Another reason for the abandonment of Ray's system can be made

---

[*] *A Short History of Biology,* copyright © 1964 by Isaac Asimov. Reprinted by permission of Doubleday & Co., Inc.

explicit by considering the system that replaced it. Largely through the work of the Swedish naturalist Carolus Linnaeus, naturalists first came to group animals by species, i.e., according to interbreeding animals, and then to successively group species according to genera, genera according to family, family according to order, order according to class, class according to phylum, and phylum according to kingdom. The merit of Linnaeus's system, beyond its economy, was (1) that the animals within a given class showed more likenesses, (2) that it highlighted likenesses between classes, and (3) that it led to fruitful speculations about the relations among the species, genera, orders, families, and so on.

Linnaeus' classification, beginning with extremely broad groups and dividing into successively narrower groups, seemed like a literal "tree of life." Looking upon the representation of such a tree, however diagramatic, it was almost inevitable that one would wonder whether the arrangement could be entirely accidental. Might not two closely related species have developed from a common ancestor, and might not two closely related ancestors have developed from a still more ancient and primitive ancestor? (Asimov, p. 38)

Thus, the order given to descriptive data by the taxonomy leads naturally to the question, "How can we account for the existence of this order?" Or, "What kind of a deductive system can we invent such that this order is a logical consequence of it?" For any given order there is, presumably, a number of possible accounts, some of which might be regarded as scientific and some of which might be regarded as other than scientific. Linnaeus, himself, for example:

insisted that every species had been separately created and that each had been maintained by divine providence so that no species had been allowed to become extinct. (Asimov, p. 38)

Nor was this the only alternative. Cuvier's extension of Linnaeus's work and his application of it in the classification of fossils led Cuvier to postulate a series of catastrophes during which all life on the earth was extinguished, and after which new forms of life that were quite different from those of previous eras emerged. Modern forms of life were viewed as having been created after the most recent catastrophe.

In this view, evolutionary processes were not needed to explain the fossils, and the biblical story, supposed to apply only to events after the last catastrophe, could be preserved.

Cuvier felt that four catastrophes were needed to explain the known distribution of fossils. However, as more and more fossils were discovered, matters grew more complicated and some of Cuvier's followers eventually postulated as many as twenty-seven catastrophes. (Asimov, p. 44)

In time, the issue was resolved on the basis of empirical evidence.

In 1830 the Scottish geologist, Charles Lyell, . . . marshalled the evidence indicating that earth underwent only gradual and noncatastrophic changes. And, to be sure, continuing studies of fossils backed Lyell. There seemed no points at all in the records of the strata where all life was wiped out. Some forms survived each period where a catastrophe was suggested. Indeed, some forms now alive have existed virtually unchanged for many millions of years. (Asimov, p. 35)

In chemistry, a good deal of experimental and theoretical work was done prior to the development of the taxonomy of chemical elements, the periodic table. The phlogiston theory had been advanced and then demolished; Dalton had formulated the beginnings of the atomic theory of matter; empirical confirmation had been obtained for the laws of fixed proportions, multiple proportions, and reciprocal proportions; a variety of new elements had been identified; and atomic weights had been assigned to the known elements.

With the discovery and examination of more and more elements it became possible for Newlands (1838–1898), a chemist in a London sugar refinery, to expound a so-called *law of octaves* in papers published between 1863 and 1866. He pointed out that when the elements were arranged in order of increasing atomic weights, each element showed a family likeness to elements which were seven, or some multiple of seven, places before or after it. He was however discouraged by the cold reception of his idea, especially when a member of an audience of the Chemical Society of London asked him whether he had ever thought of looking into an alphabetical arrangement!

Other chemists pursued the idea of a systematic classification, and in 1869 the Russian chemist Mendeleev . . . published a comprehensive arrangement known as the "periodic system," in which he showed that the elements, when arranged in the order of increasing atomic weights, fell into definite families or groups, showing a periodicity of chemical and physical properties. (Reed, 1961, pp. 178–179)

This had the effect of placing the rare gases of the atmosphere (helium, neon, argon, and others), which are alike in their unusual chemical stability and unreactivity, in one group; the alkali metals (lithium, sodium, potassium, and others), which are alike in their tendency to decompose water, liberating hydrogen, and in their tendency to form strongly alkaline solutions in another group; and so on. As in the case of biology, such similarities and relationships gave rise to much speculation concerning the "underlying cause," and attention came increasingly to be focused on the nature of the atom. This, in turn, brought into question Dalton's conception of the atom as an unbreakable particle having no structure of its own.

It seems clear that what one does when he engages in taxonomic inquiry is, first, an attempt to identify relationships of likeness among the entities classified, and second, to raise questions about, and identify relationships among classes of entities. Once one has succeeded in identifying the likenesses that lead one to speak of species, genera, and so on, the next step is to determine the relations among these. Each science, and each branch within a science, has its own set of categories, its own set of relations among them, and its own set of operations or events. In early biology, as we have seen, the categories were species, genera, and so on, and the relations among the categories were primarily those of similarity, and at a theoretical level, those of ancestor-descendant. In mathematics, the categories are numbers, and the relations among them are equal to, more than, less than. Each science also has its set of operators. In biology, these are perhaps such notions as interbreed, adapt, and the like. In mathematics they are add, subtract, and multiply. Operators, or operations, are those things that happen, or that one does to bring about certain results. In biology, one might write the sentence, "Tall peas crossed with dwarf peas yields——." In mathematics, it might be equals added to equals yield equals.

Both mathematics and the biological taxonomy, as well as other scientific languages, are in one respect classificatory systems. Both permit one to identify an entity or events as kind of a specific—e.g., one *war* is composed of *many* battles. And having made that identification, both systems permit one to make certain deductions concerning the relations between that entity or event and other entities and events classified within the system, and concerning the results of certain operations on these entities, whether the operations are "natural" or experimental. Mathematics, of course, is a much more fully developed instrument both in terms of the discriminations that can be made in classification and in terms of the relational and operational deductions in which it permits one to engage.

To translate this into Gorn's language, what one does when he engages in taxonomic inquiry is to invent the abstract nouns (subjects and predicates) in terms of which one writes sentences that are general enough to replace a number of more specific sentences each having different nouns. Once one has succeeded in that endeavor he moves to the invention of verbs that specify relationships among the nouns and specify the operations that can be performed on the nouns and the outcomes of those operations. Given the nouns and the verbs, further investigation makes it possible to write the sentences "2 dogs plus 3 dogs equals 5 dogs," "2 horses plus 3 horses equals 5 horses," and eventually to write the summary sentence, "$2 + 3 = 5$." Exactly the same processes are involved here as are involved in first writing the sentences, "A body falls 16 feet in the first second of its fall," "A body moves 64 feet in the first 2 seconds of its fall," "A body moves 144 feet in the first three seconds of its fall," "A body moves 256 feet in the first four seconds of its fall," and then writing the general sentence $S = 16t^2$ of which each of these sentences is a special case. Precisely the same process is illustrated again in substituting the general sentence "All mammals are vertebrates," for a number of specific sentences such as, "The elephant is a vertebrate." Above that, of course, is the level of developing a syntax for the language, a syntax that specifies what kinds of operations can be performed and what kinds of sentences can be written.

Whether we talk about taxonomic inquiry, or about more specific investigations of processes and relationships, the basic approach of science is one of seeing likenesses, inventing words to stand for those likenesses, and using those words to write "scientific" sentences. Thus, the dreaded scourge of seamen, scurvy, was brought under control when the Scottish physician James Lind noted that the disease was not confined to seamen, but occurred in prisons, in besieged cities, and, in general, wherever the diet of persons was severely restricted. Similarly, the carrier of typhus was identified when the French physician Charles Nicolle noted that patients in the hospital who had been stripped of their clothing and bathed on admission did not seem susceptible to the disease, a fact which led him to suspect the body louse.

Finding similarities between the conditions associated with a number of occurrences of scurvy is basically no different from finding similarities in the reproductive characteristics of a given class of animals. And, in both cases, the identification of likenesses is the occasion for asking the question, "Why these likenesses (or differences)?" Mendel's work with tall and dwarf pea plants enabled him to write such sentences as, "Self-pollinated dwarf pea plants breed true," and "Cross-pollinated hybrid plants yield true breeding tall plants, true breeding dwarf plants, and hybrid tall plants on the proportions of 1:1:2." How does one account for these facts? That is, what kinds of sentences can one write so that these sentences are logical consequences of them? The language developed by Mendel to talk about these first-order sentences included such terms as *growth-factors,* and the operation *combination.* Nearly fifty years later it was possible to rewrite these sentences using such terms as chromosomes, sperm cell, egg cell, and mitosis.

An Illustrative Example

It is time now to pull together the rather scattered reflections reported in the preceding pages. In order to do this, I should like to utilize an analogy that I have found useful in working with students. Imagine, if necessary, that you have no familiarity at all with the game of chess. Imagine also, that you are a scientist who, for reasons best known to yourself, has decided that the world of chess is worthy of investigation. How do you proceed? Although the steps may not occur in any precise sequence, there are certain steps that must come before other steps. Certainly, one of the very first things to be done is to devise some way of discriminating one piece from another (remember, you don't know a pawn from a bishop). An obvious point of discrimination is color. This may or may not turn out to be significant, i.e., it may be related to other likenesses.

A sufficient amount of observation would reveal that there are sixteen pieces that, except for their color, are very nearly identical in appearance (pawns). Of course, if the name *pawn* was adopted for use in connection with pieces with certain characteristics, we could encounter some difficulty in deciding whether a black piece with those same characteristics should be called a pawn. In addition, there are three cases in which there are four nearly identical pieces (rooks, bishops, knights), and two cases in which there are two nearly identical pieces (kings and queens). For the sake of abbreviating the story, let us assume that the names pawn, rook, knight, bishop, king, and queen have been adopted. There still remains, of course, the problem of distinguishing one pawn from another, one knight from another, and so on, but that can be solved. One might proceed as an ornithologist might when studying the behavior of members of a flock of birds, by marking each bird with a different colored dye.

Given the classification of the pieces and the identification of the members within each class, one would seem to be in a position to begin writing sentences about what happens in this world. But, here we encounter another problem. One cannot describe action apart from a frame of reference. In order to write a sentence describing what happens in the world of chess, one must have, or devise, a language for talking about events. In order to describe the movements of the pieces, we must have some sort of reference system within which it is possible to identify the location from which and to which the piece moved. Change of any kind can be described fully only if we can identify both the initial and terminal states.

We may note parenthetically, that descriptions, or discriminations based on identifying properties, involve the location of an object in a similar reference system, sometimes referred to as a property space. Thus, describing a chess piece in terms of its size, color, or shape, is locating the piece on a number of variable dimensions on which all other pieces may also be located. Some properties, of course, change too rapidly to be used for identification purposes, but others are sufficiently stable to be used reliably. The latter are sometimes referred to as *structural properties of units*.

As a reference system for the description of what happens in chess, one might adopt the fairly standard practice of treating the chess board as a matrix, identifying rows with letters of the alphabet, and columns with numbers. Since there are eight rows and eight columns, there are sixty-four possible locations on the chess board, and in the absence of any prior knowledge, any piece can potentially move from any location to any other location, i.e., any state can be followed by any other state. At this point, we can not know what actually is the case, so we must begin by making careful observations and keeping detailed records. That is, we must begin writing sentences for the information file, sentences such as "Pawn number 1 moved from a2 to a4," or more economically, "P1, a2–a4." Given a very large number of such sentences about all pieces, one then examines the sentences to see if more general sentences can be written to take the place of those about each specific piece. With persistence, one might write the sentence, "All knights move along an L-shaped track in which the L is formed by three squares." No doubt, certain sentences would be introduced that, on subsequent observation, required modification. The sentence, "All pawns move two spaces forward," would have to change to a conditional statement such as, "For all pawns, if the pawn is in state X, then it may move one or two spaces forward" (state X being the starting point at the beginning of the game).

There seems little doubt that this procedure would enable one eventually to discover the "laws of chess" much as one might discover the law of falling bodies. If we imagine that there are several varieties of chess and that each has been investigated in this manner so that the laws of each is known, then a new task is set. Just as Euclid wrote a small number of very general sentences from which theorems concerning circles, triangles, and rectangles could be deduced, so could the chess scientist write sentences from which the laws of all chess games could be deduced.

This account leaves out a number of very important considerations. Few sciences develop from descriptions to deduction in so straightforward a manner. There is also the business of adding more specific sentences to the file, of making finer discriminations. At any number of points in the general pattern of development, more specific areas of likeness and difference might have arisen to capture the attention of the investigator. One might find, for example, that it was more interesting to focus attention on the behavior of kings. If so, instead of attempting to discover the manner in which the behavior of kings differed from that of other pieces, he might concern himself with variations in behavior among kings, that is, to look for laws within laws. Although we have to begin stretching the rules of chess to make the point, it might be observed that some kings capture far more opponents than do others, leading to an interest in studies of "capturing" designed to determine the similarities among the instances of high capture rates and similarities among the instances of low capture rates. It may be found, for example, that in all cases of high capture rate the king moves in a particular manner.

Observation Reconsidered

The central point developed thus far has been that science may be characterized as an enterprise devoted to the development of specialized languages that provide more adequate symbolic representations of the structure of the environment than can be provided within ordinary language. That characterization may be useful, as far as it goes, but it does not go far enough. It leaves out of consideration altogether an extremely important complicating factor that was mentioned very briefly in the introductory section of this paper; a factor that, when ignored, makes much of what was said in succeeding sections seriously misleading. It may be recalled that we spoke of "the emancipation of elementary experience from the common-sense objects to which those experiences are attributed." It is that ambiguous notion that must now be examined with care.

In a preceding section, the biologists on whose work Darwin built were portrayed (at least by implication) as simply observing what there was to be observed in the plant and animal world, and writing factual descriptions that constituted symbolic representations of that world. The complication that arises here concerns the nature of observation, and, since factual descriptions purport to represent what is observed, the nature of statements of fact. From the common-sense, naïve realistic point of view, observation is a simple, straightforward matter of opening one's eyes and looking. Objects in the external world are perceived just as they are and description is a matter of representing them symbolically.

Stated differently, this view holds that providing common-sense, natural-history descriptions of the type provided by the predecessors of Darwin and Copernicus is a simple matter of applying linguistic terms to concrete objects and events that are immediately apprehended, or given directly to one's senses. To say that objects are given directly to one's senses implies that they are experienced (perceived) in such a way that, in the case of visual experiences, for example, all persons with normal vision have the same visual experience when directing their attention to the same object from the same vantage point. It implies that one who acquires the capacity to see after having been blind from birth, will immediately "see" what others whose vision was never impaired see; that on turning his attention toward a house, he will "see" it as a three-dimensional object enclosing space that could be entered and occupied.

There is no doubt that such a view is admirably suited to the demands of everyday living. Were it not, it seems doubtful that it would be so widely held. But there is even less doubt that such a view is inadequate. There is too much evidence to the contrary. For example, persons who gain their sight late in life have to *learn* to see solid or

TABLE 5-1

SUMMARY OF PAIR-WISE RELATIONSHIPS BETWEEN SOCIAL CLASS,
BUREAUCRATIZATION, ALIENATION, AND ACHIEVEMENT

	SOCIAL CLASS	BUREAUCRA-TIZATION	ALIENATION	ACHIEVEMENT
Social Class	————			
Bureaucratization	———	————		
Alienation	——	——	————	
Achievement	——	——	——	————

Again, the point here is not to fault Anderson on his procedure, but to suggest that the whole set of relationships "cries out" for an explanation. On the bases of his speculations, Anderson concludes:

the data so far examined indicate that it would be highly desirable from the point of view of student achievement were school administrators to attempt to minimize the number of behavioral constraints placed on students [bureaucratization] and to attempt to develop in students a sense of control over their own destinies. (Anderson, 1971, p. 22)

I would argue that the cause of knowledge and ultimately of practice would be better served by answering the "why" question than by moving so hastily to making recommendations for practice.

Suppose one theorized as follows about the reason for the set of relationships: schools have a number of goals among which are the protection of students, the socialization of students in the role of student (bringing them to accept the status of student and to share the values of the school), and the socialization of students in the broader sense of developing the commitments and capacities required for performance in adult roles. These goals constitute a system in the sense that there is a temporal sequence involved such that success in the "socialization in role" goal is a condition of success in the "protective" and "broad socialization" goals. The difficulty arises as a consequence of the fact that in lower-class homes and neighborhoods the socialization undergone prior to school entrance has been in a set of values and norms that are different from those characterizing higher class homes and neighborhoods, and most importantly, the school. This, in turn, leads to severe difficulties in socializing the student in role, and hence to problems of control and of low achievement. This is not advanced as any model of theorizing, or even as a "good" hypothetical explanation. But given such an explanation, one can derive test implications of the following kind. If there is anything to this account, then it follows logically that if one devised school and a school program such that the role of the student, and the broader socialization efforts of the school were consistent, or compatible, with the preschool socialization of lower-class children, then the frequency of application of behavioral controls to students would diminish, alienation would be lessened, and achievement would increase.

Whatever practical difficulties might be encountered, there is no problem in the "in principle" feasibility of such a study. In fact, with some ingenuity and careful investigation one might be able to identify the functional equivalent of schools in subsocieties within a society.

One final observation concerning the "state of the art" in research in educational administration can be phrased in terms of the "chess science" analogy. Researchers in our field seem to be engaged so intensively in writing more specific sentences about such subjects as the "capturing behavior" of kings that they never get around to writing more general sentences about the behavior of kings in relation to other pieces. Thus, we know a great deal more about the capturing behavior of kings than we do about the rules of the game as a whole, to say nothing about the rules of which those rules are special cases.

REFERENCES

ANDERSON, BARRY, "Socio-economic Status of Students and Schools Bureaucratization," *Educational Administration Quarterly* (Spring, 1971), pp. 12–24.

ASIMOV, ISAAC, *A Short History of Biology* (Garden City, N.Y.: The Natural History Press, 1964).

BLAU, PETER M., and SCOTT W. RICHARD, *Formal Organizations* (San Francisco: Chandler Publishing Co., 1962).

BRONOWSKI, JACOB, *The Common Sense of Science.* (Hamondsworth, England: Penguin Books, Ltd., 1960).

————, *The Identity of Man,* (Garden City, The Natural History Press) 1965.

————, "Science as Foresight," in Newman, James R., ed., *What is Science?* (New York: Washington Square Press, 1961).

CARLSON, RICHARD O., "Environmental Constraints and Organizational Consequences: The Public School and Its Clients," in Daniel Griffiths, ed., *Behavioral Science and Educational Administration,* the 63rd Yearbook of the National Society for the Study of Education, Part II (Chicago: The University of Chicago Press, 1964).

COUGHLAN, ROBERT J., "Social Structure in Relatively Closed and Open Schools," *Educational Administration Quarterly* (Spring, 1970), pp. 14–35.

DINGLE, HERBERT, *The Scientific Adventure* (London: Sir Isaac Pittman & Sons, Ltd., 1952).

VON FOERSTER, H., "From Stimulus to Symbol: The Economy of Biological Computation," in Buckley, Walter, ed., *Modern Systems Research for the Behavioral Scientist* (Chicago: Aldine Publishing Co., 1968), pp. 170–181.

GEERTZ, CLIFFORD, "Religion as a Cultural System," in Banton, Michael, ed., *Anthropological Approaches to the Study of Religion* (New York: Frederick A. Praeger, Publishers, 1966), pp. 1–46.

GORN, SAUL, "The Computer and Information Sciences and the Community of Disciplines," *Behavioral Science,* **12** (1967), pp. 433–452.

GRIFFITHS, DANIEL E., *Developing Taxonomies of Organizational Behavior in Educational Administration* (Chicago: Rand McNally & Co., 1969).

HANSON, NORWOOD RUSSELL. *Patterns of Discovery* (Cambridge: Cambridge University Press, 1965), p. 19.

HAWKINS, DAVID. *The Language of Nature: An Essay in the Philosophy of Science* (San Francisco: W. H. Freeman & Co., 1964).

HELSEL, A. RAY. "Value Orientation and Pupil Control Ideology of Public School Educators." *Administrative Science Quarterly,* **16** (Winter 1971), pp. 24–33.

KATZ, DANIEL, and ROBERT L. KAHN. *The Social Psychology of Organizations* (New York: John Wiley & Sons, Inc., 1966).

KUHN, ALFRED. *The Study of Society: A United Approach* (Homewood, Ill.: Richard D. Irwin, Inc., 1963).

NORTHROP, F. S. C. *Man, God and Nature* (New York: Pocket Books, Inc., 1963).

PARSONS, TALCOTT. "Durkheim's Contribution to the Theory of Integration of Social Systems." In Kurt H. Wolff (ed.), *Emile Durkheim, 1858–1917* (Columbus, Ohio: The Ohio State University Press, 1960).

REED, JOHN. "Chemistry." In James R. Newman (ed.), *What Is Science* (New York: Washington Square Press, 1961).

STEBBING, L. SUSAN. *A Modern Introduction to Logic.* New York: Harper & Row, Publishers, Inc., 1961, p. 294.

P A R T II

AUTHORITY, BUREAUCRACY, AND SOCIAL SYSTEM

6

AUTHORITY, BUREAUCRACY, AND SOCIAL SYSTEM: AN INTRODUCTION

William G. Monahan

THE GENESIS (and genius) of bureaucracy is associated with Max Weber—the nineteenth century giant of sociophilosophical German thinkers. But, of course, Weber did not invent bureaucracy; perhaps he did not really even discover it, but unquestionably, he rigorously defined, explained, and formulated it. Moreover, it is generally agreed that succeeding generations of scholars have added little to his essential and relatively complete depiction.[1]

To that extent, it is not inappropriate to treat bureaucracy as "a" theory. As Weber treated it, it is, however, a theory in quite another sense; in this other sense, it exemplified a kind of unobtrusive aspect of all really good theorizing—it is exciting.

The excitement that can be generated by dealing with ideas in theoretical fashion is familiar to anyone who has taught in such areas and, in essence, represents the core of what any science is really all about. No one stated it any better than Max Weber himself: "Without this strange intoxication, ridiculed by outsiders; without this passion . . . you have no calling for science and you should do something else."[1a]

The *idea* of theory is, thus, in some respects more important, and certainly a prerequisite to, its formulation. Weber was captivated by analysis and inquiry; that he was equally gifted in the exposition of his explorations is his additional distinction and our good fortune. And nowhere is his attention to rigor and analytical detail more clearly manifested than in his treatment of rationality.

Of Prophets and Priests

If there is a central focus in Weber's work, it is *rationalism*. Not only did rationality govern Weber's research and teaching but the *idea* of rationality itself is a theme that lays at or very near the surface of his

[1] It might be helpful for the reader to refer to "the institutionalization of Charisma" in Chapter 2.

[1a] H. H. Gerth and C. W. Mills, *From Max Weber: Essays in Sociology* (New York: Oxford University Press, 1946), p. 135.

expressions. Weber's attitude toward whatever system of phenomena interested him was analytically pure and rigorously systematic. At the same time, his knowledge was immense, encyclopedic. His grasp of economics, social mores and cultures, religions, law and history, and philosophy is little short of incredible. Yet, always, Weber's methods were scientifically systematic and his comparisons embraced the quality of logical development.

This concern with rationality is at the heart of Weber's explication of bureaucracy and makes his concern with the "ideal type" more meaningful. His descriptions of bureaucratization are evolved from a beginning analysis of certain special forms of legitimacy—of authority. (Weber uses the term *domination*.) The three types of domination that Weber deals with are charismatic, traditional, and legalistic (or administrative). And in Robert Nisbet's excellent treatment of *authority*, which follows, these concepts and the relationships among them are given a clear perspective.

The evolutionary pattern in the progressive development of authority, according to Weber, is from charismatic through traditional to legalistic. For Weber, this is seen almost as a compelling historical progression—a teleological phenomenon with rational considerations as the ultimate goal. In the introduction to Part I of this volume, brief comment was made regarding the nature of the change from charismatic to legalistic authority; Nisbet's chapter deals with this in broader detail within its historical context. This interest is also to be found in Weber's religious sociology. Freund, for example, points out that Weber's religious analyses begin with certain concepts—the divine, sin, magic, sorcerers, prophets, priests, doctrine, and so forth. Then he proceeds to deal with certain distinctions that illuminate the whole system with which he is interested. Freund explains the treatment of concept differentiation in the following manner:

> There are various ways of distinguishing priest from sorcerer. The latter acts on demons by magical means, while the former is by vocation the minister of a cult intended to honor the divinity. . . . Moreover, where there is no organized clergy, there is no rationalized religious life either. . . .
>
> In this he differs, first of all, from the priest. The priest is at the service of a sacred tradition; the prophet is the man with a personal revelation, who claims authority in virtue of a new law. It is seldom, moreover, that the prophet arises from the ranks of the priesthood; he is usually a layman. . . . The prophet differs from the sorcerer . . . in that he announces a revelation whose content does not consist of magical practices but of a doctrine or an obligation. . . . but there is one feature that is absolutely fundamental: the prophet promotes his idea for its own sake, and never against renunciation of any kind. His activity is wholly gratuitous.[2]

2 Julian Freund, *The Sociology of Max Weber* (New York: Pantheon Books, Inc.), 1968, pp. 194–196.

Although the priest is subject to the boundaries of a doctrine with its bases in traditional and legalistic authority, secular organizations tend progressively to deal with authority in a rational fashion. Nisbet has defined authority as, "the structure of the inner order of an association . . . given legitimacy by its roots in social function . . ." and he defines status as, ". . . the individual's position in the hierarchy of prestige and influence that characterizes every community or association."[3]

In Weber's "ideal type," authority and status are clearly implicit. For Weber, the ideal bureaucracy incorporated a number of elements that altogether constitute a formal structure. He repeatedly emphasized the "form" of the structure and although he did not hold that any specific bureaucractic organization had to include all of the characteristics, the more that it did include, the more persistent it would be over time. There are five basic elements that taken together constitute the form of his ideal type:

1. *Hierarchical structure.* Each official in a higher office has control and supervision of an official in a lower office.
2. *Functional specialization.* Individual office holders are selected on the basis of their ability to perform particular tasks.
3. *Prescribed competence.* This is derived from number 2; it stipulates that each position in the hierarchy has particular and known rights and obligations attached to it (*certification* of such "status and ability" is a logical consequence).
4. *Files and records.* Pertinent acts, decisions, and so on should be recorded and retrievable to provide bases for the establishment of policy guides. This is essential for reducing alternatives and promoting predictability.
5. *Rules of behavior.* Unless there is a codified apparatus, the problem of unpredictability is omnipresent. Codes of behavior established through policies represent an essential process in the rational structure.

Perhaps the most familiar problem, both theoretically and actually, presented by such a highly structured formal system is its tendency to feed upon itself; to grow in size without clear and distinct relationship to productivity. Weber was aware of this problem and asserted that where rationality also governs this aspect of structure, growth would come about in terms of scope rather than detail. He does, however, explicitly distinguish persistence from Parkinsonian expansion. Consider the following:

3 Robert Nisbet, *The Sociological Tradition* (New York: Basic Books, Inc.), 1966 p. 6.

Once it is fully established, bureaucracy is among those social structures which are the hardest to destroy. Bureaucracy is *the means* of carrying "community action" over into rationally ordered "social action." Therefore, as an instrument for "societalizing" relations of power, bureaucracy has been and is a power instrument of the first order—for the one who controls the bureaucratic apparatus.[4]

and also:

Bureaucratization is occasioned more by intensive and qualitative enlargement and internal deployment of the scope of administrative tasks than by their extensive and quantitative increase.[5]

Whether Weber was simply not in a position—in terms of his time and circumstance—to take into consideration some of the social-psychological factors in organizations that have come into vogue during the twentieth century is speculative. Perhaps his single-mindedness in guarding against value judgments precluded an interest in what has felicitously been labeled in contemporary thought as "informal" organization. In any case, he saw bureaucracy as ". . . an adaptive device for using specialized skills,"[6] and, since his central concern was with rationality, the extent of consideration accorded *persons* as a major variable in his system is not explicit.

When scholars examine extensions of Weber's work, they are quick to point out that little has been added to the original theoretical formulation. But in building upon his work, modern students of organization have tended to emphasize those aspects of the bureaucratic model that focus on personnel and hold that unintended consequences (the problem of predictability) swing largely in terms of the "human side of enterprise."

It is by virtue of the fact that increasing structural rationality tends toward the impersonalization of person-relations that led more recent theoretical views to focus on the person/organization interface. For example, Merton, Selznich, Gouldner, Coser, Argyris, and Anderson, to mention only a few examples, have focused on such relationships. Merton was particularly concerned with dysfunctional consequences and anomie that, although of much broader social perspective than that of organizations per se, are derived from the internalization of values and motivated by generalized responses to rules. Coser is also interested in such dysfunctions but treats them in the context of *conflict;* and Selznich,

4 Max Weber, "Bureaucracy," in H. H. Gerth and C. W. Mills, *From Max Weber: Essays in Sociology* (New York: Oxford University Press, 1946) (Galaxy Books), p. 218.

5 Ibid., p. 212.

6 J. G. March and H. A. Simon, *Organizations* (New York: John Wiley & Sons, Inc., 1958), p. 37.

who is more organizationally anchored, is interested in the way authority flows (is delegated) through the system. In all of these views, regardless of pattern, the general concern is relationships among organizational incumbents. Weber was clearly aware that changes in structure inevitably will affect the relationships of offices. He was pessimistic about the problems that were likely to be generated by the highly rationalized society. Merton states that melancholy condition into literate perspective.

The political and social as well as economic by-products of an advancing technology variously affect the structure of society at large. This wider context suggests that workers' attitudes toward the new technology are determined not by it *per se*, but by the collateral uses to which it can be and, at times, has been put as an *instrument of social power*. Technology has been employed not only for the production of goods but also for the management of workmen. It has, in fact, been repeatedly defined as a weapon for subduing the worker by promising to displace him unless he accepts proffered terms of employment.[7]

The impact of certain social-structural conditions on authority and those who wield it is perhaps an even better example of the kind of condition that Weber seemed to ignore and that captivates the interest of contemporary scholars. Again, as one manifestation of this condition, consider Merton's discussion of one aspect of group norms in organizations; his frame of reference is "visibility" and authority:

. . . authority tends to isolate those who possess it to a high degree. Since they normally interact with near-equals in the hierarchy, the more complex the organization the greater the possibility that they will be shut-off, for a time, from changes in attitudes and norms in the lower (and not only the lowermost) strata of the organization. This circumstance of social structure often makes for an informational lag. Considerable numbers of people in the organization may become alienated from established norms long before this comes to the attention of the authorities whose job it is to uphold these norms. As a result of this structural insulation, they may not know about changes in the operating norms until these changes have become far advanced. . . . Under such circumstances and to this extent, authority dwindles. Belated concessions to the now-potently changed norms of the organization serve only to make apparent to all how much the previously existing authority has declined. In some cases, when this process has run its course before it is recognized by those ostensibly in command, authority is abdicated."[8]

Thus, whereas Weber emphasized the importance of, if not the *non*-personal, the *im*personal aspects of authority, we see Merton now suggesting that at least certain significant aspects of personality are essential and desirable. Of course, in this, Merton does not advocate a "traits"

7 Robert Merton, *Social Theory and Social Structure* (New York: The Free Press, 1963), p. 565.
8 Ibid., p. 348.

approach to leadership (". . . an advanced case of platitude complicated by redundancy"); a "traits" approach should thus not be given too much credulity; rather that ". . . specific *attributes* of personality are required to maintain effective observability of group norms and role-performance. . . ."[9]

Merton builds such observations into a complex social theory and his concerns with structure are never far removed from the functions that are vital to it.

Agreeing with Merton, Anderson's article in the following section begins with the assertion that organizations do tend to both "structure and impersonalize" relationships. That this is accomplished through organizational rules is confirmed from his research with junior high schools.

THE PARSONIAN APPROACH

Any attempt to build an almost exhaustive system into which rational and natural phenomena can fit an encompassing "general theory" is clearly a task of imposing dimension. Talcott Parsons has devoted the better part of his scholarly effort to that task, and although his work is controversial, he is recognized by even his critics as having made an immeasurable contribution to our understanding of social systems. Few people have equaled the efforts of R. Jean Hills in finding applications of Parsons' theories to organizations and, specifically, to educational administration.

And even though it is almost impossible to provide any meaningful overview of Parsons' general theory without both grossly oversimplifying and distorting it, Hills' article, which is itself complex, will be more valuable to the reader with some basic comment here.

There are three major components in Parsons' work. Although each constitutes an almost full-blown system in its own right, these components should more properly be seen as subsystems of a larger, total system. The theory is systematic in that his models and concepts are designed in enough abstraction that they are applicable at *any* level of the social system—as appropriate for the individual as for the larger society of which he is a part. Moreover, central to this versatility is the essential recognition, in Parsons' work, that his is an "action" theory.

Devereux states:

An adequate general theory must be an action theory: for Parsons, this means that the central mechanism must always be some notion of actors orienting themselves to situations, with reference to various sorts of goals, values, and normative standards, and behaving accordingly.[10]

9 Ibid., p. 348.
10 Edward C. Devereux, Jr., "Parsons' Sociological Theory" in Max Black (ed.), *The Social Theories of Talcott Parsons* (Englewood Cliffs: Prentice Hall, Inc., 1961), p. 19.

fession, Parsons was struck with the observation that the relationship between doctor and patient is expected to be disinterested, while that of salesman and client is expected to be self-interested. This is evidently not a question of differences in personality or personal motivation. It is rather a matter of institutional regulation: whatever his personal motivations, the businessman is expected to make decisions with his eye primarily on the balance sheet of his own firm, whereas the doctor is expected to think primarily of the welfare of the patient, placing his own economic welfare in second priority. One can easily demonstrate, Parsons argued, that a norm of caveat emptor would be drastically dysfunctional for the medical profession.

Attempting to cast this problem in more general terms, it seemed to Parsons that, in some relationships, what are essentially moral considerations are expected to be given primacy, whereas in others they are not. And what is morality, he reasoned, but the claim of some superordinate collectivity upon the individual or sub-collectivity? The problem becomes a crucial one for the relationships among different orders of systems. Does the husband-father act primarily for himself or for his family as a whole? Does the departmental executive in a business firm act primarily in terms of his own personal interests, in terms of the interests and welfare of the department he serves, in terms of the interests of the firm as a whole, or in terms of some still broader collectivity, perhaps of society in general? It should be clear that precisely the same behavior which is collectivity-oriented in terms of the individual or some sub-collectivity may yet be self-oriented in terms of the larger system reference. The dedicated businessman may selfishly serve a corporation which is essentially self-oriented in its dealings with surrounding systems.[15]

The pattern-variable "self-collectivity" is not consolidated into the "new scheme" as mentioned previously. Parsons considers this variable a special case of the internal-external axis. This is because an important function of self-collectivity comes into play when there is a problem between different levels of the hierarchy. For example, if a dean behaves in some manner that takes his college more into consideration than the interests of the university, he acts in terms of a self-orientation; if a school superintendent believes that reorganization of his school district into a larger system is better than maintaining its current status, he is acting in terms of a collectivity-orientation. There are many times when decision-makers confront this dilemma. Acting in a collectivity-orientation, however, does not mean that such action is never self-serving; on the contrary, it can be and not infrequently is. But the criterion of distinction is one of which side of the axis is being served—the internal or the external.

Much of the previous discussion, and of Parsons' general theory itself, is couched in terms of *the* social system; that is, an all-inclusive social phenomenon. Yet, obviously, at all levels of his hierarchical structure there are numerous subsystems; social systems of almost infinite variety ranging from institutionalized and formally structured systems such as

---

[15] Devereux; in Max Black, op. cit., pp. 39–43. Used with permission.

schools and universities, corporate firms, and governmental agencies to rather loosely structured and informal systems such as bridge clubs.

Yet Parsons' operational definition literally requires hundreds of pages for, in general, he assumes that his readers understand the fundamental concept. Even at those times when he provides a singular definition, it is somewhat ponderous. For example, he points out in one instance: ". . . a social system is a mode of organization of action elements relative to the persistence or ordered process of change of the interactive patterns of a plurality of individual actors."[16]

Thus, Parsons discusses a social system of *action;* his frame of reference throughout concerns "actor's" orientation to situations which, obviously, include still other actors. Action and interaction are the emphases.

Perhaps, therefore, it will be helpful to re-examine a somewhat less abstract treatment of a particular social system—that of the school. Another sociologist, Willard Waller, has provided such treatment and his definition is as valid today as it was in 1932 when it first appeared.[17]

According to Waller, the social system of a school is operationally defined in terms of five elements; (1) a definite population; (2) a well-defined political structure; (3) a network of social relationships; (4) a pervasive "we-feeling"; and (5) a particular subculture unique to the school.

Waller held that the school is a "closed" system of social interaction. By that, he essentially attempted to call attention to what, in more contemporary terminology, would be the school's more definitive institutional boundaries. He said:

if we are to study the school as a social entity, we must be able to distinguish clearly between school and not-school. The school is in fact clearly differentiated from its social milieu.[18]

The population, of course, is composed of students and teachers in large measure with administrators included as a third major demographic component. Actually, Waller talks about those involved in the "giving and receiving" of instruction and, thus, does not specify administrators in the population context. However, in discussing the political structure, he is more explicit:

Typically, the school is organized on some variant of the autocratic principle. . . . Intra-faculty relations greatly affect the relations between teachers and students. When there is favorable rapport between teachers and the administrative authorities, this autocracy becomes an oligarchy with the teacher

---

16 Talcott Parsons, *The Social System,* op. cit., p. 24.

17 Willard Waller, *The Sociology of Teaching* (New York: John Wiley & Sons, Inc., 1932).

18 Cited in W. O. Stanley, et al., *Social Foundations of Education* (New York: Holt, Rinehart and Winston, Inc., 1956), p. 70.

group as a solid and well-organized ruling class. . . . In the most happily conducted institutions, all the teachers and some of the leading students feel they have a very real voice in the conduct of school affairs.[19]

The "network of social relationships" follows from population and political structure—as a matter of fact, the particular nature of this "network" is intimately related to all other elements, as is "we-feeling" and the school's unique culture. In these latter regards, the identification with the school, its spirit, is an essential force for effecting what is fundamentally a conformity to both formal regulatory apparatus and informal norms. The school as an institutionalized phenomenon requires a variety of cultural mechanisms ranging from ascending structural specification of statuses (sophomore, junior, senior—"bluebirds," "honey bees," "butterflies") as well as generating, thereby, other less tasteful translations of hierarchical roles—the "sheep" and the "goats." These and a host of other special values are incorporated into the subculture and are partially operationalized by well-developed rites-of-passage for managing the predictive cycles through which the system pursues its goals and policies.

That some of these properties are oriented externally and others internally, and still others clearly derived from emphasis on means and ends, is abundantly clear. Moreover, the importance of ways of categorizing social objects in the school on the basis of ascriptive, or qualitative, characterizations in some cases, and performance factors in others (a very "polite student" [ascriptive], or a "hard worker" [performance]) is an important aspect of the school's social system. In addition, ways that Parsons describes as being important not only in the ability to *categorize* social objects but, as well, for establishing *orientations toward* them are also essential for effective functioning of the social system. Teachers and students have a much more *specific* orientation to each other than students with students or teachers with other teachers. A relationship between the teacher and his own child is diffuse rather than specific; that is another way of talking about the "scope or inclusiveness of the relationship."[20]

Another final comment about Waller's discussion of the school is instructive. Like Parsons, he also recognized the propensity for social systems to behave cybernetically, and when certain kinds of imbalances occur, the consequences were seen to be dysfunctional, although he put it somewhat less prosaically than Parsons. States Waller:

There is constant interaction between the elements of the authoritative system; the school is continually threatened because it is autocratic and it has to be

19 Ibid., p. 71.
20 E. C. Devereux, Jr., in Black, op. cit., p. 40.

autocratic because it is threatened. The antagonistic forces are balanced in that ever-fickle equilibrium which is discipline.[21]

AUTHORITY

It is abundantly clear from the previous discussion that in the work of theorists and critics alike, social systems are always involved with authority. Dominance and submission are facts of the existence of social systems whether differentiated by small or large scope, whether of the little school or a nation-state. Bureaucracy is a highly rationalistic operational paradigm for structuring social systems, particularly formal ones; in fact, the condition of formality may be determined by the extent to which authority is bureaucratized. On the other hand, social systems, like schools, having the development of particular indoctrinational attitudes as a major function should be clearly distinguished from *learning*, which, of course, is supposed to take place in them.

Certainly, it cannot be argued that learning does not take place in schools. But there is no necessary guarantee that what we more normally think of as learning—what scholars have to say to us about science and art and poetry and how to make sailboats—that *that* kind of learning will automatically go on there. Unquestionably, some of it does; but one also learns how to cope with the social system itself. That is, one does if one expects to survive in it and if one, in fact, wants to. Under the mandate that social systems require authority for their survival, one must learn to cope with that before the other kind of learning can truly occur. It just happens to be the case.

Some would argue and not without validity, that the *e*ducational establishment currently confronts a series of significant crises. It is probable that such crises are really all rolled into a single one—the crisis of authority. Of all the contemporary fashionable rhetoric addressed to that problem, the following small piece of dialogue is reflective; it is excerpted from an interview with Milton Mayer, consultant to the Center for the Study of Democratic Institutions, and a professor at the University of Massachusetts. The interview was conducted by Donald McDonald of the Center staff:

Mayer: . . . No man can teach another how to live. But all men somehow learn—or fail to learn—something about it without being taught. I can teach you French or Spanish, or how to whittle a stick, but I cannot teach you how to live. All I can do is raise the questions. And if you say, "Give me the answers," I say "Either you know the answers—or there are none." An artful dodge, on the face of it, but I suspect that it's the so-help-me-truth.

McDonald: That was the burden of your essay, "To know and to do." wasn't it— . . . I think you came out—again—with a very modest conclusion.

21 Waller, op. cit., p. 73.

Mayer: A very modest conclusion, to wit, that if only we can talk about important things in school we have done about as much as can be done. As to what happens to the life of the student, I sus- pect—and this is a private suspicion—that that lies with God.

McDonald: Do your students at the University of Massachusetts want you to give them answers instead of questions?

Mayer: The whole teaching establishment has fallen apart. Young people, for one reason or another, do not want to be taught. As a conse- quence, teachers do not want to teach. Their object—all sublime —for fear of being lynched—is to have their students not have what their students do not want.[22]

Thus, the notable changes in the authority pattern are really just that—changes in pattern, and like Waller, Mayer implies a function for discipline. But, of course, Mayer speaks not for the familiar "school discipline" as a structurally formalized device for insuring order within the social system; rather, for that more substantial intellectual discipline that is derived at least in part from ". . . (knowing) the difference be- tween a good book and a bad book, and to prefer the former to the latter."[23]

The discipleship of authority is at issue in either case, and authority stands at the center of administration.

[22] "If you keep moving they can't hit you,"—An interview with Milton Mayer. *The Center Magazine VI*, x/o 4 (July/August 1973), p. 21.

[23] Ibid., p. 21.

7

THE *following essay by Robert Nisbet provides a clear frame of reference for the centrality of authority in the affairs of modern man and the organizational life that so much tends to control behavior in this century.*

There are, of course, many related concepts of significant theoretical importance that are closely related or directly derivative of authority. Some of these are power, influence, dominance, rights-and-obligations, prestige, and force, to mention the more familiar ones. Although it may (and frequently does) offer a convenient excuse for intellectual dispute, Bierstedt's characterization of the relationship of authority to power and force is, nevertheless, a useful point of departure for introducing Nisbet's analysis. Bierstedt asserts that:

> *Power is not force and power is not authority, but it is intimately related to both and may be defined in terms of them. We want therefore to propose three definitions . . . (1) power is latent force; (2) force is manifest power; and, (3) authority is institutionalized power.*[1]

Somewhat further on, Bierstedt is still more definitive regarding authority. He states that, "The right to use force is then attached to certain statuses within the association, and the right is what we ordinarily mean by authority."[2] *Interestingly, this statement is qualified by a footnote to the effect that when one refers to someone as "an authority" on some matter or field, the reference has nothing to do with force but with superior knowledge or expertise. In the modern sense we refer to persons who are highly knowledgeable and/or skillful as "authorities." Modernity notwithstanding, aspects of this same connotation are clearly manifest in what Weber refers to as "traditional" authority, and it would be the greatest mistake to assume that this kind of authority— whether traditionally accorded or earned in the modern sense by, for example, a Goren in the case of contract bridge—does not nor should imply limited access to both force and power. This is the implication as a matter of fact of Bierstedt's qualifying footnote. The issue is merely a matter of the appropriateness of scope—the boundaries, of the particular area involved.*

The exercise of traditional authority implied superior knowledge just as surely as that of a Goren on bridge. The priest may be far less charismatic than the prophet but his control over dogma and ritual by virtue of training and knowledge accorded him considerable force. By the same token, a Goren is clearly able to exercise impressive impact over the definition and interpretation of rules and procedures governing contract bridge matters, and the impact of such influence surely can be conceived as forceful in that arena. Simi-

---

[1] Robert Bierstedt, "An Analysis of Social Power," *American Sociological Review,* XV, 6, in L. Coser and B. Rosenberg, *Sociological Theory* (Toronto: Collier-Macmillan Canada, Ltd., 1969), p. 158.

[2] Ibid., p. 159.

larly, the incumbent of an established status such as that of a superintendent of schools, a college dean, or a university president involves considerable traditional authority not only by virtue of status but, as well, by the authority of superior knowledge. The latter can as easily be forcefully brought to bear as the former.

The point so eloquently explained by Nisbet is that when a well-established social order begins to break up, not only traditional authority but even tradition itself is decreasingly relevant to the affairs of the people caught up in that condition. The emerging social order mandates "newer" definitions and values. Consequently, a "traditional" authority that is appropriate to the changed values and ideology requires more time to develop. Inevitably,. of course, a tradition (and a traditional authority) will come about. Under such circumstances, organizational life is surely less rigidly articulated and areas emerge that are somewhat penumbral. Thus, authority is less clearly specified in any traditional sense and probably less clearly specified in any other sense for a time.

There have not been too many definitive circumstances of this kind of condition in history and in not a few wherein the possibility of the condition was ripe, somebody or something happened that made it possible for a quality of leadership to be exerted to head it off. Some modification—some acceptable alternative—to the older order was introduced such that a clear break with the older pattern was prevented. Augustus was able to do that for Rome and it saved that civilization for another four hundred years. The same was just not possible in 1793 in France. The fact that change came about in France is really only a footnote to history. Had it not happened there it surely would have happened elsewhere and some believe that it happened at least to similar and perhaps more lasting effect in the United States. In any case although its manifestations may have seemed quite localized, it was happening to greater or lesser extent throughout the Western world in the late eighteenth century.

Augustus was able to effect a dramatic modification of an older order (rather than confront a break-up) because he was able to recognize and take advantage of the potential contribution and substance of Italian country squires as well as the growing power of Rome's provincial governors on the one hand, and the obvious decadence and decreasing effectiveness of the Patrician class within Rome itself on the other. It is generally acknowledged that, however it was brought about, Augustus prolonged the life of Rome well into the third century A.D., although how this was precisely accomplished is still somewhat obscure.

The eighteenth century, and especially in France, was simply a different environment, and Nisbet plainly describes the conditions that prevailed. Associated with his treatment of authority in that context, however, is an acutely sensitive discussion of the progressive evolution of authority from charismatic through traditional and "into" legalistic. Nisbet provides among the better such treatments in the sociology of knowledge as well as of the idea of authority itself, and no contemporary student of organizational analysis should be without familiarity with such a holistic view. Consequently, this essay is an excellent basis for the further exploration of rational/legal content-and-process, and especially to the ongoing activities of administrative behavior that are more specifically implied in the other chapters in this section.

After reading Nisbet's essay, it would be appropriate to give some consideration to such questions as whether authority is the right to power or an access to power, or both. Whether power is the use of force, or is equally the threat to use it. Whether influence is the evidence of authority and/or power, and, finally, whether justified or not, the use of either power or force tends—as some hold—to decrease the effectiveness of its use. In the latter case, I would suppose the issue is that one has a certain amount of power under certain circumstances but as any of it is utilized much less remains. In a sense, this latter situation is something akin to Gouldner's conceptualization of the application of general and impersonal rules.[3]

AUTHORITY

Robert A. Nisbet

The Specter of Power

"In our days," Tocqueville wrote,

men see that the constituted powers are crumbling down on every side; they see all ancient authority dying out, all ancient barriers tottering to their fall, and the judgment of the wisest is troubled at the sight; they attend only to the amazing revolution that is taking place before their eyes, and they imagine that mankind is about to fall into perpetual anarchy. If they looked to the final consequence of this revolution, their fears would perhaps assume a different shape. For myself, I confess that I put no trust in the spirit of freedom which appears to animate my contemporaries. I see well enough that the nations of this age are turbulent, but I do not clearly perceive that they are liberal; and I fear lest, at the close of those perturbations, which rock the base of thrones, the dominion of sovereigns may prove more powerful than it ever was.[1]

Precisely as the breakup of the old order made men aware of the loss of traditional community, it made them aware also of the loss of traditional authority: of the constraints, normative disciplines, and patriarchal bonds that had been for so long embedded in culture that they were scarcely recognized until the onset of the two revolutions dramatized them through threatened extinction. And just as the erosion of accustomed community led to sociological premonitions of mass society,

---

3 See, e.g., Alvin Gouldner, "Organizational Analysis," in R. K. Merton, L. Broom, and L. S. Cottrell, Jr., *Sociology Today* (New York: Basic Books, Inc., 1959), pp. 400–428.

1 *Democracy in America*, II, 314.

From Chapter 4 of *The Sociological Tradition* by Robert A. Nisbet, © 1966 by Basic Books, Inc., Publishers, New York.

so the decline of ancient authorities led to premonitions of disorganization, on the one hand, and, on the other, of new types of power, more encompassing and penetrating than any known before in history.

In traditional society authority is hardly recognized as having separate or even distinguishable identity. How could it be? Deeply embedded in social functions, an inalienable part of the inner order of family, neighborhood, parish, and guild, ritualized at every turn, authority is so closely woven into the fabric of tradition and morality as to be scarcely more noticeable than the air men breathe. Even in the hands of the king, authority in such a society tends to maintain this diffused and indirect character. Such is the tendency of monarchical power to become submerged in the whole ethos of patriarchalism that the power of the king seems to its subjects as but little different from that exercised by fathers over sons, priests over communicants, and masters over apprentices. The entire weight of morality—which is typically the morality of duty and allegiance—makes authority an undifferentiated aspect of the social order, the government hardly more than a symbolic superstructure.

But when men become separated, or feel themselves separated, from traditional institutions, there arises, along with the specter of the lost individual, the specter of lost authority. Fears and anxieties run over the intellectual landscape like masterless dogs. Inevitably in such circumstances, men's minds turn to the problem of authority. What, it is asked, shall be the source and nature of an authority sufficient to replace lost authority, to restrain the natural anarchy that even in civilized society thrusts itself now and then through the crevices of law and morality? And, paralleling this question: What shall be the means of checking the kind of power that always threatens to rise on the ruins of constituted authority?

Purely individual rights may not be enough. Such rights may even, as Burckhardt wrote, echoing sentiments that Burke had first uttered, intensify the growth of new and more awful forms of power. "The great harm was begun," wrote Burckhardt,

in the last century, mainly through Rousseau, with his doctrine of the goodness of human nature. Out of this, plebs and educated alike, distilled the doctrine of the golden age that was to come infallibly, provided people were left alone. The result, as every child knows, was the complete disintegration of the idea of authority in the hands of mortal men, whereupon, of course, we periodically fall victims to sheer power.[2]

[2] *The Letters of Jacob Burckhardt,* Alexander Dru, trans. and ed. (London: Routledge and Kegan Paul, 1955), 147. "There is nothing more wretched under the sun . . . than a government from under whose nose any club of political intriguers can steal the executive power, and that is left to tremble before 'liberalism,' enthusiasm, boors, and village magnates. I know too much history to expect anything from the masses but a future tyranny, which will mean the end of history" (p. 94).

Of all the faces of the French Revolution the one that was to torment post-Revolutionary conservatism most insistently was the face of power: power that seemed to the conservative mind to be born of the Revolution's vaunted system of individual liberty, rights, and equality. To the conservatives, beginning with Burke, all that had been taken away by the Revolutionists from the traditional authorities of guild, commune, church, and patriarchal family and vested precariously in individual and in popular will amounted in fact to a magnification of political power without precedent in European history. "In all senses, we worship and follow after Power," wrote Carlyle. This theme runs like a scarlet thread through nineteenth-century conservatism. The individual alone, alienated from historic community, would never prove sufficient, it was argued, despite his newly granted rights and equalities, to offset the kind of power that the revolutionary, democratic state represented.

From the point of view of the nineteenth-century sociology of power, four aspects of the Revolutionary and Napoleonic orders are notable. Each of them, as we shall see, furnishes potent stimulus and vivid theme to the works of all the major sociologists, from Tocqueville to Simmel.[3] Rarely in the sociology of ideas is the relation between social event and intellectual response as clear and direct as with respect to these four aspects of the Revolution.

1. The TOTALISM of Revolutionary power. It was not total at first, of course, but by the time of the Committee of Public Safety more than a few zealots were convinced that unless the power of the people over its enemies, internal and external, was made absolute and penetrating, the liberty of its citizens could not be secured. Hence Robespierre's ringing declaration that "the government of the Revolution is the despotism of freedom against tyranny." Given an underlying belief in the absolute morality of intent, it was an easy step to belief that the power to effect intent was also moral and must be total, must extend itself to every realm of man's life and being. Totalitarianism is not, of course, the word to describe Jacobin France, for between the aspiration of a Saint-Just and the political reality of his France there lay too many institutional barriers —persistences of traditional allegiance and authority. But it is only too clear that the *idea* of "democratic totalitarianism" was born in 1793.

2. The MASS BASE of Revolutionary power. Legitimacy of power does not lie, it was declared by the Revolutionists, in divine decree, in heredity, or in tradition. Legitimacy is given only by the mass of people who participate in it and who, by the very fact of participating, cannot there-

3 See my "The French Revolution and the Rise of Sociology in France," *American Journal of Sociology* (September 1943), 156–164. It may be said with no exaggeration that Tocqueville, Marx, Le Play, Durkheim, Weber, Simmel, Michels, and Mosca—the prime figures in the development of the sociology of power—all wrote as though the Jacobins were looking over their shoulders.

fore be said to be enslaved by it, no matter what its intensity. This thesis became steadily more important as the Revolution progressed until, in time, virtually everything came to be justified in the name of the people. It was the invocation of "the people" that made Revolutionary armies the first mass armies in Europe's history, and it was the same invocation that justified extension and penetration of governmental power beyond anything known since the age of Diocletian in ancient Rome. Not economic man, not religious man, not moral man, but *political* man, was the key figure of the Revolution. Hence the exaltation of *citizen*. Mass participation in power, as we have seen, could appear inextricably related to the cherished perquisites of freedom, equality, and brotherhood.

3. The CENTRALIZATION of Revolutionary power. French centralization, as Tocqueville was to emphasize, had begun centuries earlier, in the latter part of the Middle Ages, but it had long been checked by institutions such as guild and commune that the Revolution was able to exterminate for once and all. Paris became the capital of French society in the Revolution to a degree never achieved by the Bourbons. Centralization of administration followed from the ideal of mass participation in power. How could the people as a whole be endowed with residual power unless all the intermediate authorities, all the ancient divisions of power, were disendowed, with their historic authorities passing to the people now, for the first time, represented by their government? By 1793 it was the conviction of many Revolutionary leaders, the Jacobins foremost, that in centralized government lay the best means of discovering and expressing the real will of the people. If five hundred persons could express the will of the people, why not fifty? If fifty, why not three? And from this it was but a short step to the fateful idea that in one man might lie possibility of fulfillment of popular will—the real will—that ordinary representative government could never equal.

4. The RATIONALIZATION of power. This, too was a process that, as Tocqueville and Weber were to emphasize, had been going on ever since the late Middle Ages. But the Revolution made it vivid, dramatized it, and rationalization became a consecrated principle of government. One sees it in the Revolution at all levels of importance. There was the rationalization of the currency, of the system of weights and measures, of the calendar. There was the rationalization of the educational system, replacing the historic autonomy of educational units by the one great public system, from elementary grades to university, that would reach every part of France and be directed from Paris. The historic irregularities of political communes and provinces were abolished, to be replaced by symmetrical departments and other units that would reflect administrative reason, not tradition. There was the rationalization of the army, including its system of command and its techniques of warfare. And there was, surmounting all of these, the whole rationalized system of bureaucracy.

brought into existence save by a political centralization that would extinguish these authorities, which, it was argued, clogged the arteries of commerce and finance.[14]

The result of two centuries of preoccupation with sovereignty had thus been to make political power appear as something either independent of or antithetical to moral tradition and social authority. True sovereignty, it had been argued from Hobbes to Rousseau, has its origin in, not tradition, not the historic social authorities, but in the nature of man and in contractual assent, either actual or implicit, and it gains its majesty and its rationality from its independence of all other types of authority.

It is on this point that we may best appreciate the significance of the sociological theories of authority that appear in the nineteenth century. We find, paralleling the rediscovery of community, the rediscovery of custom and tradition, of patriarchal and corporate authority, all of which, it is argued, are the fundamental (and continuing) sources of social and political order. In this view, the political state is converted into but one of the authorities in the larger society, conditioned, circumscribed, and limited by the others. It is in these terms that we may best see the significance of the sociologists with their rejection of the abstract or formal approach to the nature of sovereignty. And it is in these same terms that political pluralism as a systematic philosohy may be seen, along with syndicalist, guild-socialist, and other decentralist ideas. Historically, sociology's relation to them is close.[15]

The Discovery of Elites

A second consequence of the impact of the Revolution on the old regime was the beginning of modern intellectual interest in political elites. This interest flowed in the first instance from the problem posed for conservative minds by the seeming discontinuity of the French Revolution in the history of Europe. That is, given the conservative premise of the stability and essential harmony of the old order, how then could it have come to so sudden and drastic an end? Or even taking the view that that more dispassionate Tocqueville was to advance—that the centralization and rationalization of the Revolution were, along with its equalitarianism, the results of processes that had begun centuries earlier—how was the traumatic character of the Revolution to be explained?

For Burke, to whom the first of these two questions was the only real one, the answer lay clearly in the machinations of the *philosophes*

---

[14] See the discussion of the physiocrats' love of centralized despotism and their hatred of intermediate groups in François Oliver-Martin, "Le Declin et la Supression des Corps en France au XVIIIe Siècle" in *L'Organisation corporative du moyen âge à la fin de l'ancien régime* (Louvain: University of Louvain, 1937), 156.

[15] See my "The Politics of Social Pluralism," *Journal of Politics*, X, 764–786.

in their struggle for power. Burke tells us that the philosophers of the Enlightenment were animated above all else by a passion for power and, with it, a hatred of the old order, which they desired to overthrow. Burke refers to the *philosophes* as "political men of letters." As a group, he notes dryly, they have rarely been averse to change and innovation. Having lost their roots, first in church and then in royal court, they were compelled to seek their own status in society. "What they lost in the old court protection, they endeavored to make up by joining in a sort of incorporation of their own; to which the two academies of France, and afterward the vast undertaking of the Encyclopedia, carried on by a society of these gentlemen, did not a little contribute."[16] They comprised, Burke tells us, a kind of cabal. Its first dedication was to "the destruction of the Christian religion. This object they pursued with a degree of zeal which hitherto had been discovered only in the propagators of some system of piety. They were possessed with a spirit of proselytism in the most fanatical degree; and from thence, by an easy progress, with the spirit of persecution according to their means." Burke puts little credence in the persecution which allegedly was visited upon the *philosophes*. The real persecution, he suggests, was *their* persecution of all who disagreed with them.

The resources of intrigue are called in to supply the defects of argument and wit. To this system of literary monopoly was joined an unremitting industry to blacken and discredit in every way, and by every means, all those who did not hold to their faction. To those who have observed the spirit of their conduct, it has long been clear that nothing was wanted but the power of carrying the intolerance of the tongue and of the pen into a persecution which would strike at property, liberty and life.[17]

Having dethroned religion, the intellectuals moved to a subversion of the social order around them. Here, too,

a spirit of cabal, intrigue, and proselytism pervaded all their thoughts, words and actions. And as controversial zeal soon turns its thoughts on force, they began to insinuate themselves into a correspondence with foreign princes; in hopes, through their authority, which at first they flattered, they might bring about the changes they had in view. To them it was indifferent whether these changes were to be accomplished by the thunderbolt of despotism, or by the earthquake of popular commotion. . . . For the same purpose which they intrigued with princes, they cultivated, in a distinguished manner, the monied interest of France; and partly through the means furnished by those whose peculiar offices gave them the most extensive and certain means of communication, they carefully occupied all the avenues to opinion.[18]

[16] *Works,* op. cit., 504.
[17] Ibid., 504 f.
[18] Ibid., 505.

Behind Burke's attack on political intellectuals lay, obviously, deep distrust of all influences which seemed to him to be antagonistic to social tradition, Christianity, and, above all perhaps, the landed class, with the gentleman as its symbol. That Burke was himself a political intellectual, with something of the same passion for party intrigue and for insinuating himself into circles of power and prestige, and with not a little of the same capacity for duplicity that he castigates in the intellectuals of the Enlightenment and Revolution, did not, of course, ever occur to him. It does not matter. From the historical point of view what does matter is the pattern of envisagement of the secular intellectual and his relation to power that Burke gave not only to conservative thought in nineteenth-century England and France but, later, to much sociology.

That distrust of the rootless intellectual and apprehension of his moth-like attraction to the circles of power should have become a fixed part of the conservative view—expressed in the writings of Coleridge, Carlyle, Maistre, and Taine—is a matter for no surprise. More interesting is the way in which it becomes translated into a "sociology of the intellectual" that was to persist from Comte to the present day.

Comte's words on the political intellectual are set in a larger context of condemnation of the politicization of thought that, he felt, was one of the worst manifestations of the "metaphysical" stage of thought. The most vital issues of polity have fallen, Comte tells us,

to the class which is essentially one under two names—the civilians and the metaphysicians, or, under their common title, the lawyers and men of letters, whose position in regard to statesmanship is naturally a subordinate one. We shall see hereafter that, from its origin to the time of the first French Revolution, the system of metaphysical polity was expressed and directed by the universities on the one hand and the great judiciary corporations on the other: the first constituting a sort of spiritual power and the other a temporal power. This state of things is still traceable in most countries of the continent; while in France, for above half a century, the arrangement has degenerated into such an abuse that the judges are superseded by the bar, and the doctors (as they used to be called) by mere men of letters; so that now, any man who can hold a pen may aspire to the spiritual regulation of society, through the press or from the professional chair, unconditionally, and whatever may be his qualifications. When the time comes for the constitution of an organic condition, the reign of sophists and declaimers will have come to an end; but there will be the impediment to surmount of their having been provisionally in possession of public confidence.[19]

Basically the same view of the political intellectuals lies in Tocqueville, particularly in *The Old Regime and the Revolution*. Like Burke and Comte, Tocqueville calls our attention "to the remarkable, not to say formidable, influence these men's writings (which at first sight might

<hr />

[19] *Positive Philosophy*, II, 180 f.

seem to concern the history of our literature alone) had on the Revolution and indeed, still have today."[20] Unlike Burke, Tocqueville can see why the eighteenth-century political intellectual, as a social type, came into existence: to combat the "ridiculous, ramshackle institutions, survivals of an earlier age, which no one had attempted to co-ordinate or to adjust to modern conditions and which seemed destined to live on despite the fact that they had ceased to have any present value. . . ." Given these conditions, it was "natural enough that thinkers of the day should come to loathe everything that savored of the past and should desire to remold society on entirely new lines, traced by each thinker in the sole light of reason."[21]

But in their distrust of past, their total inexperience with political and social realities, and in their unwavering trust in what the light of pure reason revealed to each of them, the political intellectuals became, Tocqueville tells us, in almost Burkean words, unwitting instruments of a new form of despotism: that emanating from subjection to "an imaginary ideal society in which all was simple, uniform, coherent, equitable, and rational in the full sense of the terms."[22]

"Our men of letters," Tocqueville continues, "did not merely impart their revolutionary ideas to the French nation; they also shaped the national temperament and outlook on life. In the long process of molding men's minds to their ideal pattern their task was all the easier since the French had had no training in the field of politics, and they thus had a clear field. The result was that our writers ended up by giving the Frenchman the instincts, the turn of mind, the tastes, and even the eccentricities characteristic of the literary man. And when the time came for action, these literary propensities were imported into the political arena." The French Revolution was conducted, Tocqueville observes,

in the same spirit as that which gave rise to so many books expounding theories in the abstract. Our revolutionaries had the same fondness for broad generalizations, cut-and-dried legislative systems, and a pedantic symmetry; the same contempt for hard facts; the same taste for reshaping institutions on novel, ingenious, original lines; the same desire to reconstruct the entire constitution according to the rules of logic and a preconceived system instead of trying to rectify its faulty parts. The result was nothing short of disastrous; for what is a merit in a writer may well be a vice in the statesman and the very qualities which go to make great literature can lead to catastrophic revolutions.[23]

From the literary intellectuals came a new language of politics that was, henceforth, to alter profoundly the nature and dimension of politics.

20 *The Old Regime,* 140.
21 Ibid., 140.
22 Ibid., 146.
23 Ibid., 147.

"Even the politicians' phraseology was borrowed largely from the books they read; it was cluttered up with abstract words, gaudy flowers of speech, sonorous clichés, and literary turns of phrase. Fostered by the political passions that it voiced, this style made its way into all classes, being adopted with remarkable facility even by the lowest." Tocqueville concludes his passage with dry malice: "All they needed, in fact, to become literary men in a small way was a better knowledge of spelling.[24]

THE ROOTS OF POWER—TOCQUEVILLE

Tocqueville's *Democracy in America* is the first systematic and empirical study of the effects of political power on modern society. This work is much else also, but at bottom it is a study, and a remarkably dispassionate one, of the impact of democracy upon the traditions, values, and social structures descended from medieval society. In his second major work, *The Old Regime and the French Revolution,* Tocqueville explored the sources of modern political power, with its twin aspects of centralization and bureaucratization. Logically one might say that it precedes the earlier work. And no one reading *Democracy in America* will have any difficulty in seeing, between the lines, the thesis of the later work. Both studies have to be understood in the light of Tocqueville's obsession with the Revolution and its impact upon the social order.

Tocqueville's central thesis can be stated simply. All that alienates man in modern society from traditional authority—from class, guild, church, and so on—tends to drive him ever more forcefully into the haven of power, power conceived not as something remote and fearful but as close, sealing, intimate, and providential: the power, that is, of modern democracy with its roots in public opinion. This is Tocqueville's dominant theme. The decline of the aristocratic community and the release of men from old authorities were historically required, he repeatedly emphasizes, for modern power to make its appearance in the democratic-national state.

Unlike most of his contemporaries, Tocqueville saw democracy not primarily as a system of freedom but of power. Democracy with its emphasis upon equality, liberation from traditional authority, and its sense of the centralized, unified nation, is but the logical and inevitable outcome of forces that had begun centuries earlier in monarchical centralization which had, over several centuries, reduced medieval diversity and localism in favor of widening national aggregates based upon administrative power at the center. Whereas freedom is, for Tocqueville, *immunity* from power, democracy is, by its nature, a *form* of power, potentially greater in intensity and reach than any prior form of political government.

24 Ibid., 147.

What are the sources of democratic power? Tocqueville finds these pre-eminently in the massive tendency of modern history toward equalization of status and the leveling of ranks. "In running over the pages of our history, we shall scarcely find a single great event of the last seven hundred years that has not promoted equality of condition." Equality has meant, however, the destruction of the estates, guilds, classes, and other associations which had, by virtue of the very inequality they conferred on the population, represented limits on the power of the king.

I perceive that we have destroyed those individual powers which were able, single-handed, to cope with tyranny; but it is the government alone that has inherited all the privileges of which families, guilds, and individuals have been deprived; to the power of a small number of persons, which, if it was sometimes oppressive, was often conservative, has succeeded the weakness of the whole community.[25]

The idea of the people, of the majority, the rock on which democratic power rests, could never have come into existence apart from the sterilization of hierarchical authority. In the Middle Ages men were conscious of themselves as churchmen, guildsmen, members of this or that family or province, but never as a nation, much less as a people, with independent, corporate existence. Conceptualization of the people as an entity is a gradual process in modern history; historically its basis is, first, the atomization of the medieval *social* identities of individuals and, second, the centralization and nationalization of political power, thus providing a legal atmosphere within which socially detached masses of individuals could live and have identity.

Between equality and centralization there is, therefore, a fateful affinity. Hence the necessity, in historical terms, of early powerful monarchs such as Louis XIV. By their attacks upon feudal enclaves of authority, they could not help but gradually widen the base of equality and enrich the taste for it. Similarly, all that loosened the bonds between the feudal associations and their members—such forces as war, trade, cities, the printing press—made the work of centralization correspondingly easier.

Having established the long-run tendency and roots of centralization, what are the causes of its variable intensity in modern times? Less or greater centralization in democracy is determined chiefly by whether or not a democracy comes into existence gradually, as in the United States, or as the consequence of sudden revolution. In the latter case,

As the classes that managed local affairs have been suddenly swept away by the storm, and as the confused mass that remains has yet neither the organization nor the habits which fit it to assume the administration of these affairs,

25 *Democracy in America*, I, 10.

the state alone seems capable of taking upon itself all the details of government, and centralization becomes, as it were, the unavoidable state of the country.

Napoleonism, Tocqueville writes, was inevitable in France, for "after the abrupt disappearance of the nobility and the higher rank of the middle classes, these powers devolved on him, of course; it would have been almost as difficult for him to reject as to assume them."[26]

Tocqueville notes the affinity between the lower classes and centralized power. The central government is the only means whereby the people can wrest the management of local affairs from the aristocracy. The lower classes, or their representatives, thus tend to hold an ascendancy in the early phase of a revolution. But, Tocqueville emphasizes shrewdly, this balance changes.

Towards the close of such a revolution . . . it is usually the conquered aristocracy that endeavors to take over the management of all affairs to the state, because such an aristocracy dreads the tyranny of a people that has become its equal, and not infrequently its master. Thus, it is not always the same class of the community that strives to increase the prerogative of the government; but as long as the democratic revolution lasts, there is always one class in the nation, powerful in numbers or in wealth, which is induced, by peculiar passions or interests, to centralize the public administration, independently of that hatred of being governed by one's neighbor which is a general and permanent feeling among democratic nations.[27]

In England it is the lower classes that are striving to destroy local independence and to transfer administration to the center, and the upper classes endeavoring to retain administration in the local areas. But the time will come, Tocqueville predicts, when the very reverse will be the case.

A third factor in variability of intensity is the contrasting effect of mass illiteracy under an aristocracy and in a democracy. Ignorance of the masses does not necessarily lead to centralization in aristocracies "because in them instruction is nearly equally diffused between the monarch and the leading members of the community." Very different is the case in democracy where the intermediate powers have vanished. Mass ignorance here puts the people far more directly in the hands of the central government. "Hence, among a nation which is ignorant, as well as democratic, an amazing difference cannot fail speedily to arise between the intellectual capacity of the ruler and that of each of his subjects. This completes the easy concentration of all power in his hands: the administrative function of the state is perpetually extended because

26 Ibid., II, 298.
27 Ibid., II, 298.

the state alone is competent to administer the affairs of the country."[28]

Fourth, warfare has a strongly centralizing effect on democratic administration. Success in war, Tocqueville notes, depends more on the means of easy transferral of all the resources of a nation to a single point than on the extent of those resources.

Hence, it is chiefly in war that nations desire, and frequently need, to increase the powers of the central government. All men of military genius are fond of centralization, which increases their strength; and all men of centralizing genius are fond of war. . . . Thus, the democratic tendency that leads men unceasingly to multiply the privileges of the state and to circumscribe the rights of private persons is much more rapid and constant among those democratic nations that are exposed by their position to great and frequent war than among all others.[29]

But the foremost of the causes that centralize power in a democracy is the birth and character of the ruling individual. The people are never so happy about transferring powers to their leaders as when they feel that he is one of them in origin and nature.

The attraction of administrative powers to the center will always be less easy and less rapid under the reign of kings who are still in some way connected with the old aristocratic order than under new princes, the children of their own achievements, whose birth, prejudices, propensities, and habits appear to bind them indissolubly to the cause of equality. . . . In democratic communities the rule is that centralization must increase in proportion as the sovereign is less aristocratic.

A revolution that overthrows an ancient regal family in order to place new men at the head of a democratic people may temporarily weaken the central power; but however anarchical such a revolution may appear at first, we need not hesitate to predict that its final and certain consequence will be to extend and to secure the prerogatives of that power.

The foremost or indeed the sole condition required in order to succeed in centralizing the supreme power in a democratic community is to love equality, or to get men to believe you love it. Thus, the science of despotism, which was once so complex, is simplified, and reduced, as it were, to a single principle.[30]

Tocqueville's preoccupation with conflict between political power and traditional authority leads him to examine the effects of democratic power on social institutions. That it undermines, by its nature, localism and hierarchy we have seen. But there are other instances.

There is the authority of learning, of individual distinction, and of taste—weakened in each instance, he tells us, because the diffusion of power, or at least the myth of this diffusion, leads men to distrust all

[28] Ibid., II, 299 f.
[29] Ibid., II, 300 f.
[30] Ibid., II, 302.

authority that does not seem to arise from public opinion, a power in democracy that Tocqueville declares to be more formidable than the Spanish Inquisition, which, after all, addressed itself only to the circulation of books. "The empire of the majority succeeds much better in the United States, since it actually removes any wish to publish them."[31]

There is the effect of popular power on the authority of the family.

Among aristocratic nations social institutions recognize, in truth, no one in the family but the father; children are received by society at his hands; society governs him, he governs them. Thus, the parent not only has a natural right but acquires a political right to command them; he is the author and the support of his family; but he is also its constituted ruler. In democracies, where the government picks out every individual singly from the mass to make him subservient to the general laws of the community, no such intermediate person is required; a father is there, in the eye of the law, only a member of the community, older and richer than his sons.[32]

Conflict between family and state is, then, conflict between the traditional authority of the father and the emerging power of other members of the family, the inevitable consequence of the individualization of family and the magnification of the role of each member as citizen.

When men live more for the remembrance of what has been than for care of what is, and when they are more given to attend to what their ancestors thought than to think themselves, the father is the natural and necessary tie between the past and the present, the link by which the ends of these two chains are connected. In aristocracies . . . the father is not only the civil head of the family, but the organ of its tradition, the expounder of its customs, the arbiter of its manners. He is listened to with deference, he is addressed with respect, and the love that is felt for him is always tempered with fear.

When the condition of society becomes democratic and men adopt as their general principle that it is good and lawful to judge of all things for oneself, using former points of belief not as a rule of faith, but simply as a means of information, the power which the opinions of a father exercise over those of his sons diminishes as well as his legal power.[33]

With profession, class, and religion, the case is the same so far as authority is concerned. What is taken away by political power, and by

[31] Ibid., I, 265. It is interesting to observe, however, that in the notebooks Tocqueville kept during his stay in the United States, no such characterization is to be found, though there are several references to public opinion. See *Journey to America*, George Lawrence, trans.; J. P. Mayer, ed. (New Haven: Yale University Press, 1960), *passim*. It has to be remembered constantly, as one reads *Democracy in America*, that its author did indeed, while there, see "more than America" and that it was, as he explicitly tells us, "the image of democracy" that he sought. See I, 14.

[32] *Democracy in America*, II, 194.

[33] Ibid., 194.

public opinion adapting itself to political power, from the customary authority of each of these institutions is also taken away from their function in maintaining tradition or in serving as contexts of culture. Only the legal profession shows signs, Tocqueville believes, of maintaining traditional authority, and this is because of the inordinate number of lawyers who participate in politics and, by participating, are able to protect their professional identification along with the forms and rituals that so pre-eminently mark this medieval-born profession. In religion, Protestantism thrives by its very lack of organizational intensity and although Tocqueville seeks to demonstrate that there is greater natural affinity between Catholicism and democracy—because of the mass leveling within the Roman Church that papal centralization has effected—he notes that in liturgical and hierarchical terms American Catholicism is more "Protestant" than what is to be found in Europe.[34]

A final example of the impact of power on traditional authority is found in the military establishment. The spectacle of the Revolution's mass armies—continued in every equalitarian detail by Napoleon, who was himself a product of military democracy—left a deep impress on Tocqueville's thought, and he deserves to be called the first sociologist of militarism. He notes a deep internal conflict between *civil* democracy's preference for peace—based upon the desire to continue business affairs without the hindrance of war—and the preference of democratic armies for war. The reasons for the latter lie, he believes, in the nature of democratic military command. Whereas under aristocracy, officers are almost wholly drawn from the nobility, with nothing in war to affect a status that was ascribed by birth and hence independent of military careers, the case is very different in democracy.

In democratic armies the desire of advancement is almost universal: it is ardent, tenacious, perpetual; it is strengthened by all other desires and extinguished only with life itself. But it is easy to see that, of all armies in the world, those in which advancement must be slowest in time of peace are the armies of democratic countries. . . . All the ambitious spirits of a democratic army are consequently desirous of war, because war makes vacancies and warrants the violation of that law of seniority which is the sole privilege natural to democracy."[35]

There is the related fact, galling to status aspiration, that the military tends to be ignored, even despised, in times of peace. In an aristocracy this does not matter since the officers return in any event to noble status. It is very different in a democracy, where "military men fall to the lowest rank of the public servants; they are little esteemed and no longer understood. The reverse of what takes place in aristocratic ages

34 Ibid., II, 27.
35 Ibid., II, 266.

then occurs; the men who enter the army are no longer of the highest, but of the lowest class." The successful, educated, and wealthy in a democracy shun military service, and the result is that "the army, taken collectively, eventually forms a small nation by itself, where the mind is less enlarged and habits are more rude than in the nation at large."[36]

Tocqueville finds noncommissioned officers in democratic armies more likely than others to be inclined toward war. After all, commissioned officers tend generally to have assured status in time of peace as well as in time of war. But the noncommissioned officer has none. "A desperate ambition cannot fail to be kindled in a man thus incessantly goaded on by his youth, his wants, his passions, the spirit of his age, his hopes, and his fears.

Non-commissioned officers are therefore bent on war, on war always at any cost; but if war be denied them, they desire revolutions, to suspend the authority of the established regulations and to enable them, aided by the general confusion and the political passions of the time, to get rid of their superior officers and to take their places. Nor is it impossible for them to bring about such a crisis, because their common origin and habits give them much influence over the soldiers, however different may be their passions and their desires.[37]

Democracies tend to be weak in early phases of a war but vastly stronger than aristocracies in the later phases. It is not easy in the beginning of war to separate democrats from customary civilian pursuits and attractions. But when the sheer duration of war leads inevitably to this separation, then people turn with all the more enthusiasm and even ferocity to prosecution of the war.

War, after it has destroyed all modes of speculation, becomes itself the great and sole speculation, to which all the ardent and ambitious desires that equality engenders are exclusively directed. . . . A long war produces upon a democratic army the same effects that a revolution produces upon a people; it breaks through regulations and allows extraordinary men to rise above the common level.[38]

There is, moreover, a "secret connection" between military character and democratic character. The latter is passionately eager to acquire what it covets and to enjoy it. Democratic character tends to worship chance and to fear death less than difficulty. This is the spirit that men of a democracy bring to trade and commerce, and it is a spirit that lends itself easily to the contexts of war. "No kind of greatness is more pleasing to the imagination of a democratic people than military great-

---

36 Ibid., II, 266.
37 Ibid., II, 274.
38 Ibid., II, 277 f.

character. Political power, properly so called, is merely the organized power of one class for oppressing another."[51]

This is, of course, pure Rousseau, pure Saint-Just. Despite its location in the *Communist Manifesto*, it is no mere call to action, no passing flight of tactical fancy. It reflects all that is central in the Marxian view, and this is as true of the early "philosophical" Marx as of the later "historical" Marx. From "On the Jewish Question" through the *Manifesto*, *The Class Struggles in France*, down to his final letters, there is a view of power in Marx precisely as antithetical to Tocqueville—and also, in large measure, to Tönnies, Weber, and Durkheim—as it is congruent with what we find in Rousseau's *Discourse on Political Economy* or in some of the decrees of the Committee on Public Safety. From such a view is bound to come philosophical indifference to the long-run consequences of the use of techniques of power in a revolution.

For, if men are convinced of the inevitable disappearance of power, once the proper economic and social conditions have been brought about why should not every possible technique of centralization and consolidation of power be employed during the revolution and the period immediately following it? And, if political power is indeed only the reflection of a dominant class in a class-torn society, then how can there be a problem of power in a society leveled of class (and all other social) distinctions?

Engels was but restating Marx's own view of the matter when he wrote of the state: "When at last it becomes the real representative of the whole of society it renders itself unnecessary. As soon as there is no longer any social class to be held in subjection . . . a state is no longer necessary. The first act by virtue of which the state really constitutes itself the representative of the whole of society—the taking possession of the means of production in the name of society—this is, at the same time, its last independent act as a state. State interference in social relations becomes, in one domain after another, superfluous, and then dies out of itself; the government of persons is replaced by the administration of things, and by the conduct of processes of production. The state is not 'abolished.' *It dies out.*"[52] The line between the Tocquevillian and the Marxian conceptions of the state could not be more sharply drawn than by Engels' passage. This is the view that even today underlies the nearly total indifference (scholarly as well as administrative) in Marxist nations and movements to the problems of bureaucracy, centralization, and political mechanization that, elsewhere, have proved to be the central preoccupations of liberal minds in the twentieth century.

The difference between Marx and Tocqueville may be reduced to this: for Tocqueville the greatest threats of political power must always occur in the most individualized—that is, atomized and leveled—socie-

---

[51] *Basic Writings*, op. cit., 29.
[52] Ibid., 106.

ties; for Marx the greatest threats, indeed the *only* threats, occur in societies characterized by the reverse: where class and other modes of social differentiation are strongest. Tocqueville believed that there was more personal freedom under aristocracy than under democracy—where public opinion becomes, in his view, more despotic than the medieval Inquisition. For Marx, there was no real freedom under aristocracy. It is, for Marx, the special character of modern political development that the state, most notably in its democratic form, represents the beginning of a human emancipation that will only become complete after the socialist revolution. Then and only then will men know freedom. For Tocqueville political power is simultaneously a *cause* of alienation, through its invasions of the communities of membership which form society, and a *refuge* from alienation: that is, political power in a democracy becomes increasingly a fortress of escape from the ills and frustrations of civil society. For Marx political power *is* alienation; alienation in the special Marxian sense that pertains equally to property, class, and religion. Alienation and political power will both terminate when man knows, under socialism, full emancipation from all restraints.

Political emancipation is a reduction of man on the one hand to a member of civil society, an independent and egoistic individual, and on the other hand, to a citizen, to a moral person. Human emancipation will be complete only when the real individual man has absorbed into himself the abstract citizen; when as an individual man, in his everyday life, in his work, and in his relationships, he has become a species-being; and when he has recognized and organized his own powers (*forces propres*) as social powers so that he no longer separates this social power from himself as political power.[53]

The passage just quoted comes at the end of Marx's "On the Jewish Question," and there is no better place than in this essay, written five years before the *Manifesto,* to get at the essence of the Marxian view of the nature and role of political power in European history. The essay was written by Marx (as were so many of his briefer works) in refutation of the thesis of another philosopher: in this instance, Bruno Bauer's plea for the emancipation of the Jews and their elevation to political membership as Jews. For Marx such emancipation and elevation were chimerical. Bauer, he thought, failed to recognize the historical nature of the European state and its relation to religion. Marx's reply to Bauer's plea for Jewish political emancipation is given in a masterly review of the relation of the state to *all* forms of civil membership, religion included among economic, social, and cultural memberships. The purely polemical essence, which need not detain us here, is simply that there can be no *Jewish* membership in the state for the simple reason that there can be no *Christian* membership in the state. That is, the very idea

53 *Early Writings,* op. cit., 31.

of the state is predicated on the sterilization of religious identities for purposes of citizenship. If it is Jewishness (or Christianness either) that is declared fundamental, there can be no citizenship properly so called, for the idea of political citizenship has developed in terms of the emancipation of man from his pre-political identities.

It is the conflict between civil society and the state that strikes Marx's attention. Tocqueville too had seen this conflict, as we have observed, but in altogether different terms. For Marx it is not the state that is the decisive influence but rather civil society with its varied combinations of materialistic egoism and forms of alienation. The state offers man (and here we see again the strong substratum of Rousseau) a vision of community that stands in contrast to all that civil society represents.

Where the political state has attained to its full development, man leads, not only in thought, in consciousness, but in reality, in life, a double existence— celestial and terrestrial. He lives in the political community where he regards himself as a communal being and in civil society where he acts simply as a private individual, treats other men as means, degrades himself to the role of a mere means, and becomes the plaything of alien powers.[54]

It is thus impossible, on moral grounds alone, for members of a religion as such to become members of the state, the political community. "The conflict in which the individual, as the professor of a particular religion, finds himself involved with his own quality of citizenship and with other men as members of the community, may be resolved into the secular schism between the political state and civil society." The difference between religious man and the citizen is exactly the same as that "between shopkeeper and citizen, between the day laborer and citizen, between the landed proprietor and the citizen, between the living individual and the citizen."[55]

It is, in short, the revolutionary tension between citizenship and membership in civil society that Marx, like Rousseau, is concerned with emphasizing. To be sure, political citizenship is not for Marx, as it was for Rousseau, the final answer, for it represents, as we have noted, in itself a mode of alienation. But as one reads this essay he cannot escape the thought that it is to some extent from the political ideal of citizenship —an identity man acquires through his legal and conceptual emancipation from other status identities—that Marx derives something (a model perhaps) of his apocalyptic vision of the final "human" emancipation in which he will be liberated from political as well as from all economic and religious and social identities. "Political emancipation certainly repre-

54 Ibid., 13.
55 Ibid., 14.

sents a great progress," Marx writes. "It is not indeed the final form of human emancipation, but it is the final form of emancipation within the framework of the prevailing order. It goes without saying that we are speaking here of real, practical emancipation."[56]

What Marx writes on the state and its role in European history is penetrating. European man, Marx tells us, has emancipated himself politically from religion "by expelling it from the sphere of public law to that of private law." Religion, from being a part of the fabric of the state, becomes, through such events as the Reformation and the rise of nationalism, a part of civil society only. "It has become the spirit of civil society, of the sphere of egoism and of the *bellum omnium contra omnes*. It is no longer the essence of community, but the essence of differentiation."[57]

Such a passage gives us the clue to Marx's view of civil society—an arena of economic, religious, and social tyrannies to which the individual is still subjected. Unlike Hegel, who found in civil society—family, class, and local community—the necessary complement of the state, Marx sees in civil society only fragmentation and alienation from which man must someday be extricated. He has Rousseau's repugnance for all that emphasizes man's separate, differentiated identity and all of Rousseau's love for that which emphasizes man in his communal, or what Marx calls "species," identity. It is in these terms indeed that Marx scorns the natural-law school's insistence upon *individual* rights—precisely as Rousseau had. Rousseau, in his *Social Contract*, had declared that once man entered into the true political community, he would surrender all of his individual rights and acquire new ones based upon his membership as a citizen. "None of the supposed rights of man," Marx writes, "go beyond the egoistic man, man as he is, as a member of civil society: that is, an individual separated from the community, withdrawn into himself, wholly preoccupied with his private interest and acting in accordance with his private caprice."[58] In *The Holy Family* Marx wrote again on this point: "It has been shown that the recognition of the rights of man by the modern State has only the same significance as the recognition of slavery by the State in antiquity. The basis of the State in antiquity was slavery; the basis of the modern State is civil society and the individual of civil society, that is, the independent individual, whose only link with other individuals is private interest and unconscious, natural necessity, the slave of wage labour, of the selfish needs of himself and others."[59]

56 Ibid., 15.
57 Ibid., 15.
58 Ibid., 26.
59 *Selected Writings in Sociology and Social Philosophy*, T. B. Bottomore, trans.; T. B. Bottomore and Maximilien Rubel, eds. (New York: McGraw-Hill Book Company, 1956), 218.

Whenever the state, as a historical type, comes into being there must be conflict between it and the religious and economic elements of civil society.

Certainly, in periods when the political state as such comes violently to birth in civil society, and when men strive to liberate themselves through political emancipation, the state can, and must, proceed to abolish and destroy religion; but only in the same way as it proceeds to destroy private property, by declaring a maximum, by confiscation, or by progressive taxation, or in the same way as it proceeds to abolish life, by the guillotine. At those times when the state is most aware of itself, political life seeks to stifle its own prerequisites—civil society and its elements—and to establish itself as the geniune and harmonious species-life of man. But it can only achieve this end by setting itself in violent contradiction with its own conditions of existence, by declaring a permanent revolution.[60]

Given that passage, one does not have to search for extraneous, tactical influences to account for Marx's growing preoccupation with political power and the use of power to atomize remaining centers of privilege and hierarchy in society and to form a general association within which individuals, not groups and classes, would be the elements of polity. If it was from Hegel that Marx got his sense of the historical role of the state in Europe, it was from Rousseau (who had of course influenced Hegel) that he acquired his sense of the state as a structure resting on the unmediated loyalties and devotions of individuals, each freed of conflicting loyalties.

Like Rousseau, Marx could combine in a single passage elements of the rigorously analytical and the chiliastic. The individualizing functions of the historic state in its relation to feudal society served admirably for Marx, as for Rousseau, as the framework of speculation on the future. Rousseau's adjuration that within the general will and its exclusive association individuals shall become as completely as possible separated from competing relationships—thus forcing them to achieve their individualities—has reflections in the following passage from Marx on the subject of future society: "Religion, the family, the state, law, morality, science, art, etc., are only particular forms of production and come under its general law. The positive abolition of private property, as the appropriation of human life, is thus the positive abolition of all alienation, and thus the return of man from religion, the family, the state, etc., to his human, i.e. social life."[61] For Marx, as for Rousseau, there is always implicit a conception of man as containing naturally within himself sentiments and faculties which, over the course of social development, have become alienated from him and vested in external institutions which enslave him. Revolution is the only means by which the end of

---

[60] *Early Writings*, 16.
[61] *Selected Writings*, 244.

this alienation can be effected and man's faculties returned to him. Hence the vital political function of revolution in Marx's thought.

The political aspect of a revolution consists in the movement of the politically uninfluential classes to end their exclusion from political life and power. Its standpoint is that of the state, an abstract whole, which only exists by virtue of its separation from real life, and which is unthinkable without the organized opposition between the universal idea and the individual existence of man. A revolution of a political kind also organizes, therefore, in accordance with this narrow and discordant outlook, a ruling group in society at the expense of society.[62]

Following this passage comes a key paragraph that extends analytical vision to messianic hope: hope of termination, for the first time in history, of the omnipresence of political power.

Revolution in general—the overthrow of the existing ruling power and the dissolution of existing social relationships—is a political act. Without revolution socialism cannot develop. It requires this political act as it needs the overthrow and the dissolution. But as soon as its organizing activity begins, as soon as its own purpose and spirit come to the fore, socialism sheds this political covering.[63]

The last sentence is the crux, of course. This passage was written five years before the *Manifesto* appeared, and it is in many ways the single most important sentence Marx ever wrote so far as the future politics of socialism was concerned. It is the seed of the myth that permitted generations of Marxist intellectuals to combine without difficulty in their minds programs for the ruthless capture and absolute centralization of political power with fanatical confidence that, once the spirit and purpose of socialism had become morally sovereign, political power in the existential sense would disappear. Not without cause did Lenin style the Bolsheviks as "the Jacobins of contemporary Social-Democracy."

In the same way that organized power of the French Revolution served as a model for Marxian acceptance of the necessary totalism of revolutionary power, of atomization of traditional authorities and of rationalization and generalization of revolutionary political power, it served also as a model of the centralization that Marx and Engels never doubted would be crucial to socialist objectives in the first stages of a revolution. Marx expressed his admiration for the centralization of the French Revolution that had, like a "gigantic broom," swept away all the localism, pluralism, and communalism of traditional French society. "The centralized state power," he writes in opening words reminiscent of Tocqueville,

[62] Ibid., 237 f.
[63] Ibid., 238.

with its ubiquitous organs of standing army, police, bureaucracy, clergy, and judicature—organs wrought after the plan of a systematic and hierarchic division of labor—originates from the days of the absolute monarchy, serving nascent middle-class society as a mighty weapon in its struggles against feudalism. Still its development remained clogged by all manner of medieval rubbish, seignorial rights, local privileges, municipal and gild monopolies and provincial constitutions. The gigantic broom of the French Revolution of the eighteenth century swept away all these relics of bygone times, thus clearing simultaneously the social soil of its last hindrances to the superstructure of the modern state edifice raised under the First Empire. . . .[64]

For Napoleon too Marx had an appreciation not unlike Tocqueville's. Napoleon, Marx tells us, clearly understood the nature of the modern state, and he represented the last struggle of the revolutionary terrorism against civil society and its policy that had been begun by the Revolution. Napoleon, however, "practiced terrorism by substituting permanent war for permanent revolution." Marx's tactical understanding of the steps taken by Napoleon to nationalize, monopolize, and centralize economic and intellectual life in France is clear. And there is little doubt that the model of both Jacobin and Napoleonic centralization was in his mind when, in the *Communist Manifesto,* he and Engels came to the steps that would be a necessary part of the Revolution in "the most advanced countries." These included centralization of credit and banking, of placing the means of communication and transport in the hands of the state; extension of factories and other productive facilities owned by the state; establishment of industrial armies, and so forth.[65]

Marx was capable of writing highly sophisticated appreciations of the role of bureaucracy in the development of European government.

This executive power with its monstrous bureaucratic and military organization, with its artificial state machinery embracing wide strata, with a host of officials numbering half a million, besides an army of another half million, this appalling parasitic growth, which enmeshes the body of French society like a net and closes all its pores, sprang up in the days of absolute monarchy, with the decay of the feudal system, which it helped to hasten. The seignorial privileges of the landowners and towns became transformed into so many attributes of the state power, the feudal dignitaries into paid officials and the motley pattern of conflicting medieval plenary powers into the regulated plan of a state authority, whose work is divided and centralized as in a factory. The first French Revolution, with its task of breaking all local, territorial, urban

[64] *Basic Writings,* 363.

[65] Ibid., 28 f. Marx's insight into *l'idée Napoléonienne,* though limited by its strict economic perspective and therefore less revealing than what Michels was to write a generation later, is nevertheless penetrating. For Marx there are, in fact, *four* aspects of the Napoleonic Idea: (1) the enslavement of peasant under the guise of his liberation, (2) strong and unlimited government in order to hold the urban proletariat in harness, (3) a "well groomed bureaucracy, large in size," and (4) domination of clergy as an instrument of government. See *Basic Writings,* 341–344.

and provincial independent powers in order to create the bourgeois unity of the nation, was bound to develop what the absolute monarchy had begun—centralization, but at the same time the extent, the attributes and the agents of the governmental authority. Napoleon perfected this state machinery.[66]

Tocqueville could not have improved on those words. They were written in 1852, seventeen years after the publication of *Democracy in America,* three years before publication of Tocqueville's study of the old regime. But there the matter stopped.

That socialism might have its own problems of bureaucracy in the light of the centralized assumption of economic powers that the *Communist Manifesto* prescribes for the revolution seems to have given Marx's mind little trouble. In the same way that political power loses its political character once the capitalist class has been overthrown, so presumably does governmental administration lose its bureaucratic nature. Lenin must have felt in keeping with Marxist understanding of these matters when he wrote of socialist administration:

The bookkeeping and control necessary for this have been simplified by capitalism to the utmost, till they have become the extraordinarily simple operations of watching, recording, and issuing receipts, within the reach of anybody who can read and write and know the first four arithmetical rules. . . . When most of the functions of the state are reduced to this bookkeeping and control by the workers themselves, it ceases to be a "political" state. The public functions are converted from political into simple administrative functions. . . . The whole of society will have become one office and one factory with equal work and pay.[67]

Although Marx and Engels were indifferent to any problem of *political* power that might emerge within classless society, they had, like Bentham before them, a rather well-developed conception of the factory as the embodiment of social authority within industrialism. In "On Authority," an essay written in 1874, Engels expressed his disdain for the anarchist expectation of the cessation of all authority once capitalism was overthrown. Far from any nirvana of surcease from all authority, there will be, Engels tells us, there *must* be, under socialism, the kind of continuing authority that is bound up with the disciplines of technology and the large-scale factory. Engels' words on the future work under socialism are emphatic.

All these workers, men, women, and children, are obliged to begin and finish their work at the hours fixed by the authority of the steam, which care nothing for individual autonomy. . . . [T]he will of the single individual will always have to subordinate itself, which means that questions are settled in an authoritarian way. The automatic machinery of a big factory is much more despotic than the small capitalists who employ workers ever have been. At least with regard to the hours of work one may write upon the portals of these factories: *Lasciate ogni autonomia, voi che entrate.* If man, by dint of his knowledge and inventive genius, has subdued the forces of nature, the latter avenge themselves upon him by subjecting him, in so far as he employs them, to a veritable despotism, independent of all social organization. Wanting to abolish authority in large-scale industry is tantamount to wanting to abolish industry itself, to destroy the power loom in order to return to the spinning wheel.[68]

There was, it is plain enough, little of the utopian or romantic in Engels, and even if his words did not perfectly and wholly embody Marx's views on the subject, they certainly entered into the mainstream of the Marxist tradition that was to reach its culmination in Russia in 1919. And there is every reason to suppose that his words did in fact substantially express Marx's views, for Marx never repudiated them, and in any event they correspond to the view that he tirelessly proclaimed from earliest years, to wit: it is *history* that produces, within the womb of each stage of development, the true outlines and the true substance of the next stage. For Marx the glory of capitalism was the industrial and technological system that had formed within it. Capitalism as a set of social relations would be extinguished, along with political power, but not large-scale industry and technology and the disciplines they represented.

THE RATIONALIZATION OF AUTHORITY—WEBER

Contrast between traditional and modern society forms, for Weber as for Tocqueville and Marx, the essential background of his theory of power. In moral terms, there is the same gulf between Weber and Marx that lies between Tocqueville and Marx. There is, if possible, even more pessimism about the future of Western political power in Weber than in Tocqueville. All of the essential elements of Weber's analysis of the history of political power have their prototype in Tocqueville's treatment of the affinity between social equalitarianism and centralization of political power. The principle of rationalization serves Weber's purposes in much the same way that Tocqueville's were served by the principle of equality. In each instance a single, dominating aspect of modernism is endowed with dynamic, even causal, historical significance. What for Tocqueville is epitomized by "aristocratic" is epitomized for Weber by "traditional."

Weber, however, gives the central elements of his theory of power a degree of universality, a generality of sociological application, that is lacking in Tocqueville. There is little of the deliberately taxonomic in Tocqueville's treatment of authority, no effort to extract from the concrete materials of Western European or American society calculated per-

[68] *Basic Writings,* 483.

spectives of analysis to be used toward the clarification of the ancient world or non-Western societies. That Tocqueville could on occasion use the concrete as the basis of reflections having abstract and universal application is clear enough. But this is very different from Weber's determinedly scientific effort to formulate concepts that could be used, irrespective of time and place, in the study of society. Weber's success in his effort is amply attested by the almost universal incorporation of his basic categories in contemporary studies. It is hardly an exaggeration to say that the bulk of inquiries today into large-scale, formal organization and into the transitions of the new nations of the non-Western world from traditional to modern types of government take their departure from the categories that Weber used to account for the history of authority and power in the West. And Weber's analysis of bureaucracy, including its role in non-governmental spheres of society and culture, is not merely the point of departure of present inquiries; it is, with the rarest and most minute exceptions, still the sum of them. No one has yet added to Weber's theory (vision is the more accurate word) of bureaucracy any theoretical element that is not at least implicit in his own statements on the subject.

Let us begin with the three types of "domination" that Weber finds, in one degree or another, in all societies: the traditional, the rational, and the charismatic. The first two are, for analytical purposes, the more important in the sociology of authority. The third, the charismatic, exists, on Weber's own account, in pure form only for brief moments in history; its fate is to be converted almost immediately into the traditional or the rational. On this we shall be brief, for I believe the more relevant place for extended examination of the charismatic is in the chapter on the religio-sacred.

TRADITIONAL

A system of imperative co-ordination will be called "traditional" if legitimacy is claimed for it and believed in on the basis of the sanctity of the order and the attendant powers of control as they have been handed down from the past, "have always existed." The person or persons exercising authority are designated according to traditionally transmitted rules. The object of obedience is the personal authority of the individual which he enjoys by virtue of his traditional status. The organized group exercising authority is, in the simplest case, primarily based on relations of personal loyalty, cultivated through a common process of education.[69]

Traditional authority thus draws its legitimacy not from reason or abstract rule but from its roots in the belief that it is ancient, that it has inherent and unassailable wisdom transcending any one man's reason. Its social essence is the direct personal relation between those affected: teacher to student, servant to master, disciple to religious leader, and so

[69] *The Theory of Social and Economic Organization,* op. cit., 341.

on. No clear differentiation in such a system is made between "political" and "moral" authority. The king's authority is primarily personal, not territorial, and is mediated through ranks of other rulers—dukes, earls, and so on—all of whom have a relation to vassals below them comparable to the king's relation to them. The "apparatus" appropriate to such a system consists either of personal retainers—household officials, relatives, favorites—or personally loyal vassals and tributary lords. The essential model for traditional authority for Weber is, as it was for all other sociologists, the Middle Ages.

RATIONAL AUTHORITY differs sharply in kind. It is characterized by bureaucracy, by rationalization of the personal relationships which are the substance of traditional society. Legal domination exists in a society when "a system of rules that is applied judicially and administratively in accordance with ascertainable principles is valid for all members of the corporate group."[70] Although this mode of authority is not equalitarian —it has its own strata of function and responsibility—it cannot help but place an emphasis on equality that is lacking in the traditional order. All are equal under the rules governing them specifically. The emphasis is on the rules rather than on persons or on mores. The organization is supreme and, by its nature, strives toward increasing rationalization of itself through reduction of the influence played by kinship, friendship, or the various other factors, including money, that so strongly influence the traditional system. Function, authority, hierarchy, and obedience all exist here, as they do in the traditional order, but they are conceived to flow strictly from the application of organizational reason.

CHARISMATIC AUTHORITY is that wielded by an individual who is able to show through revelation, magical power, or simply through boundless personal attraction, that he possesses *charisma,* a unique force of command that overrides in popular estimation all that is bequeathed by either tradition or law. Charismatic leadership, whether found in religion or politics, almost always involves at some key point in its arrival a dramatic stroke, whether of state or church. Jesus, Buddha, Mohammed, Caesar, Cromwell, Napoleon (whose own *coup d'état,* as I have noted, was the prime source of the nineteenth century's fascination with this type of authority), all represent not merely the eruption of individual genius (in the Latin sense) but of a dramatic conflict with either sacred tradition or rational administration. Revolution, whether religious or political, is the very essence of the exercise of charismatic leadership, for its very impact on the people must have a profoundly dislocating effect upon the traditions or rules by which men normally live. In its pure form, charismatic authority is not, however, indeed cannot be by its very nature, stable and lasting. "It is the fate of charisma," wrote Weber, "whenever it comes into the permanent institutions of a community, to

70 Ibid., 333 f.

Michels' words are set in the context of consideration of governmental—and particularly Prussian—bureaucracy, but the essence of his book lies in the characterization of mass democratic and socialist movements in precisely these terms. Where Weber had contented himself, for the most part, with the bureaucratization of official and governmental agencies. Michels carries the analysis forward to those working-class movements—Marxist among them—which were supposedly challenging the structure of bureaucratic government and bureaucratic capitalism. What we find, Michels concludes, is little else than a reordering of socialist organization and thought in the enemy's terms.

"The Marxist economic doctrine and the Marxist philosophy of history cannot fail to exercise a great attraction upon thinkers. But the defects of Marxism are patent directly we enter the practical domains of administration and public law, without even speaking of errors in the psychological field and even in more elementary spheres." Socialist theory has either collapsed in a cloudland of impossible individualism or else "it has made proposals which (doubtless in opposition to the excellent intentions of their authors) could not fail to enslave the individual to the mass."[79] For over half a century, Michels observes, the socialists have been working toward a model organization.

Now when three million workers have been organized—a greater number than was supposed necessary to secure complete victory over the enemy—the party is endowed with a bureaucracy which, in respect of its consciousness of its duties, its zeal, and its submission to the hierarchy, rivals that of the state itself; the treasuries are full; a complex ramification of financial and moral interests extends all over the country. . . . Thus from a means, organization becomes an end.[80]

It is in the light of what Michels regards as the inevitability of bureaucratization of political action—once it is successful and attracts large numbers—that he refers to "the iron law of oligarchy":

Organization implies the tendency to oligarchy. In every organization, whether it be a political party, a professional union, or any other association of the kind, the aristocratic tendency manifests this very clearly. The mechanism of the organization, while conferring a solidity of structure, induces serious changes in the organized mass, completely inverting the respective position of the leaders and the led. . . . With the advance of organization, democracy tends to decline. Democratic evolution has a parabolic course. At the present time, at any rate as far as party life is concerned, democracy is in the descending phase. It may be enunciated as a general rule that the increase in the power of the leaders is directly proportional with the extension of the organization.[81]

79 Ibid., 386
80 Ibid., 372 f.
81 Ibid., 32 f.

Such for Michels is the iron law of bureaucracy.

It was not to socialist democracy alone that Michels directed his mordant analysis, but to democracy in general. The paragraph with which he somberly concludes his book is in the straight tradition of Tocqueville and Weber.

The democratic currents of history resemble successive waves. They break ever on the same shoal. They are ever renewed. This enduring spectacle is simultaneously encouraging and depressing. When democracies have gained a certain state of development, they undergo a gradual transformation, adopting the aristocratic spirit, and in many cases also the aristocratic forms, against which at the outset they struggled so fiercely. Now new accusers arise to denounce the traitors; after an era of glorious combats and of inglorious power, they end by fusing with the old dominant class; whereupon once more they are in their turn attacked by fresh opponents who appeal to the name of democracy. It is probable that this cruel game will continue without end.[82]

The Function of Authority—Durkheim

Authority runs like a *leitmotif* through all of Durkheim's works. Second only to community, it is the dominant theme of his sociology and philosophy. In the beginning, indeed, he took law as the only real measure of social solidarity.[83] That he was led to abandon this stringent emphasis did not, however, in any way lessen his insistence on the proposition that true society and true morality exist only when authority over individual mind and behavior is clearly present.

The centrality of authority in Durkheim's thought may be inferred from some words he wrote on the relation between discipline and personality. "Ordinarily," he writes, "discipline appears useful only because it entails behavior that has useful outcomes. Discipline is only a means of specifying and imposing the required behavior. But . . . we must say that discipline derives its *raison d'être* from itself; it is good that man is disciplined, independent of the acts to which he thus finds himself constrained."[84]

Why is discipline good? The answer forms the explicit substance of *Moral Education*, though it could be deduced easily from each of the other works. Discipline is authority in operation, and authority is inseparable, even indistinguishable, from the texture of society. Society, he has already told us in *The Division of Labor* and in the *Rules*, is manifest only in the diverse forms of constraint which rescue, as it were, the individual from the void. Authority and discipline form the very warp of personality; without authority man can have no sense of duty, no real

[82] Ibid., 408.
[83] *The Division of Labor*, op. cit., Preface.
[84] *Moral Education*, op. cit., 31 f.

freedom even. Only when traditions, codes, and roles have the effect of coercing, directing, or restraining man's impulses can it be said that society is genuinely in existence.

He is critical of Bentham, and other utilitarians for their false view of the role of authority.

For Bentham, morality, like law, involved a kind of pathology. Most of the classical economists were of the same view. And doubtless the viewpoint has led the major socialist theoreticians to deem a society without systematic regulation both possible and desirable. The notion of an authority dominating life and administering law seemed to them to be an archiac idea, a prejudice that could not persist. It is life itself that makes its own laws. There could be nothing above or beyond it.[85]

In his *Professional Ethics*, Durkheim continues the theme. "There is no form of social activity which can do without the appropriate moral discipline. . . . The interests of the individual are not those of the group he belongs to and, indeed, there is often a real antagonism between the one and the other."[86] Such interests are only dimly perceived by him: he may fail to perceive them at all. There must, therefore, be some system which brings them to mind, "which obliges him to respect them, and this system can be no other than a moral discipline. For all discipline of this kind is a code of rules that lays down for the individual what he should do so as not to damage collective interests and so as not to disorganize the society of which he forms a part."[87]

Authority, in its relation to man, not only buttresses moral life; it *is* moral life. Authority "performs an important function in forming character and personality in general. In fact, the most essential element of character is this capacity for restraint or—as they say—of inhibition, which allows us to contain our passions, our desires, our habits, and subject them to law."[88] This last suggests that Durkheim was not unaware of Freudians and others of his day who found in the rigor of moral authorities the immediate source of psychological disabilities. The contrast between Durkheim and Freudianism on the matter of discipline is of considerable interest.

Durkheim's views on authority bring him, of course, to the problem of freedom, and he does not hesitate to stress the absolute priority of authority in the establishment of any scene in which freedom is imaginable.

In sum, the theories that celebrate the beneficence of unrestricted liberties are apologies for a diseased state. One may even say that, contrary to appearances, the words "liberty" and "lawlessness" clash in their coupling, since

---

[85] Ibid., 35 f.

[86] *Professional Ethics and Civic Morals*, Cornelia Brookfield, trans. (London: Routledge and Kegan Paul, 1957), 14.

[87] Ibid., 14.

[88] *Moral Education*, 46.

liberty is the fruit of regulation. Through the practice of moral rules we develop the capacity to govern and regulate ourselves, which is the whole reality of liberty.[89]

In several places, starting with *The Division of Labor* and continuing through his last major work, Durkheim made plain that he considered the modern age one in which breakdown of authority was conspicuous. The necessity of moral authority, he writes, is a truth especially to be remembered at the present time:

For we are living precisely in one of those critical, revolutionary periods when authority is usually weakened through the loss of traditional discipline—a time that may easily give rise to a spirit of anarchy. This is the source of the anarchic aspirations that . . . are emerging today, not only in the particular sects bearing the name, but in the very different doctrines that, although opposed on other points, join in a common aversion to anything smacking of regulation.[90]

It is his theoretical concern with authority, in all its breadth and depth, that has so frequently invited charges of "collectivism," "authoritarianism," and "nationalism." Such charges are, however, incorrect. In the first place, such terms as these have political connotations, and their inevitable effect is to identify Durkheim with the unitary nationalist collectivism that was coming to flower in Europe. Such identification is false. In clear fact, Durkheim's political thought comes close to the opposite extreme. His analysis of the state and its relationship to social order, as we shall see in this section, is much nearer that of the syndicalists of his time than to either the integral nationalism of French conservatives or the more idealized variety that we find in England in the works of such men as T. H. Green and Bernard Bosanquet.

In terms of practical politics, Durkheim was a *Dreyfusard*, a term covering beliefs that went well beyond the innocence of Alfred Dreyfus to include such principles as legal equality, civil rights, the rule of law, and political liberty. The term also included anti-clericalism, and because of the emotional intensity with which all matters pertaining to the Church in political affairs were then charged, this could sometimes result in a degree of apparent anti-religious sentiment sufficient to alienate a few like Péguy. Durkheim never abandoned *Dreyfusard* principles and, given his known agnosticism, it was only too easy for supporters of the Church to distort his anti-clericalist, agnostic views into tacit support of political domination of all religious, intellectual, and moral matters.

But however easy such distortion may have been, it is not made the more acceptable. Far from being a monist, a nationalist, or a collectivist, Durkheim must be placed, like Tocqueville, among the pluralists. Durkheim's ideas were very close to those advanced in his day by such men

89 Ibid., 54.
90 Ibid., 54.

as Duguit and Saleilles in France and by Maitland and Figgis in England. Durkheim's emphasis upon society, order, and authority is clear enough. But to make this synonymous with unitary nationalism or centralized economic collectivism, as many critics have, misses the essence of a theory of man's relation to society that culminates in *pluralism* of authority and rigorous insistence upon what he called the *corps intermédiaires*. These latter, associations lying intermediate to man and the state and forming the multiple substance of society, are the real units of Durkheim's theory of authority, just as abstract individuals are the units of utilitarian theory. Criticism of individualism does not mean, in Durkheim's thought, repudiation of freedom and acceptance of collectivism. Such criticism is, on the contrary, one of the very salients of any genuine critique of the traditional theory of monistic sovereignty.

Authority is the bedrock of society. But for Durkheim authority is plural, manifest in the diverse spheres of kinship, local community, profession, church, school, guild, and labor union as well as in political government. From the premise of the necessity of continuing authority over the individual in each of society's associations, and hence a limitation on legal and social individualism, Durkheim reaches a critique of the state every bit as pointed as that of the individualists and a good deal more securely grounded in history.

When Durkheim began his work he made juridical rules the only reliable manifestations of consensus in society. In *The Division of Labor* he had chosen law as the only clear and reliable means of identifying social solidarity. There he wrote: "It will be distinctly seen how we have studied social solidarity *through the system of juridical rules;* how, in the search for causes, we have put aside all that too readily lends itself to personal judgments and subjective appreciation, so as to reach certain rather profound facts of the social structure, capable of being objects of judgment and, consequently, of science."[91]

This is one of the most quoted remarks in all of Durkheim's work, and while it may be taken properly enough as important in *The Division of Labor,* it is too seldom realized that its significance is confined to that work alone. In that work, in principle anyhow, he makes repressive law the identifying attribute, the hallmark, of mechanical solidarity, just as he makes restitutive law the essence of organic solidarity. But he did not really restrict himself even there to juridical data alone. We find him admitting that the legalist approach fails to "take into account certain elements of the collective conscience which, because of their smaller power or their indeterminateness, remain foreign to repressive law while contributing to the assurance of social harmony. These are the ones protected by punishments which are merely diffuse."[92]

91 *Division of Labor,* 36 f.
92 Ibid., 110.

Fortunate for us is the fact that Durkheim, the scholar and scientist, did not let himself be cribbed and confined by Durkheim the methodologist—for if he had not let himself go beyond "juridical rules," we would today be without, not merely *Suicide, Elementary Forms of Religious Life, Moral Education,* but even large sections of *The Division of Labor* itself.

The main point here is that Durkheim's approach to the study of authority cannot be limited by the processes of either law or the state, and it is in the sharp distinction he makes between society and the state —the same distinction made by all pluralists—that we are able to see how an emphasis on authority is compatible with a political position that is incontestably liberal, by the standards of that day and now. Only when the individual is securely rooted in a system of social and moral authority is political freedom possible.

"Imagine," he writes,

a being liberated from all external restraint, a despot still more absolute than those of which history tells us, a despot that no external power can restrain or influence. By definition, the desires of such a being are irresistible. Shall we say, then, that he is all-powerful? Certainly not, since he himself cannot resist his desires. They are masters of him, as of everything else. He submits to them; he does not dominate them.[93]

Authority, for Durkheim, is rooted in moral values which ultimately make for legitimacy or it is not authority, only the shell. And freedom is simply inconceivable save within the context of the rules and norms which define it.

Although the roots of Durkheim's pluralism lie in *The Division of Labor,* his first serious concern with the problem of the individual's triangular relation to social authority and the power of the state is to be found in the final pages of *Suicide.* Here we find him reflecting on the measures necessary to a restoration of the kind of authority sufficient to check the moral disorganization of which suicide is a conspicuous manifestation. First to be considered is a possible revival of the extreme penalties which were formerly visited on suicides and their families. But these must be rejected today, for they "would not be tolerated by the public conscience." The reason is that suicide "emanates from sentiments respected by public opinion"—even if the act itself is not—and, given these sentiments, the public would not bring itself to harsh measures. "Our excessive tolerance of suicide is due to the fact that, since the state of mind from which it springs is a general one, we cannot condemn it without condemning ourselves; we are too saturated with it not to excuse it in part."[94]

93 *Moral Education,* 44.
94 *Suicide,* 371.

The family is no solution. It might have been once, but the modern family, the conjugal family, is not only too small to absorb the ills of the human spirit, it has been separated by the forces of modern history from centrality in the economic and political processes that govern man's life and attract his allegiances. The family, far from being a haven for man's fears and inadequacies, is itself in need of the kind of reinforcement that can come only from a role in a larger and more relevant form of association, something comparable functionally to the ancient but now defunct kindred or extended family. The problem of suicide and the present condition of the conjugal family are both, Durkheim concludes, instances of the modern decline of authority. His treatment of the family—in terms of loss of functional significance—must certainly be regarded as among the first, if not the first, in what has proved to be a long line. Others had distinguished the nuclear from the extended family, but Durkheim gave it relevance to the problems of contemporary authority and disorganization.

Education is irrelevant to the problem. Education "is only the image and reflection of society. It imitates and reproduces the latter in abbreviated form; it does not create it. The evil is moral and deepseated, and to expect education, which, after all, has but a part of each of its students, and for but a short time, to overcome deficiencies in the whole social order is absurd."[95]

The only remedy

is to restore enough consistency to social groups for them to obtain a firmer grip on the individual, and for him to feel himself bound to them. He must feel himself more solidary with a collective existence which precedes him in time, which survives him, and which encompasses him at all points. If this occurs, he will no longer find the only aim of his conduct in himself and, understanding that he is the instrument of a purpose greater than himself, he will see that he is not without significance. Life will resume meaning in his eyes, because it will recover its natural aim and orientation. But what groups are best calculated constantly to reimpress on man this salutary sentiment of solidarity?[96]

Not political society, which is "too far removed from the individual" to affect him uninterruptedly and with sufficient force. The state, in any event, is one of the principal *causes* of the social atomization and moral emptiness of which suicide is an outcome.[97] Hardly more efficacious would be religious society. Once, yes, but not today, when so many currents of secular thought have made it impossible for most persons to return to the degree of dogmatic certitude required of a religion if it is

95 Ibid., 372 f.
96 Ibid., 373 f.
97 *Suicide*, 389.

to possess the authority sufficient to restrain individuals from suicidal impulses. Roman Catholicism's statistically demonstrable effectiveness is based on a degree of organizational and intellectual rigidity that would be intolerable, Durkheim thinks, for most persons today. New religions will indeed come into being, but they are likely to be even more liberal in doctrinal matters than the most liberal Protestant sects of the present, and these, as the demographic data show, have virtually no restraining influence.

We are preserved from egoistic suicide, Durkheim concludes, only

insofar as we are socialized; but religions can socialize us only insofar as they refuse us the right of free examination. They no longer have, and probably never will have again, enough authority to wring such a sacrifice from us. . . . Besides, if those who see our only cure in a religious restoration were self-consistent, they would demand the re-establishment of the most archaic religions. For against suicide Judaism preserves better than Catholicism, and Catholicism better than Protestantism.[98]

And, as one is justified in concluding from Durkheim's systematic later study of religion, it is *primitive* religion, with its total subordination of the individual to the cult, that would be most efficacious of all. In primitive society, where everything is surcharged by the sacred, where all values are set in unremitting contexts of community, suicide, except in its rare "altruistic" form, is unknown. But modern European society can hardly be supposed capable of returning to this type of religion.

In the revival of an adapted form of the guild—that is, in an occupational association specifically adapted to the character of modern industry—Durkheim finds the mode of authority and type of membership most likely to supply the social substance now lacking in individual lives. Modern man is encompassed by economic life to a degree unknown in all earlier ages. But, at present, "European societies have the alternative either of leaving occupational life unregulated or of regulating it through the state's mediation, since no other organ exists which can play this role of moderator."[99] Hence, new forms of social organization must be devised to escape the contradiction involved presently in a horde of individuals whose lives are regulated but not really ruled by the distant, remote, and impersonal state.

The only way to resolve this antinomy is to set up a cluster of collective forces outside the state, though subject to its action, whose regulative influence can be exerted with greater variety. Not only will our reconstituted corporations satisfy this condition, but it is hard to see what other groups could do so. For they are close enough to the facts, directly and constantly enough in contact with them, to detect all their nuances, and they should be sufficiently

98 Ibid., 376.
99 Ibid., 380.

autonomous to be able to respect their diversity. To them, therefore, falls the duty of presiding over companies of insurance, benevolent aid and pensions, the need of which is felt by so many good minds but which we rightly hesitate to place in the hands of the state, already so powerful and awkward.[100]

Such corporations would be, in the very relevance of their goals to economic and social need, repositories of moral authority sufficient to restrain the egoistic (and hence suicidogenic) impulses of human beings now scattered like so many grains of dust.

Both anomic and egoistic types of suicide would be checked, for the corporation would become, even as was the medieval guild, the center of legitimate moral authority.

Whenever excited appetites tended to exceed all limits, the corporation would have to decide the share that should equitably revert to each of the cooperative parts. Standing above its own members, it would have all necessary authority to demand indispensible sacrifices and concessions and impose order upon them. By forcing the strongest to use their strength with moderation, by preventing the weakest from endlessly multiplying their protests, by recalling both to the sense of their reciprocal duties and the general interest, and by regulating production in certain cases so that it does not degenerate into a morbid fever, it would moderate one set of passions by another, and permit their appeasement by assigning them limits. Thus, a new sort of moral discipline would be established, without which all the scientific discoveries and economic progress in the world would produce only malcontents.[101]

It is important that these new structures of authority be granted a measure of legal as well as strictly moral and social authority, for moral authority only follows legal recognition. Our historical development, Durkheim writes in a passage of Tocquevillian intensity, has swept away all older forms of intermediate social organization. "One after another, they have disappeared either through the slow erosion of time or through great disturbances, but without being replaced."[102] Originally kinship, through clan and family, possessed the requisite authority, but it soon ceased to be a political division and became only the center of private life. Territorial unities—hundreds, villages, communes—guilds, monasteries, and other forms of association followed, but they too have suffered dislocation and atomization.

The great change brought about by the French Revolution was precisely to carry this leveling to a point hitherto unknown. Not that it improvised this change; the latter had long since been prepared by the progressive centraliza-

---

100 Ibid., 380. This is the proposal (at which charges of "medieval corporatism" were flung by some of Durkheim's critics) that he expanded into the long Preface to the second edition of *The Division of Labor* which was published in 1902, five years after the appearance of *Suicide*.

101 *Suicide*, 383.

102 Ibid., 388.

tion to which the old regime had advanced . . . Since then, the development of means of communication, by massing the populations, has almost eliminated the last traces of the old dispensation. And since what remained of occupational organizations was violently destroyed at the same time, all secondary organizations of social life were done away with.[103]

Only the state has survived the tempest of modern history. Here we come to the true heart of Durkheim's political sociology. The modern state's action has involved profound paradox. Even as it has absorbed functions previously embodied in other groups, thus swelling further an already swollen bureaucracy, it has tended, by this very action, to level social ranks, to atomize social groups, leaving populations in the form of a sand heap.

It has often been said that the state is as intrusive as it is impotent. It makes a sickly attempt to extend itself over all sorts of things which do not belong to it, or which it grasps only by doing them violence. . . . Individuals are made aware of society and of their dependence upon it only through the state. But since this is far from them, it can exert only a distant, discontinuous influence over them; which is why this feeling has neither the necessary constancy nor strength. . . . Man cannot become attached to higher aims and submit to a rule if he sees nothing above him to which he belongs. To free him from all social pressure is to abandon him to himself and demoralize him. These are really the two characteristics of our moral situation. While the state becomes inflated and hypertrophied in order to obtain a firm enough grip upon individuals, but without succeeding, the latter, without mutual relationships, tumble over one another like so many liquid molecules, encountering no central energy to retain, fix and organize them.[104]

It is in these terms, and they are, at bottom, Tocquevillian terms, that Durkheim sets the juridical context for the establishment of his occupational associations. These will be the essential units of society— recognized equally by the state and by the families of their members— and, being units of society, they must have grants of *legal* authority that will render their moral authority as sufficient to the necessities of integration and morality.

I have dealt with this aspect of Durkheim's thought at some length for reasons that go beyond the ephemeral importance of occupational associations. These are now well behind us in terms of historical likelihood. But too often they have been treated by students of Durkheim as random fragments of his thought. The reverse is true. In their first proposal, in the concluding pages of *Suicide*, published in 1896, lies the origin and essence of a *theoretical* approach to the problem of authority and power that was to influence a considerable number of historians, jurists, and ethnologists, all of whom found in Durkheim's dichotomy

103 Ibid., 388.
104 Ibid., 389.

between social authority and political power a perspective of extraordinary utility in their studies of other cultures and historical periods.

Let us look more carefully at this theoretical approach to the relation between authority and power. What, for Durkheim, is political society? First, in its normal state, it is pluralistic. Durkheim quotes Montesquieu to the effect that political society involves "intermediary, subordinate, and dependent powers." Without these secondary authorities, the state, except in pathological form, is impossible. "Far from being in opposition to the social group endowed with sovereign powers and called more specifically the state, the state presupposes their existence; it exists only where they exist. No secondary groups, no political authority—at least no authority that this term can apply to without being inappropriate."[105]

But this is only a part of the picture. For, dependent though the normal state is on the body of secondary authorities which undergird it, there is nevertheless to be seen a *conflict*, sometimes actual, always potential, between the state and these authorities. The individual represents the third point of a triangular relation of forces. His freedom from the state's power is measured by his absorption in one or more of the secondary authorities—family, church, guild, and so on. Conversely, the individual's protection from the often overwhelming authorities of these groups is granted, history shows, and protected by the state, through the means of *private rights*. Private rights are created by the state.

This triangular relationship is universal in the history of human societies. In the beginning it is only latent. Both state and individual are but dimly conceived realities. It is the social group—clan, tribe, association—that is sovereign. "In the early stage, the individual personality is lost in the depths of the social mass and then later, by its own effort, breaks away. From being limited and of small regard, the scope of the individual life expands and becomes the exalted object of moral respect. The individual comes to acquire ever wider rights over his own person and over the possessions to which he has title. . . ."[106]

It is interesting to compare this branch of analysis with its root in *The Division of Labor*. There, in one of the most brilliant paragraphs on power and its relation to individualism ever written, Durkheim reveals an aspect of his mind that is (*mirabile dictu*) as Rousseauian as it is Tocquevillian.

Rather than dating the effacement of the individual from the institution of a despotic authority, we must, on the contrary, see in this institution the first step made toward individualism. Chiefs are, in fact, the first personalities who emerge from the social mass. Their exceptional situation, putting them beyond the level of others, gives them a distinct physiognomy and accordingly confers individuality upon them. In dominating society, they are no longer forced

105 *Professional Ethics*, 45.
106 Ibid., 79.

conflicting elements within the late medieval church; the judicial role of William the Conqueror between Anglo-Saxons and his own Normans.

Closely related is his elaboration in sociological terms of *divide et impera*. Here a familiar and oft-noted tactic in politics is converted into an abstract form, one observable in contexts ranging from family to state or empire: in this a third party gains power by adroit promotion of division between two other parties. Simmel's examples include the relation of the Roman emperors to religious and economic associations; the position of Anglo-Norman kings with respect to the manors of feudal lords; and the factionalism promoted among Australian aborigines by colonial rulers, and the efforts of rulers of medieval Venice to divide the citizenry. Simmel may be primarily concerned with the forms that can be abstracted from the circumstances of history, but no one can accuse him of rootless abstraction.

When we turn to Simmel's major work on the nature of authority, *Superordination and Subordination,* we find the same contextual relation between his formal types of authority and the concrete historical development of modern Europe that we observed in Weber. Just as Weber's categories of "traditional" and "rational" turn out to be conceptualizations of phases through which Europe had passed, and was passing, in its transition to modernism, so do Simmel's three essential types. Behind what Simmel calls "individual centralization," "subordination under a plurality," and "subordination to a principle" lie, quite as clearly as in Weber, the historical models presented by the successive phases of modern European polity in its movement from monarchy to republic to domination by impersonal organizations and norms. Nearly all of his illustrations of the three types are drawn from European history. To observe this is in no way to diminish the scientific applicability of the three types to the comparative study of authority and power. It is merely to emphasize once again the deep roots that the central concepts of modern sociology have in a special set of historical circumstances.

Superordination and Subordination begins with an analysis of the nature of domination and its relation to the minute elements of human association. Authority, Simmel tells us, is by its nature *interactive*. Domination, far from being one-sided, as it might at first sight appear to be, is in fact determined by expectation of the nature of the *obedience* it will receive. In the most extreme cases of personal subordination, Simmel tells us, there is still a considerable measure of personal freedom. So-called absolute coercion is always relative; its condition is our desire to escape from the threatened punishment or from other consequences of our disobedience. Only in cases of direct physical violation can it be said that the subordinate's freedom has been wholly destroyed in a super-subordination relationship. Obedience, in short, shapes domination quite as much as domination shapes obedience. No one, Simmel observes, "wishes that his influence completely determine the other individual. He rather wants this influence, this determination of the other, to act back upon *him*. Even the abstract will-to-dominate, therefore, is a case of interaction. This will draws its satisfaction from the fact that the acting or suffering of the other, his positive or negative condition, offers itself to the dominator as the product of *his* will."[119]

In the most extreme case of domination—master and slave—there is still, Simmel insists, a residual degree of sociation that robs domination of the unilateral character commonly ascribed to it. But when, through processes of "objectification"—that is, the reduction of persons to objects—individuals become known chiefly as classes of *things* (as in the modern working class where individual workers are unknown to those hiring them and where an impersonal commodity, "labor," is sold), then there is "as little ground for speaking of sociation as there is in the case of the carpenter and his bench."[120] Authority of persons, in contrast to domination of things, "presupposes in a much higher degree than is usually recognized a freedom on the part of the person subjected to authority. Even where authority seems to 'crush' him, it is based not *only* on coercion or compulsion to yield to it."

The unique character of authority is significant for social life in the most varied ways. One of the most significant is the relation of authority to the gradually acquired sense of objectivity in human perception and judgment. A person of superior authority acquires " an overwhelming weight of his opinions, a faith, or a confidence which have the character of objectivity." . . . By acting "authoritatively," the quantity of his significance is transformed into a new quality; it assumes for his environment the physical state—metaphorically speaking—of objectivity.[121] Here too, plainly, Simmel and Durkheim are very close.

Reciprocity is the essence of personal authority, but something else comes into the picture with the large assemblage: a diminution of reciprocity and an intensification of sheer domination. "It is the absence of this reciprocity which accounts for the observation that the tyranny of a group over its own members is worse than that of a prince over his subjects." Simmel's development of this point is different from Tocqueville's but the result is approximately the same: the inexorable expansion of the tolerable limits of power over oneself when this power is conceived as arising from relationships of which one is a part. "The group—and by no means the political group alone—conceives of its members, not as confronting it, but as being included by it as its own links. This often results in a peculiar inconsiderateness toward the members, which is very different from a ruler's personal cruelty. Wherever there is, formally, confrontation (even if, continually, it comes *close* to submission), there is interaction; and, in principle, interaction always contains some limitation

[119] Ibid., 181.
[120] Ibid., 182.
[121] Ibid., 183.

of *each* party to the process (although there may be individual exceptions to this rule). Where superordination shows an extreme inconsiderateness, as in the case of the group that simply *disposes* of its members, there no longer is any confrontation with its form of interaction, which involves spontaneity, and hence limitation, of both superordinate and subordinate elements."[122] What Tocqueville saw in public opinions, using large-scale political democracy as his framework, Simmel sees at every level of association, in the sociologically precise terms of subordination of individual role and identity to membership in the group.

We may turn now to Simmel's three fundamental types of superordination and subordination: (1) that wielded by an individual, as monarch, the father in a patriarchal family, manorial lord, or business proprietor; (2) that wielded by a group or association over its members, as in modern republics and democracies; and (3) that wielded by an objective principle in which office or impersonal organization or technology, rather than the personalities of human beings, is dominant. All three, as noted above, may be seen as conceptual distillations of European historical experience.

Individual Centralization of Authority. What Simmel calls superordination by a single individual is reflective, he tells us, of the earlier history of Europe: in commonwealth, family, and church.

It is the rule of the single person that underlies the first unification of the group. The historic success of Judaism and Christianity in bringing individuals out of diverse tribal and kinship loyalties was the consequence of centralization: in these cases, centralization of deity. The rise of the modern state would not have been possible save in terms of the focal point represented by the one—the monarch. Only rule by one makes the *ruled* conscious of itself as a society with its own interests. This may result in conflict, in dissociation, but Simmel shows how such conflict may be the further basis of unity. He notes, as had Tocqueville, the interactive relation between centralization and leveling. There are, however, different types of leveling. "The leveling most welcome to despotism . . . is that of differences in rank, not in character. A society homogenous in character and tendency, but organized in several rank orders, resists despotism strongly, while a society in which numerous kinds of characters exist side by side with organically inarticulate equality, resists it only slightly."[123] He observes the fondness of despots for persons of middle range of ability. Despots, he writes in a Tocquevillian epigram, "only love servants of average talent."

How does one rationalize normatively the disproportion involved in one-man rule? "The point is that the structure of a society in which only one person rules while the great mass lets itself be ruled makes normative

122 Ibid., 187.
123 Ibid., 198.

sense only by virtue of a specific circumstance: that the mass, the ruled element, injects only *parts* of all personalities which compose it into the mutual relationship, whereas the ruler contributes *all* of *his* personality. The ruler and the individual subject do not enter the relationships with the same quantity of their personalities."[124] Here, under the rubric of authority, Simmel comes back to the theme that we found in his analysis of the group: the unequal "giving" by the individual, from group to group, of himself. Groups are characteristically "different according to the proportion between the members' total personalities and those parts of their personalities with which they fuse in the 'mass.' The measure of their governability depends on this difference in quanta."[125]

But leveling is not the only correlate of domination by a single individual. There is a second; one "in which the group takes on the form of a pyramid. The subordinates face the ruler in gradations of power. Layers whose volume becomes ever smaller and whose significance becomes ever greater lead from the lowest mass to the top of the pyramid."[126] The pyramid may originate in either of two ways: first, in the full autocratic power of the ruler who lets the content of his authority "glide downward" while holding its form and title to himself. Generally, over a period of time, the power of the highest echelons then tends to wither, resulting in ever increasing autonomy of the lower elements of the pyramid. Second, in the conversion of authorities previously autonomous into ordered phases of the power pyramid. Here the process begins at the bottom, autonomy is traded, as it were, for the security of membership in the pyramid. Both of these types originate clearly in the political history of Europe, and Simmel is as sensitive to this as Weber. But here, as elsewhere, it is their applicability to non-political structures—to church, school, class, and clan—that also interests him. There can be a mixture of the two types of gradation, and, as Simmel notes, the history of Western feudalism illustrates this mixture.

There is, Simmel concludes with Durkheim, an indestructibility and eternality of one-man rule. The image of the one remains long after revolution and change have swept away monarchs and emperors. "It is the peculiar strength of domination by one person to survive its own death, as it were—by transferring its own color to structures whose very significance is the negation of such domination."[127] Even revolutionary democracy, he notes, is conceived as "nothing but royalty turned upside down, and equipped with the same qualities. Rousseau's 'volonté générale' to which, he teaches, everybody must submit without resistance, has entirely the character of the absolute monarch."[128]

[124] Ibid., 201 f.
[125] Ibid., 203.
[126] Ibid., 206.
[127] Ibid., 217.
[128] Ibid., 218.

Simmel notes the recurrent phenomenon in history of the group subjecting itself by preference to the *outsider:* the person whose lack of inner knowledge of the group is magnificently compensated for by objectivity on, and immunity to, the group's inner hostilities and suspicions. In medieval society, Simmel remarks, it was unthinkable that anyone—noble, guildsman, churchman, or family member—be governed, judged, by one not of his own social kind. Modern life is more variegated, however. It has introduced a new attitude toward this.

In general . . . we can say that the lower a group is as a whole and the more, therefore, every member of it is accustomed to subordination, the less will the group allow one of its members to rule it. And, inversely, the higher a group is as a whole, the more likely it is that it subordinates itself only to one of its peers. In the first case, domination by the member, the like person, is difficult because everybody is low; in the second case, it is easier because everybody stands high.[129]

Subordination Under a Plurality.   As the image of the monarch underlies the ideal type of the first, it is the image of the republic that underlies this second general type. Three points made by Simmel are deserving of emphasis.

In the first place, the *objectivity* of plural rule—that is, its incorporation of dominance within the laws and processes of the entire group rather than within the one symbolic figure—is matched by its tendency toward greater *impersonality*. This can have good consequences. The ancient slaves of Sparta, the feudal peasants of Prussia, and the modern inhabitants of India all showed understandable preference for governance by the state—state slavery, state domain, English state—over governance by private interests. But, by the same token, cruelties committed by republics to those outside often exceed those committed by individual rulers. The lot of subject peoples was harsher under the Roman republic than under the emperors and there are few examples of harsher treatment of groups—Irish, Dissenters, Scotch, Papists—than those revealed by the modern history of England, which on the other hand has the most resplendent record of all nations in its justice to *individuals*.[130] And repeatedly in European history we are struck, Simmel observes, by the greater proneness of the monarch to render popular aid than anything to be found in the collective will of the feudal nobility or the later republic. And, Simmel observes, while the modern state can legally condemn an individual to death, it cannot pardon him; pardon remains the prerogative of the individual monarch or president or governor.

The second point that Simmel makes is the historical tendency toward *increasing corporateness* of plural will or governance. Although personal

129 Ibid., 219.
130 Ibid., 226 f.

rule is required to bring the identity of the group into being in the first instance, it is the gradual transference of the center of gravity from person to collectivity that gives the latter durability. Thus,

the growth of democratic consciousness in France has been derived (among other things) from the fact that, since the fall of Napoleon I, changing governmental powers followed one another in rapid succession. Each one of them was incompetent, uncertain, and trying to gain the favor of the masses—whereby every citizen was bound to become deeply aware of his own social significance. Although he was subject to every one of these governments, he nevertheless felt himself to be strong, because he formed the lasting element in all the change and contrast among the successive regimes.[131]

Simmel is also concerned with the process of what he calls the outvoting of minorities by majorities, by which he means the modern (in contrast to the medieval) practice of minority views becoming overruled, even dissolved, by the majority. To some students of Simmel this section has had the appearance of archaic oddity. What his often rarefied terminology covers, however, is the significant problem of the maintenance of cultural, ethnic, and geographic pluralism in a society which, having become increasingly politicized, reduces more and more matters of survival to the political processes of the vote. Groups, which in the ages of the past could maintain identity even in the face of armed hostility, find it increasingly difficult to do so when all issues and tensions are assimilated by the political process and, hence, at the mercy of majority vote. It is significant, he remarks, that only rarely has majority outvoting been defended on the simple ground of the superior right of the majority. More often, distinguishable will of the whole association is presumed to lie latent and majority supremacy is rationalized as the majority's revelation by vote of what the total or real will actually is. This, of course, is what Rousseau declared the legitimate function of voting to be in its relation to the General Will.

Subordination to a Principle.   Here Simmel is concerned with objective circumstance. He describes it as the "fundamental transition of the relationship of obedience from personalism to objectivism, a transition which cannot be derived from anticipation of utilitarian consequence."[132] He compares subordination to *objects*—for example, land or machines—with personal subordination, finding the former generally a "humiliating harsh and unconditional kind of subordination. For, inasmuch as a man is subordinate by virtue of belonging to a thing, he himself psychologically sinks to the category of mere thing."[133]

It is easy to see the relation of this type of domination to the whole pattern of modernism, with its triumph of process, organization, and

131 Ibid., 233 f.
132 Ibid., 252.
133 Ibid., 253 f.

sheer physical matter over the individual. Modern society leads, Simmel argues, to a multiplication of situations in which individuals find themselves under this "objective" type of power. The status of the 'modern worker is a case in point. As long as the relationship of wage labor was conceived of as "rental contract" something was retained of the worker's subordination to a *person*—to the entrepreneur." "But once the work contract is considered, not as the renting of a person, but as the purchase of a piece of merchandise, that is, labor, then this element of personal subordination is eliminated . . . The worker is no longer subject as a person but only as the servant of an objective, economic procedure."[134] Objective power, metropolis, alienation: the three comprise, for Simmel, an unholy trinity.

But there is a second connotation of objectivism: one that may ultimately amount to the same kind of impersonal power but that nonetheless requires differentiation. Objectivism can also mean a transfer of power from person or group to social *norm*. Thus, objectification of power is revealed by such conceptions as the supremacy of the law, of the office, of the command, of abstract moral commandment. In the beginning the adjuration against killing had force only because of the identity of the person who commanded against it—chief, king, or god. But in time, "thou shalt not kill" came to assume an impersonal, objective force. Simmel's discussion of objectivism, while very close to Durkheim's treatment of the authority of the collective conscience, differs in one important respect: for Durkheim, the collective precedes, historically, and always gives force to the personal; for Simmel, however, the personal precedes the collective and supplies the lasting element of the authority that inheres even in objective circumstance.

There remains the relation between domination and freedom. Like Tocqueville, Simmel sees freedom not only as the gain by an individual or group of liberation from power, but, equally, as the utilization of freedom for domination of others. "If liberation from subordination is examined more closely . . . it almost always reveals itself as, at the same time, a gain in domination—either in regard to those previously superordinate, or in regard to a newly formed stratum that is destined to definitive subordination."[135] He uses Puritanism in England as a case in point and also the role of the Third Estate in France during and after the Revolution. On the latter Simmel's words are perceptive and profound: "By means of its economic power, the Third Estate made the other, previously higher estates dependent upon itself; but, this effect and the whole emancipation of the Third Estate derived its rich content and its important consequences only because there existed (or, rather, there was formed in the same process) a Fourth Estate which the Third

[134] Ibid., 263.
[135] Ibid., 273.

could exploit and above which it could rise."[136] A final example Simmel adduces is that of the history of the church in Western Europe. Freedom of the church, he writes, "usually does not consist in the liberation from superordinate secular powers alone but, through this liberation, in dominion over these powers. The church's liberty of teaching, for instance, means that the state obtains citizens who are inculcated by the church and stand under its suggestion; whereby the state comes often enough under the domination of the church."[137]

The freedom granted a group, Simmel observes, can have two aspects, depending on the spirit in which it is granted and the status of the group receiving it. On the one hand it can represent "esteem, a right, a power." But on the other hand it can reflect "exclusion and a contemptuous indifference on the part of the higher power." He cites the history of the Jews, in their relation to the society around them, as striking instances of each—either in single or mixed form.[138]

Between freedom and equality there is an eternally ambiguous relation. "To the extent that general freedom prevails, there also prevails general equality. For general freedom only entails the negative fact that there is no domination." But equality, although appearing as the early consequence of freedom, proves to be only a kind of transitional state. Simmel is virtually quoting Tocqueville when he writes: "Typically speaking, nobody is satisfied with the position he occupies in regard to his fellow creatures; everybody wishes to attain one which is, in some sense, more favorable." Thus the first affinity of freedom is broken quickly, for the impulse that generates, in the name of freedom, the first striving to become *equal* to the power that dominates continues to generate the desire to *exceed* that power and others like it.[139]

[136] Ibid., 274 f.
[137] Ibid., 276.
[138] Ibid., 277.
[139] Ibid., 275.

8

COMMENTARY

FEW men in any field of endeavor have gained enough stature to become truly controversial in their intellectual and academic enterprise, and fewer still have stimulated such a level of discourse about their ideas as to have had volumes published about them. Among these rare individuals is Talcott Parsons, who has been variously characterized as a genius, obscure, nonempirical, and a theoretical giant.

In the introductory chapter to a collection of analytical essays on Parsons' work that grew out of a study by a group of Cornell University social scientists, Edward C. Devereux, Jr., made the following observation:

> Talcott Parsons describes himself as an incurable theorist. On this point even his severest critics would hasten to agree. Certainly he has done more of theorizing than any other contemporary American sociologist; and it is also probably true that he has done rather less of anything else.[1]

In the same volume Parsons stated rather matter-of-factly and not necessarily in his own behalf:

> I am not at all prepared to discount entirely the view that there are peculiar and unnecessary obscurities in my writings. At the same time I can claim to be somewhat sophisticated in the sociology of knowledge and hence in the interpretation of resistances to certain types of intellectual innovation. . . . In any case, it is not possible for an author to be fully objective about the reception of his work; any more ultimate judgment will have to be left to the outcome of the process of natural selection through professional criticism by which scientific reputations ultimately come to be stabilized.[2]

Devereux, without intending criticism, also asserts that, "At a time when others have been turning more and more to empirical research, Parsons has never published a paper reporting directly on data derived from a specific empirical investigation."[3] Some three hundred plus pages beyond those assertions, Parsons again states, although not directly in response to Devereux:

> I hope to be believed in expressing the deepest respect for competent empirical research and the conviction of its central importance in the building of a science. However, at the same time I wish to contend for the justification of specializing in theory. If one is to be a specialist, his concern with empirical materials may justifiably be couched in terms of consideration of their

[1] Edward C. Devereux, Jr., "Parsons' Sociological Theory," in Max Black (ed.), *The Social Theories of Talcott Parsons* (Englewood Cliffs, N.J.: Prentice-Hall, Inc., 1961), p. 1.

[2] Talcott Parsons, "The Point of View of the Author," Ibid., pp. 320–321.

[3] Edward C. Devereux, Jr., Ibid., p. 1.

theoretical *significance, and with their codification in relation to such prob-*
*lems rather than their original production.*4

Suffice it to say that Parsons's theoretical propositions have been more sub-
stantial as bases for certain conclusions than have empirical analyses of great
sophistication on similar subjects. Moreover, many of his theoretical proposi-
tions have been found to "stand-up" when empirical studies have been carried
out on them.

Interestingly, an "empirical" study of notable sociologists based on a count of
names that appeared most often in citations in journals, graduate reading lists,
references in undergraduate texts, and so forth included only one contemporary
scholar in addition to such giants as Durkheim and Weber—Talcott Parsons,
*whose impact on his field is appropriately immense.*5

Parsons's generalized theory of action has as much appeal for students of edu-
cational institutions as any other theory and more than most, perhaps because
his pattern variables, his concept of hierarchical structure, and his more recent
*conceptualization of the "four functional imperatives"*6 *strike a note of im-*
mediate "sympatico" with educational administrators. It is somewhat ironic
that sociologists in general *have not apparently recognized the unique nature of*
formal elementary and secondary schools as the linkage "agents" between the
family role-system and other more extended societal institutions and societal
*norms.*7 *The "closeness" of schools (and, therefore, as well, their management)*
to the local mores and dominant values of the communities in which they are
embedded generates an almost automatic sensitivity to a kind of "naive" so-
ciology, or sociological intuition, in "school people." Thus, when Parsons talks
about adaptation problems as a consequence of the dichotomization of external
and means-oriented contingencies, and that is explained to school administrators
in terms of the importance of procurement and public-relations issues, the
meaning requires little elaboration. By the same token, when I have talked to
school administrators and teachers about the "ascription/achievement" pattern
variable in terms of the assignment of marks to students in terms of "who" they
are as opposed to "what" they do, I see all the heads nodding for they clearly
understand the categorization involved and the sociopolitical implications in-
tended.

I remember clearly when I was a graduate student at Michigan State Uni-
versity and closely associated with an incisive social scientist named Leo Haak
(who generated more researchable questions in a week than many people do
in a lifetime), who became intrigued by the isolated datum that a surprisingly
large number of our freshmen students left school in the first quarter because
of low grades. He one day mused in my presence that perhaps it was because

4 Talcott Parsons, Ibid., p. 318.

5 See e.g., M. J. Oromaner, "The Audience As a Determinant of the Most Important Sociologists," *The American Sociologist* (November 1969), pp. 332–335.

6 See at this point the Introductory chapter to this section, "Authority, Bureaucracy, and Social System."

7 I emphasize "in general" because a number have effectively established this
recognition. To mention just a few: James Coleman; Ronald Corwin; Wilbur Brook-
over; and, much earlier, Willard Waller.

too many young people from small communities were marked on the basis of "who" they were rather than "what" they could do. I then also became intrigued by this question. Haak had a simple "theory." Perhaps, he imagined, these young people, when they came to this large and almost totally impersonal institution, discovered to their chagrin that nobody in this new environment really cared very much who their fathers were or what their annual incomes were. We examined a small and very carefully selected sample of these students and learned that, in fact, about one third of those who had been recommended to us as "B" or better students were really not "B" or better students at all. Moreover, we found that about another one third of those who had been recommended to us as "B" or better students were appropriately bright enough to achieve that sort of performance. Because, however, they had been typically marked on the basis of Parsons' "ascription/achievement" variable (on the ascription side, of course) they had never really been challenged to do anything like "B" work and found themselves in real difficulty in an environment that was, at least, impersonal enough by virtue of its size and culture not to either know or care very much about personal status. This latter group of young people struggled valiantly and the overwhelming majority of them made a strong comeback by the end of their sophomore year and leveled off as "C" students. Another about one third of these ascription/achievement victims who had sailed through high school with little or no problems seemed also to sail through their early quarters in the university with little change either in attitude or performance. It was concluded that these students were that charmed group for whom it would have made little difference under any circumstances for they were not only adaptive but bright enough to be adaptive. It was also concluded that for about 30 per cent of the entering freshmen in a major university it makes little difference what has happened to them at school specifically, at home specifically, or in the community specifically—they will succeed in spite of everything. We were, however, much concerned about those students who had high potential in both of the other groups who could not cope with the "new" environment without considerable attention. The extent to which that study ultimately resulted in Michigan State's developing a residence hall program that gave attention to such students is speculative. But the residence hall program, now much changed, did in fact deal precisely with that problem, and a great many of the entering freshmen were salvaged by the program.

All of this is not by way of expressing a particularly notable victory for humanity as much as it is testimony to the application of a rather singular Parsonian hypothesis as expressed in a single pattern variable.

I have also talked to school administrators about the nature of the pattern variable dealing with self/collectivity, and again I have found a very understanding attitude. I have asked school administrators if they were located in a system in which there is great and apparent educational justification for consolidation or merger of some attendance centers into larger and, therefore, much more efficient learning environments, what would they do? On the one hand, if your community attitudes are opposed to such consolidations or mergers, and if you "go along," then by all means, you could be classified as an effective organizational leader. On the other hand, if an administrator clearly knows that such a reorganization is in the best long-term interest of students and that they will thereby have access to better education despite the fact

Thus far, we have indicated that all living systems are confronted by two general categories of functional problems—*external* and *internal*—and that within the system there tends to be two corresponding sets of parts and processes. Both of these categories are further differentiated in terms of a second, equally fundamental basis of system differentiation. Living systems maintain their distinctive patterns over more or less extended periods of time, and it cannot be assumed that either the required environmental interchanges or the internal adjustments occur instantaneously and without the establishment of prior conditions. To put the matter positively, some system-environment relations, and some intrasystem relations, can be established only if preparations have been made, or the conditions of their establishment have been met, in advance. This is a temporal, or sequential, basis of differentiation; a distinction between functions that are directly related to the maintenance of the distinctive pattern of the system on the one hand and those that are related indirectly, through the first kind, as preconditions of their solution, on the other. Thus, for example, the oxidizable materials that are the basis of metabolism are often not immediately available for ingestion, and their availability is contingent on action undertaken by the animal to secure them. However, the preconditions for the solution of a given functional problem may also be conditional to the solution of a variety of other problems. Hence, there is the possibility of establishing generalized conditions for the solution of a wide range of future problems.

If what have been referred to as future problems are termed *consummatory* problems, then we may distinguish between *instrumental* problems, which concern the establishment of the general conditions for the solution of a range of consummatory problems, and consummatory problems themselves. In the external context, this means that one category of functional problems (the *adaptive*) concerns system-environment relations, or interchanges, related to the establishment of the general conditions for the solution of the second category, that of consummatory problems in relation to the environment (*goal attainment*). Similarly, in the internal context, one category of problems concerns the maintenance of consummatory relations among the differentiated parts of the system (*system integration*), whereas the other concerns the establishment of the general conditions of their maintenance (*pattern-maintenance*).

The four major categories of functional problems of living systems, then, that is, problems concerning the maintenance of, and the development of the potential inherent in, the system's distinctive pattern, are: (1) *adaption*, establishing in the system environment relation the general conditions of the attainment of a plurality of goal-states. Long-term stability of the system depends on the development of a generalized adaptive capacity that is relatively emancipated from particular goals.

(2) *goal-attainment*, the achievement of system ends in relation to the environment on the basis of pre-established conditions, involving the ultimate consummatory processes of approaching system goal-states. (3) *pattern-maintenance*, establishing the general conditions of the maintenance of states of mutual adjustment in the relations among functionally differentiated system parts. This is a problem of maintaining the states of the parts that are preconditions of the maintenance of consummatory relations, or relations of mutual adjustment, among them, and; (4) *integration*, the maintenance of relations of mutual adjustment necessary to effective system functioning among differentiated parts on the basis of pre-established conditions (see figure).

Internal Differentiation. The primary basis of the internal differentiation of living systems, then, is functional. Such systems must solve four basic categories of problems if they are to maintain their distinctive patterns of organization and functioning, and subsystems, units, or parts become differentiated from each other in terms of the type of problem to which their functioning is addressed. The primary contribution of the subsystem is an output to its own environment, that is, to the other subsystems of the larger system. This implies, of course, that subsystems are systems in their own right, subject, on their own level, to the same types of functional problems as the more inclusive system of which they are parts. That is to say, a subsystem has its own distinctive pattern of organization and functioning (which must be compatible with that of the larger system) to maintain, and that maintenance requires input-output interchanges with its environment. Its environment, of course, consists, above all, of the subsystems of the larger system. With respect to the primary output of the subsystem (its contribution to system functioning) there is the problem of establishing in the subsystem-environment relation the general conditions of its production. Hence, the production of the primary contribution of the subsystem constitutes its

	Instrumental	Consummating
External	Adaption	Goal-Attainment
Internal	Pattern-Maintenance	Integration

Functional Problems of Living Systems. (From Table 1, Chapter 1, "General Theory in Sociology" by Talcott Parsons. In Sociology Today: Problems and Prospects, *edited by Rodert P. Merton, Leonard Broom, and Leonard S. Cottrell, Jr. © 1959 Basic Books, Inc., Publishers, New York. Used with permission.)*

goal-attainment, or external-consummatory problem. Recalling this treatment of the integrative problem as one concerning the mutual adjustment of consummatory relations among parts, we may now say that it is primarily a matter of maintaining states of mutual adjustment, balance, or coordination, among the goal-outputs, or essential contributions to system functioning, of the several subsystems. "Thus a unit differentiated from others (i.e., specialized) in terms of adaptive function for the system will contribute not directly to the system's goal-attainment but to the adaptive level which facilitates attainment of an indefinite number of specific system goals" (Parsons, 1959, 641).

As noted previously, units are themselves systems subject on their own level to the four types of functional problems. Hence, they will tend to have not only distinctive goal outputs and inputs but also distinctive patterns of adaption, integration, and pattern-maintenance. Moreover, "Not only must the goals of units be integrated in the system, but all their other functions must also be integrated" (Parsons, 1959, 642).

Social Systems and Their Environments. Early in this chapter we emphasized the functional significance of system-environment relations, particularly in connection with the interchange of inputs and outputs. We also suggested that much of what we include as part of the organization in the common-sense treatment of organizations lies outside the boundaries of the social system of the organization. That is to say, much of what we include as part of the organization in common-sense terms is part of the environment of the social system of the organization.

Perhaps this point can be clarified by noting that the theory of social systems is a *theoretical*[4] subsystem of a more inclusive *theoretical* system called the theory of action. The empirical subject matter of the theory of action is *learned* behavior. It is not concerned with genetically *programmed* behavior, metabolic processes, physico-chemical processes, or the anatomical structure of the organism. It is concerned with behavior insofar as it is organized and controlled symbolically. The treatment of symbolically organized human behavior within a theoretical system that consists of four subsystems reflects the view that concrete human behavior involving more than a single person over time involves four *analytically* independent *empirical* systems. To say that the relevant systems are analytically independent means that any concrete behavior involves all four systems. Stated conversely, the four subsystems are all abstractions from the *same* behavior.

Our primary concern here is social systems. These may be defined as the normatively regulated interactions of pluralities of individuals. The individual person, however, participates in a wide variety of interactive relationships, and in none of these does he interact with his whole

---

4 We emphasize the term *theoretical* here to call attention to the distinction made earlier between theoretical and empirical systems.

personality. Even as small a group as a nuclear family always involves its members in a variety of interactive relationships, which call for different types of behavior. For example, married couples typically have children and the role of *spouse* is differentiated from that of *parent*.

The point we wish to emphasize here is this:

From the perspective of the social system the personalities of its participating members are at the same time, in different respects, *both part of the social system*, through interpenetration, *and part of its environment*. The zone of interpenetration is that of the expectations about role performance, since they are both institutionalized in the social system and internalized in individual personalities. (Parsons, 1968a, 438)

It was to the nonincluded parts of the personalities of members, as well as the noninstitutionalized aspects of culture, that we referred when we spoke of the exclusion of much of the concrete society or organization from the social systems of these entities. This is a perspective that, although difficult to maintain, is critical in the present context.

The Social System of Society

Functional Problems of Societal Systems. Having set the stage with the preceding preliminary considerations, we may now turn to an examination of the functional imperatives at the level of societal social systems. These imperatives, of course, are specific interpretations for this particular type and level of system of the general functional problem definitions provided previously.

Pattern-maintenance concerns the imperative of maintaining the stability of the highest-order governing, or controlling, patterns of the system, which in the terms outlined previously establish the preconditions of the maintenance of relations of mutual adjustment among differentiated parts. In systems of social action the highest order governing patterns are the value patterns that are institutionalized in the system. The maintenance of the stability of these patterns requires their internalization in the personalities of the members of the society so that those members are motivationally committed to act in accordance with them. Socialization, the acquisition of value commitments, or the internalization of values, and other cultural elements is thus a central pattern-maintenance mechanism.

Integration refers to the ordering of relations among the parts of the societal system—persons in roles, collectivities, and normative standards —so as to promote harmonious functioning in their various involvements with each other in the system. Integration has both positive and negative aspects. The latter concerns the prevention or minimization of action that would disrupt the harmonious functioning of the system by either intentional or unintentional mutual destructiveness or blockage. The former concerns the promotion of mutual support and facilitation among units of the system in the interest of the functioning of the system as a whole as in the case of cooperation in the accomplishment of a common task.

Goal-attainment. As social systems, societies have collective goals and must, therefore, come to some collectively binding decisions and implement them effectively. Effective collective action in the attainment of collective goals depends on capacity to coordinate the actions of diverse contributing units and to assure that each will do its part. The goals of social systems are always the elimination, or reduction, of discrepancies between desired states of the system environment relation and actual or expected states. From that point of view, goal-attainment concerns the making of collectively binding decisions with regard to the implementation of the values of the system in relation to changing environing conditions. It includes not only the determination of which among the possible goals shall be pursued as collective goals in what order of priority but also the mobilization of collective resources in the interest of their effective attainment.

Adaptation concerns the problem of generating a supply of disposable facilities for use in the attainment of various unit and collective goals. In order to be readily disposable, that is, available for flexible utilization in coping with unforeseen contingencies, facilities must be highly generalized or be tied in advance to no particular goal. In somewhat more familiar terms, this is the economic problem of producing highly generalized resources for the attainment of a wide variety of societal, subsystem, and individual goals, that is, of producing disposable wealth.

All societies, and all social systems of any duration, are confronted by these four problems, and their continued existence depends on the achievement of a satisfactory solution to them. However, societies typically do not assign equal importance to the problems but establish priorities among them. Some societies place greatest emphasis on adaptation, on the development of generalized capacity for the pursuit of a variety of goals, that is, on economic development. The United States is a prominent example of this emphasis. Other societies give first priority to goal attainment, to the achievement of a state that is an end in its own right. Communist societies striving to attain a state of communism are examples. Still other societies emphasize internal harmony, that is, integration, or pattern-maintenance, that is, the perpetuation of the relations among its members. Classical China and India, respectively, are examples of these two emphases.

A society's value system applies most directly to the society itself. It provides a conception of the desirable in terms of which the actual may be evaluated. Only derivatively does it provide the standard in terms of which individual members of the society may be evaluated. Thus, "*The values which come to be constitutive of the structure of a societal system are* . . . the conceptions of the desirable *type of society* held by the members of the society of reference and applied to the particular society of which they are members" (Parsons, 1968a, 136). In the adaptive case the desirable society is conceived as oriented to active mastery over the environment in the interest of goals that are transcendental in relation to the society itself, that is, in the interest of religiously sanctioned ideals. There is no definitive goal for the society as a whole, and hence, it is seen as an instrument in the attainment of the good life for its members. In terms of the derivative standard that applies to individuals, the adaptive pattern emphasizes performance, or achievement, not in relation to a societal goal, but in relation to worthwhile goals of the individual's own choosing. The emphasis is on rational, technically efficient action in the interest of goals with relatively little concern for what those goals are, so long as they are somehow "worthwhile." The important consideration is whether the individual achieves his goals by utilizing the best means available. The goals themselves need no justification beyond being a contribution to the building of a "good society."

In the case of the society with a goal-attainment emphasis, however, the situation is very different. The good society is conceived as oriented to mastery over the environment in the interest of the attainment of an ultimate objective. Consequently, the standard applied to members emphasizes achievements that contribute to the realization of that goal. The adaptive value emphasis yields a pluralistic society, that is, one that places heavy responsibility for goal selection on the members. The goal-attainment society tends to be monolithic, it has a single paramount goal that defines what contributions are expected from the members. The good member is he who contributes to the realization of *the* societal goal.

The integrative emphasis is internal rather than external, and oriented toward maintenance rather than mastery. The good society is one that is oriented to harmonious accommodation with environment and characterized by harmonious, mutually supportive relations among units. Hence, the good member is not the one who achieves either in relation to individual or societal goals, but the one who expresses the attitudes that are appropriate for a member of the society. The emphasis is on adherence or conformity, to the standards of the groups in which membership is held. Achievement is secondary to acceptance of one's belongingness in the group.

The fourth emphasis, the pattern-maintenance, is also inward and on maintenance. It differs from the integrative in that the primary concern is not external and internal harmony, but uncompromising adherence to the values ascribed to the society in its status as a part of a transcendental order. Above all, the obligation of the society is to maintain the integrity of its commitment to values independently of the consequences of that emphasis for adaptation, goal-attainment, or integration. Internally, the emphasis is on the strict maintenance of the pattern of relationships that holds among units in the society. Relational patterns among units are carefully prescribed; the caste system is an outstanding example. The evaluative standard applicable to individuals emphasizes the expression or implementation of the values ascribed to one in his status in the society. That is, the good person is one who knows his place, or station, and behaves accordingly. Acceptance of the world and one's place in it as given in the order of things takes precedence over achievement and harmony.

The order of priorities among the four problems defines a society's value system, but all value systems provide some degree of emphasis on each of the four. Whatever the priority arrangement, there is a tendency, more pronounced in modern than in "underdeveloped" societies, for the units of a society to become differentiated from one another in terms of the problem to which their activities are most directly related. That is to say, subgroups within a society tend to specialize in the solution of these problems, and activities of one kind tend to become segregated from activities of another kind. In a primitive society very little differentiation or segregation of activities occurs. Political, economic, and other types of units tend to overlap greatly as in the agrarian society in which the family is the basic economic unit, and a feudal society in which the fiefdom was both an economic and political unit. Societal evolution has thus consisted of a long-term trend for economic, political, and other types of units to become differentiated from multipurpose units.

We may, then, think of the social system of society as being differentiated into four major functional subsystems (not concrete organizations) each of which specializes in the solution of one of the four functional problems of the society. These subsystems, in turn, consist of units that are the social systems of organizations and individuals in roles engaged in certain types of activities. Each of these subsystems, and hence the units within them, is governed by a value standard defining the approved system-environment relation; in the attainment of its goals (which arise as a consequence of discrepancies between the actual and approved system-environment relation) each produces a particular category of outputs; each is subject to a differentiated set of legal and informal norms or institutions specifying legitimate and illegitimate means of producing its output as well as sanctions for compliance and noncompliance; and each utilizes a particular system of symbols as a medium of exchange in acquiring resources, and as a measure of the value of resources and outputs.

Business firms, commercial enterprises, and economic organizations are differentiated primarily with reference to adaptation, that is, they contribute to the generation of generalized facilities that serve in the pursuit of a number of goals. The governing value standard is *utility* and the generalized goal of such units is maximizing the utility (want satisfaction capacity) of available resources through the production of goods and services of economic value. The institutions, or normative standards, regulating economic activities are those of contract, property, and employment. The institution of contract, for example, defines the kinds of economic relationships that can be entered into, the kinds of things that can be contracted for, and the rights and duties of contracting parties. The symbols that serve as a medium of exchange and a measure of value in economic activities are monetary. Monetary value (price) is a measure of the economic value, that is, of the utility, of goods and services. At the same time, money (including credit instruments) is a medium of exchange that can be utilized to secure control of the factors of production. Primitive economic systems rely on barter as a means of exchange, and one can readily see the restrictive nature of such a system. One can barter his pig for corn only if he can find someone who both wants a pig and has a surplus of corn. Money, on the other hand is free of these restrictions. Within limits, money can be exchanged for whatever one wants, at whatever time, and, of course it presents few problems of storage, and so on.

From the point of view of the societal system, however, economic production may be said to be a process of value implementation, or fulfillment of value commitments. ". . . it is the use of factors of production (resources) to increase the utility (want satisfaction capacity) of the goods and services available in the economy as a system and, through its outputs, for consumption" (Parsons, 1968a, 139). Production is a "combinatorial," "value-added" process. The utility of both resources and products is measured in terms of monetary price and is a *condition of the survival* of the firm that it combine resources in such a way that all the monetary costs of production are covered by the proceeds of sales. Only when the monetary price of the product exceeds the monetary cost of the resources utilized can the firm be said to have made a contribution that *adds* value in the sense of enhancing the utility of available resources. To state the matter very simply, the standard of successful contribution to the adaptive, or economic, function is *solvency*. A variety of enterprises are subsidized on grounds other than economic, for example, national interest, but in the general case the economic producer is expected, in the long run, to meet that standard.

Governmental bodies and agencies, including the military and police forces, are the units that are differentiated primarily around the goal-attainment function. Here the problem is the attainment of goals defined in social processes as those of the societal collectivity, or subsystems of it. The goals involved may concern relations with the cultural environment, as in the case of research goals; the social environment, as in the case of relations with other societies; the organic environment, as in the case of health goals; or the psychological environment, as in the case of educational goals. Whatever the content of the goals, the value standard governing goal-attainment is *effectiveness*, and, since the attainment of collective goals requires collective action, it is "effectiveness of collective action." Thus, just as the function of the economy, and of its units, is to add to the utility of available resources, the function of the polity and its units is to add to the effectiveness of collective action in the attainment of collective goals.

Since effective collective action depends on the coordination of the actions of diverse contributing units, to assure that each will do its part, the obvious ways of adding to the effectiveness of collective actions are the promulgation, implementation, and enforcement of authoritative decisions that bind the actions of participants. These are the goals outputs of the polity and its units.

Like economic activity, political activity is subject to regulation by a set of institutions, or normative standards, which define the rights and duties of parties to political exchange. These may be identified as authority, leadership, and regulation. Authority, for example, is the set of legitimate rights to promulgate decisions that impose binding obligations on members of a collectivity in the interest of the attainment of collective goals. In slightly different terms, it is the right to acquire and use power.

The medium of exchange and measure of value (effectiveness) operative in the political realm that parallels money in economic activity is power. Although power is not a tangible thing like money, it can be thought of as that which the political unit spends in producing binding decisions and that which it receives in return for the decisions produced, for example, in being re-elected to office. Just as the firm that efficiently produces goods and services for which there is sufficient demand receives a monetary return that exceeds its expenditures, so does the political unit that successfully produces decisions that produce effective collective action for which there is sufficient demand receive a return of power that exceeds its expenditures. That is, the decision maker "spends" power in making decisions, and if successful, he receives a return of power greater than his expenditures. Just as the amount of money one has is a measure of the amount of goods and services of economic value he can command, so is the amount of power one has a measure of the amount of compliance he can command. And just as spending more money in producing commodities than one gets in return leads to bankruptcy, so does spending more power in producing compliance than one gets in return lead to political bankruptcy, or loss of sovereignty. The political agency that spends more power than it earns can no longer buy compliance (just as the firm that spends more money than it earns can no longer buy goods and services) and can continue in operation only by borrowing power at the cost of its sovereignty.

Interest groups and political parties (as distinguished from political administrations) are examples of units differentiated with reference to the integrative function. Their generalized goal-output, their contribution to the functioning of the societal system, and the value standard governing their operation is *solidarity*. The solidarity of a system is the degree to which its members are committed to common interests through which their discrete interests can be integrated, and by means of which conflicts among competing interests can be resolved. Common interests provide the basis for justifying the allocation of benefits and burdens, and the solution of competing claims. Since common interests are, by definition, matters of consensus, one obvious contribution to system solidarity is the extension of consensus. Another, of course, is the justifiable solution of competing claims that, if unsatisfactorily resolved, could threaten solidarity.

The symbolic medium of exchange and measure of value (solidarity) that parallels money in the economic case and power in the political case is influence. Influence is the medium of persuasion that relies for its persuasiveness not on the intrinsic argument presented, but on the prestige or reputation of the source of the argument (Parsons, 1966). It is the generalized capacity to achieve consensus with other members of an associated group through persuasion without having to give fully adequate, intrinsically convincing information. The prototypical case of the exercise of influence is the patient's acceptance of the advice of the physician without fully understanding the reason for that advice (Parsons, 1968b).

Integrative units, for example, political interest groups and political parties, "spend" influence to secure the resources required to produce outputs that are evaluated as contributions to system solidarity. For example, they attempt to persuade decision makers to promulgate decisions they favor by justifying them in terms of the common interest. Commitments to membership and favorable policy decisions are among the resources required to produce the principal integrative goal output of political support. But, just as genuine contributions to the utility of resources must be both efficiently produced and valued by consumers, genuine contributions to system solidarity must be both consensually produced and consensus producing. That is, not only must the support producing agency achieve consensus internally but also the recipients of its output of support must view its position as justifiable in terms of the common interests. Viewed from the side of the consumer of support outputs, i.e., candidates for office, the available support must be seen as having sufficient value as a contribution to system solidarity to make it worth purchasing with his own influence. In short, successful contributions to system solidarity must be based on consensus, they must be justifiable in terms of the common interest, and they must be made available to consumers of support on a consensual basis, that is, the consumer must secure support by persuading groups that it is in their own and the collective interest to do so, he must achieve consensus with them.

From this it follows that the standard of success in integrative action, parallel to solvency in the economic area, is consensus. The interest group that fails to achieve consensus internally, or to justify the policies it advocates in terms of the consensually based common interest, is faced by the threat of "bankruptcy."

Since influence involves the exercise of persuasion or the achievement of consensus, on the basis of the prestige or reputation of the persuader, the normative standards governing integrative action must obviously have to do with the ordering of prestige relations among members of the system. The institutional complex that is relevant here is the stratification system of the society that orders members and collective units in a prestige hierarchy. Just as authority is the institutional code within which the use of power is legitimized, and property is the code within which the use of money is organized, prestige is the institutional code that is central to the stability of influence systems. Prestige is the aspect of a status in a social system by virtue of which the incumbent is put in a position to exercise influence.

The fourth societal subsystem and type of social unit is differentiated in relation to the performance of pattern-maintenance functions for the societal system. Prominent among the units involved here is the public school, but families, religious organizations, and higher education organizations are also included. The public school, which concerns us most directly here, may, like the business firm, be characterized as a system that is oriented to the attainment of relatively specific collective goals. It is ". . . an agency through which individual personalities are trained to be motivationally and technically adequate to the performance of adult roles" (Parsons, 1964, 130). The product output of the school, that which parallels commodities in the case of the firm, may be identified as "change in the character, knowledge and skill levels of *individual* pupils" (Parsons, 1960, 76). Just as understanding the business firm requires a knowledge of its place in the economy, however, an understanding of the school requires a knowledge of its place in the pattern-maintenance subsystem of the society. As we have seen, the highest-order elements of a societal system are the patterns of normative culture, especially, but not only the values that are institutionalized in the system's norms, collectivities, and roles. It is a condition of the stability and/or orderly change of the system that the integrity of the value pattern, and of the members' motivational commitments to its implementation, be maintained. Clearly, a critical aspect of the maintenance of the pattern is the development of motivational commitments in each oncoming generation.

Like economic production, education may be seen as a process of value implementation. The relevant value standard, however, is not utility, as measured in monetary terms, but *integrity*. That is to say, the product output of the school may be seen as a contribution to the maintenance and/or enhancement of the integrity of the system of cultural patterns that constitute the normative order of the societal system. The basis of that order lies in the fact that units of social systems, whether individuals

Integration—insuring organizational adherence to practices and procedures that are compatible with those in use in the larger community. (4) Pattern-maintenance—legitimizing the existence of the organization, i.e., public-relations activities that pursuade the general public of the importance of the attainment of organizational goals for the society and its subsystems.

With that brief mention of the external aspects of organizational functions, we can now turn to internal matters. Since organizations are goal-directed collectivities, those activities that are most directly related to goal-attainment will be emphasized. That is, in general, goal-attainment values will be paramount throughout the organization, and the performance standard applied in the evaluation of personnel will emphasize contributions to the attainment of organizational goals. This also means that the goals of the several functionally differentiated units will be the production of decisions, that the norms regulating their activities will be within the general category of authority, and that the media utilized are different kinds of power.

Internally, adaptation is concerned primarily with the maintenance of the effective system of facilities for the performance of technical, educational functions. This involves the maintenance and improvement of the patterns of allocation and organization necessary to provide the facility base for adequate performance on the part of operative personnel. Included here are both matters concerning the flow of materials (patients in hospitals, students in schools), the replacement of personnel, and the flow of facilities and matters concerning allocative organization, that is, the organizational framework within which resources are distributed and responsibility for their utilization is assigned. In the latter case, the fundamental consideration is the allocation of responsibility, that is, deciding who should make what decisions.

Goal-attainment within the organization is concerned primarily with the authorization and enforcement of measures that are necessary to implement the organization's goal commitments. Changes in external commitments and readjustment of priorities require corresponding adjustments in the allocation of responsibilities and rewards. In short, goal commitments have to be implemented, and implementation requires the selection, authorization, and enforcement of the appropriate concrete activities or measures.

Pattern-maintenance in organizations consists of those activities that express, or implement directly, the basic values of the organization. These are the activities of technical, operative personnel, production workers in industry, physicians in hospitals, teachers in schools, and so on. They are pattern-maintaining in the sense that they do not involve changes in the instrumental capacity, goals, or level or integration of the organization.

Finally, integration in organizations concerns the prevention and resolution of the inevitable conflicts that arise among adaptive, goal-attainment, and technical functions. The inevitability of conflict arises as a consequence of the fact that personnel specializing in adaptation emphasize the adaptive component of organizational values, personnel specializing in goal-attainment emphasize goal-attainment values, and technical personnel emphasize pattern-maintenance values. Integrative, or coordinative, personnel emphasize integrative values, and the function of that emphasis is to keep conflicts among the other three to an acceptable level.

The economy, or adaptive sector, of a society will reflect the value system of the society so that it fits into the general pattern. Thus, the American, British, and Russian economies differ to a considerable extent. The Russian economy reflects the goal-attainment values of the society in that solvency is a less important determinant of continued operation for a firm than is contribution to national objectives. Nevertheless, there is a tendency for those involved in economic activity to emphasize the economic standards of efficiency and solvency, and even in the U.S.S.R. there are indications of disagreement between the economically and politically oriented personnel. The same point may be made with respect to organizations. The adaptive suborganization of an organization will reflect the general organizational value system so that adaptation in a business firm will be quite different from adaptation in military and educational organizations. The adaptive sector of a business firm will place far more emphasis on efficiency than the other two organizations, and solvency is not even a consideration for military and educational enterprises. Even so, those who specialize in adaptation in educational and military enterprises will tend to emphasize economic values and concern themselves with the consequences of performance and alternative courses of action for the financial standing of the organization.

Of course, the same point can be made concerning the goal-attainment, integrative, and pattern-maintenance subunits in organizations. Although their views will be considerably modified by pattern-maintenance values, those who specialize in goal-attainment in educational organizations will tend to emphasize the degree to which performances contribute to the realization of organizational goals as an evaluative standard, Hence, goal-attainment personnel will tend to emphasize the consequences of performances and alternative courses of action for relations between the organization and its environment and "markets."

Similarly, pattern-maintenance personnel will tend to reflect the basic value pattern of the organization so that the technical, operative level performer in the business, military, medical, and educational organization will tend in general to reflect adaptive, goal-attainment, integrative, and pattern-maintenance values. In each case the basic concern will be the expression and implementation of the fundamental organizational values, that is, the performance of the basic function that is the raison d'être of the organization. The general tendency here is to continue to perform the technical function without concern for changing the general pattern of the organization. The values of pattern-maintenance units call for the maintenance of integrity of commitment to technical values and standards. That is, the responsibility of technical personnel is to perform their technical duties, not to make changes in allocative arrangements, in goal-commitments, or in integrative procedures, and the good technician is one who is committed to the relevant standards.

In general, this pattern cuts across all sorts of organizations. It applies to soldiers, lower level administrators in governmental agencies, physicians in hospitals, teachers in public schools, and professors in universities. But it is modified and works out differently in each case, as a consequence of the basic values of the organization. Quite naturally, the type of organization in which technical personnel most strongly emphasize pattern-maintenance values is the pattern-maintenance organization, for example, educational organizations. In these organizations the emphasis on implementation of the basic "professional" values without concern for the adaptive, goal-attainment and integrative implications of their implementation comes to be not only a general inclination but also a right that restricts the freedom of administrative personnel to establish new goal-commitments, reallocate responsibilities and resources, and make organizational changes.

Stated another way, technical personnel in pattern-maintenance organizations not only share the general emphasis on the performance of technical functions without regard for organizational consequences, they are, in the most extreme cases, granted the right to veto administrative decisions that would interfere with their performance. This is especially the case when there are grounds for believing that technical personnel are more knowledgeable about the basic technical processes than are administrators. In such cases, technical personnel not only have the right to veto administrative decisions but they also frequently participate directly in the making of decisions that, in other organizations, would be considered the sole province of the administrator.

The outstanding example is the university. There are wide variations among universities, but the general tendency is for faculty members, particularly those at the higher professorial levels, to participate in the appointment of new faculty members in granting tenure, in making promotions, in creating new programs, and so on. The widely espoused principle of "academic freedom" institutionalizes the right of the faculty member to maintain the integrity of his commitment to academic values even in the face of administrative opposition.

When technical personnel not only possess knowledge that is not possessed by administrators but are also affiliated with an association of similarly qualified peers, they are no longer merely members of the organization and subject to its regulations. They hold dual membership and are subject to dual, and often conflicting standards. There are some important distinctions to be made in this context. Technical personnel may possess knowledge and information that is not available to administrators, for example, sociology professors may know a great deal more about sociology than the administrators and become members of a nationwide, or international, association of sociologists. In such cases, the development of the field of sociology and the professor's status in that field may be more important to him than the realization of organizational objectives and his status in the organization. In another case, technical personnel may possess skills in the application of knowledge that are not available to administrators, for example, physicians not only have greater command of a field of knowledge than hospital administrators but they are also skilled diagnosticians and clinicians. Hence, their claim to freedom from administrative intervention is even more compelling than that of the professor.

In a third case, technical personnel may have neither knowledge nor skill that is not possessed by administrative personnel, and hence, no technical claim to freedom from intervention. Nevertheless, we do find personnel in such positions forming associations based on a common desire to restrict what are viewed as unfair management practices and to improve their economic position. We ordinarily refer to such associations as *unions*. There is a general tendency among the cynical to lump all technical associations into the broad category of unions. On the part of some, however, there is an equally pronounced tendency to apply the term *profession* to a wide variety of associations. Either of these tendencies seems to obscure some important distinctions. Regardless of the terminology applied, teaching, at either the university or public school level, cannot be equated with medicine or with automobile production.

It is reasonable to assert that teachers at all levels possess knowledge of a field that administrators do not share. In this respect teachers are similar to physicians. However, one is hard put to demonstrate that teachers, in either the university or public school, have knowledge about conveying that knowledge to students that is not shared by administrators, and even by reasonably well-educated citizens. In this respect teachers are very different from physicians to the extent that public school teachers neglect both disciplinary and clinical expertise, and they resemble the disciplinary associations of the academician. To the extent that teachers emphasize both areas of expertise, they resemble those in the medical profession. For those who wish to "professionalize" teaching, the course of action seems clear; develop both the disciplinary and clinical expertise of teachers.

Backtracking now to the point at which we were discussing the general proclivities of pattern-maintenance or technical personnel in educational organizations, these considerations seem to have important implications for any discussion of innovation in education. Within the analytical framework utilized here, the primary function of the teacher role in the social system of the school is directly analogous to that of the school in the social system of the society. That is to say, technical functions, those that directly implement the values of the collectivity, are by definition pattern-expressing; that is, they are implementing and maintaining of functions. Thus, what has been said in the preceding sections with respect to the orientation of the school to its environments can be repeated with respect to the teacher. In the social system of the school, the teacher's obligation, above all, is to engage in actions that are expressive of, and implement, the pattern-consistent complex of values ascribed to him in his status in that system, independently of system adaptation, goal-attainment, and integrative problems. The primary concern of the teacher is neither organizational efficiency, effectiveness, nor solidarity, but his own professional integrity. Again, the intrinsic properties of new elements—performances, practices, and procedures tend to be less important than their "goodness of fit" with the system. Those that fit are readily accepted; those that are incompatible with, or threaten to disturb, the organization of the system, are rejected or modified. In our view, the empirical evidence accords well with this view. Jackson, for example, has pointed out that:

When teachers look back on a day's activities and ponder the wisdom of their actions, the criteria they apply to what they have done are not limited to the achievement of educational objectives. They also worry about whether they were just or unjust in the distribution of praise and reproof, sensitive or insensitive to the nuances of the events that transpired, consistent or inconsistent in the standards and regulations they enforced. They are interested, in other words, in stylistic qualities of their own performance as much as in whether specific goals were reached and specific objectives attained. At such moments, the engineering virtues of speed, efficiency, accuracy, and economy are not uppermost in their minds. (Jackson, 1968, 167–68)

Tentative findings from another source (Lortie, 1967) reveal that teachers report their angry behavior, or loss of self-control in the classroom, as a source of shame with three times the frequency of any other category, including inadequacy of instruction and conflict with colleagues. In Lortie's terms, "It is interesting that teachers may feel regret at errors or unfortunate, unintended consequences of their actions; they clearly feel shame at anger" (Lortie, 1967, 165). To Lortie's surprise, "emphasis on the teacher's mastery of subject matters occurred rarely and indirectly; no teacher, for example, confessed to shame at not knowing his subject matter sufficiently well to teach it effectively" (Lortie, 1967, 166).

When asked to identify the personal characteristics that qualified them to teach, Lortie's respondents tended heavily toward qualities or dispositions, rather than competencies, or performances.

teachers volunteered such responses such as affection for children and wanting to work with people, patience, an understanding and kindly nature, the capacity to establish rapport with the young, and a sense of humor and easygoing disposition. (Lortie, 1967, 168)

Elsewhere, Lortie suggests that:

One may, in fact, attribute a special work ethic to teachers (including, probably, social workers and clergy) a "dedicatory ethic" which elevates service motives and denigrates material rewards as proper motivation to work. Proper orientation lies in willing service to children and little thought to economic and other extrinsic rewards. (Lortie, 1969, 40)

Lortie's observations support the general conclusion that teachers' orientations are focused on the classroom to a degree that leaves them relatively unconcerned about matters that do not bear directly on teaching activities. Thus, their interest in schoolwide problems, general school affairs and policies, curriculum committees, and collegial ties is minimal.

If technical personnel tend to value those performances that maintain the integrity of their commitments, then we ought not to be surprised when teachers do not suggest or initiate changes that have implications beyond their immediate concerns. At this point I am reminded of the frequent complaint of administrators to the effect that teachers cannot see beyond the four walls of their classrooms. About the only occasion on which we might reasonably expect teachers to initiate organizational changes would be when they believe that the organization is hindering, rather than facilitating, the implementation of the values to which they subscribe.

Nor should we be surprised if and when teachers only go through the motions of implementing administrative innovation. From the teachers' point of view this is more than justified if the innovation in any way restricts his freedom to implement basic values. For example, to the extent that, in the view of teachers, the good teacher is one who maintains high standards of academic achievement that all students must meet, any attempt to introduce such practices as anecdotal report cards, "social" promotion, and the like, will be strongly resisted. Similarly, to the extent that, in the view of teachers, the good teacher is one who maintains a warm, personal relationship with students, new devices such as teaching machines will be utilized unwillingly and sparingly, if at all. In short, the primary concern of the teacher in evaluating any proposed course of action is, "Is it consistent with what constitutes 'good teaching?'" Matters of economy, the satisfaction or dissatisfaction of external agents, and the minimization of conflict within the organization are irrelevant to the teacher. Good teaching is good teaching no matter what the business manager, the central office, the community member, or the coordinator thinks. Those who wish to change teaching practice will have to change the teachers' conception of good teaching or be satisfied with innovating at the organizational level.

All this is not to say that teachers are opposed to all innovation. Given the preceding analysis, one would expect teachers to respond favorably to any innovation that enabled them, within their conception of good teaching, to be better teachers. Thus, teachers for whom the good teacher is a subject matter specialist would be inclined to favor any change that tended to increase their specialization, for example, a change that involved a reduction of the number of different classes taught. On the other hand, those for whom the good teacher is one who knows all there is to know about each student and accommodates his teaching to the "needs" of the individual student, would tend to seek out and respond favorably to changes that provided more opportunities to get acquainted with students. These considerations suggest another alternative for those who wish to promote change in the practice of teaching. One might find it possible to demonstrate to teachers that current practices simply are not implementing the values they think they are. If the good teacher is held to be one who develops students' critical reasoning skills, and if firm evidence can be presented to indicate that current practices are having precisely the opposite effect, then the emphasis on consistency makes change probable. Similarly, if the good teacher is one who helps each student proceed at his own rate on his own level, and if one can demonstrate that students in the normal heterogeneous classroom have a range of seven to eight years in a particular subject, then one can make a convincing case for the abandonment of the single book, single lesson approach.

However, this approach is bound to fail sooner or later, for the values of teachers do not constitute an internally consistent system. Their values, like those of others, and of organizations as a whole, contain conflicting emphases, and the device that is eminently suited for the implementation of one value will be utilized less than fully because it conflicts with the implementation of another value.

To repeat the conclusion stated at the end of the preceding section, this particular way of answering the question, "What is education all about?" leads us to predict precisely those features of the educational enterprise that seem to be occasions for amazement, dismay, and concern. Given this account, we should be surprised to find an absence of conflict between technical and the several categories of administrative personnel, for conflict is a predictable consequence of opposing value orientations. Moreover, we should be surprised, except under special conditions, to find technical personnel actively involved in the initiation of organizational changes.

Conclusion

To conclude this analysis before it gets completely out of hand, I should like to indicate that what I have "really" been doing here is demonstrating that a particular set of statements of fact couched in the language of the educator is deducible from, and hence explained by, other statements couched in the language of social systems theory. Or, to state it in another way, certain relationships known to educators have been shown to be embedded in a more extensive system of interrelationships. From still another point of view, a set of relatively specific generalizations concerning educational organizations and personnel have been shown to be special cases of more inclusive generalizations about the nature of organizations.

The fact that there is a number of ways of saying what I "really" did should serve to underscore the point that it is nonsense to speak of what educators "really" do in some absolute sense. Not only is the same set of facts deducible from more than one theoretical account but also entirely different and equally accurate statements of fact can be made within frames of reference other than the one adopted here.

REFERENCES

JACKSON, PHILLIP W. *Life in Classroom.* New York: Holt, Rinehart and Winston, Inc., 1968.

LORTIE, DAN C. "The Teachers' Shame: Anger and the Normative Commitments of Classroom Teachers." *The School Review* (Summer 1967), 155–171.

PARSONS, TALCOTT. "An Approach to Psychological Theory in Terms of the Theory of Action." In Sigmund Koch (ed.), *Psychology, a Study of a Science.* New York: McGraw-Hill, Inc., 1959, Study I, Vol. 3, pp. 612–711.

———. *Structure and Process in Modern Societies.* New York: The Free Press, 1960.

———. *Social Structure and Personality.* New York: The Free Press, 1964.

———. "The Political Aspect of Social Structures and Process." In David Easton (ed.), *Varieties of Political Theory.* Englewood Cliffs, N.J., 1966, pp. 71–112.

———. "On the Concept of Value Commitments." *Sociological Inquiry,* 38:2 (Spring 1968), 1968a, pp. 135–139.

———. "Social Systems." In David L. Sills (ed.), *International Encyclopedia of the Social Sciences.* New York: The Free Press, 1968b, pp. 458–472.

———. "Some Problems of General Theory in Sociology." In Edward A. Tirygkin and John McKinney (eds.), *Theoretical Sociology: Perspectives and Developments.* New York: Appleton-Century-Crofts, 1970, pp. 27–68.

9

COMMENTARY

THE following article by James Anderson will surely invoke some to assert that it is the only "empirical" article in the book. With that, I would quickly disagree, unless by empirical one has reference to form and structure rather than to content and explanation. In this regard, Kaplan provides some instructive observations for which those interested in theory and theory development would do well to consider. He states:

> no observation is purely empirical—that is, free of any ideational element —as no theory (in science, at any rate) is purely ideational. The classical positivists attempted a reconstruction of knowledge on a phenomenological basis, whose first premises were "protocol sentences" describing here-and-now sensations. But the terms of even the barest description carry us beyond the here-and-now, if only because they must be capable of more than one utterance to have usage. When I say, "This object is red," I am inescapably relating the present occasion to others in which "red" is properly used. And this relation is in some way inferential: it is always possible that I am mistaken. All inferences implicate theories, in the broadest sense of the term. Error is of our own making; it has no part in God's world.[1]

Accordingly, "empirical" has customarily come to mean what many have tended to agree that it means rather than what it may surely mean. The point is made neither to initiate argument nor to belabor the inclusion of the Anderson article in this section; on the contrary, the point holds that differences in terms, ". . . are not to be construed ontologically, as though observations name other kinds of things than theoretical terms do. (. . . 'lunch' and 'dinner' do not identify dishes but the circumstances of the eating.)"[2]

Consequently, the inclusion of this excellent small study here serves two very important and useful purposes. First of all, it is an appropriate way of following up on the previous discussions of authority and bureaucracy with a specific treatment of some elements in organizational structure/function that are demonstrated as not being the result of the bureaucratic structure itself. On the contrary, the conditions of bureaucracy are much more pervasive than structural considerations alone or in concert with still other typically bureaucratic characteristics—rules, roles, satuses, and formalized ritual. Thus, the diffusion of authority, whether by virtue of an emphasis on legalistic or administrative considerations, is perhaps as much (or more?) an increasingly acculturated phenomenon as it is an organizationally systematic one. Second, and related to the first, the particular assumptions and hypotheses that guided Anderson in this investigation have relevance for the discussion that follows,

[1] Abraham Kaplan, *The Conduct of Inquiry* (San Francisco: Chandler Publishing Co., 1964), p. 58.
[2] Ibid., p. 60.

concerned with some exploration of the tendency for contemporary organizational structure to compound certain aspects of alienation in contemporary life and thereby to inhibit the normative evolution of systematic change as implied from Malinowski's model of a cultural, or institutional system.

This latter consideration is directly at the heart of the "hunches" that Anderson pursued. He recognized that several scholars had been provoked by the apparent dysfunctional aspects of bureaucratic structures on incumbents, that impersonality in relations between organizational members and clients would vary with the degree of bureaucratic rules existing within organizations.

In this article, Anderson deals with this notion and substantiates it in large measure since his study of junior high schools revealed that "bureaucratic impersonality" appears quite strongly related to the degree of rules that circumscribe teacher behavior. Moreover, Anderson has discovered that this characteristic seems to be a function of the teacher's sex, the subject matter taught, the size of the school, and the socioeconomic level of the student body.

These findings seriously bring into suspicion the accepted view that organizational constraints are the major determinants of dysfunctional behavior; on the contrary, although such constraints are nowhere questioned as contributing to such dysfunctions, the familiar assumption of causality is immensely overdrawn. Such constraints are apparently, if not less important, certainly not more so than certain psychological characteristics of organizational participants, as well as the substantive activity of the organization, professional differences, environmental influences, and—as important as anything else—the backgrounds of the clientele served by the organization.

Perhaps some will argue and, probably not without persuasiveness, that these latter phenomena are permeated by a variety of extraorganizational constraints; that is, that ours is an organizationally pervasive society and that whether or not one is targeted as demographically identified with some particular organization, constraints of a structural nature are affective in a larger sense, and thereby the "other" factors that Anderson notes are merely implications of the larger organizational culture. Thus, bureaucratic constraints are the same. Perhaps. But within a larger view, it must be remembered that really good theory, substantiated by rigorous inquiry, leads to still better theory, and by raising such questions, one is able to move another step ahead.

This article does indeed provide such a perspective. Furthermore, it demonstrates in a micronistic way that human behavior in contemporary society must still be examined both theoretically and methodologically within the broad context of the interpenetration of personality, culture, and social system. The specificity of concerns within that large interrelationship is the stuff of which both knowledge production and knowledge utilization are ultimately derived. This is the basis from which curious scholars ask their "silly" questions and thereby generate novel theoretical notions, and hopefully move us not only to better understand ourselves and our institutions but to make both, somehow, better. This article is thus an excellent example of the theory-research relationship.

THE CONSEQUENCES OF BUREAUCRATIC STRUCTURE

James G. Anderson

WITHIN complex organizations there is a continuous attempt to structure and impersonalize relationships so that individual personalities will have little or no effect on the accomplishment of organizational goals. In this manner the formal organization becomes a rational system pursuing certain defined goals in a predictable, organized fashion. However, no organization can be completely rational (Bendix, 1947). In the first place, it must involve individuals who bring with them diverse experiences, training, and attitudes. Also, these individuals can and do interact outside of the formally assigned roles that they play in the organization. Second, the formal and informal structures of the organization are affected by pressure from the environment in which the institution exists. Third, the historical perspective with which persons both within and without the organization regard the goals of the organization and the methods used to accomplish these goals will have a decided effect upon the organization.

The structuring of the organization involves an allocation of authority and the delineation of responsibility and jurisdiction for each role within the organization. However, even Max Weber, in his initial formulation of the characteristics of a bureaucracy, seems to have realized that although the rational-legal system of authority institutionalized in the modern bureaucracy is the most efficient and rational form of administration, it is also the most unstable form. Talcott Parsons has cogently observed:

a system of rational-legal authority can only operate through imposing and enforcing with relative efficiency, seriously frustrating limits on many important human interests, interests which either operate, independently of particular institutions, in any society, or are generated by the strains inherent in the particular structure itself. One source of such strain is the segregation of roles, and of the corresponding authority to use influence over others and over non-human resources, which is inherent in the functionally limited sphere of office. There are always tendencies to stretch the sanctioned limits of official authority to take in ranges of otherwise "personal" interests. In other words this form of institutionalization involves a kind of "abstraction" of a part of the human individual from the concrete whole which is in a certain sense "unreal" and hence can only be maintained by continual discipline. (Weber, 1947: 68)

Furthermore, participants in the organization are assigned particular roles that are functionally specified and impersonalized. Authority is

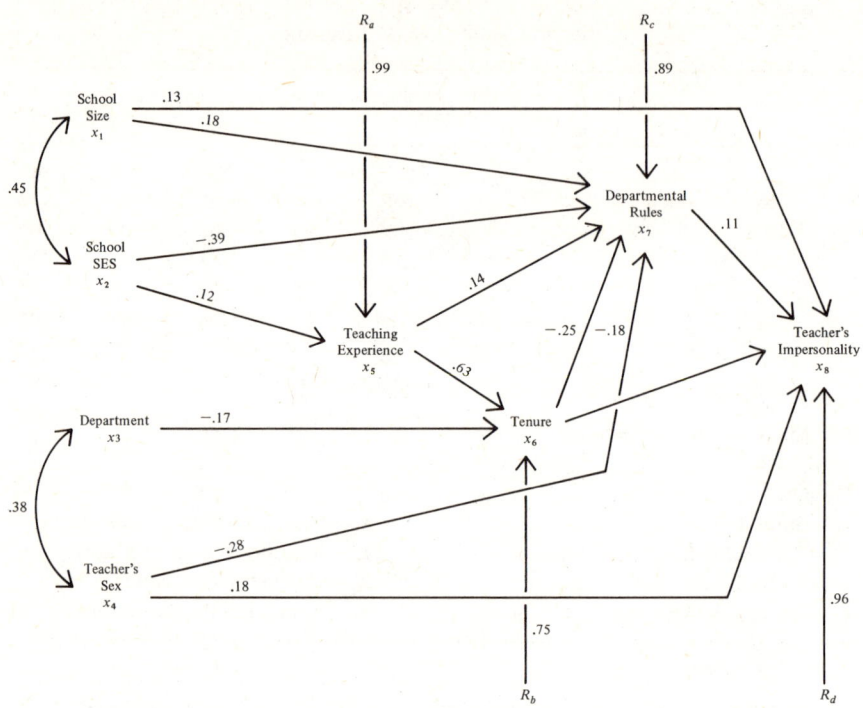

a Path coefficients and the corresponding arrows for values less than .10 have been omitted in order to simplify the diagram.

such as the one used here, path coefficients are standardized partial regression coefficients and can be estimated by ordinary least squares. Path coefficients for the present model are shown in Table 9-2.

Once the model has been formulated, a set of structural equations can be written (Duncan, 1966; Land, 1969). These equations permit the correlation between any two endogenous variables or between an endogenous and an exogenous variable to be expressed in terms of the paths leading from an antecedent variable to a dependent variable. The zero-order correlation between the two variables or total effect can be broken down into a direct effect as measured by the path coefficient, an indirect effect through intervening variables, and a joint or spurious effect caused by the correlation of the two variables with other variables included in the model. Table 9-3 provides a breakdown of the total effect of each endogenous and exogenous variables included in the mode on teachers' impersonality scores.

Results of the analysis indicate that, as hypothesized, the degree of institutional control in the form of rules concerning classroom instruction affects the teacher's relationships with his students. As rules increase within a department, the teacher spends less time counseling individual

TABLE 9-2
MULTIPLE CORRELATIONS AND STANDARDIZED PARTIAL
REGRESSION COEFFICIENTS

DEPENDENT VARIABLE	INDEPENDENT VARIABLE	MULTIPLE CORRELATION COEFFICIENT	STANDARDIZED PARTIAL REGRESSION COEFFICIENT
Impersonality	Rules	.29	.11
	Tenure		−.18
	Experience		.06
	Sex		.18
	Department		−.04
	Socioeconomic Status		.06
	School Size		.13
Rules	Tenure	.46	−.25
	Experience		.14
	Sex		−.28
	Department		−.01
	Socioeconomic Status		−.39
	School Size		.18
Tenure	Experience	.66	.63
	Sex		.04
	Department		−.17
	Socioeconomic Status		−.07
	School Size		.00
Experience	Sex	.15	−.07
	Department		−.05
	Socioeconomic Status		.12
	School Size		−.03

TABLE 9-3
CONTRIBUTION OF VARIABLES TO THE TEACHER'S
IMPERSONALITY SCORE

VARIABLE	TOTAL EFFECT	DIRECT EFFECT	INDIRECT EFFECT THROUGH OTHER VARIABLES	JOINT OR SPURIOUS EFFECT
Rules	.08	.11	—	−.03
Tenure	−.17	−.18	−.03	.04
Experience	−.07	.06	−.11	−.02
Sex	.15	.18	−.04	.01
Department	.06	−.04	.04	.06
Socioeconomic Status	.08	.06	−.04	.06
School Size	.16	.13	.02	.01

students and adopts a more universalistic grading scheme, two of the components that make up the impersonality score. This effect occurs even when the teacher's discipline, sex, experience, and tenure status are controlled as well as attributes of the school and its student body. This finding is of particular importance since the original analysis of these data (Anderson, 1968) did not detect such a direct effect of bureaucratic structure on teacher-student relations.

Tenure appears to have a negative direct effect on impersonality. The model reveals that tenured teachers make a greater effort to personalize their teaching. On the whole, they spend more time with individual students and are more particularistic in their grading practices regardless of discipline, sex, experience, or the size or social class of the school in which they teach. Quite possibly tenured teachers may feel more secure in dealing with students and with their superiors since they are not as closely supervised as nontenured teachers and can only be dismissed for cause. Moreover, a selection process has occurred by the time teachers are elected to tenure that also may account for their greater tendency to individualize instruction. The indirect effect of this variable is small but reinforces the direct effect. Tenured teachers are subject to fewer instructional regulations in the schools. As a result of this decrease in bureaucracy, there is a slight tendency for teachers to personalize their relationships with students. This indirect effect is −.03.

The effect of experience on teacher-student relations is mostly indirect. With experience comes tenure that, as we have seen, has an important effect on the way in which teachers respond to students. The indirect effects of this variable are −.11, indicating an overall decrease in the impersonal treatment of students as experience increases. Part of this effect, however, is offset by the direct effects of experience. When the other variables in the model are controlled, experience results in a small increase in impersonality scores among teachers. Nevertheless, the combined direct and indirect effects of this variable are still negative.

The teacher's sex also influences the manner in which he relates to students. Male teachers are more impersonal in their treatment of students. The direct effect in this instance is .18, whereas the indirect effects of this variable through other variables is negative. Female teachers are subject to a greater degree of instructional control through rules in the school. The path coefficient between sex and rules is −.28. Increased bureaucracy with its resultant effect on teacher-student interaction then slightly reduces the difference between male and female teachers on the impersonality index.

The effect of the teacher's discipline on teacher's relationships with students is revealing. Science teachers appear to make more of an attempt to personalize their instruction and their relationships with students than do English teachers in the junior high school. Moreover, fewer science teachers are tenured, which results in an increase in bureaucratic rules in these departments that adversely affects student-teacher relations. The result is that the effects of the bureaucratic structure completely offset the direct effect of the teacher's discipline on the manner in which he treats students.

Exactly the same pattern is evident when we examine the effects of school context on teacher-student relations. Teachers, regardless of their sex, experience, or tenure status appear to respond to lower-class students by attempting to personalize their instructional practices. The direct effect of this variable is .06. School administrators, on the other hand, respond to a lower-class clientele by increasing the instructional rules to which teachers are subject. It would appear then that the bureaucratic structure of the school then largely vitiates the efforts of teachers to respond to lower-class students.

The size of the school, as predicted, directly affects teacher-student relations. Teachers who are assigned to large schools are more impersonal with students. Also, larger schools are more bureaucratic with an attendant increase in impersonality. Such an effect may result in large part from the complexity of large schools offering several academic curricula and providing a large number of extracurricular activities for students since several other studies suggest that complexity rather than size accounts for increased bureaucracy (Terrien and Mills, 1955; Anderson and Warkov, 1961).

Conclusions

When one considers the general implications of these findings, it would appear that bureaucratic impersonality is a much more complex phenomenon than suggested in the literature on bureaucracy. Merton (1940), for example, views dysfunction within organizations as a consequence of the hierarchical demand for control. Rules and procedures are formulated in an attempt to ensure predictability of behavior. As a result, organizational members react to one another and to persons outside of the organization in terms of the specified rights and duties inherent in their positions; in other words, in a formal, impersonal stereotyped manner. Emphasis is transferred from the goals of the organization to the means of attaining them, which results in a means-ends inversion.

The findings of this study support Merton's theory. Bureaucratic structure, in particular instructional rules, were found to have a direct effect upon the relationships established between junior high school teachers and their students. An increase in bureaucracy resulted in more impersonal treatment of students. Teachers responded to the increased control over the performance of their classroom duties by spending less time with individual students and by adopting more universalistic criteria in grading students. Bureaucracy with its adverse effect on teacher-student relations appears to be, at least in part, a function of characteristics of the teacher as well as of the school. Female teachers were found to be subject to more rules than their male colleagues. Also, more bureaucratic constraints were imposed on nontenured teachers than on tenured teachers. In both instances this resulted in less personalized instruction.

Also, as the school grows in size its bureaucratic structure changes. Larger schools were found to be more bureaucratized and consequently exercised a deleterious effect on teacher-student relations. A far more significant finding is the effect of the composition of the student body on its bureaucratic structure. Schools that enrolled students from predominantly lower-class homes were found to be more bureaucratized. Teachers were found to be subject to more instructional rules than their colleagues. The resultant impersonal treatment of students largely offset the tendency of teachers in these schools to adopt a more individualized instructional approach with children from lower-class families. Professional-client relations also appear to be a function of the sex of the professional, the substantive nature of his professional activity, the size of the organization, and the background of the clients served by the organization.

The first of these variables is definitely related to teacher impersonality. This is evidenced by the impersonality scores of male teachers that are significantly higher than those of their female counterparts. Differences between male and female teachers in interest, attitudes, temperament, and expectations is a major determinant of the degree of individualized instruction. In general, female teachers are much more likely to make an attempt to assist individual students and to consider personal factors in grading. For a number of reasons, women appear to become more personally and emotionally involved and demonstrate more empathy for students than do males in the junior high school.

Since it has been ascertained that female teachers are much less prone to impersonal stereotyped behavior in instruction, it might be suggested that the personality, temperament, background, and experience of an individual may be important factors in the degree of personal interest that he shows in dealing with those served by the organization. Sex as well as emotional and psychological factors may be important determinants of an individual's proclivity toward impersonal treatment of clients of the organization. Since no attempt has been made to determine other characteristics of the persons involved in the research, this discussion is entirely speculative but suggests that the relation of psychological factors, attitudes, and background characteristics of organizational participants to the degree of impersonal behavior that they manifest should be examined in future research. These factors may be as important in determining behavior as organizational constraints imposed on the individual.

Furthermore, although the degree of impersonality appears to be directly related to the substantive activity carried on by the organizational participants, it appears to be a less significant factor than the three factors previously mentioned, at least in the schools. Teachers in science departments are significantly lower on the index of impersonality than other teachers. In this case, differences in sex, experience, or tenure status between the departments cannot account for this finding. Consequently, this finding must be largely the result of intrinsic departmental differences.

Generally, this finding would suggest that professional recruitment, training, expectations, and practices all profoundly influence a person's disposition toward the organization's clients. An impersonal attitude toward clients may be indigenous to certain professions and certain subgroups within broader professions. The validity of this hypothesis, in general, can only be ascertained by comparing various professional groups and subgroups outside of the educational profession.

Impersonality was also found to be related to the background of the clientele served by the organization. If the socioeconomic level of the school is considered, it is found to be related to the proportion of teachers whose scores are high on the index of impersonality. Teachers assigned to schools serving lower-class neighborhoods had the lowest scores on this index.

Earlier this finding had been tentatively accounted for in terms of the empathy and dedication of the teachers in dealing with disadvantaged students. However, it has wider implications for the theory of bureaucracy that has consistently viewed dysfunction as being an outgrowth of organizational constraints.

Environmental factors may occasion organizational dysfunction to a much greater extent than is recognized. The subtle interaction of clientele with lower participants of an organization appears to shape attitudes and the degree of individualized attention afforded people outside of the formal organization. In the present study of the behavior of school teachers, it was learned that socioeconomic status is directly related to this dysfunctional element but in a manner that can only be explained in terms of the empathy between teachers and students. This relationship, an inverse one since the lower the socioeconomic status the more personalized is the attention accorded students, may be peculiar to organizations dealing with youth. Conceivably, an entirely opposite relationship may hold in other types of organizations. A comparative study might prove or disprove this notion.

Moreover, the impact on organizational behavior of the clientele served by other organizations needs to be examined. Possibly environmental factors, such as the gap between the social and economic levels of organizational members and clients, the heterogeneity of the group served by the organization, the urgency of the organizational task as perceived by employees, the degree of emotional involment of participants, and the effect of these factors on the complexity of the organization's substantive activity, may be related to the degree to which organizational participants attempt to personalize relations with those persons that the organization serves.

Finally, the size of the organization also has proven to be related to impersonalized behavior of subordinates. As the organization grows in size teachers score higher on the impersonality index. Here again, it is not clear whether the important factor is size per se or one or more of the variables that are concomitant with size, such as frequency of contact with other organizational members, number of contacts with clients, degree of supervision, complexity of activity, diversity of goals, and heterogeneity of clientele. All of these organizational characteristics vary with the size of the organization that, in turn, appears to be related to the degree of impersonalized behavior manifest by participants. At this point it can only be pointed out that additional research is badly needed to unscramble the true effect of organizational size from that of these other variables.

If these findings concerning bureaupathology are borne out by research in other types of organizations, it will be necessary to modify the accepted notions as to the causes of dysfunction in organizations and to include professional background and psychological makeup of the individual members, substantive nature of the organizational endeavor, size of the organization, and environmental factors that affect the relationship between organizational members and clients, in addition to bureaucratic structure.

REFERENCES

ANDERSON, J. G. *Bureaucracy in Education.* Baltimore, Maryland: The Johns Hopkins University Press, 1968.

ANDERSON, T. R. and S. WARKOV. "Organizational Size and Functional Complexity." *American Sociological Review,* 26 (1961), 23–28.

BECKER, H. S. "The Career of the Chicago Public School Teacher." *American Journal of Sociology,* 57 (1952), 470–477.

BENDIX, R. "Bureaucracy: The Problem and Its Setting." *American Sociological Review,* 12 (1947), 493–507.

DUNCAN, O. D. "Path Analysis: Sociological Examples." *American Journal of Sociology,* 72 (1966), 1–16.

GOULDNER, A. W. *Patterns of Industrial Bureaucracy.* New York: The Free Press, 1954.

•LAND, K. C. "Principles of Path Analysis." in E. F. Borgatta (ed.) *Sociological Methodology.* San Francisco: Jossey-Bass, Inc., Publishers, 1969, pp. 3–37.

MERTON, R. K. "Bureaucratic Structure and Personality." *Social Forces,* 17 (1940), 560–568.

SELZNICK, P. "Foundation of the Theory of Organization." *American Sociological Review,* 13 (1948), 25–35.

TERRIEN, F. W. and D. L. MILLS. "The Effects of Changing Size upon the Internal Structure of Organizations." *American Sociological Review,* **20** (1955), 11–13.

WEBER, M. *The Theory of Social and Economic Organization,* trans. A. M. Henderson and T. Parsons. New York: Oxford University Press, 1947,. p. 68.

IO

IN *the literature concerned with organizational analysis, there are three major focuses of concern, the organization itself (the "formal" structure), various groupings of the incumbents (the "behavioral" structure), and the concrete individual. Almost any theoretical treatment of organizational phenomena takes these factors into consideration, and yet certain views will emphasize one or the other or combinations of these.*

Golembiewski, for example, within an O and M framework (Organization and Method) emphasizes the small group.[1] *In so doing, he refers to the behavioral organization in terms of groups of incumbents—the "small group." The function of this group is assumed to be based on some kinds of cohesive identification. States Golembiewski:*

> *the small group could complement the technical organization by providing control in areas into which the technical organization has not been extended . . . by providing affiliation and affection for its members, can make them more secure.*
> *(it) can lay claim to a substantial importance in organizations (and) is a universal element of the "informal organization" which develops within any formal organization. Thus the small group has been called one of the by-products of any attempt at coordinated human behavior.*[2]

Certainly there can be no question of the importance of the work group and one needs only to remember the work of Mayo and his associates for proof. There are also aspects of the relationship of the individual to his group affiliations within the organization as well as to the organization's goals and expectations, (and even to societal values and norms) that to some extent govern or influence all of these and tend to complicate analysis. Not the least of such "other" factors is the personality of the individual. It was an emphasis on this dimension that led Getzels to examine human behavior in a social-process sense in organizational analysis. Getzels was concerned, in a sense, with the focuses of the individual on the one hand and both the small group and the organizational structure on the other.[3]

The "nomothetic" dimension of the Getzels-Guba scheme actually includes aspects of what the "group" might expect of the role of any organizational incumbent as well as what the organization, as an apersonal system, might expect. For if the "role" is defined by the "institution," then the latter

---

1 Robert T. Golembiewski, *Behavior and Organization: O & M and the Small Group* (Chicago: Rand McNally & Co., 1962).

2 Ibid., pp. 97–98.

3 See, Jacob Getzels, "A Psycho-sociological Framework for the Study of Educational Administration," *Harvard Educational Review* (Fall 1952), XXII, 235–246.

*obviously must include phenomena derived from both groups and structures.*4

Parsons has attempted to build all of these focuses into his general systems view. He has, however, been criticized for attempting so much that his reasoning often becomes overly complex and difficult to follow. Yet familiarity with Parsons's work makes much of the work of others more meaningful. His definition of "levels" of organization, of the "functions" they are expected to perform, and of the unique relationships they must mediate with reference to both the immediate and the remote environments in which they are embedded all lie not very far from the necessity of our attention when we are attempting to learn more about why things happen, explain them, and hopefully thereby be better able to predict what might happen next.

In all of this, of course, we in the social sciences are not yet close to a sophisticated codified knowledge. Kenneth Boulding reminds us of our "newness" when he observes:

> The full impact of the social sciences may not be felt for a hundred years simply because we are still so far from any really adequate knowledge process in the study of the whole sociosphere. Our sampling system is imperfect to the point of being embarrassing; we have no centralized information collection and processing; we operate in bits and pieces, by lights and flashes, and there is up to now no steady process of cumulation, prediction, and feedback in the sociosphere as a whole.5

The essential problem with which we are dealing in educational administration and with organizational life wherever it occurs is fundamentally the dilemma of authority and freedom. In large measure, we have dealt with that dilemma by studying a variety of problems that are inherent in the conflicts between the individual and the organization. That is implicit in Golembiewski's concern with the "formal organization" and the "behavioral organization"; with Getzels's and Guba's "idiographic-nomothetic" model, and is implicit in most other analyses.

Clearly, the conditions within organizations or within the larger social system that impinge on these concerns for the person and the system can also be treated in terms of the nature of the goals and means involved at either level— that of person or organization. This seems so apparent that it need not be said. Yet, the issue of goals and their pursuit constitutes either an explicit or implicit aspect of most of our theorizing about the problems of organizations and human behavior within them. Consequently, in the following article, I have attempted to deal with two dimensions of the goals-and-means conceptualization: first in an examination of the ways alienation, or anomie, occurs within that context and, second, a treatment of the relaionship of goals-and-means to the cultural structure itself. These issues, treated either broadly or more molecularly, are essential in the development of a "feeling" for what Boulding has labeled the "sociosphere." We continue to strive for a (not yet, certainly the) frame of reference for fitting in some of our own bits and pieces.

4 For one of the best and most succinct treatments of the Getzels-Guba work, see R. F. Campbell, J. E. Corbally, Jr., and J. A. Ramseyer, *Introduction to Educational Administration*, 2nd ed. (Boston: Allyn & Bacon, Inc., 1962), pp. 182–209.

5 Kenneth Boulding, *The Impact of the Social Sciences* (New Brunswick, N.J.: Rutgers University Press, 1966), p. 20.

ANOMIE AND CULTURE STRUCTURE IN SCHOOL SYSTEMS

William G. Monahan

Anderson, in his concluding comments in the previous chapter, observed that not only were very large schools more bureaucratized but that when schools enrolled a student body drawn largely from predominantly lower socioeconomic strata, the tendency toward bureaucratization and impersonality was even more pronounced.

This observation serves as an important point of departure for some consideration of two different, but related "sets" of conceptualizations. On the one hand, I want to provide some discussion of certain aspects of the *idea* of alienation within the context of the institutionalized and bureaucratized school organization; leading from that, I want also to deal with a kind of anthropological system, which, although the term may be somewhat inexact, I nevertheless refer to as "the Malinowski model."

In order to set the stage for my point of view, I deal, for the purposes of descriptive example, with conditions contributing to alienation in large city school systems. I am convinced that *size* is less impacting as a variable in the propensity toward organizational alienation than many of us have tended to assume. As Anderson so incisively noted, size *seems* the likely suspect but there are other *unobtrusive* variables that suggest that "size" is somewhat deceptive. In fact, it is just as likely that size is merely a convenient *ex post factum* explanation and thus has impressive plausibility. Consequently, other variables such as those referred to by Anderson are obscured.

On the contrary, similar alienating syndromes have been observed in smaller schools and organizations for which without doubt size, as a convenient explanation, is altogether without substance. Increasing intensification as a result of size a direct tendency for accelerating alienation and also for compounding it. But size alone is not the major factor, for there are entirely too many exceptions. Large schools, ranging toward two thousand plus students, provided they are located in reasonably "well-off" suburban areas, seem to function with relatively little anomie vis-à-vis the typically expected frequencies to which we have become accustomed in such large indoctrinational organizations. The sociocultural environment is thus a significant factor.

Although my comments, therefore, are directed to alienation largely within the frame of reference of the large inner-city school system and clearly within certain boundaries peculiar to such large structures, one should be aware that the generally chaotic sociological conditions that

wherein they can excuse their rejection of the pupils by blaming the dehumanizing factors in the organization and in the external environment. In this fashion a form of intersystem equilibrium is created that could be described as intercultural symbiosis. Admittedly naïve, this analysis suggests some directions for more rigorous examination.

The nature of the disorganizing influences in the central city are well documented. In general, empirical findings are predominantly concerned with low-status persons but it is this stratum around which the most critical school problems cluster.

With reference to low-status persons, the social stratification literature strongly suggests that poverty is almost a closed culture. Evidence indicates that friendship patterns, spouse selection, geographical mobility, and extensiveness of interests are well confined among low-status persons.[7] Moreover, analysis of group memberships has disclosed that without exception, in every type of group there is less membership on the part of low-status persons.[8] As another example, a number of ecological studies—those by Farris and Dunham,[9] Green,[10] Mowrer,[11] Shroeder,[12] and Hadley[13]—all disclosed that when one considers the distribution of mental disorders, higher rates are concentrated in the centers of cities with declining rates toward the edges of cities. There is no reason to assume that these studies are not still valid. An interesting study by Clark and his associates examined psychoses rates in terms of occupational groups.[14] They recognized the fact that a disorganized environment is highly likely to affect persons in terms of the strength and nature of the disorganization, and although all persons do not react to such influences in the environment, the fact remains that where there is a greater proportion of such disorganizing factors there will be a greater proportion of persons who are adversely affected by them. But they went further than that; they assumed that different occupational groups would also differ regarding certain traits that would have some bearing on the likelihood of their becoming psychotic. A salesman, for example, might be "put together" in some way that would make him either more or less likely

7 Genevieve Knupfer, "Portrait of the Underdog," *Public Opinion Quarterly*, **XI** (1947), pp. 103–114.

8 Ibid.

9 R. E. L. Farris and H. W. Dunham, "Mental Disorders in Urban Areas," cited in Robert E. Clark "Psychoses, Income, and Occupational Prestige," *American Journal of Sociology*, vol. 14 (March, 1949), pp. 433–440.

10 H. W. Green, "Persons Admitted to Cleveland State Hospital," cited in Clark, Ibid.

11 E. Mowrer, "A Study of Personal Disorganization," *American Sociological Review*, IV, Aug. 1939 39, pp. 475–487. Cited in Clark, op. cit.

12 C. W. Shroeder, "Mental Disorders in Cities," *American Journal of Sociology* (July 1942), pp. 40–47. Cited in Clark, op. cit.

13 E. Hadley et al., "Military Psychiatry: An Ecological Note," *Psychiatry*, **VII** (November 1944), pp. 379–407.

14 Robert E. Clark, op. cit.

to become psychotic than, say, a lawyer or a garage mechanic or a stenographer. They point out that: "The psychoses rates for native-white and foreign white males show that in general the low rates are found in occupations having high prestige and high income, while the high rates are found in occupations having low prestige and low income."[15]

The point to be made, very simply, is that the low-status person seems to function in a condition of sociocultural isolation; he reinforces this through a kind of voluntary perpetuation of these conditions. It was this kind of isolation, internalized in the low-status person to which C. C. North referred forty years ago when he said that low status: "limits the sources of information which retards the development of efficiency in judgment and reasoning abilities, and confine(s) the attention to the more trivial interests of life."[16]

There is at least some logical similarity between assessments of low-status culture and bureaucratic orientation in large organizations. Consider Thompson's description of the latter:

The bureaucratic orientation is conservative. Novel solutions, using resources in a new way, are likely to appear threatening. Those having a bureaucratic orientation are more concerned with the internal distribution of power and status than with organizational goal accomplishment. This converts the organization into a political system concerned with the distribution of these extrinsic rewards.[17]

Thomson suggests, however, that other things promote provincialism in the organization beyond this concern with the internal deployment of power and status. Again, there is a striking similarity to the kind of conditions that characterize low-status socioeconomic strata. Thompson states:

there are other factors which strengthen tendencies toward parochialism. The organization seems to factor its activities into narrow single-purpose, exclusive categories and assign these to sub-units composed of superior and subordinates. Very often strong sub-units and sub-goal identifications arise from this pattern so that members of any unit know and care little about what other units are doing.[18]

Finally, there is some reason to believe that the big city teacher's internalization of feelings of frustration regarding the organization on the one hand, and inadequacies of technical competence in dealing with low-status pupils on the other, may lead to an almost pathological guilt complex. Bonney points out that:

[15] Ibid., p. 435.
[16] C. C. North, *Social Differentiation* (Chapel Hill: University of North Carolina Press), 1927, p. 247.
[17] Victor A. Thompson, op. cit., p. 7.
[18] Ibid., p. 8.

guilt feelings demand some kind of punishment, which in lieu of any form of external punishment generally eventuates in some kind of self-punishment such as working unnecessarily long hours at tedious tasks, putting up with unfavorable working conditions that could be changed, and leading restricted and self-denying lives.[19]

It is likely, however, that the behaviors that Bonney describes do not characterize the big city teacher any more than they do the teacher in smaller metropolitan communities. In the big city, the teacher is more likely to have become disillusioned regarding the general "status" that teaching was thought to provide and has responded more in terms of what he interprets the *particular organization* expects of him rather than of what the *institution of education* expects. Contributing to this condition is the greater social isolation that the teacher confronts in the large, anonymous city. It provides him greater freedom from the traditional imposition of a highly constraining "teacher morality" but its price is indifference to his status.

Organizational Anomie and Information Structures

The foregoing discussion suggests that teachers in very large school systems (and particularly those in the old large cities) are characterized by what Merton refers to as "simple" anomie. He distinguished between "simple" and "acute" anomie as follows:

Simple anomie refers to the state of confusion in a group or society which is subject to conflict between value systems, resulting in some degree of uneasiness and a sense of separation from the group; acute anomie, to the deterioration and, at the extreme, the disintegration of value-systems, which results in marked anxieties.[20]

Merton postulates a typology of response patterns to anomic conditions based on the dichotomization of culturally sanctioned goals and socially acceptable means for their achievement.[21] His discussion of that mode

---

[19] M. E. Bonney, *Mental Health in Education* (Boston: Allyn & Bacon, Inc., 1960), p. 399.

[20] R. K. Merton, *Social Theory and Social Structure* (New York: The Free Press, 1957), rev. edit., p. 163.

[21] The five types of adaptation schematically presented by Merton; in this scheme, (+) signifies acceptance; (−) signifies rejection; and (±) represents "rejection of prevailing values and substitution of new values."

MODES OF ADAPTATION	CULTURAL GOALS	INSTITUTIONALIZED MEANS[a]
I. Conformity	+	+
II. Innovation	+	−
III. Ritualism	−	+
IV. Retreatism	−	−
V. Rebellion	±	±

[a] R. K. Merton, *Social Theory and Social Structure* (New York: The Free Press, 1957), rev. ed., p. 140. Used with Permission.

of adaptation, which he calls "ritualism," is particularly reminiscent of Thompson's previously cited description of "desk classes." (See p. 9.) Merton states:

The syndrome of the social ritualist is both familiar and instructive. His implicit life-philosophy finds expression in a series of cultural clichés: "I'm not sticking my neck out," "I'm playing safe," "I'm satisfied with what I've got," "Don't aim high and you won't be disappointed." The theme threaded through these attitudes is that high ambitions invite frustration and danger whereas lower aspirations produce satisfaction and security.[22]

I am not willing to assert that big city teachers are necessarily characterized by ritualist modes of adaptation to anomie more so than by other response patterns. I am suggesting that anomie reflects the chaotic factor in big city schools if, for no other reasons, by virtue of the fact that anomie-generating factors more clearly characterize the big city itself.

Under any circumstances, the need to re-examine the social systems and organizational correlates of schools wherever they are found is clearly apparent. Although the present state of theory and methodology might not be all we should like for mounting the kind of penetrating analysis that is required, it nevertheless constitutes a level of sophistication that encourages the initiation of such an attempt. It is my contention that there is a qualitative dimension to aspects of system equilibrium that deserves more rigorous analysis from those interested in educational administrative theory. If we can refer to an organizational system as "open," then we are implicitly assigning a positive quality to the system. If, on the other hand, a system can be described as "closed," it is clearly of a negative quality in this context. There is a third condition, perhaps, which may be characterized as neutral equilibrium, whereby a system is in process of "moving toward" either clear-cut positive or negative status. These states of system-balance are roughly correlative with Merton's responses to anomie. If a system could be characterized by measuring "levels" of anomie, then "conformity" and "innovation" might be hypothesized as characterizing open/positive systems, whereas "ritualism" and "retreatism" would characterize closed/negative systems, and "rebellion" would characterize a neutral-dynamic system. The latter could not be assigned to either open or closed status because the degree of interchange at the boundaries of such a system would be fragmented. As stated previously, such a system would be in some stage of "becoming."

It seems reasonable that the theoretical position of Halpin and his associates in the development of the Organizational Climate Description Questionnaire (OCDQ) is similar in many respects to this point of

[22] Ibid., p. 150.

view.[23] The six climates that the Halpin work postulated do not fit the positive/negative/neutral categorization scheme as neatly as do Merton's response patterns to anomie but there is still something of a correspondence. We can consider Open, Autonomous, and Familiar climates as positive (although admittedly of varying degrees thereof), whereas Controlled, Paternal, and Closed climates can be categorized as negative. There are no climates that specifically fall into the neutral category. Yet, it is possible that this quality of "becomingness" about neutral systems is precisely the source of the difficulty that vexed Halpin and his associates in dealing with the concept of "authenticity."[24] In a phenomenological sense, "authenticity" as defined by Halpin, can *only* be brought into question in circumstances in which the incumbents or organizations are in some acute stage of internalizing new values that are themselves products of the interaction of personality, culture, and social system. Aspects of this same process represent a major focus in the equilibrium theories of such people as Festinger (cognitive dissonance,[25]); Newcomb (co-orientation toward X,[26]); Heider (balance states,[27]); and Osgood, Suci, and Tannenbaum (the principle of congruity,[28]). I do not deal with particular analysis of these views here, but they are intimately concerned with social judgment, attitude formation, and interpersonal perception, all of which constitute important aspects of personhood. What is imperative has not to do merely with our need to know more about the humanizing and dehumanizing factors that permeate school systems; we know a lot about that already. What we need to know more about is the *operational* conditions within which such factors are activated and the particular relationships of organizational to ideographic variables that somehow continue to generate them. In large measure, the work of Halpin and his associates moved us substantially in that direction. Unfortunately, the manageability of the OCDQ confines researchers to the elementary schools. Beyond that, the control of variables become too unmanageable for reliable treatment.

Even were it possible to exercise tighter measures within the complex structures of the more mobile patterns characterized by departmentalized secondary schools, the difficulty would not be close to resolution because

[23] A. H. Halpin, *Theory and Research in Administration* (New York: Macmillan Publishing Co., Inc., 1966).

[24] Ibid., p. 216.

[25] Leon Festinger, *A Theory of Cognitive Dissonance* (New York: Harper & Row, Publishers, Inc., 1957).

[26] Theodore Newcomb, *Social Psychology* (New York: Holt, Rinehart and Winston, Inc., 1950).

[27] Fritz Heider, *A Psychology of Interpersonal Relations* (New York: John Wiley & Sons, Inc., 1958).

[28] C. Osgood, et al., *The Measurement of Meaning* (New York: The Free Press, 1957).

the extent to which the immediate (much less, the remote) environment comes into function, is not incorporated either in the models currently available or in the assumptions on which they are based. It is this problem that Bennis gives attention to in his following article, which is concerned with the issue of the integration of persons and organizations.

Some Catching Up

As has been pointed out repeatedly in this book, any attempt to conceptualize, measure, predict, or otherwise deal with human behavior in organizational (or any other) situations—in other words to develop theory about such behaviors—must begin with the assumption that the broad concepts of personality, culture, and social system are interacting.

Where some particular scheme about any aspect of such conditions is posited with reference to these broad categories—or specialized variables that might represent linear descendants of any one of them—the others are implied. In such cases it is no great task to discern the implicitness of the other broad categories even though either, or both, may not be the essential concern of the moment. The point is simply that if a model or theory focuses on social system, for example, personality and culture lie lurking very near that surface.

Consider the previous discussion of alienation. Alienation may be viewed in innumerable ways but at the heart of that concept is the simple idea that one is "turned" in some way. Now he may be turned in peculiar ways; some may be turned "inward," whereas others may simply change the direction of their valences. Karen Horney once characterized a typology of patterns of response to other persons by pointing out that some people move *toward* other people, others *against* them, and still others *away from* them. These were distinctly *interpersonal* patterns. By the same token, personalities may move toward, against, or away from *social structures*. That is, institutions, such as organizations, businesses, and schools may have appeal and challenge, but, may generate hostility or apathy for others. The same is true of certain specifically cultural factors such as values, traditions, ritual, or similar ideas that are more to be associated with the particular *patterns* of institutional expectations (that is, *culture*) than with either social systems or personality per se. But in none of these cases is it distinctly possible to separate any one of the major categories for each and all in combination are brought to bear. Alienation then may be seen as a turning-away-from.

That may seem an almost trite observation; yet it represents a major idea in the study of organizational theory. When one adds the notions of time, and space (territoriality), one has the basic ingredients for any study of human conditions.

The importance of alienation in the affairs of mankind is, therefore, only one avenue of departure for analysis. As Merton has suggested in his treatment of this aspect of social structure, time is an important implication. If one is concerned with the "belief" in some normative goal (the good life, let's say), he must also make some choices regarding how that goal shall be pursued. To pursue the goal at all assumes time— time to become expert, time to "case the job" (if he chooses some "innovative" path to the goal), time to cultivate people with power if that is his alternative—in any case, the simple idea of moving-toward-the-achievement-of-a-goal is a temporal idea. By the same token, the pursuit of a goal or end requires some access and perhaps control over territorial conditions. It requires access to the "tools of the trade" and thus, artifacts have certain spatial connotations; it requires access to the special *spaces* or spatial components essential to pursuit—to buildings, offices, streets, fields, factories, schools, and so forth. Finally, it requires access to the particular institutional structures that the society or some subset of society has developed for governing the normative processes of that movement-toward-goal. These institutional structures are operationally defined by a whole variety of social systems—or organizations, associations, and coteries—which specify generally accepted behaviors. And even in those cases in which some *deviant* responses are chosen, those also have their own norms and organizational correlates. Moreover, if one decides that both the goals and the means toward their achievement are unacceptable (rebellion), the ultimate consequence of the "new order" will obviously require the *institutionalization* of the substitute goals and means if that "new" order is to have any chance of survival. The new goals and the appropriate means for pursuing them will require internalization by those involved. Although this internalization may come about in the immediate postrevolutionary period largely as a consequence of commitment and zeal, it can no more be sustained over time by such enthusiasm than can the antiestablishment changes initiated by charismatic authority. Systems of indoctrination must usually be actuated and commitment must be reinforced with both policies and procedures that assure conformity to the norms of the new order.

This is a familiar pattern to be sure but its repetition in organizations below the societal level are not so apparent. That is the case simply because the extent and the intensiveness of *institutionalization* is so pervasive.

Goffman has referred to some such organizations as "total." He states:

The central feature of total institutions can be described as a breakdown of the barriers ordinarily separating these three spheres of life. First, all aspects of life are conducted in the same place and under the same single authority. Second, each phase of the member's daily activity is carried on in the immediate company of a large number of others, all of whom are treated alike and required to do the same thing together. Third, all phases of the day's activities are tightly scheduled, with one activity leading at a prearranged time into the next, and the whole sequence . . . imposed from above. . . .[29]

Compared to prisons, mental hospitals, monasteries, and convents, schools are clearly not "total" organizations. Yet, to the extent that dependence upon rather explicit formality, as reflected in bureaucratic rules, becomes progressively more pervasive, the incumbents of such organizations will exhibit behaviors that are also characteristic of conditions wherein "breakdowns of barriers" between the three spheres of life, referred to by Goffman, seem likely.

Bureaucratic Isolation

Clearly, there is a relationship between the anomic condition and isolation. But, here, my frame of reference is a little different from that generally defined as a mode of response wherein one is somewhat apart-from the societal norm; in other words, as Seeman has suggested, "Those who . . . assign low reward value to goals or beliefs that are typically highly valued in the given society."[30]

This context is typically that of the intellectual who is not only "apart-from" but "above" the normative societal system. This form of alienation clearly leads to what Merton refers to as the "innovator" and, Seeman maintains, to the "rebel" responses as well.

I refer to it differently in the bureaucratic sense and see it more related to a kind of meaninglessness. When one finds himself caught up in an almost oppressive standardization and the depersonalizing environment of highly redundant bureaucratic systems, there is a tendency to feel identification with the "lonely crowd." Instead of a weakening of collective standards, these are merely routinized and consequently not only strengthened thereby, but the condition of "normlessness" becomes curiously a condition of norm-*full*-ness. Norms thus do not emerge as patterns of individual behavior but of quite *rigid* organizational expectations that are continually reinforced by the organizational incumbents' willingness to abide by and gradually depend upon them. One's behavior day-by-day is increasingly automatic. His "pace" is highly predictable. Isolation is thus a consequence of the conformity imposed by the system and reinforced as the individual acquiesces to it.

My reference here is not so much to the "bureaucrat." Such a person usually enjoys some level of control by virtue of a status within the hierarchy no matter how minor it may be. The reference instead is to

---

[29] Erving Goffman, "On the Characteristics of Total Organizations: The Inmate World," in D. R. Cressey (ed.), *The Prison, Studies in Institutional Organization and Change* (New York: Holt, Rinehart and Winston, Inc., 1961), p. 17.

[30] Melvin Seeman, "On the Meaning of Alienation," in L. A. Coser and B. Rosenberg, *Sociological Theory* (London: Collier Macmillan, Ltd., 1969), p. 518.

those of largely similar status and role who function at what Parsons refers to as the "technical level" of organization. In schools, these would be teachers, but teachers are still somewhat different from, say, office workers.

Accordingly, tendencies toward anomie among teachers are somewhat mitigated by two other conditions—professionalism and collectivization. These, interestingly, are also somewhat anomalous. That is, the conditions and attitudes that tend to reinforce and sustain the professional orientation of the teacher are diluted by other conditions and attitudes that tend to reinforce and sustain militant collectivization. I deal only briefly with these for the purpose of returning to a consideration of organizational size as an intervening variable.

Regardless of the scope of a school organization or of the general style of management—harsh and dictatorial, or open and nondirective—many aspects of the particular situation that might otherwise promote forms and degrees of alienation are effectively softened by the quasiprofessional character of the role. Since teaching claims allegiance to outside reference groups, requires extensive and license-monitoring pre-entry preparation, and has some definitive aspects of a professional/client role system, it is characterized by a professional orientation. But unlike the physician whose professional competence cannot be judged very well by a layman because the latter has little rational basis for such assessments,[31] teachers are so judged as a matter of legalized policy—appointed and assessed as a matter of course by lay boards of education. Obviously, this function is typically delegated to professional managers but the distance between lay opinion and professional performance is rather narrow. Thus, to some extent the professional *orientation* may be real but the professional *status* is largely mythical. Consider, for example, the following comments:

Students of the professions have pointed out that the autonomy granted to professionals who are basically responsible to their consciences (though they may be censured by their peers and in extreme cases by the courts) is necessary for effective professional work. Only if immune from ordinary social pressures and free to innovate, to experiment, to take risks without the usual social repercussions of failure, can a professional carry out his work effectively.[32]

Does that describe the schoolteacher? On the contrary, teaching is far more consonant with "administrative" rather than "professional" authority. In the former, ". . . the ultimate justification of an administrative act . . . is that it is in line with the organization's rules and regulations and that it has been approved . . . by a superior rank."[33] In many re-

---

[31] Amitai Etzioni, *Modern Organizations* (Englewood Cliffs, N.J.: Prentice-Hall, Inc., 1964), p. 65.

[32] Ibid., p. 76.

[33] Ibid., p. 77.

spects, the "fixed-role" model is more descriptive of the teacher.[34] This view assumes that regardless of outside reference groups, the organization itself is the single definer of functions. Persons entering the system need only know what the existing role patterns and status performances are as determined by the organization or its immediate managers. Clearly, numbers of such employees do not fit this set of assumptions whether in schools, large or small, or in other types of bureaucratic structure. These persons, indeed, do look "outside" the organization for certain ways of performing their roles. But the cost of this to the organizations' tolerance for other than minimal disturbance is such that the professionally oriented person can become a problem. In a study by Haga and his associates that investigated aspects of professional orientation in a typically bureaucratic organization, this proved to be the case:

"supervisors made clear distinctions among their subordinates about the forms and extent of supervisory attention they required. Apparently, they made these along the lines of their subordinates' professional orientation for all eight leadership issues . . . supervisors indicated that *the high professional subordinates required more attention than the low.* [35] (Italics added)

It should also be mentioned, however, that when a span of time was examined—a period of almost a year—the professionally oriented managers in the Haga study were actually *shaping* both the role as well as the role-expectations of supervisors. In other words, the "highly" professionally oriented subordinates were working longer hours, assuming more responsibility, and so forth, and, as a consequence, participated more in policy-formulation, achieved more autonomy over their work, and engaged more in planning and communicating behaviors. These were not only substantially different from similar activities by "low" professionally oriented managers but, after nine months on the job, their supervisors apparently expected them to behave that way! Thus, according to Haga and his associates, "Once these managers entered their new role situations, the supervisor's ideas of what they ought to be doing became a function of what they were doing."[36] We do not know from this study the extent, if any, that these role-making behaviors on the part of more professionally oriented managers resulted in different expectations of supervisors for the less professionally oriented managers. Nor do we have any information as to whether the opposite was the case for low professional-oriented managers. That is, did those managers who generally accepted and followed the fixed-role model tend to also

34 See Robert Kahn, et al., *Organizational Stress* (New York: John Wiley & Sons, Inc., 1964).

35 W. J. Haga, George Graen, and Fred Dansereau, Jr., "Professionalism and Role Making in a Service Organization: A Longitudinal Investigation," *American Sociological Review*, 39:1, Feb., 1974, pp. 127–128.

36 Ibid., p. 131.

thereby shape that role-expectation such that their supervisors also came to expect them to perform *that* way? One gets the feeling from the reported study that such is indeed the case. Again, it would seem that conformity and acquiescence to it is reinforcing.

The problem itself is a familiar one to students of organizational analysis. Argyris, for example, has based much of his work on the conflicts—real and presumed—that result from the dilemma of organizational demands for passive conformity and the individual's needs for variety and change in his work.[37]

A particularly appropriate study of this problem with reference to schools and teachers and of special relevance to these comments was conducted by Ronald Corwin.[38]

Corwin takes that curious anomaly that I stated earlier, namely, professionalism and collectivization, and constructs a general working hypothesis to the effect that the tensions arising from the professional/employee dichotomy in schools moves professionalism toward a *militant* process. He developed scales of items relating to both "professionalism" and "bureaucratic" role expectations and administered these to 284 teachers in seven secondary schools. The schools were both large (one hundred and twenty teachers) and small (nine teachers). Corwin's professionalism scale included sixteen items judged to be appropriate to several significant concepts: for example, centralization, standardization, and specialization. Certain *dimensions* of these concepts constituted the item selection and these, in turn, constituted subscales.[39]

In addition to analysis of the scale data, Corwin also randomly selected teachers for interviews regarding incidents of friction involving themselves or other staff. What he found was that the higher the mean of professional orientation, the higher was the rate of conflicts. He states:

The seven schools were grouped into three categories on the basis of their rank or mean professional orientation (2-high, 3-middle, and 2-low schools). The two high ranked schools (combined) reported a rate of open or heated discussions or major incidents per interview several times as great as that of the low-ranked schools. . . . The reverse also tended to be true; schools with higher rates of conflict had higher mean professional scores than schools with lower professional orientations.[40]

37 Chris Argyris, *Personality and Organization* (New York: Harper & Row, Publishers, Inc., 1957), pp. 50–51. See the Bennis article that follows.

38 Ronald Corwin, "Professional Persons in Public Organizations," in W. Lane, R. Corwin, and W. Monahan, op. cit., pp. 401–421.

39 The subscales were *Employee orientation*—administrative orientation, loyalty to organization, competence based on experience, interchangeability of personnel, standardization of work, stress on rules and procedures, and public orientation. *Professional Orientation*—Client orientation, orientation to profession and colleagues, competence based on monopoly of knowledge, decision-making authority, and control over work. Ibid., p. 420, note 25.

40 Ibid., p. 414.

in fact, defines *institution* as the organized types of activities generally to be clearly associated with the particular functions assignable to a set of related activities. It follows that each set of organized types of activities has a definite structure, and that all of this is *functional* by virtue of the fact that function is defined as response to a need. Malinowski states: "Function . . . can be defined as the satisfaction of an organic impulse by the appropriate act. Form and function, obviously, are inextricably related to one another. It is impossible to discuss the one without taking account of the other."[45]

Although in retrospect, Malinowski's obvious leaning toward biological analogy (generally attributed to the influence of Herbert Spencer, and reinforced by the work of his colleague Radcliffe-Brown) has brought his particular brand of "functionalism" into some contemporary contention,[46] his systematic analysis of the relationship of the institutional *ideal* and *real* is an impressive structural contribution. It is that contribution that I want to deal with here, for there is little question that it has useful application to educational administration.

The model proposed by Malinowski is now presented and explained.[47]

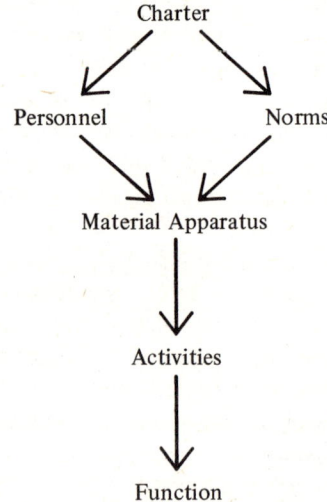

45 Bronislaw Malinowski, *A Scientific Theory of Culture and Other Essays* (Chapel Hill: University of North Carolina Press, 1944), p. 83.

46 See, e.g., Melville Jacobs, *Patterns of Cultural Anthropology* (Homewood, Ill.: Dorsey Press, 1964). Jacobs suggests of the biological or organismic frame of reference for "functionalism" that it stands, ". . . as an antique fallacy of analogic thinking . . ." and that both Radcliffe-Brown and Malinowski, ". . . toodled the same monotonous tune" (p. 32). Perhaps truth is more clearly perceived in 1964 than in 1920 or, at least, one can always look into the past with rather unobstructed vision.

47 Malinowski, op. cit., p. 53 ff.

The key to a fundamental understanding of this simple diagram has to do with the relationship between what we might like to have happen—the "ideal"—and what in fact actually does occur—the "real." This becomes clear when the particular elements of the scheme and the relationships among them are explained.

The "charter" of any organization or systematized social configuration specifies the system of values for the pursuit of which the thing is initiated in the first place. It is something like a constitution, although obviously certain aspects of a charter may or may not be formalized. In other words, the extent to which an organization is progressively institutionalized, or some legalistic definition of its legitimacy is clearly established, may have a bearing on the necessity for "putting-it-in-writing" so to speak, but a coterie (say, for example, an afternoon bridge group) has little compulsion to develop a formal statement of goals and values yet that does not mean that such a system of values is not implicitly presumed and explicitly pursued. In any case, the *charter* is an idealized definition of what *ought* to be accomplished and what *ought* to be accomplished obviously relates to some identifiable group of people—the personnel. In addition, this system of values must be operationally defined or structured in some fashion such that the prescriptions for pursuing these values are known to the personnel. This is usually determined in formal organizations by policies, regulations, and rules. In the institutional sense and for less formal social arrangements, the determination is by normative standards that are internalized by the personnel. Again, these norms or rules specify *ideal* behaviors or activities.

In any type of organized activity there must be some manner of interaction with the environment; there must be some manner of material apparatus for carrying out the rules in pursuit of the charter's ideals. Even a bridge group must have playing cards and scoring pads, and a surface for play.

The two last components, or perhaps I should say "bottom" components of the diagram, shift from what *ought* to be to what *is*. Just as the norms are designed to specify the particular behaviors that are appropriate and desirable, the *activities* are manifestations of reality. These represent what the personnel actually do. Finally, the *functions* represent the real or actual outcomes.

There is this kind of relationship between certain key components of this simple model: the functions are the *real* and demonstrative manifestations of the charter, and the activities are the *real* and demonstrative manifestations of the rules. The *charter* specifies what *ought* to happen and the *rules* specify rather precisely how it *ought* to happen; the activities on the other hand represent the way we actually go about the *doing* of "it" and the *functions* constitute the reality of the *results*.

Let us pose some theoretical postulates on the basis of this interesting model. These are presented as rather simplistic "if-then" statements.

1. *If* the activities deviate too far from the rules, *then* either the rules must be modified or the activities must be "brought into line" (whatever that might mean.)
2. *If* the functions, or outcomes, deviate too far from the system of values specified or otherwise internalized by virtue of the charter, *then* the functions must be either
   a. sanctioned, whereby the charter must be modified;
   b. restrained or otherwise inhibited such that the integrity of the charter is reasonably sustained.

What are the generalized consequences of these hypotheses? In the first place, Malinowski has shown us how change takes place over time. Moreover, he has provided us with a particularistic definition of organizational equilibrium. It clearly remains for research to provide us with definitive data for predicting whether the charter will be revised or whether the outcomes will be sanctioned; all the same a theoretical pattern is outlined. If some set of activities are such that deviation from the rules is so great (whatever that might ultimately mean) that some state of disequilibrium is manifest, then obviously something has to "give." Either the rules must be modified to accommodate the contemporary activities or the contemporary activities must somehow be brought into conformity with the rules. The same is obviously true of the functions—either the manifest functions, if they are clearly too deviant from the charter, must be brought back into conformity with the charter or the charter must somehow be revised to accommodate the deviance in outcomes. By and large, it is a reasonable generalization to assert that something of a compromise between these two extremes occurs. That is, certain activities and the functions that are a direct outgrowth of them are accommodated by appropriate revisions in both the charter and the norms such that deviations are reasonably well satisfied while at the same time these deviations are inhibited enough that neither the fundamental system of values nor the norms that constitute the behaviors related and derived from the charter are rendered nonfunctional thereby. Change occurs consequently more by evolutionary modification than by clear-cut revolutionary destruction, but even the latter is accounted for. Revolutionary behaviors may indeed occasionally occur but the interesting aspect of this process supports the observation that such events are atypical rather than normative. The ultimate risk of total revolution is that the persistent urge for the organization to survive is threatened. There is thus little argument with the notion that the overarching objective of organizations and institutions is for survival itself and anything that might be proposed that brings that very survival into issue can be as risky to the "rebel" as it is to the "ritualist."

As pointed out previously, an organization is a derived structural device for operationalizing and actualizing the institutionalization of some rather coherent system of values—education, religion, politics, or the like. The dismemberment of some particular organization does not imply that the institution it serves is also dismembered thereby; the institution leads a kind of separate existence. If it were possible to eliminate all currently constituted religious organizations—churches, denominations, synods, and theocratic systems—the fundamental necessity for some manner of metaphysical and religious orientation as a human/cultural universal would still remain and in order to service that "set" of cultural mandates, new patterns would undoubtedly emerge. These new patterns might not rely much or at all on previous definitions of values and process, but the abstract and analytical *functions* of some system of tenets involving ardor, conviction, devotion, and belief would continue to require adherence. One may turn from a belief in God to a belief in man, but that does not alter the necessity or the sociocultural function of belief itself.

Moreover, and this is important, there is also a systematic equilibrium, dynamic to be sure, that governs the relationships across and within the total institutional structure. Consider only the two institutions of religion and education. If it could be agreed that, among the hierarchy of values that abstractly defines the function of education in the life of man (and regardless of any particular organizational configurations that are designed to articulate it) that high in that system of values or "charter" is the notion that education is instituted in order to *prepare the young for assuming adult roles in the society*. Then as that statement of values is pursued and as whatever organizational configurations are initiated to promulgate it become progressively more refined, learning is brought to bear that may raise rather serious misgivings as to the logical consistency of accepted practice in those other institutionalized behaviors that define the appropriateness of religious activities. Some reasonably intelligent and energetic "student" with a potential for leadership in the society by virtue of his participation in the socialization process of education may one day stand in class and say, "Hey man, we can't get it all together and make some really effective progress as long as people continue to believe that whether they do or don't have a good crop this year is because they haven't paid proper homage to the Sun-god. I think on the basis of some things that I've learned here that the Sun-god is a myth. The problem is not the Sun-god; we haven't given enough appropriate reverence to the Rain-god." If that young person has a little charisma and enough energy, he might be able to get a group together who favor the Rain-god and thus a new sect is born. Either point of view may or may not be terribly functional for the pursuit of bountiful crops but in the process, a new point of view is progressively built in and the educational institutions of that culture will have to take that into account the "next time around."

Sometimes, a dramatic change in conditions that impinge on the charter, rules, activities, and functions of institutional and organizational systems can be almost accidental, or such dramatic changes may be due to the effectiveness of one or another of the institutions that altogether constitute the operational definition of a culture. But in any case, when such events occur, the total flavor on the society is affected. Charters are significantly revised in the face of insurmountable pressures of deviance from accepted patterns, and by virtue of that, "new orders" come about. In essence, that was the case in modern Western European society with the advent of the industrial and French revolutions as has been described in Part I by Nisbet. Perhaps a way of characterizing the patterns of this process of interinstitutional relationship is through providing a particular illustration from a simpler culture. The following is an account of some interesting changes that occurred in the culture of a group of people known as the Tanala. These are a hill people in western Madagascar, and the basic economic source of their subsistence until about two centuries ago was through the cultivation of dry rice. In order to pursue this pattern of subsistence, it was necessary to cut and clear the land and burn the jungle vegetation. Consider then the following account.[48]

The Tanala are a hill tribe of western Madagascar. . . . Prior to about 200 years ago the economic basis of their life was the cultivation of dry rice by the cutting and burning method. Under the local conditions this method gave a good crop the first year and a moderately good one from the same land five to ten years later. After this the land had to be abandoned until it had once more produced a fairly heavy growth of jungle, twenty to twenty-five years as a minimum. Since the newly cleared land produced the best crops, the usual native method was to utilize all the original jungle which could be profitably exploited with the village as a center, then move the village to a new locality and begin the process again. Under these conditions there was no opportunity for individual ownership of land to develop. The village as a whole held a territory within which it moved from site to site, and forest products such as game taken from this territory belonged to the man who obtained them. Joint families owned the crops growing on jungle land which they had cleared, but the division of land for this use was made as equitable as possible. According to one account, the village elders staked out equal frontages of land to be cleared and assigned one of these to each joint family. The family members, working in a group, then cleared back from the line as far as they thought necessary to provide for their needs. If a family had had bad luck with its crops one year, it would be given an advantage the next. As a result, no marked inequalities in wealth between the joint families ever developed. As there was no market for any surplus, there was no attempt to cultivate more land than

---

[48] Ralph Linton, *The Study of Man* (New York: Appleton-Century-Crofts, 1936). Cited also in W. O. Stanley, et al., *Social Foundations of Education* (New York: Holt, Rinehart and Winston, Inc., 1956), pp. 41–44. Used with permission of Appleton-Century-Crofts.

was actually needed, and the product was divided by the joint family's head, each household receiving according to its needs.

The cultivation of wet rice appeared first among the clans on the eastern edge of the Tanala territory, having been borrowed from the Betsileo. It began as a simple adjunct to dry rice, the new crop being planted in naturally wet places in the bottoms of the valleys. From the first this work seems to have been done by households rather than joint families, the task being too small to necessitate the coöperation of the whole group. Later came small systems of terraces, also borrowed, but by the time this improvement was accepted the pattern of household cultivation of the new crop had become thoroughly established, so that joint families, as such, rarely built terrace systems or shared the produce.

Even before the introduction of wet rice the Tanala had well-developed patterns of personal property, and these, in combination with the idea of family rights to land during the brief period in which it bore a crop, opened the door to individual ownership of land and the exclusive right of a household to the rice patch it cultivated. Since rice terraces were actually growing crops throughout most of the year and had to be kept in repair even between seasons, the land which they occupied never really went out of use and therefore never reverted to the village to be reassigned. Only a limited amount of land could be utilized for this purpose due to soil, height of water available for irrigation, and other natural factors. Hence those households which had not had the energy and foresight to take up rice land at first soon found themselves permanently excluded. Insensibly there grew up within what had formerly been a classless society a class of landholders, and with this went a weakening of the joint family organization. Loyalty to this unit had been maintained largely by the economic interdependence of its members and their constant need for coöperation. But a household could tend its fields of irrigated rice unaided, and its head felt a not unnatural reluctance to share the produce with persons who had contributed nothing toward it.

The rise of individual land tenure did not affect the expropriated very seriously at first, since they could continue with the older method of exploiting village land not available for irrigation. However, land within easy reach of the village would be increasingly exhausted, and the landless households had to go farther and farther afield to find jungle. Often their fields were so far away that they could not possibly go and return in the same day, so they developed the custom of building combined granaries and sleeping quarters there. These distant fields also became increasingly household rather than joint family enterprises. Perhaps the breakdown of the joint family patterns of coöperation had already progressed too far when the system was instituted, or the joint family may have been unwilling to risk any large number of men so far from home. This camping-out was dangerous since a hostile war party could cut off a small group with ease.

One of the greatest stresses within the culture arose in connection with the periodic moving of the village. This was a deep-rooted custom, but now the villages were split into the landless, who needed to move, and the landowners, who had a capital investment in the locality and were unwilling to move. A further breakdown of the joint family system resulted. Under the old conditions villages not infrequently split and formed new units, but such splits were always along joint family lines. At most, a man who stood at the head of three or four households within the lineage would secede with his group and found a distinct lineage in the new village. Now when villages split it was the ex-propriated who moved, so that the immigrant group formed a cross-section of the original lineages. In the new locality the same process went on again until the land which had formed the range of the original mobile village was dotted with descendant villages, each held in place by the irrigated fields about it.

The combination of increasingly settled life and breakdown of the joint family into its component households had still further results. The mobile villages had been socially self-contained, endogamous units. The settled villages were much less so. The joint family retained its religious importance, based on the worship of a common ancestor, after it had lost much of its functional importance and even after its component households had been scattered. Family members from different villages would still be called together on some ceremonial occasions, and this going and coming helped to break down the old patterns of village isolation. Intermarriages became increasingly common, especially among the clans of the Menabe division whose pattern of cross-cousin marriage often made such matings necessary. Thus the original pattern of independent village groups was increasingly transformed into a tribal one.

The new conditions also had important repercussions on the patterns of native warfare. The mobile villages had always fortified themselves with a simple ditch and stockade, but there was little point in expending a vast amount of labor on a site which would presently be abandoned. An enemy war party, using surprise, had a fair opportunity of taking such a village, seizing a rich booty of cattle and personable young women and driving the group out of its territory, which could then be added to the enemy's own range. In fact this was a normal procedure whenever a village felt itself crowded. Now that permanent residence in a village was assured, the villagers could set themselves seriously to the work of fortification, and by the time the Europeans arrived some of the eastern villages, which had gotten wet rice first and hence been settled longest, had made themselves impregnable to anything short of artillery. I was told of one village which was protected by concentric ditches each twenty feet wide and of the same depth, straight-sided and with hedges of prickly pear planted between. The Tanala probably copied this form of defense from the Betsileo, although they had not adopted it while they still followed the mobile pattern. The new conditions made what was already a well-known foreign trait desirable, and it was accepted accordingly.

Since the natives had no siege machinery, these great fortifications reduced war to a stalemate. It was impossible for an attacking party to take a village except by treachery, and the large, determined war parties of the earlier period degenerated more and more into small groups of raiders who aimed to cut off stragglers. This tendency was increased by an increase in the value of slaves. The presence of Arab, European, and Imerina slave-traders, who gave guns in exchange, had something to do with this, but their activities were never carried on on a large scale. In part, at least, this increased importance of slaves was correlated with the new crop. Under the old system slaves were of little economic value, while now they could be put to work in the rice fields. With the rise of slavery there came an increasing need for techniques of ransom and other relations involving captive slaves, and these were gradually developed. In particular, a technique arose for regularizing the relations between a slave woman and her master, her family paying half her market value and thus promoting her to the status of a legal wife. In this way still further bonds were established between villages, even when these belonged to different clans, and the whole tribe was drawn more and more together.

The last step in this drama of change came less than a century ago. In the early mobile period Tanala organization was highly democratic. The head of one of the lineages in a village acted as a magistrate and executive, but there was no formal investiture of any sort and he had no real power. Outside the village there was no recognized authority of any sort. The settled tribes to the east, on the other hand, had had kings for some centuries and were in process of developing a sort of feudal system which cut across the old clan-locality lines and strengthened the central authority. About 1840 one of the Tanala clans established domination over several of the other northern clans, declared itself royal, and announced that the hereditary head of its senior lineage was now King of the Tanala Menabe. Incidentally, the control of this king always remained rather weak and he never really controlled any of the groups who were still mobile. Over the settled clans he was able to exercise some real authority, but the kingdom came to an end before adequate machinery for government could be developed or borrowed. This first king introduced two new elements of culture, both taken from the Betsileo. He built himself an individual tomb, thus breaking a long-established Tanala custom, and after his death the Tanala accepted the belief that the souls of their kings passed into snakes.

Regarding Educational Administration

What has all this to do with the administration of schools? As a matter of fact, I think anyone who has ever been involved in one way or another with the particular difficulties confronted when attempting to bring about organizational restructuring of educational systems will find the progressive rearrangements that came about in the Tanala culture somewhat familiar.

At one time, for example, I worked in the area of trying to help local school districts deal with some of the difficult problems of reorganization. I did this as a member of the staff of a state department of education. My mission was quite explicit; many local organization structures were too small to provide the diversity of content contemporarily required and moreover, the maintenance of such small and inefficient schools was inimical to the best interests of the pupils to be served.

There could technically be little argument with that premise; we had a "wet-rice" world with too many "dry-rice" systems. My job was to bring various systems-components together for the purpose of working out whatever details of change were vital to at least ensure that what was operational was consistent with what was realistic. It was, needless to state, a frustrating and frequently fragile chore. The first thing I had to recognize was that concern for appropriate education was far less important than concern for holding on to what was traditionally known and believed in. In recent times, the surprisingly aggressive and organized defense of the "neighborhood" school has far less to do with convenience and security than it does with identification and territorial ownership. The quality of education and of the basic concern for pluralistic sensitivity is beside the point. The same thing was as much a factor when issues of race, ethnicity, and social class were totally irrelevant. I found rural high schools with enrollments of less than one hundred in which curricula were little more than primitive assaults on fundamental ignorance. The clientele of these schools was all white, Protestant, and of uniform socioeconomic standing; yet these school's patrons were just as resisting of efforts to provide more efficient and effective educational programs as I have found in neighborhoods that have succumbed to the panic of ethnic and socioeconomic integration.

On several occasions where I have seen attempts at school district merger move so far along that one district was agreeable to giving over to the other millions of dollars in capital outlay, the management of operations to one or the other of the older systems, deciding whether a certain fourth grade teacher would be assigned similarly to last year, and dozens of other major and minor items of merger—all of this and more came to no particular avail because someone wonders, along toward the end of a long and difficult evening of negotiations, as to what our "colors" are going to be, or what we shall call the new high school. And that would end things for another long period of tension! One would like to believe that these fiduciary boards are basically guided by a concern for what kind of educational program is the most appropriate for the young people in their charge, how such a program can be most efficiently mounted within the resources available, and what kinds of configurations can be determined that most optimally move in those directions, but the truth is much simpler and perhaps much more intensive: how can we readjust our identity, our allegiance, and our "we-feeling" for this thing that is new and foreign to us? That is most complex to deal with. If somehow one can convince these "powers-that-be" that they will surely win the state high school basketball championship next year, the task is somehow made easier, but that only reflects further on the concerns with the cultural structure rather than with institutional function.

Summary

If it is presumptuous to talk about "principles" derived from these ideas, perhaps it is useful at least to suggest some plausible hypotheses that might be drawn from a discussion of alienation and the cultural structure as these might have application to schools. And since our purpose is to deal with certain theoretical dimensions of education, that seems reasonably appropriate in either case. Whether hypothesis or principle may depend upon the extent that rigorous inquiry tests the validity of such speculations. In any case, certain notions are warranted and I conclude with a discussion of these possibilities.

Regarding great size, there is always the risk that persons performing basic functions will be confused regarding their identification and allegiance to, as well as their ability to articulate roles, in reference to the charter of the organization. Acute anomie in any of the response patterns we have discussed is probably rare in school organizations and in those instances in which it might be likely to occur, administrators, particularly at the level of the activities themselves, must be sensitive to it. But simple anomie in school systems is much more likely and systematic procedures must be invested that are designed to mitigate it. In smaller systems, ritualistic modes of alienation are just as likely as in large, highly impersonal and bureaucratized organizations, although obviously the sources of the condition are quite different; again, sensitivity to these concerns is vital in organizational managers and systematic attempts through wider and more secure communication frameworks are required.

The relationship between the theoretical treatment of alienation on the one hand and of the "Malinowski model" on the other is fundamentally reconciled in terms of the relationship of means-to-ends and of goals-to-activities. The two sets of ideas are exactly related even if the differences of contexts might require explicit clarification.

Both sets of ideas are concerned with the operational relationship between goals on the one hand and the accepted and internalized procedures designed for the effective pursuit of said goals on the other. It is the *arena* in which these processes occur that is distinctive. With reference to our discussion of alienation, the issue is whether any particular individual can make some sense of the relationship of goals-to-means for *him;* consequently, if he recognizes that the goals are meaningful, appropriate, and worth pursuing, he does so; but if the goals are so remote from his recognition of their worth and function that he perceives an inability to pursue them, he may decide that the so-called and typically prescribed *means* shall be his major source of concern.

On the other hand, Malinowski provides us with a more macronistic system. Here the issue is not so much the individual but the total system that is of concern. Again, the overall goals in the form of the "charter" are of major interest, but here again it is the totality of function that need be remembered. That particular individuals performing particular roles and occupying particular statuses is important to that overall pattern is without question, but the major focus shifts from the individual to the organization. And, again, the definition of goals in that context must be in terms of systematic values and idealized representations of what constitutes "good" and "right" and "appropriate" purposes. Still, the rules or norms that also specify the ideal behaviors designed to achieve those value systems are *organizational* rather than institutional.

Finally, if the outcomes according to Malinowski's scheme are too far deviant from the system of values specified in the charter, either the charter must be changed to accommodate those outcomes or the outcomes must somehow be inhibited, brought back into line, or otherwise modified to adjust to the changed situation. With reference to anomie, the same situation prevails; if one rejects both the goals as well as the institutionally constituted means for their pursuit, it is incumbent on that source of power that the goals and the means shall be substituted for by new goals and new means, or one decides to concentrate only on means, only on goals, or quite simply rejects both and withdraws from or becomes indifferent to the whole thing.

If a major, overall principle is derivable from this discussion, it is that one needs quite clearly to be familiar with the systematic relationship between what wants-to-be-accomplished and how-one-wants-to-go-about-accomplishing-it.

Perhaps that is trite—yet, such a relationship between the idea of goals, ends, and purposes, and the *means* available for their pursuit is the issue of evaluation, of assessment, of "management by objective," of concern for budget planning, and almost anything else that one wants to conjure up as a measure of what constitutes administrative activity. Even if one wants to fall back on the common-sense notion that administration is the so-called art-of-the-practical, the issue remains that of the relationship between what one wants, thinks, believes, or is otherwise able to persuade somebody else to believe—and what one does or persuades others to do to bring it about.

Many managers have never quite understood this notion, and those who do not cannot be successful. The issue is simply that of what do you want and how do you go about getting it, but there are significant complications involved in knowing what *ought* to be wanted and knowing what *ought* to be done in getting it. The strategies, techniques, skills, knowledge, patience, energy, and commitment required, and for knowing "how" is perhaps as much a matter of wisdom and of wit as it is disciplined training and professional competence, but undoubtedly theory helps.

Moreover, the kinds of theoretical ideas that are discussed in this chapter undergird the motives that guide emerging techniques for more systematic analysis of the relationship between means and ends. These systematic concerns are discussed in Part III of this book, "Developmental Activity and the New Rationalism." Implicit in all of that discussion is the centrality of the relationship between organizationally and institutionally valued purposes and the most appropriate definition of the means and activities that are vital to their effective realization.

demands and constraints of some supraindividual entity.[5] History has presented us with this explosive legacy, transformed and ossified through many stages and forms, but ultimately reducible to the age-old puzzle of the uneasy balance between individual and organizational needs, between freedom and authority.

On the surface, the conflict seems inevitable. To make matters worse, it probably is deepened by the dominant emphasis in American ideology that tends to understress principles of authority in favor of exalting the rights of the individual.[6] Perhaps the best recent demonstration of this riddle is the presidential campaign of 1972, or any presidential campaign for that matter. Candidates typically seem to be promising greater national purpose and a strong executive office while preserving the verities of freedom and individuality. Perhaps what has been happening in 1973–74 will change all of that somewhat, but one is, by virtue of history, charitably allowed to doubt. It is more likely that a new candidate will simply assure us that as a strong executive, he will exercise that central authority with more sensitivity to those verities of freedom and individuality.

Organizational and group theories are similarly honeycombed with this duality. For Chester I. Barnard, satisfying the requirements of efficiency (personnel relations) and effectiveness (productivity) is the prime task of the effective manager;[7] Harold J. Leavitt refers to "pyramids and people";[8] Argyris to the essential conflict between the restricted nature of the formal organization and the individual "self-actualization"; McGregor to "Theory X" and "Theory Y" stressing either the organization's or the individual's goals.

How these seemingly incompatible demands can be fulfilled simultaneously presents today's managers with their most formidable challenge. It is my contention that *effective leadership depends primarily on mediating between the individual and the organization in such a way that both can obtain maximum satisfaction.* But aside from the practical considerations, this conflict and its resolution provide a sharp analytical

[5] For a concise, popularly written account of the history-of-ideas point of view, see J. Bronowski and Bruce Mazlich, *The Western Intellectual Tradition: From Leonardo to Hegel* (New York: Harper & Row, Publishers, Inc., 1960). Whereas earlier writings deal with the relationship of man to the state, the church, and the nation, our present-day concern appears to be mainly with man and the organization. Witness the popularity of the polemic, W. H. Whyte, Jr.'s, *The Organization Man* (New York: Simon & Schuster, Inc., 1956). It is still being read and reread.

[6] One of the better books still on the social and philosophical undertones of this issue is Kenneth Benne's, *A Conception of Authority* (New York: Teachers College Bureau of Publications, 1943). My debt to this book is shown throughout.

[7] Chester I. Barnard, *The Functions of the Executive* (Cambridge, Mass.: Harvard University Press, 1950).

[8] Harold J. Leavitt, *Managerial Psychology* (Chicago: University of Chicago Press, 1958), pp. 257–262.

tool with which we can analyze the tortuous twists and turns, the zigzag fads, and the massive reversals-of-emphasis in leadership theory.

Before we consider some recent books on leadership in organization, we must review recent history and map out, rather arbitrarily, some landmarks which provide the building blocks of contemporary thought.[9] The two major pillars upon which current theory stands I will refer to here as *scientific management* and the *human relations* approach.

SCIENTIFIC MANAGEMENT

The first approach, really scientific management *and* bureaucracy, describes a body of theory (prevalent from 1910 to 1935) which tended to view organizations as if they existed without people. Max Weber, the German sociologist, contributed the first fully developed theory of bureaucracy.[10] For Weber, bureaucracy was a descriptive term—not an epithet—for characterizing what we now call formal, large-scale organizations.

Two main influences on Weber probably contributed to his later theory: (1) he was deeply impressed by the growth of industrial organizations in his native country and his military experience in the German army, and (2) he was concerned with human frailty and the general unreliability of human judgment and passion.

His answer was to develop an apparatus of abstract depersonalization, a system that would rationally dispense solutions without the friction of subjective coloring and human error. Weber, in fact, once likened the organization to a "modern judge who is a vending machine into which the pleadings are inserted together with the fee and which then disgorges the judgment together with its reasons mechanically derived from the code." [p. 9]

Writing about the same time as Weber (1910) was an American engineer, Frederick W. Taylor, who more than any other individual advanced the professionalization of management.[11] Taylor, the "father of scientific management," attempted to rely on a "third force" that would mediate between man and the organization. Whereas Weber emphasized the legal domination of "role" or position in a status hierarchy, Taylor stressed the impersonal rationality of measurement.

Loosely speaking, then, classical organizational theory developed from these roots. But possibly even more important than those structures

9 A more detailed explanation of these factors, and of a great many other points only touched on here, can be found in my article, "Leadership Theory and Administrative Behavior: The Problem of Authority," *Administrative Science Quarterly,* Vol. 4, No. 3, December 1959.

10 Reinhard Bendix, *Max Weber: An Intellectual Portrait* (Garden City, N.Y.: Doubleday & Company, Inc., 1960), p. 421.

11 Frederick W. Taylor, *Scientific Management* (New York: Harper & Row, Publishers, Inc., 1948).

which took shape from the theories were the assumptions, both hidden and explicit, which the classical theorists made about "human nature." They created organizations which could be construed as predesignated, omniscient machines, and any deviation from prediction was probably occasioned by the fact that man is regrettably unpredictable and unstable or by outright engineering inadequacies. Henry Ford, the prophet of this earlier age, put it neatly when he said, "All we ask of the men is that they do the work which is set before them." Man was viewed as a passive, inert instrument, performing the tasks assigned to him.

In classical theory, then, the conflict between the man and the organization was neatly settled in favor of the organization. The only road to efficiency and productivity was to surrender man's needs to the service of the bloodless machine.

HUMAN RELATIONS

The second group of theories (thriving from 1938 to 1950) appropriately is called the *human relations* approach. Here people are regarded essentially as if they existed without organizations. It is often jokingly said that the Ford Motor Company has grown so much that if "old Henry" were alive today, there would be no place for him in the organization. What happened to create this change, this shift away from the mechanical resolution typified by Weber and Taylor and characterized by Henry Ford?

What precipitated the change was the formulation of the human relations model, crystallized in the early 1930's by Fritz Roethlisberger and W. J. Dickson in *Management and the Worker*.[12] Now, the dominant focus of organization was transformed from a rational model, free from the friction of man's emotions, to a model which appears less determined (or mechanistic) and hence more unfathomable. That is, the new look in organizational theory took cognizance of unanticipated consequences of organizations—workers' feelings, attitudes, beliefs, perceptions, ideas, sentiments (exactly those elements of passion Weber believed escaped calculation).

Management—partly through the seminal work of several social scientists—began to take seriously not only the formal organizational chart, but also the informal and interpersonal contexts. The major assumption of the human relations model was that man could be motivated to work more productively on the basis of fulfilling certain social and psychological needs. This "new look" of organizations was no less "rational" than the earlier machine model, except that man's motivation was a trickier and more elusive concept than was the concept of the machine.

The names primarily associated with this pioneering work are Elton Mayo, with his emphasis on the significance of the human group and

[12] Fritz J. Roethlisberger and William J. Dickson, *Management and the Worker* (Cambridge, Mass., Harvard University Press, 1939).

affiliation as the strongest human need; Kurt Lewin, who stressed the promise of democratic and group decision making as well as the importance of *participation* in motivating people; J. L. Moreno, with his emphasis on *positive feelings* and liking as fundamentals in effective group action; and Carl Rogers, the founder of "nondirective therapy," who underscored the need for understanding, *empathy*, and self-realization. These men and their associates, spanning the range of the behavioral sciences, forged the conceptual framework of the human relations approach.

Let us now return to our original focus, the conflict between man and the organization. For the human relations model, there is no essential conflict; satisfying the workers' social and psychological needs is entirely congruent with the organization's goals of effectiveness and productivity. Thus there is no need for an authority to govern between these forces.

The leader is seen as a facilitator in this context—as an agent who helps smooth the pathway toward goal-achievement. This model assumes that there is no essential conflict between individual satisfaction and organizational satisfaction, that the former (whether described as "morale," "job satisfaction," or whatever) will lead to greater efficiency, and that authority, insofar as it exists, attempts to facilitate forces which will increase personal satisfaction.

If the reader feels that in my description of the classical and human relations models of organization I have been guilty of exaggeration and of building straw men, he is right. I have not meant to imply that Weber et al. were proposing a "brave new world" where all of man's impulses are controlled and dictated wholly by the organization. Nor do I really believe that the human relations proponents were postulating a world of "Huck Finns" actualizing themselves.

I have tried, however, to dramatize in fairly stark terms the key differences between the two models. And when the contrast is made between the broad outlines of the theories, it is clear that the earlier vision elevated the apparatus, the structure, and took man as a given, while the more recent focus on human relations has worked the other side of the street.

Undoubtedly, the building of knowledge goes on in this way. Otto Neurath, the mathematician, once compared the development of science to a man repairing a leaky boat. As he patches up one side while standing on the other, dry side, the latter starts leaking, so he shifts over to the new dry side, and so on and so forth. If such jerky rhythm and patchwork characterize most knowledge building, then in any reversal of emphasis, such as that evoked by the human relations movement, exaggeration of and inattention to some factors inevitably occur. After any revolution in thought, the debris—in terms of fads, unsubstantiated theories, and overstatements—has to be put in perspective and incorporated into more formal theory.

THE REVISIONISTS

Accordingly, since 1950 a number of authors have attempted to reconcile and integrate classical and modern organizational theory. I will refer to these theorists as the *revisionists*. In general, they share a common concern for revising the native, unsubstantiated, and unrealistic aspects of the human relations approach without sacrificing its radical departure from traditional theory. These revisionists, only three of whom will be discussed here,[13] have modified their view for any number of reasons, but the chief ones are probably related to new research findings and some "reality" considerations.

As to research findings, the idea that productivity is strongly correlated with morale turns out to be more a wish than reality. As Rensis Likert put it:

On the basis of a study I did in 1937, I believed that morale and productivity were positively related; that the higher the morale, the higher the production. Substantial research findings since then have shown that this relationship is much too simple.[14]

The fact of the matter is that we are not at all clear today about the relationship of morale to productivity, or, indeed, even if there *is* any interdependence between them; Likert and his associates have found organizations with all the logical possibilities—high morale with low productivity, low productivity with low morale, etc.

Other research findings as well have challenged some of the basic assumptions of the human relations model—for example, whether attention to group process factors leads to greater efficiency of group operations, whether the leader who attempts to get close to the men is a more efficient leader, and whether the leader can or should avoid hostile and aggressive attitudes directed toward him by his men.

In general, then, the revisionists recognize clearly that organizational theory must take into account such factors as purpose and goal, status and power differentials, and hierarchy. And, finally, they have come to know that leadership ultimately has to act in ways other than, or in addition to, leading a group discussion.

In this connection, it is particularly illuminating to note that Douglas M. McGregor, an early advocate of human relations and a colleague of

---

[13] Other writers such as Philip Selznick, Mason Haire, William F. Whyte, Rensis Likert, Herbert Shepard, Alvin W. Gouldner, Herbert A. Simon, Abraham Zaleznik, Robert L. Katz, and many others deserve to be mentioned.

[14] Rensis Likert, "Developing Patterns in Management," *Strengthening Management for the New Technology* (New York: American Management Association, 1955), p. 13.

Kurt Lewin, began formulating his new theories (which I will discuss later) after six years of line experience as a college president.

I think McGregor's final note to the alumni and faculty of the college deserves to be printed in full, for its honesty and for its attempt to spell out a significant change in attitude—a change which typifies the prevailing currents in recent organizational theory. Space considerations do not permit this, but the following excerpt captures the main point:

> I believed, for example, that a leader could operate successfully as a kind of adviser to his organization. I thought I could avoid being a "boss." Unconsciously, I suspect, I hoped to duck the unpleasant necessity of making difficult decisions, of taking the responsibility for one course of action, among many uncertain alternatives, of making mistakes and taking the consequences. I thought that maybe I could operate so that everyone would like me—that "good human relations" would eliminate all discord and disagreement.
>
> I couldn't have been more wrong. It took a couple of years, but I finally began to realize that a leader cannot avoid the exercise of authority any more than he can avoid responsibility for what happens to his organization.[15]

The utopian wish to escape conflict, to avoid tough decisions, to create "the happy family," and to stress group and interpersonal factors, tinctured the writings of the early human relations students. Yet this was an indispensable antidote, a required emphasis, given the apersonal models of the classical era.

Now the revisionists are concerned with external, economic factors—with productivity, formal status, and so on—but not to the exclusion of the human elements that the traditional theorists neglected. At this point, let us consider the works of some of these revisionists.

PESSIMISTIC RESOLUTION

Robert N. McMurry has presented a cogent case for a Weberian model of organization led at the top by strong and mature personalities. What is needed, he concludes, is "benevolent autocracy."[16] His reasoning is rather interesting. While he believes that "bottom-up" or consultative management (a species of the human relations model) is preferable ideologically, it is not practical—nor is it congruent with what he knows about personality functioning. (He holds a Ph.D. in psychology, and he has had considerable experience as an industrial consultant in this area.)

Managers are hard-driving entrepreneurs and include many stubbornly destructive people. Only about 10 per cent of them *really* believe in the human relations approach. Furthermore, the bureaucratic personality does not want responsibility and independence; it prefers regimentation, routinization, structure. "It just isn't possible in business," McMurry

---

15 Douglas M. McGregor, "On Leadership," *Antioch Notes* (May 1954), pp. 2–3.
16 Robert N. McMurry, "The Case for Benevolent Autocracy," *Harvard Business Review,* 36 (January–February 1958), p. 82.

claims, "to delegate much autonomy below the top echelons of management." [p. 12]

This melancholy view of the "bureaucratic personality" (whatever that truly is) goes on to show that, even if preferred, a human relations viewpoint—which McMurry equates with a radical version of group dynamics—is not really practical.

Benevolent autocracy, on the other hand, gets its results because it rigidly structures and controls the relation of the supervisors to their subordinates. Its major virtue is that it works and makes the best out of the worst. It works because a strong autocrat, who can evoke binding loyalty, respect, and distant worship, dictates, commands, and controls the organization by occupying the only room at the top. "The typical bureaucrat," McMurry says, "is incapable of conceiving or applying sound leadership principles on his own initiative." [p. 90]

Let us assume, for the moment, that McMurry's position is valid. What we see in this approach is a virtuous and popularized psychoanalytic justification for rigid autocracy on the presumptive basis that this is the way people are. McMurry's strong autocrat, whom he does not discuss in any detail (nor does he account for his recruitment or his development), sounds like a nostalgic and romantic image of the old-time entrepreneur —strong, wise, smart, aggressive, the good father, a man utterly independent.

While McMurry's writing seems to have a close kinship to the classical model of organization, with the resolution of the conflict clearly favoring the organization, he does not hold with the legal and/or scientific rationales of Weber or of Taylor. Rather, he creates the "great man" (the benevolent autocrat).[17]

When we examine McMurry's thesis more closely, we see that it resolves the conflict between man and the organization by postulating certain human needs that appear to be compatible with a tightly controlled hierarchy: man wants to be dependent, man is incapable of taking responsibility, man needs a strong leader, and so forth. And, most importantly, McMurry appears to assume these needs are fixed and immutable.

Here is where the rub comes. If McMurry's diagnosis of the situation is correct (and I strongly question it, for I have never seen a "typical bureaucrat"), is there no possibility for change, no possibility for producing more mature and able personnel, no possibility for creating organizational conditions where individuals can take responsibility? McMurry's answers are not very clear.

And if the human relations model has tried to feature man as it would have liked him to be (denying reality), then McMurry appears to be

---

[17] For a renewed plea for the great man, see Eugene Jennings, *The Anatomy of Leadership* (New York: Harper & Row, Publishers, 1960).

taking man as he is—i.e., denying the possibility of change. Even Freud, known for his tragic view of man and his recognition of the difficulty of human change, once said: "Certainly men are like this, but have you asked yourselves whether they need be so, whether their inmost nature necessitates it?"

UTOPIAN RESOLUTION

Chris Argyris's *Personality and Organization* provides a neat counterfoil to McMurry. For, while they both start with the nature and importance of the human condition within organized settings, they end up with totally opposite diagnoses and conclusions.

Argyris, more than any other recent author, comes directly to grips with the man–organization problem. He feels that the individual's needs and the formal organization's demands are basically incompatible. The outcome of this frustration can be inferred and observed through a variety of defense mechanisms and other pathological behaviors on the part of the individual which ultimately lead to the attenuation of the organization's goals and his own mental health.

Let us take a closer look. Argyris postulates a "total personality" signified by a number of dimensions: passivity to activity, dependence to independence, behavioral inflexibility to flexibility, subordinate to superordinate positions, and the like. His model assumes that these dimensions reside on a continuum and that the healthy personality develops along the continuum toward "self-actualization."

In contrast, formal organization is characterized by conditions which stultify this "growth": task specialization, chain of command, unity of direction, span of control, and other repressive and restrictive devices. The picture we get from Argyris, then, is that of an organizational behemoth slowly but surely grinding down the individual's need for growth and actualization.

The contrast between Argyris and McMurry now becomes focused:

• For McMurry, most personnel are children (according to Argyris's and his own criteria), and that is *the only way they can and want to be.*
• Argyris argues, on the other hand, that that is the way they are, to be sure, but that the organization forces them into this mold and they can be vastly different.

Argyris does not pretend to solve this dilemma, but suggests three possibilities which would enhance work in the industrial organization, and thus lead to greater human potentiality: (1) job enlargement, (2) employee-centered leadership, and (3) reality leadership.

These suggestions are not fully developed, nor is their meaning clear. Mason Haire comments, for example, that reality leadership is "flexible leadership tailored to the situation, not too directive, not too non-directive, not too employee-centered, but firm when it should be firm, and like the song in *South Pacific*, broad where it should be broad."[18]

What these proposals lack in clarity, they make up in promise. Through improved "diagnostic skill" on the part of the manager (meaning greater competence in interpersonal relations), and through the use of a staff specialist who will help management and the organization to attain these skills, a fusion process will occur which will help to bring about the optimal actualization of both the organization and the individual.

There are two main difficulties that I have with Argyris's thesis. The first has to do with his notion of "self-actualization," the second with what he means by "optimal":

(1) Self-actualization is a term used rather loosely by some psychologists to explain that an individual will "realize his full potential." It is a fuzzy term, drenched in value-connotations both of what people are like and of what they can become. I have as much difficulty in seeing concretely the self-actualized man as in seeing the typical bureaucrat.

In order for an abstraction to be meaningful, there must be empirical and experiential validity for it. And when I ask for examples of the self-actualized person, the proponents suggest people like Einstein, Goethe, Spinoza, William James, Schweitzer, Beethoven, and Thoreau.[19]

The criteria used are not at all obvious, for when they are explored, it is clear that individuals like Lucky Luciano and Adolf Hitler deserve equal consideration as candidates. It is also clear that, for the most part, those public figures who are termed self-actualizers rarely fall into the category called managerial leadership (or, for that matter, rarely are they alive now!), but fall rather within the area of the arts and sciences.

The heart of the matter is that the assumptions about human behavior made by Argyris and McMurry lead them to construct totally different organizational models. For McMurry, humans are slothful and need leading; for Argyris, humans, if left free, will move naturally toward growth. As for my own belief, I, like Machiavelli, hold that man is both good and evil, and that certain conditions in the organization will lead to accentuation of one or the other expression. Man's goodness and/or badness, this ambivalence, is part of the human condition and, as such, has to be considered in any theory of organization.

(2) Related to this point is the idea of "optimizing." This term refers to Argyris' notion that effective leadership can successfully fuse the organization's and the individual's needs in such a way that both will arrive at some peak point.

If this is so, then what becomes of the inevitable conflict between the two? If Argyris is correct, his solution is very similar to the human relations one: greater need-satisfaction on the part of the workers yields higher productivity for the organization. Yet this solution tries to avoid, unsuccessfully, the calculus of values so essential to the problem. For it is clear that simultaneous optimi-

18 Mason Haire, "What Price Value," *Contemporary Psychology* (June 1959), p. 181.

19 See particularly Abraham Maslow, *Motivation and Personality* (New York: Harper & Row, Publishers, 1954).

zation is not feasible, that there is accommodation and relinquishment of some objectives on both sides, and that the best possible solution will be one wherein neither employer nor employee is at his peak value, but where sufficient personnel satisfaction is reached at a viable rate of organizational efficiency.

THE TRAGIC VIEW

Another system of thought, in many ways similar to Argyris's, is now developing; it attempts to deal with the inherent tension between individual needs and organizational demands. It has taken shape in the form of McGregor's recent book, *The Human Side of Enterprise.*

Unlike the quest for optimization, this view seeks no more than a satisfactory resolution. Unlike actualization, this view settles for a "commitment toward maturity." Instead of a unidirectional tendency toward growth, it recognizes the basic ambivalence and conflicts within the personality. At its most hopeful, this view asserts that from this basic conflict, new and creative resolutions *may* emerge—but not necessarily. In that sense, this view is tragic.

Taking Peter Drucker's phrase, "management by objective," McGregor has recast four principles that outline a new approach to organizational leadership:

(1) The starting point is the clear recognition that "if there is a single assumption which pervades conventional organizational theory it is that authority is the central, indispensable means of managerial control." [p. 18] McGregor shows the limitations of various forms of organizational authority, and then transforms authority based on role or status into authority based on task or goal demands—i.e., objectives. Under this concept, management by objective comes about through "target setting," a joint effort where superior and subordinate attempt to develop the ground rules for work and productivity.[20]

(2) There is the principle of "interdependence"—or collaboration—between superior and subordinate. This is essential if the two parties are to agree on some mutually satisfactory target.

(3) Another principle has to do with "the belief—evidenced in practice—that subordinates are capable of learning how to exercise effective self-control."[21] Self-control, because it is not governed by external forces, is apparently one of McGregor's indications of maturity.

(4) This position asserts the need for "integration"; i.e., the bringing together and working through of the differences between individual and organizational needs. This idea was missing in the earlier conclusion of proponents of the human relations approach. According to McGregor, "The central principle which derives from Theory Y is that of integration: the creation of conditions such that members of the organization can achieve their own goals *best* by directing their efforts toward the success of the enterprise." [p. 49]

20 For further elaboration see Douglas M. McGregor's, "An Uneasy Look at Performance Appraisal," *Harvard Business Review* (May–June 1957), p. 89.

21 Douglas M. McGregor, "Notes on Organizational Theory" (Cambridge, Mass.: Massachusetts Institute of Technology, mimeographed, 1957), p. 11.

Self-control, collaboration, and integration—these are the main ingredients of the McGregor approach. Although this approach does not claim theoretical completeness, a number of questions must be raised.

Take the concept of self-control. As I understand it, self-control comes about through the internalization of standards, not through external incentives; and through satisfying tasks, not on the basis of reward-punishment schedules.

But do all or most jobs in industry induce this "instinct of workmanship"? Can we expect assembly-line workers, maintenance personnel, or other workers performing relatively repetitive tasks to be motivated from within? Or is self-control more likely and possible in those jobs where there is a high degree of responsibility and autonomy?

McGregor bases a good deal of his theory on collaboration—between subordinate and superior. Like Argyris, he recommends training in human relations to facilitate a process whereby both parties can develop skills and engage in this collaborative activity.

But we have to ask: Can individuals working in organized settings manage to deal and work collaboratively with their superiors? Can superiors and subordinates manage to perceive each other as human beings with all their limitations and strengths, as helpers, coordinators, as well as persons with *realistic* power? These questions have to be deferred for empirical investigation, but, right now, we can see no simple solution.

Along these lines, Samuel Goldwyn was reputed to have said to his staff one day, "I want you all to tell me what's wrong with our operation—even if it means losing your job!" And this is the point. Authenticity in a relationship—which depends on "leveling" and honesty—is a prime requisite for collaboration. Authenticity and authority seem almost antithetical to each other. Can they be combined? McGregor feels they can, over a period of time, as long as there is a "commitment to maturity."

But the main strength of McGregor's position is that he, more than other recent students of organizational behavior, has attempted to stress the sticky problem of integration of task requirements with the individual's growth. Role incumbency, personal factors, coercion, external rewards and punishments, and "selling and persuasion" are replaced by objective stress on organizational purpose and attainment. It is the "tragic view" because it comes to grips fully with the calculus of values and because it recognizes the trading, negotiations, and accommodations necessary to realize a true integration.

These brief summaries of the revisionist authors do not do full justice to their ideas; they are far more complex and provisional than I have indicated here. They also provide hope for future research and theory in organizations, work that can illuminate even more clearly the thorny issues that they raise and leave exposed to scientific scrutiny. They are to be praised, moreover, for realizing that leadership is the fulcrum on

2. The problem of *social influence* is essentially the problem of power and how power is distributed. It is a complex issue and alive with controversy, partly because of an ethical component and partly because studies of leadership and power distribution can be interpreted in many ways, and almost always in ways which coincide with one's biases (including a cultural leaning toward democracy).

The problem of power has to be seriously reconsidered because of dramatic situational changes that make the possibility of one-man rule or the "Great Man" not necessarily "bad" but impractical. I am referring to changes in the role of top management. Peter Drucker, over twelve years ago, listed forty-one major responsibilities of the chief executive and declared that "90 per cent of the trouble we are having with the chief executive's job is rooted in our superstition of the one-man chief."[28] The broadening product base of industry, impact of new technology, the scope of international operations, make one-man control quaint, if not obsolete.

MANAGING CONFLICT

3. The problem of *collaboration* grows out of the very same social processes of conflict and stereotyping, and centrifugal forces that divide nations and communities. They also employ furtive, often fruitless, always crippling mechanisms of conflict resolution: avoidance or suppression, annihilation of the weaker party by the stronger, sterile compromises, and unstable collusions and coalitions. Particularly as organizations become more complex they fragment and divide, building tribal patterns and symbolic codes that often work to exclude others (secrets and noxious jargon, for example) and on occasion to exploit differences for inward (and always fragile) harmony. Some large organizations, in fact, can be understood only through an analysis of their cabals, cliques, and satellites, where a venture into adjacent spheres of interest is taken under cover of darkness and fear of ambush. Dysfunctional intergroup conflict is so easily stimulated, that one wonders if it is rooted in our archaic heritage when man struggled, with an imperfect symbolic code and early consciousness, for his territory. Robert R. Blake in his experiments has shown how simple it is to induce conflict, how difficult to arrest it.[29] Take two groups of people who have never been together before, and give them a task that will be judged by an impartial jury. In less than one hour, each group devolves into a tight knit band with all the symptoms of an "in-group." They regard their product as a "masterwork" and

---

[28] D. Ron Daniel, "Team at the Top." *Harvard Business Review* (March–April 1965), 74–82.

[29] Robert R. Blake, Herbert A. Shepard and Jane S. Mouton, *Managing Intergroup Conflict in Industry* (Houston, Texas: Gulf Publishing, 1964).

the other group's as "commonplace," at best. "Other" becomes "enemy;" "We are good; they are bad. We are right; they are wrong."[30]

Jaap Rabbie, conducting experiments on the antecedents of intergroup conflict at the University of Utrecht, has been amazed by the ease with which conflict and stereotype develop.[31] He brings into the experimental room two groups and distributes green name tags and green pens to one group and refers to it as the "green group." He distributes red pens and red name tags to the other group and refers to it as the "red group." The groups do not compete; they do not even interact. They are in sight of each other for only minutes while they silently complete a questionnaire. Only ten minutes is needed to activate defensiveness and fear.

In a recent essay on animal behavior, Erikson develops the idea of "pseudo-species."[32] Pseudo-species act as if they were separate species created at the beginning of time by supernatural intent. He argues:

Man has evolved (by whatever kind of evolution and for whatever adaptive reasons) in pseudo-species, i.e., tribes, clans, classes, etc. Thus, each develops not only a *distinct sense of identity* but also a conviction of harboring *the* human identity, fortified against other pseudo-species by prejudices which mark them as extraspecific and inimical to "genuine" human endeavor. Paradoxically, however, newly born man is (to use Ernst Mayr's term) a generalist creature who could be made to fit into any number of pseudo-species and must, therefore, become 'specialized' during a prolonged childhood. . . .

Modern organizations abound with pseudo-species, bands of specialists held together by the illusion of a unique identity and with a tendency to view other pseudo-species with suspicion and mistrust. Ways must be discovered to produce generalists and diplomats, and we must find more effective means of managing inevitable conflict and minimizing the pseudo-conflict. This is not to say that conflict is always avoidable and dysfunctional. Some types of conflict may lead to productive and creative ends.

4. The problem of *adaptation* is caused by our turbulent environment. The pyramidal structure of bureaucracy, where power was concentrated at the top, seemed perfect to "run a railroad." And undoubtedly for the routinized tasks of the nineteenth and early twentieth centuries, bureaucracy was and still is an eminently suitable social arrangement. However, rather than a placid and predictable environment, what predominates today is a dynamic and uncertain one in which there is a

---

[30] Carl Rogers, "Dealing with Psychological Tensions," *Journal of Applied Behavioral Sciences* (Jan.-Feb.-March 1965), 6–24.

[31] Personal communication, Jan. 1966.

[32] Erik Erikson, "Ontogeny of Ritualization." Paper presented to the Royal Society in June 1965.

deepening interdependence among the economic and other facets of society.

5. Finally, the problem of *revitalization*. As Alfred North Whitehead says:

The art of free society consists first in the maintenance of the symbolic code, and secondly, in the fearlessness of revision. . . . Those societies which cannot combine reverence to their symbols with freedom of revision must ultimately decay . . .

Growth and decay emerge as the penultimate conditions of contemporary society. Organizations, as well as societies, must be concerned with those social structures that engender bouyancy, resilience, and a "fearlessness of revision."

I introduce the term *revitalization* to embrace all the social mechanisms that stagnate and regenerate and with the process of this cycle. The elements of revitalization are:

- An ability to learn from experience and to codify, store, and retrieve the relevant knowledge.
- An ability to "learn how to learn," that is, to develop methodologies for improving the learning process.
- An ability to acquire and use feedback mechanisms on performance, to develop a "process orientation," in short, to be self-analytical.
- An ability to direct one's own destiny.

These qualities have a good deal in common with what John Gardner calls "self-renewal." For the organization, it means conscious attention to its own evolution. Without a planned methodology and explicit direction, the enterprise will not realize its potential.

Integration, Distribution of Power, Collaboration, Adaptation, and Revitalization are the major human problems of the next twenty-five years. How organizations cope with and manage these tasks will undoubtedly determine the viability and growth of the enterprise.

Organizations of the Future[33]

Against this background I should like to set forth some of the conditions that will determine organizational life in the next two or three decades:

1. *The Environment.* Rapid technological change and diversification will lead to interpenetration of the government with business.

Partnerships between government and business will be typical. It will be a truly mixed economy. Because of the immensity and expense of the

33 Adapted from my earlier paper, "Beyond Bureaucracy," *Trans-Action* (July–August 1965).

projects, there will be fewer identical units competing for the same buyers and sellers. Organizations will become more interdependent.

The four main features of the environment are:

- Interdependence rather than competition.
- Turbulence and uncertainty rather than readiness and certainty.
- Large scale rather than small scale enterprises.
- Complex and multi-national rather than simple national enterprises.

2. *Population characteristics.* The most distinctive characteristic of our society is, and will become even more so, education. Within fifteen years, two thirds of our population living in metropolitan areas will have attended college. Adult education is growing even faster, probably because of the rate of professional obsolescence. The Killian report showed that the average engineer required further education only ten years after gaining his degree. It will become almost routine for the experienced physician, engineer, and executive to go back to school for advanced training every two or three years. Some fifty universities, in addition to a dozen large corporations, offer advanced management courses to successful men in the middle and upper ranks of business. Before World War II, only two such programs existed, both new, both struggling to get students.

All of this education is not just "nice," it is necessary. As Secretary of Labor Wirtz recently pointed out, computers can do the work of most high school graduates—cheaper and more effectively. Fifty years ago education was regarded as "nonwork" and intellectuals on the payroll were considered "overhead." Today the survival of the firm *depends* on the effective exploitation of brain power.

One other characteristic of the population that will aid our understanding of organizations of the future is increasing job mobility. The ease of transportation, coupled with the needs of a dynamic environment, change drastically the idea of "owning" a job—or "having roots." Already 20 per cent of our population change their mailing address at least once a year.

3. *Work Values.* The increased level of education and mobility will change the values we hold about work. People will be more intellectually committed to their *professional* careers and will probably require more involvement, participation, and autonomy.

Also, people will be more "other-directed," taking cues for their norms and values from their immediate environment rather than tradition. We will tend to rely more heavily on the temporary social arrangements.[34] We will tend to have relationships rather than relatives.

34 "On Temporary Systems." In M. B. Miles (ed.). *Innovation in Education,* (New York: Bureau of Publications, Teachers College, Columbia University, 1964), 437–490.

4. *Tasks and goals.* The tasks of the organization will be more technical, complicated, and unprogrammed. They will rely on intellect instead of muscle. And they will be too complicated for one person to comprehend, to say nothing of control. Essentially, they will call for the collaboration of specialists in a project or a team-form of organization.

There will be a complication of goals. Business will increasingly concern itself with its adaptive or innovative-creative capacity. In addition, meta-goals will have to be articulated; that is, supra-goals which shape and provide the foundation for the goal structure. For example, one meta-goal might be a system for detecting new and changing goals; another could be a system for deciding priorities among goals.

Finally, more conflict and contradiction can be expected from diverse standards of organizational effectiveness. One reason for this is that professionals tend to identify more with the goals of their profession than with those of their immediate employer. University professors can be used as a case in point. Within the University, there may be a conflict between teaching and research. Often, more of a professor's income derives from outside sources, such as foundations and consultant work. They tend not to be good "company men" because they divide their loyalty between their professional values and organizational goals.

ORGANIC-ADAPTIVE STRUCTURE

5. *Organization.* The social structure of organizations of the future will have some unique characteristics. The key word will be "temporary"; there will be adaptive, rapidly changing *temporary systems.* These will be "task forces" organized around problems-to-be-solved by groups of relative strangers who represent a diverse set of professional skills. The groups will be arranged on an organic rather than mechanical model; they will evolve in response to a problem rather than to programmed role expectations. The "executive" thus becomes a coordinator or "linking pin" between various task forces. He must be a man who can speak the diverse languages of research, with skills to relay information and to mediate between groups. People will be evaluated not vertically according to rank and status, but flexibly and functionally according to skill and professional training. Organizational charts will consist of project groups rather than functional groups. This trend is already visible today in the aerospace and construction industries, as well as many professional and consulting firms.

Adaptive, problem-solving, temporary systems of diverse specialists, linked together by coordinating and task evaluating specialists in an organic flux—this is the organizational form that will gradually replace bureaucracy as we know it. As no catchy phrase comes to mind, I call this an organic-adaptive structure.

6. *Motivation.* The organic-adaptive structure should increase motivation, and thereby effectiveness, because it enhances satisfactions intrinsic

to the task. There is a harmony between the educated individual's need for meaningful, satisfactory, and creative tasks and a flexible organizational structure.

There will, however, also be reduced commitment to work groups, for these groups, as I have already mentioned, will be transient structures. I would predict that in the organic-adaptive system, people will learn to develop quick and intense relationships on the job, and learn to bear the loss of more enduring work relationships. Because of the added ambiguity of roles, time will have to be spent on continual rediscovery of the appropriate organizational mix.

AMERICANS PREPARED

The American experience of frontier neighbors, after all, prepares us for this, so I don't view "temporary systems" as such a grand departure. These "brief encounters" need not be more superficial than long and chronic ones. I have seen too many people, some occupying adjacent offices for many years, who have never really experienced or encountered each other. They look at each other with the same vacant stares as people do on buses and subways, and perhaps they are passengers waiting for their exit.

Europeans typically find this aspect of American life frustrating. One German expatriate told me of his disenchantment with "friendly Americans." At his first party in this country, he met a particularly sympathetic fellow and the two of them fell into a warm conversation which went on for several hours. Finally, they had to leave to return to their homes, but like soul-mates, they couldn't part. They went down into the city street and walked round and round on this cold winter night, teeth chattering and arms bound. Finally, both stiff with cold, the American hailed a cab and went off with a wave. The European was stunned. He didn't know his new "friend's" name. He never saw or heard from him again. "That's your American friendship," he told me.

That *is* American friendship: intense, spontaneous, total involvement, unpredictable in length, impossible to control. They are happenings, simultaneously "on" and transitory and then "off" and then new lights and new happenings.

A Swiss woman in Max Frisch's *I'm Not Stiller* sums it up this way: "Apparently all these frank and easy-going people did not expect anything else from a human relationship. There was no need for this friendly relationship to go on growing."[35]

Training Requirements for Organizations of the Future

How can we best plan for the organizational developments I forecast? And how can training and development directors influence and direct

35 Max Frisch, *I'm Not Stiller* (Harmondsworth, Middlesex: Penguin Books, 1961), p. 244.

this destiny? One thing is clear: There will be a dramatically new role for the manager of training and development. Let us look at some of the new requirements.

1. *Training for change.* The remarkable aspect of our generation is its commitment to change, in thought and action. Can training and development managers develop an educational process which:

- Helps us to identify with the adaptive process without fear of losing our identity?
- Increases our tolerance for ambiguity without fear of losing intellectual mastery?
- Increases our ability to collaborate without fear of losing individuality?
- Develops a willingness to participate in our own social evolution while recognizing implacable forces?

Putting it differently, it seems to me that *we should be trained in an attitude toward inquiry and novelty rather than the particular content of a job;* training for change means developing "learning men."

2. *Systems counseling.* It seems to me that management (and personnel departments) have failed to come to grips with the reality of *social systems.* It is embarrassing to state this after decades of research have been making the same point. We have proved that productivity can be modified by group norms, that training effects fade out and deteriorate if training goals are not compatible with the goals of the social system, that group cohesiveness is a powerful motivator, that intergroup conflict is a major problem facing modern organization, that individuals take many of their cues from their primary work group, that identification with the work group turns out to be the only stable predictor of productivity, and so on. Yet this evidence is so frequently ignored that I can only infer that there is something naturally preferable (almost an involuntary reflex) in locating the sources of all problems in the individual and diagnosing situations as functions of faulty individuals rather than as symptoms of malfunctioning social systems.

If this reflex is not arrested, it can have serious repercussions. In these new organizations, where roles will be constantly changing and certainly ambiguous, where changes in one subsystem will clearly affect other subsystems, where diverse and multinational activities have to be coordinated and integrated, where individuals engage simultaneously in multiple roles and group memberships (and role conflict is endemic), a systems viewpoint must be developed. Just as it is no longer possible to make any enduring change in a "problem child" without treating the entire family, it will not be possible to influence individual behavior without working with his particular subsystem. This means that our training and development managers of the future must perform the functions of *systems counselors.*

3. *Changing motivation.* The rate at which professional-technical-managerial types join organizations is higher than any other employment category. While it isn't fully clear what motivates them, two important factors emerge.

The first is a strong urge to "make it" professionally, to be respected by professional colleagues. Loyalty to an organization may increase if it encourages professional growth. Thus, the "good place to work" will resemble a super-graduate school, abounding with mature, senior colleagues, where the employee will work not only to satisfy organizational demands but, perhaps primarily, those of his profession.

The other factor involves the quest for self-realization, for personal growth which may not be task-related. That remark, I am well aware, questions four centuries of encrusted Protestant Ethic. And I feel uncertain as to how (or even *if*) these needs can be met by an organization. However, we must hope for social inventions to satisfy these new desires. Training needs to take more responsibility for attitudes about continuing education so that it is not considered "retread" or a "repair factory" but a natural and inescapable aspect of work. The idea that education has a terminal point and that adults have somehow "finished" is old-fashioned. A "drop-out" should be redefined to mean anyone who *hasn't returned* to school.

However the problem of professional and personal growth is resolved, it is clear that many of our older forms of incentive, based on lower echelons of the need hierarchy, will have to be reconstituted.

4. *Socialization for adults.* In addition to continuing education, we have to face the problem of continuing socialization, or the institutional influences that society provides to create good citizens. Put simply, it means training in values, attitudes, ethics, and morals. We allot these responsibilities typically to the family, to church, to schools. We incorrectly assume that socialization stops when the individual comes of age. Most certainly, we are afraid of socialization for adults, as if it implies the dangers of a delayed childhood disease, like whooping cough.

Or to be more precise, we frown not on socialization, but on conscious and responsible control of it. In fact, our organizations are magnificent, if undeliberate, vehicles of socialization. They teach values, inculcate ethics, create norms, dictate right and wrong, influence attitudes necessary for success and all the rest. The men who succeed tend to be well socialized and the men who don't, are not: "Yeah, Jones was a marvelous worker, but he never fit in around here." And most universities grant tenure where their norms and values are most accepted, although this is rarely stated.

Taking conscious responsibility for the socialization process will become imperative in tomorrow's organization. And finding men with the right technical capability will not be nearly as difficult as finding men with the right set of values and attitudes. Of course, consciously guiding this process is a trying business, alive with problems, not the least being the ethical one: Do we have the right to shape attitudes and values? We really do not have a choice. Can we avoid it? How bosses lead and train subordinates, how individuals are treated, what and who gets rewarded, the subtle cues transmitted and learned without seeming recognition, occur spontaneously. What we can choose are the mechanisms of socialization—how coercive we are, how much individual freedom we give, how we transmit values. What will be impermissible is a denial to recognize that we find some values more desirable and to accept responsibility for consciously and openly communicating them.

5. *Developing problem-solving teams.* One of the most difficult and important challenges for the training and development manager will be the task of promoting conditions for effective collaboration or building synergetic teams. Synergy is where individuals actually contribute more and perform better as a result of a collaborative and supportive environment. They play "over their heads," so to speak. The challenge I am referring to is the building of synergetic teams.

Of course, the job isn't an easy one. An easy way out is to adopt the "zero synergy" strategy. This means that the organization attempts to hire the best individuals it can and then permits them to "cultivate their own gardens." This is a strategy of isolation that can be observed in almost every university organization.

[Until universities take a serious look at their strategy of zero synergy, there is little hope that they will solve their vexing problems. The Berkeley protests were symptomatic of at least four self-contained, uncommunicating social systems (students, faculty, administration, trustees) without the trust, empathy, interaction (to say nothing of a tradition) to develop meaningful collaboration. To make matters even more difficult, if possible, academic types may, by nature (and endorsed by tradition) see themselves as "loners" and divergent to the majority. They all want to be independent together, so to speak. Academic narcissism goes a long way on the lecture platform but may be positively disruptive for developing a community.]

Another approach has the same effect but appears different. It is the pseudo-democratic style, in which a phony harmony and conflict-avoidance persists.

In addition to our lack of background and experience in building synergy (and our strong cultural biases against group efforts), teams take time to develop. They are like other highly complicated organisms and, just as we wouldn't expect a newborn to talk, we shouldn't expect a new team to work effectively from the start. Teams require trust and commitment and these ingredients require a period of gestation.

Expensive and time-consuming as it is, building synergetic and collaborative frameworks will become essential. The problems that confront us are too complex and diversified for one man or one discipline. They require a blending of skills, slants, and disciplines for their solution and only effective problem-solving *teams* will be able to get on with the job.

6. *Developing supraorganizational goals and commitments.* The President of ABC (the fictitious name of a manufacturing company) was often quoted as saying:

The trouble with ABC is that nobody aside from me ever gives one damn about the overall goals of this place. They're all seeing the world through the lenses of their departmental biases. What we need around here are people who wear the ABC hat, not the engineering hat or the sales hat or the production hat.

After he was heard muttering this rather typical president's dirge, a small group of individuals, who thought they could wear the ABC hat, formed a group they called the ABC HATS. They came from *various* departments and hierarchical levels and represented a microcosm of the entire organization. The ABC HATS group has continued to meet over the past few years and has played a central role in influencing top policy.

It seems to me that training and development managers could affect the development of their organizations if they would encourage the formation of HATS groups. What worries me about the organization of the future, of specialized professionals and an international executive staff, is that their professional and regional outlook brings along with it only a relative truth and a distortion of reality. This type of organization is extremely vulnerable to the hardening of pseudo-species and a compartmentalized approach to problems.

Training and development can be helpful in a number of ways:

- They can identify and support those individuals who are "linking pins" individuals who have a facility for psychological and intellectual affinity with a number of diverse languages and cultures. These individuals will become the developers of problem-solving teams.
- They can perform the HATS function, which is another way of saying that training and development managers should be managers who keep over-all goals in mind and modulate the professional biases which are intrinsic to the specialists' work.
- They can work at the interfaces of the pseudo-species in order to create more inter-group understanding and interface articulation.

Today, we see each of the intellectual disciplines burrowing deeper into its own narrow sphere of interest. (Specialism, by definition, implies a peculiar slant, a segmented vision. A cloak and suit manufacturer went to Rome and managed to get an audience with His Holiness. Upon his return a friend asked him, "What did the Pope look like? The tailor answered, "A 41 Regular.") Yet, the most interesting problems turn up at the intersection between disciplines and it may take an outsider to identify these. Even more often, the separate disciplines go their crazy-quilt way and rely more and more on internal standards of evidence and competence. They dismiss the outsider as an amateur with a contemptuous shrug. The problem with intellectual effort today (and I include my own field of organizational psychology) is that no one is developing the grand synthesis.

Organizations, too, require "philosophers," individuals who provide articulation between seemingly inimical interests, who break down the pseudo-species, and who transcend vested interests, regional ties, and professional biases in arriving at the solution to problems.

To summarize, I have suggested that the training and development director of the future has in store at least six new and different functions: (1) training for change, (2) systems counseling, (3) developing new incentives, (4) socializing adults, (5) building collaborative, problem-solving teams, and (6) developing supraorganizational goals and commitments. Undoubtedly there are others and some that cannot be anticipated. It is clear that they signify a fundamentally different role for personnel management from "putting out fires" and narrow maintenance functions. If training and development is to realize its true promise, its role and its image must change from maintenance to innovation.

I have seen this new role develop in a number of organizations not easily or overnight, but pretty much in the way I have described it here. It might be useful to review briefly the conditions present in the cases I know about:

The personnel manager or some subsystem within personnel (it might be called "employee relations" or "industrial relations" or "career development") took an *active, innovative* role with respect to organizational goals and forcibly took responsibility for organizational growth and development.

Secondly, this group shifted its emphasis away from personnel functions *per se* (like compensation and selection) and toward organizational problems, like developing effective patterns of collaboration, or fostering an innovative atmosphere or reducing intergroup conflict, or organizational goal-setting and long-run planning.

Thirdly, this group developed a close working relationship to various subsystems in the organization, an organic, task-oriented relationship, not the frequently observed mechanical "line-staff" relationship.

Fourthly, they were viewed as full-fledged members of the management team, instead of the "head-shrinkers" or the "headquarters group." This was the hardest to establish in all cases, but turned out to be the most important. In fact, in one case, the man responsible for spearheading the organizational development effort has recently taken an important

Parsonian social system theory into: (1) integrated concepts capable of answering and posing questions; (2) operational concepts that provide blueprints for investigation; and (3) generalizable concepts capable of application to a wide variety of issues. Getzels describes the model:

We conceive of the social system as involving two classes of phenomena which are at once conceptually independent and phenomenally interactive. There are first the institutions with certain roles and expectations that will fulfill the goals of the system. And there are second the individuals with certain personalities and need-dispositions inhabiting the system, whose observed interactions comprise what we generally call "social behavior." We shall assert that this social behavior may be understood as a function of these major elements: institution, role and expectation, which together constitute what we shall call the *nomothetic* or normative dimension of activity in a social system; and individual, personality, and need-disposition, which together constitute the *idiographic* or personal dimension of activity in a social system.[4]

The school represents a social system within which teachers and principals interact as organizational members. In this sense schools direct their efforts toward the attainment of goals, and, in the words of Parsons, "contribute to a major function of a more comprehensive system, the society."[5] Bidwell[6] lends credence to this point of view as he discussed the first classic sociological study of the school, Waller's *The Sociology of Teaching*. In Waller's analysis the school is not just a formal organization but a social system or small society.

Social systems theory, and specifically, the social systems model represents a theoretical framework from which one can derive a conceptualization of the climate of a school and the behavioral characteristics of principals.

Organizational Climate and Role

Lonsdale wrote of organizational climate:

Indeed, organizational climate might be defined as the global assessment of the interaction between the task-achievement dimension and the needs-satisfaction dimension within the organization, or in other words, of the extent of the extent of the task-needs integration.[7]

4 J. W. Getzels, "Administration As a Social Process," in A. W. Halpin (ed.), *Administrative Theory in Education* (New York: Macmillan Publishing Co., Inc., 1967), p. 152.

5 Talcott Parsons, "Suggestions for a Sociological Approach to the Theory of Organizations—I," *Administrative Science Quarterly*, No. 1 (June 1956), p. 63.

6 C. E. Bidwell, "Some Effects of Administrative Behavior: A Study in Role Theory," *Administrative Science Quarterly*, No. 2 (1957), pp. 978–980.

7 R. C. Lonsdale, "Maintaining the Organization in Dynamic Equilibrium," in D. Griffiths (ed.), *Behavioral Science and Educational Administration*, 63rd Yearbook of the NSSE, Part II (Chicago: University of Chicago Press, 1964), p. 166.

Lonsdale uses the terms *task-achievement dimension* and *need-satisfaction dimension* synonymously with the terms *nomothetic* (institution) and *idiographic,* (individual), respectively. The nomothetic and idiographic dimensions represent two conceptually independent classes of phenomena; (1) the normative activities of the social system (role, expectation), and (2) the personal activities of the social system (personality, need-disposition).

Normative activities or prescribed behavioral expectations are dealt with in considerations of role theory. From this point of view every individual in the social system occupies a position that carries with it certain norms for behavior. They carry out their duties in a rational hierarchy of subordinate-superordinate interactions. As organizational members encounter each other in the performance of their roles, the setting usually elaborates the need for reciprocal adaptations to the others' behavior. Organizational roles are, therefore, complementary.

Lonsdale wisely notes that the term *organizational climate* "has a psychosocial flavor that reflects more concern with the need-satisfaction dimension than with the task-achievement dimension."[8] In so doing he calls attention to the fact that the institutional roles are implemened by members, each one of which brings his unique characteristics as a person into his role. These characteristics, his personality and need-disposition, give to each role in varying degrees the mark of the individual assigned.

Conceptually, organizational climate is that state of the organization that results from the interaction that takes place between organizational members as they fulfill their prescribed roles while satisfying their individual needs. Guba illustrates this concept in operation as he writes about the task of the administrator:

The unique task of the administrator can now be understood as that of mediating between two sets of behavior-eliciting forces, that is, the nomothetic and the idiographic, so as to produce behavior which is at once organizationally useful as well as individually satisfying.[9]

The concept of organizational climate can be operationalized to refer to the resulting condition within the school from the social interaction between the teachers and the principal.

Principal Behavior

Principal behavior within the conceptual framework of the social system is that which results as the principal-delegate attempts to cope with an environment made up of expectations for his behavior (roles) in

[8] Ibid.

[9] Egon Guba, "Research in Internal Administration—What Do We Know," in R. F. Campbell and J. M. Lipham (eds.), *Administrative Theory As a Guide to Action* (Chicago: Midwest Administration Center, 1960), p. 121.

ways consistent with his own individual pattern of needs (personality). Getzels[10] illustrates the behavioral act by the general equation: $B = f(R \times P)$, where B is observed behavior, R is a given defined role, and P is the personality of a given role incumbent.

In the process of actualizing his personality through the expectations of his role, the principal exchanges his behavior for rewards.[11] Simon, Smithburg, and Thompson include this exchange principle in their theory of organizational equilibrium:

1. An organization is a system of interrelated social behaviors of a number of persons whom we shall call the participants in the organization.

2. Each participant and each group of participants receives from the organization inducements in return for which he contributes to the organization.

3. Each participant will continue his participation in an organization only as long as the inducements offered him are as great or greater than the contributions he is asked to make.

4. The contributions provided by the various groups of participants are the source from which the organization manufactures the inducements offered to participants.

5. Hence, an organization is "solvent"—and will continue in existence —only as long as the contributions are sufficient to provide inducements in large enough measure to draw forth these contributions.[12]

Barnard[13] believed that one of the essential elements of organizations is the willingness of members to contribute their efforts to the system. This contribution is predicated upon an exchange wherein each member, in this case the principal, has more than one course of behavior open to him. The issue of the variations in the rewards and costs of organizational members to the frequency distribution of behavior chosen among alternatives is taken up by Parsons and Shils in a discussion of "double contingency."[14] The choice of an alternative by one may well

[10] Getzels, op. cit., p. 158.

[11] This exchange principle is referred to in Parsons, Talcott and E. A. Shils, *Toward a General Theory of Action* (Cambridge, Mass.: Harvard University Press, 1951), p. 180; G. C. Homans, "Social Behavior As Exchange," in A. P. Hard, et al. (eds.), *Small Groups* (New York: Alfred A. Knopf, Inc., 1966), pp. 170–183; J. G. March, H. A. Simon, *Organizations* (New York: John Wiley & Sons, Inc., 1964), p. 84; and B. M. Bass, *Leadership, Psychology, and Organizational Behavior* (New York: Harper & Row, Publishers, Inc., 1960), p. 36.

[12] H. A. Simon, et al., *Public Administration* (New York: John Wiley & Sons, Inc., 1950), pp. 381–382.

[13] C. E. Barnard, *The Functions of the Executive* (Cambridge, Mass.: Harvard University Press, 1964), p. 139.

[14] Parsons and Shils, op. cit.

determine in part or whole the alternative of another. The reciprocal nature of this intraorganizational social behavior has a significant effect upon the interaction variables that make up the organizational climate. In this regard, as the principal contributes his behavior to the organization for rewards he is at the same time influenced by it.

The social system model elaborates personality as need-disposition, which Getzels defines as the central analytic unit of personality. Moreover, Parsons and Shils define need-dispositions as "individual tendencies to orient and act with respect to objects in certain manners and to expect certain consequences of these actions."[15] Parsons and Shils suggest that each concrete need-disposition involves a combination of values. Values are those aspects of the member's orientation that commit him to norms, standards, and expectations when he is in a situation requiring him to make a choice. On this basis a principal's value orientations will guide him to his choices whenever he is forced to choose among various goal objects and need-dispositions. Furthermore, the value orientations that commit him to the observance of certain rules and behaviors are not random but tend to form a system of value orientations that commit him to some organized set of rules. Culturally, the organized set of rules are system values to which the member is committed through his own personal values that are elaborated as need-dispositions. It is with these considerations in mind that the behavioral characteristics of principals are considered as outgrowths of his prescribed role and his personal values and orientations.

The Principal in the School Climate

The history of the role of the principal illustrates shifts in emphasis from the strict custodial orientation in the Taylor era to the occasional *laissez faire* practices of the 1930's in the name of human relations. In this regard the shifts in the manner of viewing the influence of the principal over the school and the school over the principal have varied throughout the history of public education. The interest of this inquiry is focused on the relationship of principal behavior, role, and school climate in the present era of public education. Specifically, the interest is in an analysis of principal behavior, role, and school climate in the conceptual social system of the school.

Although Getzels does not speak directly to the subject of the socialization of member behavior, he does state that the organization establishes what he calls "imperative functions that are to be carried out in certain routinized patterns."[16] Parsons,[17] on the other hand, observes the

15 Ibid., p. 114.

16 J. W. Getzels, "Conflict and Role Behavior in the Educational Setting," in W. W. Charters, Jr., and N. L. Gage (eds.), *Readings in the Social Psychology of Education* (Boston: Allyn & Bacon Co., 1963), p. 311.

17 Talcott Parsons, *The Social System*, op. cit., pp. 481–482.

organizational forces built about the processes of maintenance of equilibrium. The social system maintains the stability of its interactive processes by balancing motivations toward deviant behavior with motivation toward organizational restoration, for example, the school climate once established will tend to prevail over forces to change it. Furthermore, Parsons cites the processes of socialization as fundamental to the maintenance of equilibrium within the social system in that it is the means whereby the members acquire necessary orientations to the performance of their roles and integration of their personalities.

Merton asked the question two decades ago to which one aspect of this inquiry addresses itself; "To what extent are particular personality types selected and modified by the various bureaucracies (private enterprise, public service, and quasi-legal political machine, religious orders)?"[18] Subsequent to Merton's question the influence that the school climate bears upon principal behavior was evidenced in the research of Chase[19] and Moyer,[20] which suggests that teachers will not accept the leadership of a principal unless he fulfills, to a considerable extent, the expectations of the teacher group. Effective principal behavior in this regard is dependent upon the role, the principal's concept of his role, the need-dispositions of his personality, and the expectations of the group.

Following Merton's question, Presthus[21] presented an analysis and a theory of the organizational society. A basic assumption upon which Presthus based his analysis is that social values and the climate of the social system mold individual personalities through the process of socialization. Although man has a broad scope for individual choices, the influences of the social system through the forces of socialization significantly influence the conditions under which choices are made. The principal can expect to find that his behavior is largely subject to the control of the school climate. The school as an organization represents the source of the assumptions that the principal forms about his identity. In exchanging his behavior for organizational rewards, the principal subscribes to the process of socialization and becomes strongly motivated by the need for group approval and, thus, intensely subject to conventional values of success and power. Lipham[22] and Halpin[23] discovered

18 R. K. Merton, *Social Theory and Social Structure* (New York: The Free Press, 1949), p. 205.

19 F. S. Chase, "How to Meet Teachers' Expectations of Leadership," *Administrator's Notebook*, I (April 1953).

20 D. C. Moyer, "Leadership That Teachers Want," *Administrator's Notebook*, III (March 1955).

21 R. Presthus, *The Organizational Society* (New York: Alfred A. Knopf Inc., 1962).

22 J. M. Lipham, *Personal Variables Related to Administrative Effectiveness* (Unpublished dissertation, University of Chicago, 1960).

23 A. W. Halpin, "The Superintendent's Effectiveness As a Leader," *Administrator's Notebook*, VII (October 1958).

similar evidence that principals tend to pattern their leader style to a role construed for them by the school and the school district as did Charters[24] in a study of teacher socialization.

In referring to schools, Bridges posited several assumptions about the socializing influences of large formal organizations:

> sustained role-enactment in a bureaucracy should lead to reduction in behavioral variation among organizational members occupying the same role. Role performances should be characterized by uniformity rather than diversity with perspectives, outlook, and behavior shaped more and more by institutional position and less and less by personality in the course of service within a given bureaucratic role.[25]

In a discussion of the characteristics of bureaucracy and how they influence behavior, Bridges goes on to say that as tasks are distributed among various positions as official duties, the principal performs most of the same occupational operations day in and day out. Through his research, Bridges suggests that the elementary principal's perspectives, outlook, and behavior are shaped more by his role in the school and less by his personality in the course of his service.

The responsibility of the principal to the interests and demands of the school in relationship with the external environment is a component in the total system. Principals are motivated by the need for not only the internal approval of the school staff but also for external group approval from the larger school district and the school clientele. This intensifies the influence of experience. The influence of both internal and external demands upon the principal's behavior places him in a boundary or interstitial role. While his behavior is being intensely influenced by both internal and external sources he find himself frequently mediating between these two socializing forces.

The Socialization Process

THE TEACHER

Socialization is a process whereby individuals learn to become viable group members. The teacher engages his personality with the construed role that the school holds for him. In the process, the teacher role and the teacher personality become realigned to facilitate the arrival at a point of organizational homeostasis or balance. The socializing forces of the school that influence the reconciliation of the teacher to the organi-

24 W. W. Charters, Jr., "The Social Background of Teaching," in N. L. Gage (ed.), *Handbook of Research on Teaching* (Chicago: Rand McNally Co., 1963), pp. 715–813.

25 E. M. Bridges, "Bureaucratic Socialization: The Influence of Experience on the Elementary Principal," *Educational Administration Quarterly* (Spring 1965), p. 20.

zation are pervasive and effective. Compliance is almost a guarantee as the school establishes functions for teachers to carry out in a predictable pattern. Compliance is the means whereby teachers become "good" teachers, for "good" teachers are teachers whose beliefs, norms, and behavior are brought into line with those of the organization. The research of Hoy[26] and Willower and Jones[27] indicate that the influence of experience upon teacher behavior is significant:

The findings suggest that the pupil control ideology of beginning teachers is affected by teaching experience. The process of socialization within the school subculture seems important in reshaping the control ideology of organizational newcomers. New idealistic teachers appear to be confronted with a relatively custodial control orientation as they become a part of the organization. . . .[28]

THE PRINCIPAL

The most commonly shared basis upon which school districts select candidates for principalships is evidence of experience as a "good" teacher. The "good" teacher candidates for principalships in large urban school districts are almost always chosen from the ranks of the upward mobiles who already reside within the district. By the time the principal aspirant shows interest, the district has had ample time to identify the candidate as compatible with the image it holds for successful principals. One can surmise that promotions of this nature are ways that urban school districts reward compliance and make predictions regarding continued compliance in the principal role after promotion. In this sense, compliance appears to be a pervasive and highly valued phenomenon in the administrative role.

Halpin and Croft[29] found that the lives of elementary principals as children were characterized by a concept of "the good child." Principals perceived their idealized self-image of "goodness" incredibly similarly. Indeed, individuality was virtually nonexistent or buried in the importance of the identity with the idealized self-image. The research of the author[30] on principal characteristics and organizational climate showed a remarkable similarity in the behavior characteristics of principals. The sample of forty-one principals in an urban school district in California

26 W. K. Hoy, "The Influence of Experience on the Beginning Teacher," *The School Review* (September 1968).

27 D. J. Willower, and R. G. Jones, "Control in an Educational Organization," in J. D. Raths, et al. (eds.), *Studying Teaching* (Englewood Cliffs, N.J.: Prentice-Hall, Inc.), 1967, pp. 424–428.

28 W. K. Hoy, op. cit., p. 320.

29 A. W. Halpin, and D. B. Croft, *The Biological Characteristics of Elementary Principals* (Washington, D.C.: Government Printing Office), 1960.

30 T. W. Wiggins, *Leader Behavior Characteristics and Organizational Climate* (unpublished paper presented to the American Educational Research Association, Los Angeles, 1969).

were found to be highly task-oriented, kindly, and considerate of sub-ordinates, needing direction and support of superordinates, but desirous of independence to use the direction and support to arrive at their own decisions. As with Halpin and Croft's portrait, it would be difficult to deny that this is the picture of a principal in an urban area who is endowed with those characteristics that would tend to stabilize and per-petuate schools. Furthermore, it would be equally difficult to deny that a reservoir of principals such as those previously characterized could be interchanged freely as is frequently necessary in urban school districts where problems of growth prevail. This identifies the school district as the primary socializing force that influences principal behavior.

The research included an exploration of the effect of the replacement of a principal upon the climate of the school, and, like Bridges, the effect of the length of the principal's incumbency upon his leader behavior in relation to the school climate. A multivariate analysis showed no signifi-cant relationship between the principal's behavioral characteristics and the school climate. Additional analyses revealed no change in the school climate as principals were replaced, and the longer the principal had been assigned to the school the more significant was the relationship of his behavioral characteristics and the school climate.

The discovery of no general relationship between principal behavior and school climate was not expected as a result of the research. A search was conducted for plausible explanations. Recall that the principals in this study were discovered to share almost identical behavioral char-acteristics. School climates varied, but principal characteristics did not. The measurement of the school climate was predominantly that which was perceived by teachers—usually fifteen or more teachers to one principal. Inasmuch as the principals were fundamentally behaviorally alike and the school climates did not change as the principals were re-placed, one can conclude that the principals were interchangeable parts. However, the surprising factor was the general lack of relationship be-tween principal behavior and school climate. This relationship did in-crease slightly with the length of the principals incumbency, but generally it was a nonsignificant relationship. This appears to suggest a refutation of the socialization assumptions. In fact, it refutes more fundamental organizational theory regarding the relationship of individual's person-alities to institutional roles. The key to understanding these findings lies in the discovery that the socializing influences in the case of the princi-pals extends beyond the immediate school site. These principals had all been "reared" as teachers, vice-principals, and in other service positions within the same large urban district. Apparently the district and the educational establishment itself carefully prepare principals to behave in a rational, predictable, and uniform manner. This renders them more predictable and more easily interchangeable; their personalities become as one. With this in mind the research of the author measured the principal's behavior as related to the school (the subsystem) when it more appropriately should have focused upon the district (the system.). It is the district (the system) that over the years influences the behavioral characteristics of its principals in an enduring and pervasive manner a good deal more so than does the school where he is assigned. The hypotheses need to be reformulated and retested accordingly. The efficacy of the theories need re-examination accordingly.

In his analysis of the organizational society Presthus[31] makes the assumption that societal values and the climate of the social system mold individual personalities through the process of socialization. Fromm states it another way; "Those drives which make for the differences in men's character life . . . the lust for power and the yearning for submission are all products of the social process."[32] Although man in the social system may have some scope for individual choices, the influences through socialization significantly influence the conditions under which choices are made. The principal can expect to find that his behavior is largely subject to the control of the school or more accurately the school district in the urban area.

The conceptual and empirical support cited leads to the assumption that organizational socialization takes place and that the influence of internal and external organizational expectations prevails over the principals' personality characteristics as the length of their incumbency increases.

Through the socialization process the principal's personality becomes gradually dominated by the school expectations as the length of time he is in the school increases (see figure). Parsons and Shils summarize this issue as they discuss organizational adjustment as a toleration and

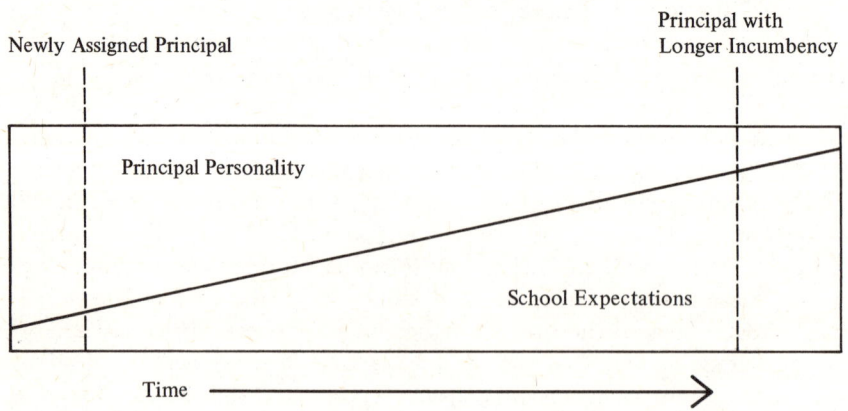

Newly Assigned Principal

Principal with Longer Incumbency

Principal Personality

School Expectations

Time

31 R. Presthus, op. cit.

32 E. Fromm, *Man for Himself* (New York: Holt, Rinehart and Winston, Inc., 1947), p. 241.

internalization within the personality of the value patterns of the organization that may not be in harmony with the member's value system.

Even after the personality has become a relatively stabilized system of need-dispositions allocated among various occasions for gratification and integrated into some approximation of a working unity, it is still continuously confronting the cultural patterns as situational objects of orientation.[33]

Over a period of time these confrontations have the continuing and pervasive effect of socializing the principal into the established as well as changing school expectations. In this sense he approaches the image of rational man, the school approaches a state of homeostasis, and stability renders organizational life more predictable.

Conclusions

The twentieth-century popularity of social systems theory has begun to have an influence on the manner in which students of educational administration view the functions of the executive. The school administrator functions in a social system wherein he is influenced by the roles and expectations of the school, the school district, and the clientele as much, if indeed not more, as he influences the school by means of his personal style as an administrator. This notion necessitates a re-examination of much of the tradition of so-called administrative leadership that presumes that the power, authority, and influence of school principals provide the major source of thrust and significance to the educational enterprise. In the systems sense the principal is an interdependent force in a school, and his behavior is analyzable only in the perspective of other forces both external and internal that make up the social system. Generalizations about principal behavior are justifiable only when they are relative to generalizations about the school and the community as a social system. The influence of experience within the system is enormous and tends to mold the principal's behavior. The implications of these assumptions for the training of school administrators are significant. Success in educational administration is predicated upon the successful adaptation of the behavioral characteristics of administrators with existing organizational forces. Concepts of the principalship as essentially a role couched in the vagaries of "administrative leadership" and "instructional leadership" are questionable under the scrutiny of the test of research. The modern school needs principals who can contribute applicable expertise to the total system and not merely perpetuate existing traditions. The training of these administrators will likely necessitate an entirely different set of assumptions and perspectives on the part of training institutions. The infusion of the behavioral sciences in the field of educa-

33 Parsons and Shils, op. cit., p. 181.

tional administration is generally accepted conceptually but yet rarely effectively operationalized. The training of administrators is still, for the most part, an apprenticeship of folklore that has been handed down from administrator to administrator. The environment and conditions of the school as a complex social system make up the medium from which administrative training programs could emerge that could enable schools to confront the demands of our enormously complex and dynamic modern condition.

It is astonishing to see how many philosophical disputes collapse into insignificance the moment you subject them to this simple test of tracing a concrete consequence. There can *be* no difference anywhere that doesn't *make* a difference elsewhere. . . .[5]

James contributed this observation as a commentary on his reconciliation of a dispute among a company of men engaged in argument as a consequence of an interesting metaphysical debate; observing a man who had somewhat cornered a squirrel on a tree trunk, they noticed that when the man went about the tree, the squirrel went ahead of him. Thus, no matter how persistent was the man in going round, the squirrel seemed always to be ahead of him. The argument rested on the issue of whether the man, having gone round the tree with the squirrel still thereon had, in fact, also gone round the squirrel? James pointed out that it would depend upon what one meant by going around; that is, what is *practically* meant by that notion of "going round." Said James:

If you mean passing from the north of him to the east, then to the south, then to the west, and then to the north of him again, obviously the man does go round him, for he occupies these successive positions. But if on the contrary you mean being first in front of him, then on the right of him, then behind him, then on his left, and finally in front again, it is quite as obvious that the man fails to go round him, for by his compensating movements that the squirrel makes, he keeps his belly turned towards the man all the time, and his back turned away. Make the distinction and there is no further occasion for dispute.[6]

Dewey suggests the same "proof" in a way and perhaps with more relevance to developmental activity when he suggests the following— it surely will make much sense to anyone contemplating the construction of a PERT diagram:

Only changes which lead to some defined or fixed outcome of form are of any account and can have any account—any logos or reason—made of them . . .

Development holds merely of the course of changes which take place within a particular member of the species. It is only a name for the predetermined movement from the acorn to the oak tree.[7]

"It is only a name for predetermined movement," indeed! Yet, here in a sense is an important part of the operational definition of a "system." Where systems occur *naturally* and can be studied—where development can be observed as a "given"—there it can also lead to modeling and to simulation. In other words, it can lead to the artificial construction of

[5] William James, *Essays in Pragmatism,* Alburey Castell (ed.) (New York: Hafner Publishing Co., 1948), p. 142.

[6] Ibid., p. 141.

[7] John Dewey, *Reconstruction in Philosophy* (New York: Holt, Rinehart and Winston, Inc., 1920). Cited in Barrett and Aiken, op. cit., pp. 300–301.

isomorphic systems. And these systems, composed of developmental phenomena can, under mathematical explanation and manipulation, be compressed in both time and space. The constraints and variables and events involved can be repeatedly and instantaneously reiterated in systematically prescribed combinations in order to generate solutions to particular problems. By "running" these patterns repeatedly and acting on the information, successive refinements can be determined until, finally, an *optimum* solution is selected. It may not be the absolutely best solution possible, of course, but it is sufficient to know that it is the best solution *under the circumstances*—that is what is meant by "optimal."

But it would be a mistake to assume that the same principles are applicable only to circumstances in which the utility of a computer is available. In some cases, particularly in terms of the overall dimensions of developmental theory, the computer is not important. When Guba talks about such "steps" in developmental activity as "inventing" and "fabricating" and "installing," he is referring as much to a fundamental *logic* as to particular ways that such a logic might be operationalized. Equally vital to Guba's position—and that sets him apart from those we more familiarly refer to as operations researchers and linear programmers —is the importance of the *environment* in which developmental activity proceeds. No matter the exquisiteness of some arrived-at solution, it must be *installed* and in an environment that, unlike any simulated or experimental condition, is real. *All* of the variables are there. Guba is concerned with an ultimate question: "It sounds like a great idea, but will it work?" All of the possible constraints cannot easily be anticipated.

All of that withstanding, developmental theory includes a variety of procedures, methodologies, techniques, and technology aimed toward the solution of practical problems and toward the institutionalization of planning processes that are, like important aspects of rationalized bureaucracy, aimed toward reducing the probability of the unintended consequence. In some circumstances, a developmental ideology may pursue a relatively simple problem, whereas in others, similar procedures generally may be applied to extremely complex ones. The morphological technique discussed in the Ignatovich article, for example, is one systematic and complex way of deterministically generating alternative futures. It requires considerable quantification, yet the fundamental notion is again that of developmentally dealing with a particular logic. Obviously, the technique would be senseless without electronic computation.

The same is true of a rather "hard-nosed" systematic approach to the design of efficient management precedures by Glans, et al. in their book, *Management Systems.*[8] The first three authors listed are all employed

[8] T. B. Glans, et al., *Management Systems* (New York: Holt, Rinehart and Winston, Inc., 1968).

by IBM, and of the five authors, only one, Richard N. Schmidt, is affiliated with a university. Yet, the overall pattern of this book is based on almost the same model that Guba deals with. These authors talk about "study and design, implementation and installation, and operation, evaluation, and modification." They treat these as three "stages" in the life cycle of management, and it is doubtful that any of them ever read Guba's excellent general analysis that says almost the same thing but, in my view, says it much better and more efficiently. (In truth, they deal with a particular and concrete, although simulated set of solutions.) The issue that Guba raises is not specifically directed to any particular problem per se, but is generalizable to any problem-solving dilemma— that the issues with which he deals are applicable to a broad set of problems is axiomatic.

In no case has anyone interested in promulgating a systematic approach to a variety of problems confronting managers in different kinds of organizations ever suggested that their particular logic is a panacea. But that such procedures are almost *assumed* to be the emerging substance of administrative activity is increasingly apparent in the view of systems proponents. This view is reasonably well stated by Deutch:

In simpler systems—where you can vary one factor at a time—the methods of conventional and automated analysis is sufficient. But in dynamic and interconnected complex systems, the alteration of one factor immediately acts as cause to evoke alterations in one or a great many others. . . . today we see societies declining, and economic systems faltering, the scientist being able to do little more than to appreciate the full complexity of the subject he is studying. But science is also taking the first steps toward studying "complexity" as a subject in its own right. [Cybernetics] respects the vaguely intuitive ideas that we pick up from handling such simple statistics as income or balance of payments data, or capital input-output data, and sets to work to a rigorous discipline of sound practical planning.[9]

By the same token, Banghart, who has developed a special reputation as one of several of the educational establishment's systems experts, has declared: "Management can no longer afford a lengthy time-lag in making decisions. This is true of the school systems as well as of government. . . ."[10]

Elsewhere, Banghart has said:

The growing utilization of quantitative techniques by administrators in military, business and government suggests the increasing role that these tech-

---

[9] Michael J. Deutch, "The Applications of Cybernetics to the Professional and Scientific Operations of the US Government," Third International Congress on Cybernetics Namur: Association Internationale de Cybernetique, 1965), p. 640.

[10] Frank Banghart, *Educational Systems Analysis* (London: Collier Macmillan, Ltd., 1969), p. 23.

niques will play in teacher and administrative decision-making. The growing scientific orientation to administrative decision-making confirms the fact that administration is indeed a discipline.[11]

Well, perhaps that is exaggerated a bit. Apart from the application and logic of a systems approach with highly specific orientation to algorithms and quantitative process, a great many theoretically astute scholars in the field of administration have been talking about "systems" approaches for many years. It should be clearly recognized that the concept of a system is much broader than those aspects that are reducible to quantification and measurement as well as to those aspects of decision-making that can be programmed into a computer.

This aspect of quantification of administrative activity has to some extent prompted me to suggest some cautions in the application of quantitative techniques at the American Educational Research Association meeting in 1969; that article is included in this section. The point very simply is this; there are certain dimensions of administrative activity in school systems that are clearly value-laden, and the issue of success in implementing a particular plan is sometimes much less a matter of what is most appropriate as it is a matter of what can be achieved. Guba's discussion of developmental activity takes this condition very much into account. There is a quite distinct difference between the application of systematic and quantitative techniques in *planning* on the one hand and to *decision-making* on the other. The best defined plans are sometimes not appropriate, perhaps because of value concerns, perhaps because of other types of contingencies. The point, again, is that such techniques have an important function in the preparation and training of administrators, but there is no magic in them if the conditions in which one finds himself functioning are incongruent with the decisions that are specified.

Much is being written in these times about systems-analysis and operations research techniques in administrative work. Much of that is prescriptive and formulated; that is, the theoretical material on which such technical activity is based is frequently obscure, or not considered —(and perhaps properly so)—essential to the level of understanding necessary for application. It is my view that the selection of a variety of such content is better left to those courses dealing rather specifically with the development of quantitative skills that are appropriate to the application of such techniques as linear programming, simulation, queuing procedures, Monte Carlo techniques, and so forth. I consider it more appropriate to present in a book concerned with theoretical dimensions of administrative activity more general statements of the *pattern* of these systematic views, and I have chosen to label that as "developmental theory."

[11] Ibid., p. 72.

Consequently, three particular statements appear in this section. The Guba article presents an excellent general treatment of development, diffusion, and evaluation, and the Ignatovich article takes a quite different methodological tack than that generally concerned with planning modes that are appropriate to developing alternative types of futuristic decisions. "Futurism" is very much in vogue in these times; that is all to the good, of course, for we must continue to give a great deal more attention to the kinds of problems and prospects that will confront us in both the "extended present" and later. This is an aspect of administrative concern that is relatively new since, typically, we have tended to believe, in public organizations, that we could not effectively plan beyond more than a few years in any case. The Ignatovich article presents a methodology that is somewhat different from the more familiar kinds of Delphic orientations to futuristic analysis, and its versatility is clearly based not only on its potential for alternative futures but also to unique analysis of any complex problem regardless of its special time frame.

It should also be emphasized that when Guba talks about attempting to "install" some systematic solution in a "world wherein all the variables are operative," he could be saying something similar to what linear programming proponents mean by "constraints." He would, I think, not argue with that; more importantly, the issue is a kind of theoretical explanation of what developmental activity is *really all about*—that, very simply, as he observes, one does not drop the proverbial feather in a vacuum, but drops it in the "real world," where everything that can have an affect does. In linear programming, one tries to anticipate and quantify such factors (constraints) and builds them in. Guba is saying fine—but they *are these*.

Finally, I have included my own article, previously referred to, regarding some of the limitations that we must be aware of in the application of quantitative techniques to decision-making, primarily to remind ourselves that the final responsibility for decisions made by administrators, regardless of how they are arrived at, is the administrator's. Such roles are performed by ordinary human beings with all of the risks that simply being human involve.

It would be far too presumptive to suggest that these three articles represent a "theory of Development," but they come much closer to the pursuit of that idea than would a variety of other statements dealing with primarily methodological explanations and push-pull-click-click recipes for the application of particular techniques to particular problems. That kind of content is available elsewhere, and much of it is not only excellent but clearly essential to the preparation of contemporary educational executives—it simply has no place here.

Since these articles speak directly for themselves, they are preceded by very brief commentaries.

14

COMMENTARY

PAUL LAZARSFELD *has suggested that the major problem in the theory-practice continuum is that there are not enough "explicators." Explicators are those who stand intellectually between the theorist and the practitioner and whose function it is to translate the language of the theorist into the language of the practitioner.*

In the field of science—in some instances, at least—these roles have been developed; for lack of a better way of characterizing these individuals, we call them "science writers."

In the following article, Egon Guba treats this issue but in a somewhat different way. Guba is concerned with helping us to understand that whether we are involved with knowledge-production or with knowledge-utilization, our major emphasis must begin with a clear understanding of the substantive differences between "research activity" and "developmental activity." These are clearly different not only because the goals and the conditions within which each (researcher and developer) operates are different but also because, owing to these factors, the processes themselves are dissimilar. Consequently, problems of diffusion and especially of evaluation are also contextually separate.

Guba, in this article, presents a compelling logic that represents a major contribution to a better understanding of the theory-practice continuum and in my view, there are probably no better statements of this complex process to be found anywhere in the literature.

DEVELOPMENT, DIFFUSION
AND EVALUATION

EGON G. GUBA

MORE than a decade ago I was a self-styled "expert" in the area of administrative staff relationships. My colleague at the University of Chicago, Jack Getzels, and I strove mightily to put the terms "nomothetic" and "idiographic" into the vocabulary of every practicing administrator in the country. I recall that we made a lot of speeches on the

---

This article was originally presented at a symposium cosponsored by the University Council on Educational Administration and the Center for Advanced Study of Educational Administration, Eugene, Oregon. It appeared in *Knowledge Production and Utilization in Educational Administration,* ed. by Terry Eidell and Joan M. Kitchell (Eugene, Oregon: CASEA, 1968). Used with permission.

subject, Jack and I, and usually there was a question or discussion period following. Almost inevitably this comment would come from someone in the audience, "What you say seems to make some sense, although I'm not sure I really know what you're talking about. Why don't you fellows come down out of your ivory tower and tell us about your ideas in language that we can understand? How about showing us how to apply those ideas 'on the firing line'?"

"Well," we would say, "practice is hardly our concern. We don't know what the practical problems are. It's up to you administrators who have to deal with these problems every day to make the application. And as for not understanding our language, well, you can hardly fault us for that. If we are in the ivory tower, then you are surely in the basement. If we should descend so as to speak your language, why don't you ascend and meet us at least halfway up?"

Thereupon the discussion would end in an impasse. The listeners would go away feeling that they had been led to the trough but kept from drinking, because the theoreticians had failed to say anything that made operational sense to them. "If applications are to be made," they would ask, "who is better able to make them than the minds that developed those ideas in the first place? It is only because they are uncooperative that we can't use what they have discovered."

We, the speakers, would go away equally disillusioned, feeling that we had been pouring the water into their open mouths but that they had refused to drink. "For who," we would ask, "should be better able to appreciate and apply what we have to say than the men who are daily involved with the very problems we have been analyzing? It is only because they are lazy and ignorant that they won't use what we have discovered."

And so, to point the moral, the uncooperative researcher-theoreticians and the lazy, ignorant practitioners would go their own self-satisfied ways, each convinced that the fault for any lack of communication lay with the other.

Now I recall also that when I made these speeches on the nomothetic-idiographic theme, I would usually start my remarks with the observation that I had never been an administrator myself and never hoped to be one. But about a half-decade after this time, I suddenly did find myself an administrator, not of a school system to be sure, but of a bureau of educational research and service, with a staff about the same size as might be found in a middle-sized school. I had the usual "honeymoon" and then my problems began. One day, perhaps six months after I had taken office, I suddenly sat up in my overstuffed administrator's chair and said, "Why most of my problems are being generated by people. People are no damn good!"

It was just at that point that the full significance of a farewell card that had been given to me by the staff associates in the Midwest Administration Center when I left Chicago hit me. "If you're so smart," it read, "why aren't you rich?" Or to quote from another idiom, the phrase "Physician, Heal Thyself" came home to me with a new forcefulness. How was it that a man of such great theoretical expertise in the staff relations area should suddenly conclude that people are no damn good? No use to claim that I couldn't understand the theoretical language—I had helped to invent it![1] No use to claim that practice was hardly my concern—I was up to my neck in it! What then was my problem? Why was I having so much trouble applying the ideas that I had myself helped to formulate?

The answer to the latter question was some years coming, and has two parts, I now believe:

1. There is a tremendous gap between knowledge production and knowledge utilization that cannot be spanned *either* by the producer or by the utilizer himself, or even by these two acting in concert, at least in the typical situation. New mechanisms and agencies using special techniques are required to perform this bridging or linking function.
2. Knowledge is at best only one of a number of input factors in any practical situation. No practical problem can be solved using knowledge alone—a whole host of economic, social, political, motivational, cultural, and other factors must be considered.

Let me illustrate these two points with some examples. First, in relation to the gap between knowledge production and knowledge utilization, education seems to be literally centuries behind other areas of endeavor in recognizing the gap and in making provisions for its reduction. In the physical sciences, for instance, engineering activities were instituted for precisely this purpose. Consider the Bell Telephone Laboratories as an agency for knowledge production and the Bell Telephone system as an agency for knowledge consumption and application. Now a great deal of knowledge production, commonly called basic research, goes on in the Bell Laboratories; to cite one instance, much of the research in solid state physics leading to the discovery and development of transistors was conducted there. But it is a long step from developing transistors as a laboratory curiosity, however exciting their potential might be, to utilizing the transistor principle in building better dialing and switching equipment. No one expects the scientists in the Bell Laboratories to make such applications; indeed, if anyone were to suggest it, the idea would be thrown out on the grounds that scientists would be diverted from what they do best and turned to a task that they could do but poorly.

---

[1] The terms "idiographic" and "nomothetic" were picked from Roget's Thesaurus by me one wintry afternoon when I had nothing better to do than to try to find some new and interesting terms to use in our theory. We justified this at the time by claiming that we had to find terms "untainted" by value connotations.

Instead, AT&T in its wisdom has interposed a vast organization between the knowledge producers and the ultimate consumers. This system, known as Western Electric, has the unique mission of making the applications and producing the ultimate devices which the various Bell systems will install and use. Western Electric has its own coterie of engineers, who are themselves divided into specialties. Some of their personnel are concerned with developing prototype applications; others with testing these out and debugging them. Still others are concerned with designing these applications in ways that will make their production feasible and economical. And finally, of course, there are production specialists who actually turn out the devices that will be installed and used by the Bell Telephone companies.

This whole system seems to us only right and natural when we think of the physical sciences. But in education, even if there were good and plentiful basic research findings, there is no mechanism similar to the Western Electric Company, unless the R&D Centers and/or the Regional Educational Laboratories eventually assume this function, to carry on the intermediate functions of development, testing, and production. And as my original example indicates, as recently as a decade ago this lack had never even crossed our minds; instead, we were content to write off the research-practice gap as stemming from the uncooperativeness of the researchers or the laziness and ignorance of the practitioners, or both.

Let me dwell now for a moment on the second part of my answer to the question of why there is so much difficulty in applying new knowledge, *viz.*, that knowledge is, at best, one of a number of input factors in any practical problem situation. Let me use a real even if somewhat absurd example. In one school district I know about in the hills of Appalachia all of the power is held by the president of the Board who happens also to be the town physician. He has always controlled enough Board votes to hire and fire superintendents as he pleases. But this physician has one great vice: he is a morphine user. Now as a physician he had easy access to morphine and was able to provide himself with all that he needed to support his habit. But recently the state drug authority discovered his vice and relieved him of his license to prescribe narcotics. Hence he has had to turn to other sources for his supply, in this case, the local county health officer who is also his close personal friend.

Now it happens that the incumbent superintendent has somehow displeased the Board president, a failing that has cost the jobs of all of his predecessors. But the incumbent has one trump card: he happens to be the nephew of the county health officer. Hence the physician is faced with the difficult choice of firing the superintendent and losing his supply of narcotics or retaining the superintendent and having to put up with his nonconformist tendencies. A Hobson's choice indeed!

If we could find a candidate for the superintendent's job in this district who had ready access to a supply of drugs, great things might be accomplished. The incumbent is not in this happy situation, and every action he takes will have to be examined in terms of its potential for upsetting the delicate balance of power that presently exists. Get the physician too angry and he may decide that he can find some other source of drugs after all. If new knowledge is to be inserted into this school system's workings, it will have to be able to survive this scrutiny.

My colleague, Henry M. Brickell, has put the case more eloquently than this homely example illustrates. He says:

> When research-based information does exist, it must take its place beside all the other information available. The research finding may coincide with and confirm the other information. In such a case, the chances of its being used are good. Or it may be the only source of information on a specific topic, in which case its chances of use are possibly only fair because it is not substantiated by experience. Or it may conflict with other information, in which case the situation is one of competition.
>
> In the United States even today, research findings do not compete well against such established, persuasive information sources as one's personal experience or knowledge of what other schools are doing. For example, when a local school asks, "What might we adopt to solve our particular problem?" a very limited number of solutions (at best) generated through a research and development process compete for its approval with a larger number of solutions which have been generated without benefit of research. The prospective adopter is not likely to select the research-based solution solely because it stands on a base of scientific knowledge, especially if something else is *less expensive, easier to install, preferred by the faculty, or otherwise attractive.* (Italics added.) (Brickell, 1967, p. 235.)

Let me call your special attention to the very last part of that quotation, which asserts that research-based solutions to educational problems are not likely to be selected if they are in competition with other solutions that are less expensive, easier to install, preferred by the faculty, or otherwise attractive. Mere knowledge, Brickell seems to be saying, is not enough; there are other economic, feasibility, and motivational factors that must be taken into account. And he might well have added social, political, cultural, and psychological factors as well. Whoever and whatever it is that will bridge the gap between knowledge production and knowledge utilization will have to be sophisticated enough and shrewd enough to assess these factors and be able to cope with them. In general I would assert that the typical researcher surely, and probably the typical administrator, do not have the special training and equipment for this purpose.

The Theory-Practice Continuum

If my analysis is correct, so that special mechanisms and agencies will be needed to fill the enormous gap between knowledge production and knowledge utilization, where are these to come from and what will their nature be? To deal with these questions I will need to digress for a moment to describe to you the categories of a theory-practice continuum which my colleague, David L. Clark and I have developed and published in other contexts.[2] I would like to begin by defining the various phases of this continuum and then proceed by discussing certain of their relationships.

Clark and I have talked about four phases or stages in this continuum, viz., *research, development, diffusion,* and *adoption.* Our concern today is with the middle two of these four, but I believe it is important to distinguish them from the other two, with which they are sometimes confused.

Research has as its basic objective *the advancement of knowledge.* The researcher is not concerned, nor should he be, with whether or not his research has an evident practical application. He needs freedom to pursue his ideas wherever they lead; he needs to be free to fail on occasion; he needs to be free from pressures for an immediate payoff. Research provides one input for the next phase, development.

Development has as its basic objective the *identification of operating problems and the formulation of solutions to those problems.* The developer, unlike the researcher, is most acutely concerned with practice. It is his job to make practice conform to the highest ideals that can be set for it, to be constantly probing the system to determine what, if anything, is keeping it from functioning at its best, and then to devise new approaches and techniques to ameliorate or eliminate whatever problems he may identify. In devising such problem solutions the developer borrows heavily wherever he can—from research, from experts, from his own experience.

But development implies more than just coming up with an answer. The answer must be one that will work in the real world. It must be one that can be adapted into the system. It must be one that is usable by the personnel available. It must get results. Thus development involves production, engineering, packaging, and testing a proposed problem solution or invention.

Diffusion has as its basic objective the *creation of awareness about new developments and the provision of opportunities for their assessment along whatever dimensions practitioners may deem necessary.* The most potent solutions that men can devise to overcome their problems have little utility if practitioners are not informed about them, or if they have

---

[2] See, for example, our papers, "An Examination of Potential Change Roles in Education," NEA-CSI Seminar on Innovation in Planning School Curricula, Aerlie House, Virginia, October, 1965; and "Effecting Change in Institutions of Higher Education," UCEA International Inter-Visitation Program, Ann Arbor, Michigan, October, 1966.

1. *He can tell.* Telling involves the word. The word may be written, as in newsletters, papers, monographs, books, articles, and the like; or it may be spoken, as in conferences, speeches, conversations, etc. My essential diffusion mode today is, obviously, telling.

2. *He can show.* Showing is a form of communication which involves a direct confrontation with the phenomena of interest, as in a planned or casual observation, or in actual participation. It may involve structured experiences such as demonstrations or simulations; or it may involve looking at materials or displays such as pictures, slides, films, dioramas, realia, and the like.

3. *He can help.* Helping consists in the direct involvement of the diffuser in the affairs of the practitioner but on the practitioner's terms. It may take the form of consultation, service, trouble-shooting, and the like.

4. *He can involve.* Involving takes the form of an inclusion or cooptation of the practitioner. Thus the diffuser may enlist the practitioner in assisting with the development, testing, or packaging of an innovation; in acting as a "satellite" or agent to diffuse the invention to others; in contributing the problems to which innovative solutions are to be sought; and the like.

5. *He can train.* Training takes the form of familiarizing practitioners with the features of the proposed problem solution or invention, or of assisting them to increase their skills and competencies or to alter their attitudes. It may be accomplished through formal university credit courses, institutes, workshops, internships, apprenticeships, extension courses, local in-service training, "T-group sessions," and similar experiences. Training may involve telling, showing, helping, and involving but differs from these other techniques in that the practitioner makes a formal commitment to learn by allowing himself to be trained.

6. *He can intervene.* Intervening consists in the direct involvement of the diffuser on his own terms, not those of the practitioner. It may take the form of mandating certain actions (e.g., adopting a statewide textbook), inserting certain control mechanisms (e.g., instituting a statewide testing program), or of intruding certain economic or political factors (e.g., arranging the purchase of language laboratory equipment or causing board dismissal of an uncooperative teacher).

The reconstructed logic of the diffusion process is thus as follows: The diffuser has the task of building awareness and understanding of an invention and causing practitioners to consider its features with a view to possible application. To discharge this function he has essentially six techniques at his disposal: telling, showing, helping, involving, training, and intervening. He will use any combination of these techniques to cause favorable consideration without resorting to hucksterism or unethical manipulation. He sees himself as a person opening viable professional alternatives to the potential adopter with a problem to solve.

ADOPTION

The purpose of adoption activity is to shape and install a problem solution or invention within a particular local setting. This phase seems to have received little conceptual attention from anyone; it is perhaps the most muddy of the four. It seems to me that at least three major steps are involved, with the second of these being divided into several sub-steps as follows:

1. *Trial.* No prudent administrator will permit the installation of a proposed problem solution on a permanent basis without having convinced himself that it will perform as claimed. Indeed, a local trial is mandatory even when national assessments have indicated that the solution performs well on the average, for the obvious reason that the situation in which installation is proposed may not be average. Local variations must be taken into account.

2. *Installation.* When a proposed solution has proved itself through a local trial, it then becomes necessary to arrange for its installation on a building-wide or system-wide basis. At least four areas of concern must be attended to:

> *Modification.* No invention will fit exactly into a local school situation for which it was not explicitly designed. Decisions will have to be made whether the fit can best be accomplished by modifications in the invention itself or in the school situation. If for example the invention requires teachers with particular skills but teachers with these skills are simply not available, some modification in the invention will be required.
>
> *Training.* Personnel expected to use the invention must be trained. No teacher will willingly risk his reputation before a class with a technique about which he is unsure. More importantly, no administrator should be willing to permit a teacher to adopt a new technique without proper training for use, lest through lack of knowledge he should

```
┌─────────────────────────────────────────────┐
│                                               │
│              Adoption Activity                │
│                                               │
│                        ⎧ Modify               │
│       Try-Test         ⎪ Train                │
│       Install............⎨                     │
│       Institutionalize ⎪ Equip and House      │
│                        ⎩ Organize             │
│                                               │
└─────────────────────────────────────────────┘
```

fail to take full advantage of whatever additional benefits are expected to accrue.

Facilities. Many inventions require particular kinds of physical arrangements. Typically a school adopting such an invention will not be suitably housed for the purpose or may not possess appropriate equipment. Flexible scheduling or multiple-size grouping cannot occur in a building arranged for conventional size classes of 25 or 30.

Administration and organization. The proposed invention may have important administrative or organizational consequences. Problems in scheduling, in budgeting, in staffing, in organizing may all produce headaches for the administrator. Unless these possibly disruptive consequences can be foreseen and obviated, the result may be a failure of an otherwise useful invention.

3. *Institutionalization.* Ultimately the invention must be assimilated into the ongoing program. At some time it must cease to be viewed as new and must become an integral and accepted component. It is not clear to me what steps might be taken to insure institutionalization. Sometimes I feel that the most important factor may simply be the passage of time. Obviously, the lack of awkward incidents in relation to the invention is helpful and the more quickly the spotlight can be taken off of it the more quickly it is likely to become accepted.

How Are We Doing on Bridging the Gap Between Research and Practice?

In my preceding remarks I have attempted to illustrate the fact that there is a large gap between knowledge production and utilization, and I have attempted to depict the flow of knowledge from initial research into final use in terms of a four-category continuum. Our concern at this conference is primarily with the middle two categories, development and diffusion, for they represent the projected means for bridging this gap. I would like now to turn briefly to a consideration of what we are doing, and how well, in operationalizing these two categories.

I will, therefore, not make any further remarks about either research or adoption. I do feel compelled to observe, however, as we leave these categories behind, that my lack of attention to them does not indicate any high degree of satisfaction on my part with the way research and adoption activities are operating. Indeed, it is well known that research results are not being utilized to any great degree in educational practice, and that almost no attention has been paid either conceptually or practically to the problems of adoption which I briefly outlined above. But my concern today is with the bridge and not with the abutments, although I hope that due attention will be paid lest we mount our bridge of steel on banks of sand, when the time comes.

Let me turn then to a more detailed consideration of development and adoption.

DEVELOPMENT

Development is a very complicated process which neither practitioners nor researchers are particularly competent to carry out. If there is any area in education that calls for reorganization and for the evolution of new professional roles, this is certainly it. Experience from industry indicates that from five to eleven times as much investment is required to develop an application from a research finding than was necessary to produce the research finding in the first place. High level specialists are required to do the job. Moreover, development depends not only upon the availability of relevant basic research but upon a host of other factors as well: the availability of resources, institutional support, experience, practical judgment, political factors, and the like. Research data provide only *one* of several critical inputs, and the blending of these inputs requires more specialized skill than either researchers or practitioners commonly possess.

Initial attempts at development in education occurred gradually and without a clear realization of what was happening. I am sure that the persons following the lead of Jerrold Zacharias in the development of the PSSC physics materials were scarcely aware of what a vanguard group they were. The several other curriculum development groups, mainly funded by the National Science Foundation in those early days, were certainly more interested in updating content than they were in establishing development patterns which others might emulate. But their pattern did seem to prove successful, and it was soon emulated, particularly in the new course content improvement projects of the U.S. Office of Education.

In more recent years we have seen further systematic attempts to establish development agencies. Clearly the research and development centers have a mandate to turn their research into practice. But as we have seen, successful development involves a great deal more than the mere availability of relevant research. We may well wonder therefore whether the primarily research-oriented R & D centers will be up to the task. Another similar effort has occurred in the establishment of the regional educational laboratories, which are mandated to identify and solve educational problems, hopefully through recourse to research but by other means if necessary. Thus far the laboratories are too new to make it profitable to venture a judgment about their probable level of success.

It seems that no existing agencies have responsibility for the full range of development activities indicated by the taxonomy presented earlier. The depicting function seems to be especially neglected. While both regional laboratories and Title III projects were mandated to make needs surveys of their regions, it is clear that these surveys were carried out in a most perfunctory way, and without the benefit of hard data in many cases. (I should note at once that this is not the fault of the agencies involved so much as it is of the Office of Education, which mandated these surveys under incredible constraints of time and resources.) More importantly, even when well done, these surveys provide but a static "snapshot" of the situation at any moment rather than a dynamic "motion picture film" over an appreciable time span.

The invention function is perhaps better managed than the others, although certainly not nearly as well as it should be. Funds are available for improvement projects and several agencies, including the new industry-education combines as well as the regional laboratories and research and development centers, are beginning to undertake massive improvement projects. Yet a conceptual underpinning for such activity is still missing. We still know far too little about effective ways of creating new solutions or even of transmitting, translating, or transforming known solutions.

Fabrication will probably be handled best by the industry-education combines, since these typically involve publishers and manufacturers of hardware that can be used to good effect. The publishing industry has shown a great deal of ingenuity in the past in placing its materials into interesting and novel formats and will probably continue to do so.

In the area of testing we came again upon a quite underdeveloped area. We shall see later that existing evaluation designs do not seem to be too appropriate for the real problems of education. We may also be concerned that if much of the fabrication is carried on by commercial agencies, they may be over eager to rush their fabrications into production without the kinds of testing that would assure a professionally warrantable product. Thus both conceptual and consumer protection innovations are needed in the area of testing.

From one point of view, then, the development picture is not too rosy. When one considers, however, how late in the day we determined to undertake development at all, and with what meagre resources we have supported it, we may perhaps be forgiven if we take a more charitable view. Now that education is fully aware of the need for development activities, is apprised of their complexity, and is being aided with resources to get development activity started, we may hope that within a decade most of the problems I have enumerated will have disappeared.

DIFFUSION

Diffusion is an activity regarded with some distaste by many members of the educational establishment, particularly the research community. It is often equated with hucksterism, and I suppose, in fairness, that one must concede that a great deal of hucksterism does take place. This fact may be the best argument one can muster in favor of well organized diffusion efforts, however, so that one can be sure that what is being diffused is a viable alternative rather than just another fad.

Traditionally educational diffusion has fallen within the domain of commercial interests, mainly the book publisher. Recently both research and development centers and regional educational laboratories were given some diffusion responsibilities, and these agencies have begun to develop new approaches, although haltingly.

The major diffusion responsibility seems to be falling squarely on the shoulders of Title III projects. There is a school of thought that suggests that research and development centers should be concerned with research, regional educational laboratories with development, and Title III projects with diffusion. This is a formulation with which I am in essential agreement, perhaps because this division of labor would fit my earlier model so well. There would be at least three of the change stages, then, for which institutional responsibility would be firmly fixed. This formulation also seems to be supported in the Office of Education.

But whatever our view may be about the appropriate institutional arrangements for carrying out the diffusion function, it is clear that that function has not to date been carried out very well. In my own opinion the major reason for this failure may be traced to our earlier failure to delineate acceptable *strategies* for diffusion. I use the word *strategy* to indicate an action plan which indicates which of the adoption techniques outlined in the earlier adoption activity taxonomy should be used when and where and in what combination. To evolve such a strategy seems to me to imply some consideration of at least the following elements:

1. *Assumptions concerning the nature of the practitioner who will be exposed to the strategy.* The practitioner may be viewed as a rational entity, who can be convinced, on the basis of hard data and logical argument, of the utility of proposed invention; as an untrained entity who does not know how to perform but who can be taught; as a psychological entity who can be persuaded; as an economic entity who can be compensated or deprived; as a political entity who can be influenced; as an entity in a bureaucratic system who can be compelled; or as a professionally oriented entity who can be obligated. We might term these respectively as *rational, didactic, psychological, economic, political, authority,* and *value* assumptions. Obviously the ways in which the earlier outlined techniques are used will depend heavily on which assumptions one makes. Therefore, telling, showing, training, etc. will certainly be different if one assumes a rationally oriented subject, i.e., one who will be convinced by facts, than if one assumes a politically oriented subject, i.e., one who can be manipulated.

2. *Assumptions concerning the end state in which one wishes to leave the practitioner.* Very little attention is typically paid to the question of

the end state in which the diffuser wishes to leave his subject. This situation may arise, of course, because the diffuser may act as a mere huckster; hucksterism may "sell" a particular invention being promoted but it may leave the practitioner with very little residual propensity ever to consider any other proposed invention. But even with "well-intentioned" diffusers this difficulty may arise because of a basic failure to consider desirable end states. What is it that the practitioner should be able to do, think, or to feel as a result of having been exposed to a diffusion strategy? Is he to be better trained? More skillful? More knowledgeable? More open? Wiser? Obviously the choice of a diffusion strategy would be considerably aided by careful attention to this factor. It seems particularly ironic that this situation of carelessness about end states should hold true in the field of education, which is so generally characterized by concern about behavioral outcomes and objectives. If we applied a little of our usual logic about specifying expected goals this difficulty would be largely overcome.

3. *Assumptions about the nature of the agency or mechanism carrying out the diffusion activity.* No sensible diffusion strategy can be evolved without careful attention to the matter of who is to carry it out. For not all strategies are within the capabilities of all agents or mechanisms. Constraints exist which mandate certain actions for certain agents and which prohibit other actions to them. So for example, a regional educational laboratory, acting as a diffusion agent, is hardly in a position to intervene, since it lacks the necessary power or authority to do so, but telling, showing, or involving come "naturally" to it. A state department of education may well intervene (and indeed may be legally mandated to do so) but would probably be very suspect if it tried to involve. An individual teacher can tell and show but probably would be thought ridiculous if she set up a training experience for her fellows. A university, however, could carry out this latter function with impunity. Since the final implementation of the strategy depends upon the agent, the strategy must be one appropriate to the agent's circumstances.

4. *Assumptions concerning the substance of the invention.* Obviously not all inventions are alike; they pose different problems of adoption, and this fact must be taken into account in developing an appropriate diffusion strategy. One way to view this situation is in terms of the amount of change mandated by the invention. Thus Chin (1963) characterizes innovations as involving *substitution, alteration* (a minor change), *perturbations and variations* (mere changes in organizational equilibrium), *restructuring* (requiring reorganization), and *value orientation change* (deep-seated value changes). Rogers (1962) talks about characteristics of inventions that make them more or less acceptable, including *relative advantage* (instrinsic superiority), *compatibility* (consistency with existing values and experience), *complexity* (difficulty in use), *divisibility* (degree to which the invention can be partitioned and/or tried

on a limited basis), and *communicability* (or diffusability). Whether these or other ways of classifying the substance of innovations are most useful is less important for us at the moment than that there be some explicit way for taking account of substance at the time that a diffusion strategy is devised.

We are thus confronted, in considering diffusion, with a picture that is, if anything, even less satisfying than that presented by development, which we reviewed earlier. There seems to be a considerable confusion about the organizational responsibilities that may exist in this important arena, with attempts to develop viable organizations being so recent as to invalidate any attempts at judgment at this time. Further, theory and practice are both relatively silent on the important issue of how diffusion strategies are best devised. All we seem to be able to do at this time is to point to the important factors that probably ought to be considered. However, as in the case for development, when one considers how recently this concern has emerged and how new are our efforts to deal with it, we may perhaps be willing to take a more long range view.

Evaluation

Thus far I have said very little about evaluation, which you may have considered rather remarkable in view of the fact that the term appears in the title of this paper. I wish to remedy that defect now. Evaluation is so important and so pervasive a concept when we think about closing the gap between knowledge production and utilization that it deserves quite detailed and separate attention.

I shall have two major points to make about it: (1) The concept of evaluation is changing rapidly, becoming in particular much more pervasive than has traditionally been the case, and (2) The methodologies currently in use for evaluation are hopelessly bad and urgently need replacement.

Let me begin with some observations about what has in the past been meant by evaluation. Typically two complementary operations are denoted by the term: (1) the comparison of some results, output, or product with a set of standards, in an absolute sense; and (2) the comparison of some two or more methods of producing the same results, output, or product, in a relative sense. In the first case the standards were usually derived in relation to some objective. Thus, the objective might be to develop reading skill, and the standard might be the 4.0 grade equivalent on the Stanford Reading Achievement Test. Pupils could then be judged, in an absolute sense, on their achievement of that objective. Or two methods of teaching reading skills might be judged to determine which produced a higher average reading skill level in two groups of pupils, in a relative sense.

Measurements taken to carry out these classic forms of evaluation are usually of the pre- and post-test type, depending upon one's preoccupation with initial status, group equivalence, and similar matters relating to control or data analysis. The term *bench mark* is frequently used to describe collection of initial status data. Between collection of bench mark data and final performance data a long period, say a semester or school year in length, could and usually did intervene, during which data might or might not be collected but during which stringent controls are maintained so that the data will not be confounded. In particular great care is taken not to alter any essential element related to the method, technique, or content being evaluated, lest the change render the evaluation invalid (one could not tell what was being evaluated). Generally speaking the traditional rules of experimental design and field control are rigorously invoked. The essential task of traditional evaluation is to judge.

Emergent evaluation however is seen as a tool to aid in decision-making. The tasks of (1) identifying an educational problem or need, (2) devising or selecting a treatment to cope with it, (3) implementing the treatment procedures, and (4) determining the treatment's feasibility, quality, effectiveness, and efficiency require a series of decisions which evaluation can aid. The process of collecting and interpreting data relevant to this series is seen as the substance of evaluation.

Daniel Stufflebeam (1967) of the Evaluation Center at The Ohio State University seems to me to have come closest to defining the new evaluation when he talks about four kinds of evaluative activity. The first of these is *context evaluation*, which, in the setting of the school, means the continuous determination of the school's status on key variables with a view to identifying needs and problems. Such an evaluation gives the decision-maker data he needs to have about important directions in which he should move. Second, there is *input evaluation*, which is concerned with assessing various possible responses to the needs or problems that may exist. There are probably a number of ways, for example, in which a school principal might revamp his reading program to take account of the special problems posed by culturally disadvantaged children; which of these ways has the highest payoff potential in his situation? Third, we need to be concerned with *process evaluation*, which is used to determine whether the selected input is working as it was expected to and which, even more importantly, provides for continuous feedback so that the selected input can be continuously refined and adjusted to better achieve its intended purpose. Finally, there is *product evaluation*, which is most like what we have traditionally meant by evaluation, i.e., the determination of the feasibility, quality, efficiency, and effectiveness of the input in responding to the need or problem involved.

It is interesting to check the terms of this analysis against the terms listed in the taxonomy of development presented earlier. What Stufflebeam calls *context evaluation* is of course very similar to what I meant by the term *depict,* i.e., a continuous assessment of the situation. We might note the similarity of this concept of continuous assessment to the older concepts of bench mark or base line, but while these latter are static concepts indicating status at some point in time like a snapshot, the continuous assessment idea is rather like a dynamic bench mark or base line, giving, as it were, a continuous motion picture film of what is going on. Needless to say attempts at continuous assessment pose some interesting methodological problems.

Next, it seems clear that Stufflebeam's idea of *input evaluation* has relevance at what I have called the "invent" stage of development. In order to determine, for example, whether the invention problem is one of transmitting, translating, or transforming existing solutions, of synthesizing new solutions from available elements, or of creating a solution *de novo,* some assessment will be required of possible inputs and their probability of useful payoff.

Finally, when a solution has been fabricated, it must be tested, and it is clear now that testing should involve both *process* and *product* measures. It is likely that the solution will not be in near-perfect form when it is first applied in a real context; hence continuous improvement is mandated. Process evaluation allows for this contingency. Further, we need to be sure that the solution is being applied in a form reasonably similar to the one its fabricators had in mind; again, process evaluation to the rescue. And of course we want to be sure that the solution does in fact achieve its objectives; i.e., meeting the need or responding to the problem. And here we have product evaluation.

Needless to say, we are a long way indeed from having the techniques necessary for applying evaluation in the way indicated by this analysis. These concepts are only now emerging, and it will take a long time before we are able to apply them systematically in operational situations. But it is clear that traditional concepts are no longer good enough.

The shortcomings of traditional evaluation can be documented in other ways than through such a theoretical analysis, however. We need only to look at the large mass of "no significant difference" findings typically produced by evaluation studies to begin to wonder about the power of the techniques, particularly when all the evidence of the senses of participants argues that there is a difference. Or consider the conclusion of the widely publicized Coleman report (1966, p. 235), which asserts, after a most careful and thorough examination of all available data, that there is only a ". . . relatively small amount of school-to-school variation that is not accounted for by differences in family background, indicating the small independent effect of variations in school facilities, curriculum, and staff upon achievements."

This conclusion is simply incredible on its face. It means, if true, that it makes no difference whether a teacher is good or bad, whether good or poor materials are available, whether the school is a barn or a geodesic dome, students will learn about the same (and not much at that!). Now anyone who has spent any time at all in a school knows that is just not so; why then do our evaluative techniques not pick this up?

I believe it can be argued that traditional evaluation has four characteristics which account for its sharply limited utility. These include *terminal availability of data, retrospective view, imposition of constraints,* and *limited generalizability.*

1. Evaluative data are usually available only upon the termination of the evaluative period. Hence they can provide information relevant only to "go," "no-go," or "recycle" decisions about the treatment being evaluated. Other kinds of decisions cannot be served.

2. Evaluative data typically afford only a retrospective view. The evaluation does not provide information during the test of the treatment which might have been used to improve it.

3. The assumptions on which evaluative designs are based (those of traditional experimental design) impose a series of constraints on the evaluator. There can be, for example, no variation in treatment or context once the evaluation is under way, since this would result in the confounding of critical variances. Thus traditional evaluations militate against any concurrent effort at improvement of the treatment and against other contextual changes, e.g., the introduction of any other innovation, during the term of evaluation.

4. The constraints imposed because of the requirements of classical experimental design in effect create a laboratory condition within which the treatment will be tested. The many sources of variation found in the real world are deliberately excluded from having any effect upon the outcome. The evaluation describes what happens under laboratory circumstances, and not under "typical" circumstances. The generalizability of the findings is thus necessarily limited.

The problem of constraints is an especially interesting one and probably deserves some special comment. Generally speaking, the constraints arise because of a variety of assumptions that must be made to support the logical and statistical structure of design theory. Three general classes of assumptions may be identified:

1. *Statistical assumptions.* Statistical assumptions support the development of the statistical techniques for analyzing and interpreting data. There are certain assumptions necessary to know that a distribution is normal before one can assert that 68 per cent of the cases are included in the interval $\overline{X} \pm s$. Other assumptions are built into the derivation of the interpretive tables in which the "significance" of analytic statistics is read; thus the derivation of the F distribution depends upon assumptions of random sampling from a population in which the variable of concern is normally distributed. Finally, still other assumptions are

MORPHOLOGICAL ANALYSIS*

Frederick R. Ignatovich

The future is what men make it, so long as they never close their minds to the heroic potential of the human mind.

—Jeffrey St. John

Dᴜʀɪɴɢ the 1940's Fritz Zwicky, a noted astrophysicist, advocated the use of a morphological approach to problem-solving in scholarly communities and social institutions.[1] Zwicky felt that despite the dedicated work of thinkers throughout the course of history, the accumulated principles of wisdom have not been utilized fully for the realization of a sound and healthy social world. He claims that in the past "real progress" has been made in the context of discovery and invention by "lone wolves," that is, those men of thought and action who cast off the prevailing dogmas in their fields of inquiry or endeavor, who ventured upon the high seas of thought and action and probed the unknown. Such persons are the creative morphologists who discover new knowledge and invent new applications. Furthermore, what typifies past and present morphologists is the adoption of a universalistic and collective orientation that enables them to ". . . visualize and comprehend all of the essential interrelations among physical objects, phenomena, concepts, and ideas, as well as evaluate the human capabilities needed for all future constructive activities."[2] They employ a morphological approach that aims at elucidating all the possible relationships among objects of consideration without prevaluing the desirability or feasibility of the analysis itself or the products of the analysis.

Those who fail to think in universal terms and vast perspectives cling to calcified beliefs and dogmas that inhibit the generation of new knowledge and new technologies. "They thus practice what might be called coastal navigation along clearly discernible shore lines of well-established knowledge and they do not dare to venture on the high seas of thought and action where the horizons are unlimited."[3] They are the custodians of existing bodies of knowledge and tinker with puzzles generated by prevailing paradigms.

---

[1] F. Zwicky, *Discovery, Invention, Research: Through the Morphological Approach* (Toronto: Collier-Macmillan Canada, Ltd., 1969).

[2] Ibid., p. 3.

[3] Ibid., p. 3.

---

* This paper was presented at the American Educational Research Association annual meeting, April 1974, and also appears in *Futurism in Education: Methodologies* by Stephen P. Hencley and James R. Yates, eds., Berkeley: McCutchin Publishing Corp., 1974. Used with permission.

Morphologists of social phenomena would be those individuals who create alternative conceptualizations and applications of social knowledge. They would be the creative social scientists and social engineers who employ morphological analyses to discover, invent, and construct alternative future social systems.

Overview

In order to facilitate the process of imaginative-creative inquiry, and to some extent routinize the process, Zwicky has developed new methods of thought and procedure to systematically probe the unknown (the discovery of new knowledge) and to systematically utilize existing and new knowledge to suggest possible inventions and technological applications to social systems. These new procedures are collectively termed *morphological analysis* and consist of:

A. identifying a problem—stated with precision and emanating from existing knowledge or experience.
B. adopting a morphological perspective—every problem consists of complexes of objects, phenomena, ideas, and concepts that are structurally interrelated.
C. employing an unbiased attitude—all problem solutions are possible unless proven impossible and
D. employing a morphological procedure—that produces alternative solutions to the problem by following the rules of the procedure.

Morphological analysis is essentially a Kantian mode of inquiry that focuses on systematic elucidation of all alternative solutions to a well-stated problem.[4] It forces the inquirer to consider all possible solutions of a problem, thereby minimizing the omission of a particular solution that results from prevaluation or prejudicial judgment.

Mitroll and Turoff provide a rationale for the use of Kantian inquiry in forecasting the future by first indicating that the future consists of hopes, dreams, plans, and aspirations. Subsequently, they indicate that a mode of inquiry that facilitates the analysis of aspirations would produce alternative or possible futures. In their words: "If the future is 99 percent aspiration or plan, it would seem that the best approach is *to draw forth explicitly as many different aspirations or plans for the future as possible. In short, we want to examine as many different alternative futures as we can.*"[5]

Morphological analysis is one of a family of exploratory techniques (for example, scenarios, delphic probes) that provide reconnaissance in-

4 See I. Mitroff and M. Turoff, "The Whys Behind the Hows," IEEE Spectrum, 10, no. 3 (March 1973), pp. 62–71, for a discussion of alternative modes of inquiry.
5 Ibid., p. 66.

formation concerning alternative futures, with the added advantage of being the only one that systematically produces a "cornucopia" of alternatives.

Morphological Analysis via the Method of the Morphological Box

In order to deduce all possible solutions to a problem, which is assumed to be multidimensional, and to ensure an unbiased evaluation of the solutions, Zwicky created the method of the morphological box. The required and sequential rules for employing this method are:

Step 1: The problem to be solved must be very concisely formulated.

Step 2: All of the parameters that might be of importance for the solution of the given problem must be localized and analyzed.

Step 3: The morphological box or multidimensional matrix that contains all of the potential solutions of the given problem is constructed.

Step 4: All of the solutions contained in the morphological box are closely scrutinized and evaluated with respect to the purposes that are to be achieved.

Step 5: The optimally suitable solutions are (being) selected and (are) practically applied, provided that the necessary means are available. This reduction to practice requires in general a supplemental morphological study.[6]

In applying morphological methods to a particular field of inquiry, one can attempt to account for all (slack morphology) or relatively few aspects (tight morphology) of the phenomena. This is analogous to the assumption of a macroscopic or microscopic perspective—the view from the captain's bridge as compared with the view from the boiler room.

In order to provide some insight and understanding of the intricacies of applying morphological methods, it seems wise to progress from simple to complex applications—simplicity facilitating clarity and complexity developing depth of understanding.

For purposes of illustration, let us consider two applications of morphological analysis. The first is an *attempt* to conduct an analysis of a problem in the field of educational administration, e.g., the problem of interface between public school systems and colleges of education.

It is a tight morphological situation that accounts for relatively few aspects or dimensions of the problem. This perspective is assumed for instructional purposes and not because of inherent simplicity in the phenomena. At best, it should be considered a useful instructional device or initial morphological probe. The second is a slack morphological situ-

6 F. Zwicky, op. cit., p. 101.

ation that accounts for a large number of parameters. It is an elaborate analysis of hypothetical jet engines and provides an illustration of the productiveness of morphological inquiry.

Application I: Alternate Interfaces Between a College of Education and Public School Systems

One of the perplexing problems faced today by colleges of education in the U.S.A. is the interface between colleges and the public school systems that form its significant environment. Awareness of interface dysfunctions have been verbalized, analyzed, and eulogized, not necessarily in that order, by those who honor the passing of unidimensional and unidirectional relationships.

For example, practitioners frequently claim that degree programs are not relevant to the needs of administrators and teachers in school systems. They claim that courses conducted on campus provide the essential building blocks for obtaining a degree but do not help resolve persistent instructional and management problems. Also, the response of a college to field problems is relatively simple and direct—create a new experimental course. If the problem persists, routinize the course. If it dissipates, drop the course.

Whether social, political, economic, or other forces have evoked cries of relevancy and responsiveness of practitioners or whether the dysfunctions in fact exist is not the substance of this application. Instead, the morphological approach leads us to inquire: What are all the possible purposive interfaces between public school systems and a college of education?

Are there alternative responses to practitioner needs that have not been attempted? Analysis of this problem can be provided by use of the method of the morphological box, as follows:

Step 1: The problem is concisely formulated. What are all possible purposive institutional interfaces between public school systems and a college of education?

Step 2: All the parameters are localized and analyzed. This is the process of enumerating the parameters and identifying elements of the parameters. Those identified will depend on the state of knowledge in the field of application and the precision of the problem statement. Since a morphological perspective assumes that every entity consists of a set of independent interrelated objects, ideas, concepts, or phenomena, the task at this point is to identify and list the set.

For illustration, let us consider some basic elements of social interaction. First, two or more concrete units must enter into a relationship and interact. In our case, this would be a unit from the school system and a unit from the college. Let us assume that the crucial units in school systems are roles (teacher, principal), work groups (administrative teams, sixth-grade teachers), organizational units (elementary, middle, high schools), the organization itself, and for the college of education, which consists of a role (professor), interest groups (evaluation, competency based education), departmental task forces (field-service unit), and college task forces (interdisciplinary teams). Second, there must be a need or purpose for entering into a relationship between units, a function that makes the units interdependent. Let us assume that the triad of instruction (transfer of knowledge), research (the production of knowledge), and service (the resolution of operational problems) are the basic needs valued by both units. Third, all interaction between units takes place in a setting or physical location. This can occur in one of three places: at the school district, at the college, or at a neutral location. Finally, a college can interfere with a single school district or a set of school districts. There are other factors that could be considered, for example, frequency of interaction. But we will stop enumeration at this point to keep the analysis simple.

Summarizing, the following parameters and elements have been identified:

PARAMETER	ELEMENTS
P_1 Number of Public School Systems	P^1_1 Single, P^2_1 Multiple
P_2 Unit of a Public School System	P^1_2 Role, P^2_2 Work Group, P^3_2 Organizational Unit, P^4_2 Total Organization
P_3 Unit of a College	P^1_3 Role, P^2_3 Interest Group, P^3_3 Departmental Task Force, P^4_3 College Task Force
P_4 Need or Purpose	P^1_4 Instruction, P^2_4 Research, P^3_4 Service
P_5 Location or Setting of Interaction	P^1_5 College, P^2_5 Neutral Turf, P^3_5 School District

Step 3: The morphological box is constructed.

$$\left[P^1_1, \ P^2_1 \right]$$

$$\left[P^1_2, \ P^2_2, \ P^3_2, \ P^4_2 \right]$$

$$\left[P^1_3, \ P^2_3, \ P^3_3, \ P^4_3 \right]$$

$$\left[P^1_4, \ P^2_4, \ P^3_4 \right]$$

$$\left[P^1_5, \ P^2_5, \ P^3_5 \right]$$

This matrix contains 288 permutations or alternate paths through the matrix arrived at by multiplying the elements of the parameters:

$$2 \times 4 \times 4 \times 3 \times 3 = 288$$

By encircling one element of each parameter and connecting them with straight lines, one path or problem solution is generated.

Therefore, the morphological box contains 288 alternative purposive interfaces between a college of education and public school systems.

It is important to note that up to this point no attempt has been made to evaluate the feasibility of any possible alternative. That is because we wish to avoid any prevaluation of alternatives.

> *Step 4:* All of the solutions are scrutinized and evaluated. First, the matrix is examined for internal contradictions that would result in meaningless solutions. This matrix appears to be free of such conflicts, therefore, individual and groups of solutions are examined. One set of solutions, those defined by P^1_1, P^1_2, P^1_3, P^1_4 or P^2_4 or P^3_4, and P^1_5, identify interfaces that are operational in most universities.

These consist of individuals from a single public school system who come to the college and interact with professors for instruction, research, and service purposes. Examples of these interfaces are numerous, such as an individual study course, research proposal development and review sessions, and general advising and counseling.

By changing parameter P_1 from P^1_1 to P^2_1, a single school system to multiple school systems, and holding all other parameter values constant, P^1_2, P^1_3, P^1_4 or P^2_4 or P^3_4, and P^1_5, we can identify interfaces, such as formal courses, a collection of individual research studies, and a file cabinet full of advisees. These are all examples of interfaces that exist and occur almost daily in a university setting.

Now let us look at some interfaces that depart from the usual type of institutional interface. For example, the interfaces defined by P^2_1 multiple school system; P^3_2 organizational units in a public school; P^2_3

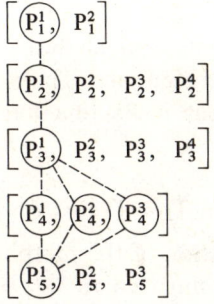

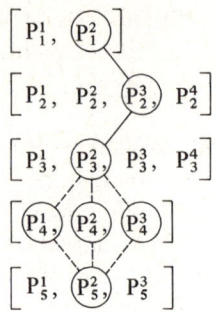

college interest groups; P^i_4 the instruction, research, and service functions; and P^2_5 neutral turf.

This set of interfaces would consist of organizational units from school systems and interest groups from a college that met in a neutral setting to transfer knowledge, develop new knowledge, and resolve operational problems. This is essentially an extern interface, which exists in very few colleges in the United States. Also, most of the existing extern programs are for administrators on an individual basis (P^1_2). The possibility of providing extern interfaces for instructional teams, administrative teams, counseling teams, and so on, from school systems with instructional, research, and service teams from interest groups within colleges of education is thus elucidated by this application of morphological analysis. Incidentally, we have examined only 10 interfaces of the possible 288. There still remain 278 possibilities or alternative futures embedded in the matrix.

> *Step 5:* The solutions are selected and practically applied. Essentially this step is one of determining the feasibility and desirability of identified alternatives. This might be accomplished by using other forecasting techniques of a normative nature or one that combines exploratory and normative techniques in a feedback loop.
>
> For example, whether a college should develop extern programs would surely be affected by such factors as institutional inertia, its future image, resources available now and in the future, and trade-off between alternative futures.

At this point the morphological analysis ends and the morphologist loops to other forecasting techniques. The analysis has produced an array of possibilities, and that is its function in planning and decision-making processes.

Application II—Types of Jet Engines

The most famous application of the morphological box was conducted by Zwicky in 1943 concerning the totality of jet engines, which were composed of simple elements and activated by chemical energy. The analysis produced 576 possible engines, which included the V-1 pulse-jet powered aerial bomb and the V-2 rocket bomb then being developed in Germany. Jantsch reports that the failure of Lindemann (scientific advisor to Churchill) ". . . to recognize the potential of the V-2 even when he was shown photographs ('It will not fly') is plausibly explained by his exclusive preoccupation with solid propellent, stubbornly rejecting the idea of liquid propellents."[7] This example is a powerful confirmation of one of the essential prerequisites of morphological analysis—avoiding prevaluations and biased perspectives.

In 1951, the body of knowledge regarding jet engines had expanded and Zwicky conducted another morphological analysis extending the number of parameters in the 1943 study.[8] The inclusion of new parameters is, in Zwicky's terminology, the addition of "new pegs of knowledge" that further enumerates the morphological structure of the problem. A complex application of the morphological box is readily understood by following an adaptation of Zwicky's 1951 analysis of jet engines:

Step 1: The problem is concisely formulated: What is the totality of all pure-medium jet engines containing single simple elements and activated by chemical energy?

Step 2: All the parameters are localized and analyzed. For jet engines · Zwicky identified the following:

	PARAMETER		ELEMENTS
P_1	Source of chemically active mass	P^1_1	Intrinsic, P^2_1 Extrinsic
P_2	Location of thrust generation	P^1_2	Internal, P^2_2 External
P_3	Source of thrust augmentation	P^1_3	Intrinsic, P^2_3 Extrinsic, P^3_3 Zero
P_4	Location of thrust augmentation	P^1_4	Internal, P^2_4 External
P_5	Jet	P^1_5	Positive, P^2_5 Negative
P_6	Possible thermal cycle	P^1_6	Adiabatic, P^2_6 Isothermal, . . . , P^4_6
P_7	Medium	P^1_7	Vacuum, P^2_7 Air, P^3_7 Water, P^4_7 Earth
P_8	Motion	P^1_8	Translatory, P^2_8 Rotatory, . . . , P^4_8
P_9	State of propellant	P^1_9	Gaseous, P^2_9 Liquid, P^3_9 Solid
P_{10}	Type of operation	P^1_{10}	Continuous, P^2_{10} Intermittent
P_{11}	Igniting of propellent	P^1_{11}	Self, P^2_{11} Nonself

Step 3: The morphological box is constructed

7 E. Jantsch, *Technological Forecasting in Perspective* (Paris: Organization for Economic Co-operation and Development, 1967), p. 177.

8 F. Zwicky, *Morphology of Propulsive Power* (Pasadena, Calif.: Society for Morphological Research, 1962).

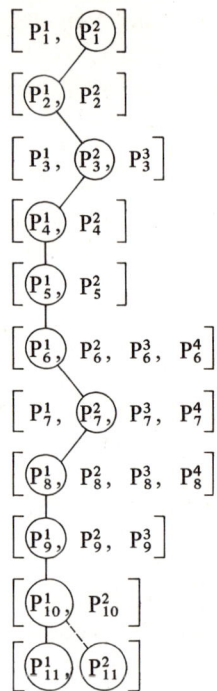

This matrix contains 36,864 permutations or alternate paths through the matrix arrived at by multiplying the elements of the parameters:

$$2 \times 2 \times 3 \times 2 \times 2 \times 4 \times 4 \times 4 \times 3 \times 2 \times 2 = 36,864$$

Therefore, the morphological box contains 36,864 problem solutions. Again, note that no attempt has been made to evaluate the feasibility of any of the possible solutions.

Step 4: All the solutions are scrutinized and evaluated.

At this point the matrix is examined for internal contradictions. Examination reveals that parameter P_4, internal or external location of thrust augmentation, is meaningless when the value of P_3, source of thrust augmentation, is zero (P^3_3). It is quite evident that it is meaningless to be concerned with the location of thrust augmentation when there is no thrust augmentation. Also, it is meaningless to suggest extrinsic acquisition of a chemically active mass (P^2_1) in a vacuum (P^1_7). Therefore, all permutations that contain P^3_3 (zero thrust augmentation) and P^1_4 (internal thrust augmentation) or P^2_4 (external thrust augmentation) plus P^2_1 (extrinsic chemically active mass) and P^1_7 (vacuum) must be deleted from the original solution set.

One procedure that may be used to arrive at the number of remaining solutions is to compute the number of permutations containing the contradictions and substract them from the original solution set. This may be done by determining the number of permutations that contain P^2_1 and P^1_7, which is:

$$1 \times 2 \times 3 \times 2 \times 2 \times 4 \times 1 \times 4 \times 3 \times 2 \times 2 = 4{,}608$$

and determining the number of permutations that contain P^3_3 and P^1_4 or P^2_4, which is:

$$2 \times 2 \times 1 \times 2 \times 4 \times 4 \times 4 \times 3 \times 2 \times 2 = 12{,}288$$

But, 1,536 of these permutations (P^3_3 and P^1_4 or P^2_4) contain P^2_1 and P^1_7, which have already been accounted for previously. Therefore, to avoid deleting the same permutations twice, the total number is reduced by 1,536:

$$\begin{array}{r} 4{,}608 \\ 12{,}288 \\ \hline 16{,}896 - 1{,}536 = 15{,}360 \end{array}$$

In the process of determining this sum, however, all possible solutions that contain P^3_3 (zero augmentation) have also been deleted. Since it is possible to have a jet engine without thrust augmentation, these possible solutions omitting parameter P_4 are:

$$2 \times 2 \times 1 \times 2 \times 4 \times 4 \times 4 \times 3 \times 2 \times 2 = 6{,}144$$

But 768 of these permutations contain P^2_1 and P^1_7, which are internally contradictory. Therefore, the number of solutions is reduced accordingly:

$$6{,}144 - 768 = 5{,}376$$

The total number of solutions, accounting for contradictory permutations, is:

$$\begin{array}{rl} 36{,}864 & \text{Original possible solutions} \\ -15{,}360 & \text{Contradictory permutations} \\ \hline 21{,}504 & \text{SUB TOTAL} \\ +5{,}376 & \text{Zero augmentation solutions} \\ \hline 26{,}880 & \text{TOTAL possible jet engines[9]} \end{array}$$

Step 5: The solutions are selected and practically applied.

Individual and sets of solutions are examined, and an evaluation of technological feasibility is conducted. This analysis resulted in the identification of several jet engines, which simulated research in various

---

[9] In the original work Zwicky reports that there are 25,344 possible jet engines. There is a 1,536 difference between Zwicky's computations and the author's calculations. This may be caused by the double deletion of contradictory permutations.

scientific fields. The permutation circled in the matrix is the interplanetary aeroduct or ramjet. This engine would acquire its chemical energy from the medium (air) in which it is traveling. It would carry no propellent. Jantsch indicates that the feasibility of this type of engine would in part depend on ". . . high atmosphere research, to find out about the nature and number of (the) excited particles (this is already well under way); research in the possibilities of de-exciting the particles and using the energy gained in aeroducts, aeropulses, and other devices for the generation of propulsive power."[10] The determination of the alternative ways of de-exciting particles would perhaps be facilitated by an additional morphological analysis.

Also included in the matrix are solutions whose realization appear to lie in distant futures. For example, any solution containing P^2_1 and P^3_7, or P^2_1 and P^4_7, would be a jet engine that acquires its chemical energy from the water or earth through which it moves.

In summary, this application clearly demonstrates the major benefits of morphological analysis—the systematic, unbiased elucidation of alternative solutions and identification of basic and applied research opportunities. The results of morphological analysis can also be used for long- and short-range planning, by conducting normative forecasts to determine the sequence of activities that would result in desired technological inventions.

Thus, we have looked at two applications of morphological analysis in the context of social and aeronautical engineering. The first is relatively simple and the second is somewhat complex. Perhaps a review of other applications would provide some insight into the state of morphological research.

TYPICAL APPLICATIONS USING THE MORPHOLOGICAL BOX

During World War II, Zwicky conducted a morphological analysis of the following problem: How many different ways are available to collect scientific journals and books for the purpose of replacing collections in various scientific libraries destroyed by war?[11] No funds were available for purchasing the materials.

By enumerating the parameters that characterize the flow of books and journals from publishers to final repositories and determining the discrete values of these parameters, Zwicky identified alternative solutions and selected those that seemed most promising for his project. This application focused on all the means, or points of intercept, available to realize a particular objective—acquisition of scientific books and journals. This morphological analysis was used to provide alternative solutions to an operational problem.

[10] E. Jantsch, op. cit., p. 178.
[11] F. Zwicky, *Discovery, Invention, Research*, op. cit., pp. 113–169.

First, morphological analysis could be used to create new social products, such as organizational structures, roles, and mechanisms to operate them. Second, new processes can be developed to realize a functional capacity, such as preparation programs for administrators and operating procedures for school districts and universities. The specific problems to be considered in each of these basic types is a matter of choice for the morphologist. What follows, then, is a sample of problem areas that the author feels might produce fruitful applications. For example, university departments that offer preparation programs for educational administrators continually evaluate the appropriateness of their programs. Perhaps a morphological analysis of possible preparation programs would identify alternatives that currently are unknown. The set of current options includes master's, specialist's, and doctoral programs. The doctoral program generally requires a period of residency at the university. Are there other program alternatives that would provide for a postspecialist program with extensive field-based experiences? A related problem is the sequence of activities that degree candidates might follow in pursuit of their programs. What are all the possible sequences of activities that would lead to the acquisition of administrative skills and competencies? Another set of persistent problems that confront administrators is planning operating systems. What are all the possible operational units that could exist in a school system? What are all the possible ways in which students could flow through these units? What types of personnel are needed to operate these units? Many other problems might be amenable to morphological analysis, such alternative ways of financing educational programs, alternative learning experiences for students, and alternative research opportunities in administrative and organizational behavior.

In addition to conducting probes in these sample problem areas, morphological analysis can be used in conjunction with other exploratory forecasting techniques. For example, a number of "think tank" organizations have used morphological techniques to systematically generate scenarios that contain a large number of variables.[19,20] Similar types of applications could be made by scenario writers wishing to systematically consider alternative futures for educational administration. Delphic probes could use morphological analysis to generate an array of possible futures that expert panels could then use as starting points for deliberations.

Whereas the use of morphological analysis for generating alternative problem solutions in educational administration seems promising, al-

[19] R. Rea, "A Comprehensive System of Long-Range Planning," in *Long Range Forecasting and Planning*, U.S. Air Force Office of Aerospace Research Symposium, Aug., 1966.

[20] T. Taylor, W. Van Cleave, and E. Kinderman, "Preliminary Survey of Non-National Nuclear Threats," Stanford Research Institute Technical Note SSC-TN-5205-83, Sept. 17, 1967.

though unproven, there are some practical difficulties and limitations for those using this method.

Practical Considerations and Limitations

First is the difficult task of formulating and stating a problem in concise terms. Although morphological literature continually reiterates the cruciality of arriving at well-formulated problem statements, it does not provide guidelines for problem formulation. Related to problem statements is the difficult task of parameter identification and comprehensive enumeration. How can a morphologist know that all the important parameters of the problem statement are included in the matrix of solutions? The severity of these problems seems to be related to the maturity of the particular field of morphological application. Those fields that have rich and elaborate conceptual and theoretical networks seem able to generate well-formulated problem statements and enumerate crucial variables. Fields, such as educational administration, do not presently have a wealth of conceptual and theoretical capital to facilitate problem formulation and parameter enumeration. The practical consequences seem clear—the educational morphologist is in for a frustrating experience when he attempts to formulate and enumerate the parameters of his problem.

Assuming that the educational morphologist overcomes these initial problems, new difficulties immediately arise. The number of problem solutions increases geometrically as the number and values of parameters increase. Although the object of morphological analysis is comprehensive identification of solutions, it is easy to visualize a situation in which the *number* of problem solutions becomes a hindrance to solution selection, especially when we realize that most of the research findings in social science testify to the multivariant and complex nature of social phenomena. If morphological analyses of social phenomena are complex, how can the great number of solution alternatives receive equal consideration? The solution to this question would require a substantial investment of human resources—even if a computer were used to generate a listing of alternative solutions.

Summary

This chapter has examined one exploratory forecasting technique that could be used to provide reconnaissance information concerning alternative futures. Further, of all the exploratory techniques, it is the only one requiring that all possible solutions (or futures) be generated, analyzed, and evaluated. Therefore, this technique minimizes the possibility of overlooking a promising solution or alternative future. Morphological analysis, although developed thirty years ago, has been infrequently used by members of the forecasting community, particularly those forecasters concerned with social phenomena. Possible morphological probes and applications in educational administration appear to be limitless. However limitless the opportunities, they will not be attempted until interested individuals draw upon their accumulated experiences and knowledge and decide to conduct first approximation morphological probes.

16

SOME LIMITATIONS AND CAUTIONS IN THE USE OF QUANTITATIVE TECHNIQUES IN DECISION-MAKING

William G. Monahan

LET ME begin by pointing out that the most precautionary aspect surrounding the use of quantitative techniques in support of administrative decisions is an obvious one; I would put it in this fashion: since computational procedure, processing equipment and technique are, in and of themselves, inert, nonhuman phenomena, *only the man can be held accountable for the decision.*

Now, that is at once both the major strength of the use of quantitative techniques and the major limitation, for all other admonitions must derive from this fundamental one. Just as the power of quantification vastly improves the precision with which optimality can be achieved, it decreases the decision-maker's familiarity—his involvement—with the elements of the decision-making process and therefore tends to accentuate the *abruptness* of his confrontation with accountability. In a sense, this merely states, in a somewhat oblique fashion, the more familiar dialectic which has and continues to take place with reference to the place of values and valuing in the "quantified society." I will return to this major issue toward the end of this paper, for it seems to me that a topic such as this one must both begin and end with this molar kind of concern of the quantitative as over and against the qualitative.

Of somewhat more molecular interest, there are, as I see it, eight areas under which limitations and cautions might be articulated with reference to the use of quantitative techniques in decision-making. These might be

This paper was first presented at the meeting of the American Educational Research Association in 1969 and subsequently appeared in *Educational Technology Magazine,* September 1969. I am grateful to the publishers of *Educational Technology Magazine* for permission to include it here.

The author is indebted to his colleague, Professor Ralph Van Dusseldorp, for critical comments; his expertise in this area is substantial. Also, the author expresses appreciation to those students in the PAERIS Fellowship Program at the Iowa Center for Research in School Administration, University of Iowa, for their critical reading of the paper. Their comments and opinions are highly valued.

subsumed under the major headings of limitations of *applicability, expertise* and *consequence.*

Consequence

I begin with the last of these first, for limitations imposed by consequence are also somewhat axiomatic—at least to the extent that we can all agree that predictability is seldom finite; to state the premise that, all other things being reasonably equal, quantitative precision enables one to reduce the probability of the unintended consequence, logically assumes that the unintended consequence can indeed occur. Put more simply, we can observe that if there is only one viable alternative, no decision process, whether intuitively vague or mathematically exact, offers anything additional to the choice.

For an empirical illustration, remember that few commercial decisions in recent years were rationally planned more thoroughly in American industry than the introduction by the Ford Motor Company of the Edsel.

Consequences and Antecedents

Another dimension of the problem of consequence is the requirement that an analyst must begin with an already established set of consequences of other antecedent decisions. It is seldom that we are able to deal with problems in a *de noveau* fashion; more likely, we turn to the seeking of more objective, quantitative devices after problems are already well-developed and some kinds of decisions have already reduced the degrees of freedom available at that point. An interesting example of this situation is illuminated by events surrounding the seizing of the Pueblo; by the time the President was clearly aware of the action taken by the North Koreans, whatever alternatives available to him were limited by the decisions already made at lower echelons. Thus, an important limitation to the use of any objective process for problem-solving is the set of given conditions that must be considered. It is for this reason that we have to be satisfied with "optimal" solutions—and, as the reader is aware these are merely the best solutions under the circumstances. Clearly, then, the circumstances must represent a significant limitation.

Applicability

One important aspect of limitations of consequence ties closely with limitations of applicability; if applicability is misjudged, then obviously consequences are going to be completely unintended. And if decisions are rendered on the basis of inappropriate applications of a technique, then they are not going to be good decisions and are not going to have predicted consequences.

This is not always so clear-cut as it may seem. Consider the situation in which a board of education and its executive staff confront the problem of the need to construct a building. Assume that by some appropriate and reliable method the decision to construct a building is arrived at, and it is one upon which there is complete conviction and confidence.

Now, obviously, this decision generates the need for hundreds of additional ones, many of which are consequential and many of which are inconsequential. At least one of the consequential decisions concerns strategies of securing enough community support to provide the resources for constructing the facility. In this case there are two very different tactical alternatives. For lack of something better to call these, let us label one tactic "efficiency" and the other "effectiveness." In an oversimplified way of characterizing the natures of these two tactical alternatives, suppose we assume that the board can either think in terms of the long range by designing a facility for low maintenance costs over time, or not give too much consideration to maintenance costs and go for the lowest possible initial costs in order to stand a better chance of getting the facility.

In this case, the use of quantitative techniques will very likely dictate in favor of efficiency, for that is the nature of quantitative phenomena. There are all kinds of arguments in favor of efficiency in this case—even basic values about thrift and quality-control and so forth indicate that the better decision is high initial cost, low maintenance costs. But having arrived at this alternative, the board may, using equally objective data and quantitative techniques, have another alternative available which says in effect that if you go for high initial costs you confront a 50/50 risk of having the bond issue turned down, whereas if you go with low initial costs you only run, say, a 40/60 risk of failure on the issue. What is the criterion of decision? If it is a conviction that the need is great enough, then the optimal decision is the lower risk; but if that conviction is not that substantial, and one wants sincerely to provide the best instructional space possible, then the other decision is perhaps optimal.[1]

In both situations, it is possible to apply certain kinds of quantification techniques. But with the tactic of "efficiency" one can be more comfortable with the measurement of variables, for he is dealing with a greater number of components which lend themselves to quantification and, in addition, the *accessibility* to, and retrieval of, the measurable data in the case of "efficiency" is more convenient. The entire quantitative process is more parsimonious. But when one is confronting the probabilities of

[1] Professor Dale Bolton, while a postdoctoral Fellow at Stanford University on leave from the University of Washington, pursued this problem as a result of this paper and has devised a quantitative solution paradigm for it based on three alternatives and their consequences. There is not space enough here to give consideration to his work, but it implies a quasi-quantitative solution for the subjective dilemma. His arguments are persuasive and imaginative.

whether a particular set of specifications is or is not *marketable,* he is dealing with a much more fluid mathematical environment. Too many of the components that he must build into his system do not lend themselves to easy quantification. Such components are likely to be characteristically idiosyncratic to a unique decision environment. The analyst must therefore assign *weights* to his various components.

When one performs this activity, he engages in a process whereby an attempt is made to objectify otherwise subjective judgments. So long as he is consciously aware of what he has done, he may proceed (albeit timidly) to pursue the particular logic involved in simulating the course of events that is probable.

However, there is ample evidence to suggest that many of us fall into the trap of forgetting that our "weights" are little more than beta-values and begin to think of them as exact quantities. That is an error of noble dimensions. Again, the applicability of a procedure is dictated by the consequences expected. In this case—and many others—the final decision is influenced by the judgment, intuition, experiences and, sometimes, sentiments, of the people who will be held accountable. These are qualitative phenomena. In some way, *any* decision must be *qualified.*

Applicability and Purpose

I suppose that the major point that I want to make in this regard is to emphasize the major difference between those conditions in which the inputs, operations, resources and outputs are easy to quantify and those other situations in which the opposite is true. The purposes to be served are of immense importance. In this connection, I remember an old story that is instructive; their was a man who was interested in knowing more about an objective approach to hiring personnel and who had a friend well experienced in this area. This friend invited the man to sit in while he interviewed a number of applicants for a stenographic position. The personnel expert asked each prospective candidate for the position a number of complicated questions, noting each response very carefully. After the series of interviews, he turned to the man who had watched the process intently and said to him, "Now you have heard all of the questions and the answers given; which one would you choose?" The man gave it only a moment's thought and then said, "Why, I would choose the one with the nice legs." No one would argue that well-proportioned legs do not lend themselves to easy quantification, but surely there is some intrusion of valued purpose into that decision.

Applicability and Scope

Again with reference to problems of applicability, there are some limitations and restraints forced upon quantification by virtue of the *scope* of the problem. The greatest success in the use of various quantitative techniques has been achieved when sub-units of the total system have been the primary target; and, furthermore, when utility is most defensible.

For example, we can solve certain school transportation problems more satisfactorily using linear programming techniques than simple experience, even if the experience is substantial and meaningful. Such a procedure is highly efficient in helping us to determine rather precisely the nature of equipment needs in terms of the kind, size, number and even optional accessories required. But that same technique may not be at all appropriate when we confront the problem of trying to determine where, when and how each bus must go. It is my understanding that attempts to use linear programming on the latter problem have not yielded satisfactory results: operations researchers, having generally recognized such limitations, are seeking solutions through different procedures. Graph theory, for example, according to some specialists, may provide much more appropriate techniques.

Problems of Expertise

Just as problems of applicability are closely related to limitations of consequence, the applicability issue is also closely related to limitations of expertise. In this context, there is always the limitation of know-how. If linear programming is the only technique one knows, then the utility of the service rendered is substantialy reduced. Moreover, that lack of sophistication can be compounded many times over if one knows only this one technique but tries to apply it to all kinds of problems. Associated with that is a condition that might be characterized as "measurement myopia." This condition may be suspected whenever a manager begins to observe that his systems people suggest quantitative techniques for attacking anything remotely problematical; or, in more advanced stages, when he discovers that they no longer seem able to communicate with anyone except each other. There is clear and present danger that having reached this stage of "measurement myopia" a *procedure* becomes more important to the technician than its *product*. In very advanced stages, a *particular* procedure becomes obsessive; and, unless a problem lends itself to that particular technique, the analyst may choose disdainfully to have nothing to do with it. He will respond by asserting that, "The problem does not excite me."

To deny that this is a potentially real shortcoming is to forget how conversationally narrow the typical graduate student can become at that point where he really begins to get going on his thesis topic. It is remarkable to him that anyone could possibly be enthused about, or care to discuss, anything else.

The extent to which quantitative techniques are maximally useful to a decision-maker is directly proportional to the versatility of the people he must depend upon to develop them. To this extent, I might also point out that one is limited clearly by the hardware available for processing one's data and—expertise again—the versatility of programmers.

The Problem of Time

There is a final limitation to quantitative procedures—they require time; and, in many decision situations, there isn't enough of it. Sir Richard Livingston, who was vice-chancellor of Oxford, once described administrative work by pointing out that it:

. . . consists in being pushed by events, finding immediate answers to immediate questions, and the difficulty (being), behind their urgency, to remain aware of anything ultimate, to avoid mortgaging the future.[2]

Finding immediate answers to immediate questions too frequently precludes a rational survey of the situation and renders codification of appropriate responses impossible.

Qualitative vs. Quantitative: the Problem of Values

Thus far in this paper, I have attempted to characterize some of the limitations that impinge upon the use of quantitative techniques; hopefully, if the paper is useful, readers will have thought of others that have not been mentioned.

At this point, I want to return to the caution that I expressed at the beginning of the paper—that only men are accountable for decisions, regardless of how they are arrived. The implications of this fact of human accountability are primarily *qualitative;* that is, judgments regarding the *value* of any decision, plan or procedure cannot be easily built-in to any quantitative system, if they can be built-in at all. Several years ago, John Wilkinson discussed this problem as follows:

"Quantity" may be defined as a species of geometrical extension, which can be measured or counted, and whose syntax is mathematics and logic. "Quality" is value as felt. That this definition of quality is unsatisfactory illustrates the principal thesis . . . , namely the exclusion of valued quality from rational discourse. The reason for this is that our mathematical and logical systems can only refer to qualities if they are quantified, that is, if they have ceased to exist as qualities as such. Price is an example of quantity, *value* of quality. How little connection price may have to value is often painfully clear. . . . In a computerized society values as such cannot get into the mathematical language of

[2] Lucian Price. *Dialogues of Alfred Worth Whitehead.* Boston: Little, Brown, and Company, 1954, p. 305.

the computer network. The numbers that are supposed to express value turn out to have a very ambiguous relationship to valuational feelings.[3]

Mr. Wilkinson's paper stirred considerable controversy, and I recommend it; what he reminds us of is the fact that the quantification of information makes it possible for man to measure the order or disorder extant in a system. On the basis of this, he proposes that the ". . . more ordered a social system becomes from the quantitative point of view, the more disarrayed it becomes qualitatively."[4]

Perhaps another way of saying something like that is to suggest that the more ordered any kind of system becomes, the more monolithic it must be, for the simple reason that it is immensely difficult—and at this point, I would guess, impossible—to put values into mathematical systems in a *multidimensional* fashion.

Whitehead once implied the nature of this dilemma when he observed two wine glasses on a table and said:

One and one make two. One and one what? One glass, or one partly filled? One and one where? On a table, in this room, or in this universe? But two glasses are not and cannot possibly be made exactly equal. Nor can they be filled with equal amounts of wine. Then do we mean "one plus one" after all of the necessary deductions and additions have been made? But the glasses are also raging with molecular activity . . . and we must remember that [they] are disintegrating before our very eyes. I refuse to be taken in by such monstrous inexactitude . . .[5]

In a real sense, then, we must cautiously remember that the use of quantitative procedures requires the making of "necessary deductions and additions," and though we may say they constitute x number of the former and y number of the latter, this ability to enumerate the *number* of deductions and additions, precise though it may be, tells us absolutely nothing about the ways they have changed the procedures we propose to use or the utility of their application.

The *decision* to apply quantitative techniques in decision-making is itself a value judgment of sizable dimensions and is dictated by qualitative assessment of the purposes it can serve. Purposes cannot be determined by quantitative techniques—only the means available to us for their most proficient pursuit can be. Bertrand Russell suggested the same thing when he pointed out that:

Broadly speaking we are in a race between human skill as to means and human folly as to ends. Given sufficient folly as to ends, every increase in the

3 John Wilkinson. The Quantitative Society or—What Are You To Do With Noodle? Occasional Paper, Center for the Study of Democratic Institutions, Santa Barbara: *The Center*, 1964, p. 2.

4 *Ibid.*, p. 2.

5 Price, *op. cit.*, pp. 329–330.

skill required to achieve them is to the bad. The human race has survived hitherto owing to ignorance and incompetence, but given knowledge and competence combined with folly, there can be no certainty of survival . . . unless men increase in wisdom as much as in knowledge, increase in knowledge will be increase in sorrow.[6]

The availability of emerging techniques in the use of quantitative concepts and procedures for assisting managers in the solution of administrative problems is a most significant development advance; judicious and appropriate use of such techniques will undoubtedly provide avenues for vast improvements in all of those activities which facilitate educational achievement. But we should occasionally remind ourselves of the obvious—the major precaution in the use of such procedures is that we must be careful not to limit ourselves to them, and more important, not to be limited by them. We must continue to emphasize that purposes and the processes by which purposes are defined must guide our behaviors. The use of any set of skills is always a matter of fundamental perspective.

---

[6] Bertrand Russell. *The Impact of Science on Society.* New York: Simon and Schuster, 1953, pp. 97–98.

University of Oregon. CASEA is easily perceived as an Educational (the capital *E* is emphasized) center for the applied behavioral sciences. It has produced some highly significant research and it has explored avenues of interest that will have impact upon our field in the future. Moreover, a half dozen or more major university presidents count themselves among the early participants in the "movement" and a great many more deans of Colleges of Education than anyone would have dared believe twenty years ago and a significant number of public school administrators as well. A variety of special centers have grown as a consequence of this interest and many others that have had a longer history have taken on a different emphasis in the process; the Mid-West Administration Center at Chicago early began to push the importance of the relationship and continues to be a major influence; the National Institute for the Study of Educational Change at Indiana University is something of an outgrowth of the relationship; the Iowa Center for Research in School Administration (which was initiated by Stephen Knezevich and carried on by Willard Lane) is also a practical application of theoretical expertise that was born of the "movement." In merely mentioning these as examples one surely confronts the typical risks of not having mentioned all of those other organizations that probably deserve even more notable identification—but that also is some testimony to the pervasiveness of the consequences of this twenty-year growth. Moreover, state and national associations—school boards, principals, superintendents, and curriculum and supervision—have been influenced by this reactive relationship and I can really think of *no* university curriculum in educational administration that does not reflect significant aspects of it.

I agree with Getzels—the effects have been undramatically cumulative but dramatically pervasive in retrospect.

That does not mean that we have really come either very far or perhaps even close to far enough in developing the best of the possibilities of a relationship with the social sciences. When Frankel advises that we must restore precision in our words, our premises, and the rules guiding our conduct, he speaks not only to our consciences as part of the great *Educational Establishment,* he speaks as well to those of us who value our interpenetration with the "sociosphere" of *our* domain—the management of educational organizations. These, need we be reminded, are *social* inventions; *cultural* institutions; *psychological* and *socialpsychological* entities; *economic* systems; and *political* realities.

That we must restore precision to our words is precisely the issue that Hills elaborates in his article in this section. He urges us to understand the distinction between knowing *what* to do as opposed to knowing *why* we know what to do. It is a simple kind of dictum but an extremely complex issue in the sociology of knowledge. Willower raises provocative questions about our premises and reminds us that the most effective use of knowledge demands of us that we know what we are about and whither we tend. His article is an elegant and literate call for us to be purposeful and sensible. Finally, Halpin, in his inimitable style and using the theme of our seduction by the magic of change, reminds us to be careful that we do not delude ourselves by marvelous nonsense, for it is easier to enjoy the fascination of the idea of change than it is to engage in productive manifestations of it.

These are all important statements with which to end a book devoted to an initial exploration of several dimensions of theory as it might apply to something called "educational administration." Still, Frankel said something else that does not fit as neatly with these articles; he admonished that we restore some precision to the rules that guide our conduct. This admonition, it seems to me, leads us somewhat away from social science and into the humanities.

Some years ago, when I was involved in the study of administration and we were visiting relatives, I was expounding eruditely on the complexities of administrative lore. My father-in-law suggested that management was all in the hands—"You keep your hands out of the cash drawer and off the female help. Why should one spend time and money to study such simple matters?"

In a sense, he was asserting a fundamental sociological *and* ethical principle. Parsons would have characterized this observation in terms of affectivity/neutrality and of the value systems that underlay my father-in-law's prescription. This is not to say that values have no place in the substance of social science but merely that values also constitute an important linkage concept between the social sciences and the humanities; between theory and philosophy; science and art.

I once had a creative and talented student who wanted to do something a little different by way of a doctoral thesis. We discussed things for some time, and one day, recognizing his interest in, and particular talent for, photography, I urged him to consider the possibilities of depicting the organizational climate of a school in ways other than typical empirical techniques—using, for example, a kind of photographic essay. He obtained a job in a Denver, Colorado, junior high school as a science teacher and started taking pictures. (He was also a superb science teacher.) Everybody there knew pretty well what he was doing and nobody really seemed to mind. After a time, the staff and the students merely came to take for granted that he was never without his camera and they went about their daily business fairly oblivious of him. He took literally thousands of pictures. He would write to me that he was discouraged; not really much satisfied with his work, and not always very clear regarding its focus. I would write back that I thought his work was exciting, and although I knew nothing about photography, I could see that he was capturing aspects of the "feeling" of this school that could be very useful contributions to our knowledge of school climate. But this was an artistic medium and he would have to "package" it in some conceptually meaningful way. He kept at it and it turned out to be a very different kind of doctoral thesis in educational administration.[3] My intent was to use his photographs in a procedure. The notion was to explore whether some of the judgments that he and others made in response to his pictures would yield typologies that were heuristically congruent. That "second phase" was never completed nor were several other unusual doctoral projects that were proposed. For example, I wanted someone interested in moving into a position as a department chairperson in music in a college or university (or elsewhere), and who thereby should have some expertise in educational administration, to go into schools and record the sounds, the rhythms, and the sequences of organizational "noise" that characterize such places, and on the basis of that, to write an original musical composition using that "data." Unfortunately, I never found such a person who was talented enough or interested enough in tackling the discipline of such a chore. I found a few who would have been willing to adapt the "sounds" to already established and recognized compositions, but somehow that did not quite suit my purposes. Probably somebody will do either or perhaps both—I hope so. The point is that I see no other way of beginning to examine ways through which the humanities, and what I have elsewhere referred to as the "art" of administrative activity, can be rigorously brought to bear in systematic ways to expand our understanding of administrative behavior and to expand it beyond the parameters to which we confine ourselves when we deal only with the so-called behavioral sciences.

The contribution of the humanities, however one may choose to treat such areas, is, I think, largely a matter of dealing with values and in a context that is somewhat free of typical social-science constraints. (Although that context may be related in a variety of ways to models and methodologies that are more within the realm of social science.)

The issue of values was explored in the extended, or "third dimension," of the Getzels-Guba scheme.[4] From this theoretical extension Abbott investigated value orientations of superintendents and board members. There have been a number of values-oriented studies, but Abbott's is

---

3 See, e.g., Michael Sexton, "Who Is the School?" *Saturday Review* (May 1972), pp. 32–37 and *Phi Delta Kappan* (February 1973), Vol. 6., pp. 397–403. Also, M. J. Sexton, *Who Is the School?* (Philadelphia: The Westminster Press, 1973). The subsequent publicity this work received made both of us, and especially Sexton, personae non gratae in Denver. The study was never intended as an exposé nor was it that. The school was little different—and better than most—inner-city junior high schools. It had a well-trained and generally dedicated staff, but his work did graphically demonstrate that such organizations have dominant custodial values and control-mentalities intensified as the year wears on.

4 See Jacob W. Getzels and Herbert A. Thelen, "The Classroom Group As a Unique Social System," *The Dynamics of Instructional Groups*, National Society for the Study of Education (Chicago: The Society; University of Chicago Press, 1960), Chap. 4, and Jacob Getzels, "Changing Values Challenge the Schools," *The School Review* LXV (Spring 1957).

probably among the best because it was derived directly from an explicit theoretical system.[5]

What is missing in most of the studies in which values are the central concern—and this was the case with Abbott's study—is a treatment that deals with the *function and operation of values and value-systems* in the behavior of administrators, rather than identification and descriptions of the effects of their perception. Typically such studies deal with this functional aspect in speculative statements in a final chapter or with suggested possibilities or "implications-for-further-research" that also appear somewhere nearby. It is unquestionably true that such methodological procedures and instruments as semantic differentials and several breeds of factor-analytic techniques provide fruitful avenues for researching the dynamics and functional patterns of values in administrative behavior. But too frequently many of us who have tended to cavalierly dismiss curiosity about such areas with the retort that "that-is-just-a-value-judgment" have implied that any topic within that broad idiosyncratic arena is really not worthy of serious investigation.

Perhaps that is both too harsh and inaccurate, for obviously much is happening that I cannot possibly know about. Yet values and value-clarification, ethics, aesthetics, and other similar or related phenomena are inseparable from administrative activity. Restoring precision to the rules that guide our *conduct* is somewhat beyond the rubric of social science but undoubtedly is related to it. Consider, for example, the following "principles" of administrative behavior; all of them seem to be little more than common sense and yet each is embedded in a variety of complex sociocultural processes and all have a value-oriented basis. Moreover, all of these "principles," although indeed they may seem little more than the proverbial "rules-of-thumb," have been supported by research (although my style of expressing them may not be in their original pristine rhetoric):

* One treats people well in order that they may get ahead, not that he may.

* One must recognize that any administrator's effectiveness is reasonably short-lived. In any case, after some reasonable amount of time, by virtue of the administrator's role, all of the people in the organization who cannot abide each other learn that they can abide the administrator even less. And, in Parsonian terms, they will learn to defer immediate gratification in favor of discipline in order to rid themselves of this monster.

* One should not be too openly critical of this town or this place or these people; the lack of conveniences and accouterments to which itinerant administrators have become cosmopolitanly accustomed is some-

5 Max G. Abbott, "Values and Value-Perceptions in Superintendent-School Board Relationships," *Administrator's Notebook* vol. 9, No. 4 (December 1960).

how not recognized by the natives. They have spent much of their lives here—or may have—and they just don't feel that way. (One should say under such circumstances that his is a challenging position!)

* One should never take to his superiors or his fiduciary board members any plan or proposition that has not been well thought through; they are likely to ask embarrassing questions for which he is unprepared.

* One should never speak of those with whom he works in other than good terms; if he can say nothing positive or at least neutral, he is better advised to say nothing at all.

* Moreover, one is well advised not to discuss his intimate antagonisms toward subordinates or superiors even with his wife (or husband as the case might be) for he, or she, might inadvertently—at the tavern or the beauty shop (both of which are communication-prone locations)—let the proverbial cat out of the proverbial bag.

* One should recognize that in administrative affairs, the first time is the time to be tough and forthright; if one folds in the pinches, he (or she) has had it. That is tantamount to a loss because those who are after you know that they have got you.

* Along similar lines, there is absolutely no substitute for forthrightness—if people cannot frighten the administrator and if it is apparent that they cannot buy him, the only alternative is simply to deal with him.

* The first year is likely to be the most rewarding and the most productive one. The first years are the best ones for requesting what one needs from those who are empowered to supply it. The latter will tend still to think of one as a "role" rather than as a "personality." When "they" start calling the administrator by his first name, the honeymoon is over! This is contrary to some of the folklore of administration. The folklore holds that one should adopt an information-absorbing attitude and a sit-back-and-look-things-over view during the first year. This view has also been formalized in many cases in which the potential successor becomes, say, a superintendent-elect, and works for a year with his predecessor. That can be very hazardous to administrative health since it becomes very difficult to plead ignorance regarding either errors or strategic achievements.

* The sensitive administrator learns quickly that neither organizational structure nor human beings are totally capable of change—there is likely a middle ground; one may change structure and discover changes in behavior or he may discover that ways of changing people make much more difference than changing structure. But more is likely to be accomplished in the long run if ways can be found of changing behavior, attitudes, feelings, skills, and motivations. People changes are more enduring than manipulating the organizational chart.

* One learns to hire the very best people that can be found and then to enjoy basking in their reflected brilliance. Excellent people who are adequately compensated and willing to do things that need to be done

without being asked can make the administrator look very able. Inferior subordinates may make a good administrator look pretty good by comparison, but the organization is likely to be in continuous difficulty, and sooner or later, he goes out with the losers he has hired.

* One must be willing to spend considerably more than a forty-hour week in administrative work; there are many ritualistic and symbolic functions that must be attended as part of the job. These are important aspects of the culture. But one should not take the organization's problems home with him. This is difficult and occasionally just not possible, but it is a useful habit to develop. Trying to learn to play the guitar is a remedial way of beginning the habit.

All of these "principles" can be rephrased in more precise theoretical language and fitted into already existing theory.[6] Although they are stated here in terms of the administrator or the person, similar statements about the organization itself can be theoretically derived. James Price has developed "an inventory" of organizational propositions by a very systematic and painstaking examination of ". . . the core of what the behavioral sciences now know about the effectiveness of organizations: what we really know, what we nearly know, what we think we know, and what we claim to know."[7] Price organized his inventory in terms of propositions related to the economic system, the political system (internal and external components thereof), and the control system. Each proposition is stated, then the key terms are defined, and the empirical work supporting the proposition is presented. It is a most interesting consolidation of much of what is known.

Accordingly, those who assert that theoretical dimensions of administrative activity have not yielded principles are simply wrong. That the principles may not yet approach codification is admitted but the theoretical work in educational administration and that which it has borrowed from other social science areas has been remarkably productive.

That we must now give more consideration to an investigation of value concerns and to personality and style in administration seems apparent.

The following three articles suggest additional dimensions of the tasks, interests, idiology, and uses of knowledge in educational administration. It is also appropriate, I think, that they are personal and lively points of view. So, yes—administration and the social sciences one more time; I am immensely confident that it will certainly not be the last.

---

6 Some of these, I learned from such people as Ernest Melby when I was a graduate student. Others, I have subsequently "collected" from my own former students.

7 James L. Price, Organizational Effectiveness: *An Inventory of Propositions* (Homewood, Ill.: Richard D. Irwin, Inc., 1968), p. 1.

18

COMMENTARY

IN *the following article by R. Jean Hills some additional and incisive comments are offered on the relationship of the behavioral sciences to educational administration.*

Hills asserts at the outset that the relevance of the one to the other still remains, at least for him, an open matter. By that, Hills is not suggesting that the relationship between the behavioral sciences and the practice of educational administration is not a highly relevant one but, with Andrew Halpin, he begins by assuming that the relationship seems not to have gotten very far beyond the courting stage, whereas some have pretended marriage. Halpin has taken a somewhat more pessimistic view; it is his belief that the time may be past when the opportunity for a truly interpenetrating interaction between the two areas was possible.[1]

Hills explores aspects of the relationship somewhat differently than others have. In typical fashion, he is concerned with the nature of the relevance of social-behavioral science to educational administration and pursues that in the context of examining the implications of knowing "what" to do as opposed to knowing "what one is doing precisely in the process of doing it." Stated differently, although perhaps falling somewhat short of his point, it is the difference between merely doing something as compared to analytically knowing why. As has been pointed out, when the ancient Chinese discovered the magnetic principle they were reasonably satisfied that the magnetized needle pointed north. But when this phenomenon found its way to the West, those peoples asked the proverbial "silly question," Why does the needle point north? It is the "silly questions" that led man to understand the immense distinction between merely "doing" and knowing about doing.

In a sense then, the relevance of social-behavioral science to educational administration is perhaps not so apparent in the practice of it as it is in the study of it. In the latter case, the issue is not so arguable even though the pattern of relevance might be far-ranging. Yet in terms of scholarly inquiry about educational administration, the debt owed to many disciplines in the social-behavioral sciences is substantial.

Continuing and expanding somewhat on the importance of language, Hills deals with organizational roles in social systems in analogy with linguistic behavior. More specifically, he develops the notion of normative behavior in organizations by suggesting that, like language patterns, ". . . it seems . . . reasonable that most of what one learns about participating in organizations (apart from technical skills) is learned long before formal preparation begins." In a sense then, just as one must learn to speak his language prior to formally studying it, one learns to internalize many aspects of organizational behavior

[1] Andrew Halpin. "Administrative Theory: The Fumbled Torch," In *Issues in American Education* ed. by Arthur M. Kroll (N.Y.: Oxford Univ. Press, 1970), pp. 156–183.

before dealing very definitively with the formal rules governing that behavior. From this, he proceeds to explain aspects of normative culture as well as the analytical tools that are vital to comparability within and across normative cultural patterns. The results of this discussion are some rather specific kinds of contributions that certain aspects of the social-behavioral sciences make to both the study and the practice of management.

THE SOCIAL-BEHAVIORAL SCIENCES AND EDUCATIONAL ADMINISTRATION

R. JEAN HILLS

Introduction

DESPITE the fact that it has received a variety of answers in the past two decades, the question of the relevance of social-behavioral science concepts, theories, and research for the practice of educational administration remains open for this writer. What remains open, however, is less a question of "Are such materials relevant?" than a question of, "What is the nature of their relevance?" Although I once took a stronger position, (Hills, 1963), I am now inclinded to agree with Getzels when he says,

The significant influence of research comes not piecemeal—study by study, technique by technique, and practice by practice. Rather it comes cumulatively through altering the general conceptions and ultimately what Kuhn calls the paradigms of the human being and of human behavior which serve as the context for educational practice. It is by examining these general conceptions and paradigms that we may trace systematically both the nature of significant educational research and the character of its contributions to the classroom. (Getzels, 1969, p. 10)

The position of Getzels is not unlike those of others who speak of "sensitizing ideas and concepts" (Gross, 1963), "alternative ways of viewing the world" (Charters, 1960), and "aids to insight and conceptual understanding that transcend prescriptions and techniques" (Halpin, 1958). The several positions have in common an emphasis on theories, analytical frameworks, or paradigms as mediators in the relation between research and practice Whatever may be the case in the future, it is held that, at this time, most specific research findings have little to contribute directly to educational practice. Insofar as they have significant implications, they are theoretical, not practical, and it is the theories and paradigms themselves that have practical significance.

Implicit Versus Explicit Relevance

Getzels has argued persuasively that long-term trends in educational practice parallel closely trends in the development of paradigms of the human being as learner, suggesting, it seems, that the contribution of such paradigms itself is a long-term cumulative one. Stated another way, his approach emphasizes the contribution of social-behavioral science materials to the field of educational practice as a whole, perhaps through gradual modification of its cognitive culture. The point that concerns us here, and that is caught up only by implication in Getzel's analysis, is the nature of the contribution of such materials to the performance of the individual practitioner. Clearly, if changes in the conception of the human being arising from research are to make a contribution to educational practice, it must be through the performance of individual practitioners. Because of the gradual, incremental nature of the process of conceptual change, however, the contribution to the performance of given individual practitioners would presumably be relatively slight. And, more to the point here, there need not, and very likely would not be, any awareness on the part of the practitioner that any such contribution had been made. In short, the process described by Getzels is one in which the practitioner works unself-consciously within an implicit conception of the human being, which, as a consequence of research, is somewhat different from that held by his predecessors. It is not a process of self-conscious utilization of explicit conceptions in the context of practice. The line of thought that I wish to develop here is that at least some social-behavioral science materials have the latter sort of relevance to the practice of educational administration (and to education more generally); that they can contribute to practice through enabling the practitioner to "know what he does when he does what he does."

A SIMPLIFIED EXAMPLE

Consider the simple example about boating. I introduced in my previous article (see Ch. 8). One who takes up boating may learn by one means or another that the more anchor line he lets out, the greater is the probability that the anchor will hold, and the less is the probability that he will experience the discomfort of finding himself adrift in the middle of the night. This highly specific bit of practical wisdom will enable the boater to anchor safely in a variety of situations. But there are situations in which it is quite inadequate. Imagine trying to anchor in a confined area, say a small cove, where letting out more than a small amount of line will allow the boat to drift aground.

Imagine a second boater in the same situation who knows that when he lets out more anchor line what he does is to decrease the angle of incidence between the anchor line and the bottom on which the anchor rests, thus reducing the likelihood that the anchor will be lifted free when the rope is taut. Whereas our first boater knows that he can increase the holding power of the anchor by increasing the length of the line, the second knows what he does when he lengthens the line. The advantage that accrues to the second boater may be seen clearly when we recognize that, given his knowledge of what he does when he increases the length of the line, i.e. decreases the angle of incidence, he can then cast about for ways of achieving that end *other* than lengthening the line. For example, he can make the line sag by fastening a heavy object to it midway between the boat and the anchor. Another alternative is to use chain instead of rope or to use rope in combination with a length of chain on the end to which the anchor is fastened. The point is that the more one knows what he does when he does what he does, the greater is the probability that he will find alternate ways of achieving his ends when a given way fails.

There are a number of ways of talking about the difference between the two boaters. One way is to say that the first knew only the relationship between the length of anchor line and holding power, whereas the second knew that fact as well as the reason for, or the why of, that relationship. Another way is to say that the first boater knew only one consequence of his action in lengthening the rope, whereas the second boater knew that as well as the mediating consequence of decreasing the angle of incidence. Still another way is to say that the first boater knew of only one relationship whereas the second knew of a set of relationships.

A REALISTIC EXAMPLE

The preceding example involves a clearly established, uncomplicated cause-effect relationship and thus presents an unrealistic picture from the point of view of what the social-behavioral sciences have to offer. Let us turn now to an example in which that element is less prominent, and in that context consider the manner in which "knowing what one does . . ." makes, or can make, a contribution to practice. To begin with a very simple and limited illustration, consider Hawkins' suggestion that:

> In social communication the literal concept of a code may be analyzed as a *standardized* sequence of questions: the sender imputes them to the receiver, and the receiver, knowing this imputation, imputes to the sender the intent to answer them. (Hawkins, 1964, p. 106)

On the one hand, I might take no note at all of such a suggestion. Indeed, it might make no sense to me. On the other hand, as a teacher, it might occur to me that, from Hawkins' point of view, much of my teaching could be seen as sending messages to people in a code known only to myself; that is, sending messages to people who do not have the questions for which the messages are intended answers. In this example there is no clearly established cause-effect relationship that gives its user an advantage over the nonuser. Still, for me, there remains an important sense in which even such a limited conception of the communication process is highly relevant to my own involvement in the practice of education. Although it does not contribute directly and immediately to my performance in the classroom, it does lead me to reflect along lines such as these: "Would I achieve better what I am trying to achieve as a teacher if I were to provide the questions before I provide the answers?" Or, linking the conception of communication with a conception of motivation, "Would it be better if I could find ways to lead students to ask the questions themselves?" The conception does not provide answers to these questions, nor does it provide proven alternative means of getting the results I seek. But it does permit me to raise questions that I probably would not otherwise have raised.

Conceptions and Self-consciousness

Still another benefit of "knowing what you do when you do what you do" can be illustrated through a consideration of the conception of language presented by linguists. In the English language there are forty-five basic "building blocks" called phonemes that correspond roughly (but obviously not exactly) to the letters of the alphabet. The use of language is, in part, a process of organizing, or combining these elementary building blocks to form a succession of higher-order linguistic units, first morphemes from phonemes, then lexical units from morphemes, and so on. Hypothetically, the initial problem confronting any would-be user of the language is learning which combinations of phonemes constitute acceptable morphemes and which do not. Given 45 distinct elements to be utilized singly or in combinations of varying numbers from 2 to 45, the number of potential morphemes staggers the imagination. If we consider only the four-element combinations these are $45^4 \cong 5,000,000$.

That, of course, is just the beginning, for once one has learned which combinations of phonemes constitute morphemes, the question of which combinations of morphemes constitute lexical units, or words, arises. Without even raising the question of sentence construction, the problem has become fantastically complex, yet every individual who learns his native tongue solves it as though it were no problem at all. And, as a matter of fact, it is not a problem, at least not of the kind suggested previously. Structurally, a language consists of a multileveled hierarchy of rules. There are rules governing the combination of phonemes, of morphemes, and of each successively higher unit of language; rules that number in the thousands (Koestler, 1967). Of all the possible combinations on any given level, only certain ones are admissible under the rules. The remarkable thing about this is that the only rules taught explicitly are the relatively trivial rules of grammar that most of us

barter-type exchange, and is thus tied to the particularities of that situation. Linguistic symbols, words, or concepts of any kind have a similar function in comparison with some nonlinguistic signs. For example, if another person and I were lying in wait for deer while on a hunting trip, and I were to point in a given direction, my companion would doubtless understand the message as, "Something is coming from that direction." That particular nonlinguistic sign, however, would be tied very closely to that particular situation or to situations very much like it. It would have very little meaning if given on the street, in my home, or elsewhere. On the other hand, the linguistic message, "Something is coming" has meaning in almost any context in which the English language is spoken. It renders comparable certain features of all sorts of situations, just as the word *dog* renders comparable (and discriminable) a wide variety of four-legged animals.

There is another extremely important parallel between the several cases under consideration here. Consider money first. By far its most important property, from the point of view of those who possess it, is its capacity to serve as a highly generalized resource. It is tied in advance to no specific use and hence can be used in the pursuit of a great variety of specific goals. Exactly the same thing may be said with respect to the symbolic representations of the world that we speak of as "knowledge." It too is a highly generalized resource capable of facilitating the attainment of a wide variety of goals. In that sense it enhances the adaptive capacity of those who possess it.

CONCEPTIONS AND THE REORGANIZATION OF EXPERIENCE

These considerations, particularly the monetary analogy, suggest a further interesting parallel. The only situation in which there is a need for a monetary medium is that in which economically valuable resources have become emancipated from ascriptive ties, and, hence, available for exchange. As long as property rights are transferable only through inheritance, and labor is allocated through hereditary succession, there is no need for money. Presumably, emancipation is a condition of the development of a monetary system. The parallel in the conceptual area would seem to be the necessity for our experience of objects to become emancipated from the objects that are the postulated sources of them. That is, the development of concepts that make wide varieties of objects and situations comparable requires the abandonment of the naïve outlook of primitive realism. Early men doubtlessly knew that the metal called lead was gray and heavy, but it never occurred to them that what they experienced directly was grayness, heaviness, solidity, and so on, and that the material object "lead" was a "construction," an inference, based on those experiences (Dingle, 1952). Failing in that, they could neither take their elementary experiences and reassemble them in more useful ways, nor abstract grayness and heaviness from the objects with which they were (in their view) associated. The modern, pratical realist has no difficulty abstracting properties from objects, but there he stops, because properties have to be properties of some object. This leads to the sort of problem that arises when we tend to think of social-system theory as a way of viewing organizations such as the school rather than as an entirely different conceptual organization of experience that does not speak directly to the organization of common sense at all. To put the matter more concretely, since all properties must be properties of objects, we try to attribute to organizations the properties of social systems.[3]

The considerations touched on previously concerning the conceptual organization of experience, or perception, suggests still another contribution of analytical conceptions. The issue is far too complex to undertake an analysis here, but there are firm grounds for asserting that our elementary experiences consist not of the objects of common sense, e.g., trees, houses, other persons, dogs, automobiles, and so on, but of shapes, colors, sounds, and textures. The objects of common sense are *inferred* objects, objects whose existence is postulated on the basis of elementary experiences. Their existence is so well verified by experience that they tend to be regarded as the primary observational data. We tend to say, "See that tree? It is red, yellow, and gold." The more accurate (although terribly cumbersome) way to put it is to say, "I perceive a red, yellow, and gold shape that, given my previous experience and my knowledge of the laws of perspective, I take as evidence of existence of the three-dimensional object known as a tree." Considerations such as these lead Northrop to say:

> meaningful knowledge of a personal self, which is, in some sense, the same person today that it was yesterday, and of external objects in public space and time, is not given by direct introspection or observation radically empirically through the "inner or outer" senses and can be known only by means of indirectly confirmed theory. (Northrop, 1962, p. 174)

As Hanson (1965) points out, seeing is a theory-laden undertaking. Perception is conceptually organized and our knowledge of the external world, however well confirmed, is theoretical knowledge. The difference between houses and electrons in terms of ontological status is only a matter of the degree of directness of confirmation.

When it is recognized that what we know directly are visual, auditory, tactile, and other sensory experiences, and that our observations of common sense and entities with definable properties is conceptually organized elementary experience, then it is clear, as Charters notes, "Each set of concepts serves . . . in effect, as a pair of spectacles bringing into focus a few selected aspects of his world which he would not have

---

3 As numerous commentators have noted, this realistic bias is a feature of English as well as other languages, built in by its subject-predicate construction.

singled out for attention otherwise" (1960, p. 179). Each satisfactorily supported conception provides the means and the opportunity to organize one's experience in a different way. Thus, to clarify an ambiguous statement made previously, social-system theory is not a way of viewing organizations. Rather it is a way of reorganizing experience that is an alternative to the habitual way that leads us to speak of organizations.

One final point must be made before concluding this discussion. That is, the higher the level of abstraction, the greater is the amount of information that is left out of the account. In the example of my own participation in faculty deliberations concerning promotions, saying that what we were doing was "ranking persons according to . . ." obviously leaves a great many things unsaid. It might also have been said that some participants were expressing loyalty to their department, some were trying to please their friends, and some were putting an upstart in his place. What this implies, however, is not that they were "really" doing one thing and not the other, but that any given elementary experience can be seen from within a variety of conceptual systems, the faculty as a system, his department as a system, the relation between himself and a colleague as a system, his personality as a system, and so on.

Conclusion

The conclusion reached on the basis of these deliberations can be stated relatively succinctly in terms of the immediately preceding discussion as follows: Although the product of the social-behavioral sciences is insufficiently explicit and detailed to contribute to the adaptive capacity of practitioners in various fields in a manner comparable to the products of the physical and biological sciences, that lack of detail does not deprive it of relevance. One may say with a reasonable degree of conviction that there are social-behavioral science conceptions that are sufficiently supported by empirical evidence to contribute to the practice of educational administration in at least the following ways: (1) Enabling practitioners to raise questions they would not have otherwise raised; (2) Enabling practitioners to take note of the obvious, to acquire an awareness of the givens of their world, and to subject them to critical examination; (3) Enabling practitioners to "see" the pattern of their world as one of a variety of possible patterns, to conceive of alternative patterns; (4) Enabling the practitioner to more adequately analyze the situations in which he acts, to know what's going on here, what are we doing here and, through a rational consideration of alternatives, to better adapt his action to the objective requirements of the situation, and; (5) Providing alternative ways of organizing his experience of the world.

In the final analysis, social-behavioral science conceptions contribute to the two generic aspects of the thought process indentified by William James, namely sagacity and learning.

Sagacity is the ability to categorize, to see in the concrete particular situation an exemplification of some abstractable characteristics, some universal, learning is the capacity, derived from past experience and education, to link the universal thus discerned with other universals, to the end that the particular be characterized in some non-obvious way that is useful for the purposes at hand. (Hawkins, 1964, p. 97)

REFERENCES

CHARTERS, W. W., JR. "Improving Administrative Theory and Practice: Three Essential Roles." In Roald F. Campbell and James M. Lipham (eds.), *Administrative Theory As a Guide to Action*. Chicago: Midwest Administration Center, University of Chicago, 1960.

DINGLE, HERBERT. *The Scientific Adventure*. London: Sir Isaac Pittman & Sons, 1952.

GETZELS, JACOB W. "Paradigm and Practice: On the Contributions of Research to Educational Practice." *Educational Researcher,* No. 5 (1969).

———"Theory and Practice: An Old Question Revisited." In Roald F. Campbell and James M. Lipham (eds.), *Administrative Theory As a Guide to Action*. Chicago: Midwest Administration Center, University of Chicago, 1960.

GROSS, NEAL. "The Use and Abuse of Sociological Inquiry in Training Programs for Educational Administrators." In L. W. Downey and F. Enns (eds.), *The Social Sciences and Educational Administration*. Edmonton: Division of Educational Administration, University of Alberta, 1963.

HALPIN, ANDREW W. "The Development of Theory in Educational Administration." In Andrew W. Halpin (ed.), *Administrative Theory in Education*. Chicago: Midwest Administration Center, University of Chicago, 1958.

HANSON, NORWOOD RUSSELL. *Patterns of Discovery*. Cambridge: Cambridge University Press, 1965.

HAWKINS, DAVID. *The Language of Nature: An Essay in the Philosophy of Science*. San Francisco: W. H. Freeman and Co., Publishers 1964.

HILLS, R. J. "Theory, Research, and Practice: Three Legs of Administrative Science." *The School Review,* 71, 4 (Winter 1963), pp. 478–492.

KOESTLER, ARTHUR. *The Ghost in the Machine*. New York: Basic Books, Inc., 1967.

NORTHROP, F. S. C. *The Logic of the Sciences and the Humanities*. New York: Meridian Books, Inc., 1959.

PARSONS, TALCOTT. "Evolutionary Universals in Society." *American Sociological Review* vol. 29 (June 1964).

———"Durkheim's Contribution to the Theory of Integration of Social Systems." In Kurt H. Wolff (ed.), *Emile Durkheim, 1858–1917: A Collection of Essays*. Columbus, Ohio: Ohio State University Press, 1959.

———"Culture and the Social System." In Talcott Parsons, et al. (eds.), *Theories of Society Vol. II*. New York: The Free Press, 1961, pp. 963–993.

19

COMMENTARY

WITH *"bite and wit and, occasionally, a little literate frustration,"* Donald
Willower of the Pennsylvania State University emphasized to his colleagues in
the University Council for Educational Administration in his presidential ad-
dress that professors of educational administration are again in need of some
serious purpose-definition activity.

Willower discusses a variety of issues within that charge; the constraints
within universities themselves as well as the patterns of client-orientation that
frequently compound them; the importance of generalizable experience, and
the crucial value of critical analysis of educational organizations; that too much
of what has happened has either been "ornamental" or similarly trivial. He
cites some examples and raises the question that perhaps we have too often
presumed that administrators are only interested in "how" questions rather
than "why" questions, and he points out the error of this. He concludes with
a plea for a greater commitment of effort toward substantive ideas.

EDUCATIONAL ADMINISTRATION AND THE USES OF KNOWLEDGE

DONALD J. WILLOWER

Great Expectations and Modest Explanations

MORE than fifteen years have passed since the academic study of
educational administration turned toward the social sciences and
eventually embraced at least some of their conceptual frameworks and
methods. This shift was dubbed the theory movement and had some
features of a movement such as a mission, adherents committed to its
virtues, and some antagonists who saw it as alien, if not sinister.

Clearly, it was neither salvation nor catastrophe. In a fundamental
sense, it was more maturation than movement. It meant that what was
passed on in educational administration increasingly would be based on
explanations rather than personal experiences, on theories and hypotheses
and the inquiries they generated rather than on nostrums whether in-
spirational, informational, or inane. In short, educational administration

This article is adapted from Willower's Presidential address at the annual meeting
of the University Council for Educational Administration, Atlantic City, N.J.,
February, 1974. Used with permission.

emerged from its alchemical age into a more scientific one, albeit a scientific infancy.

We lost our prophets and gained a cadre of serious, often rather specialized scholars. On the whole, this was healthy, if somewhat hard on heroes. After all, the wisdom of prophets requires a measure of faith but unwise scholars suffer a public unwisdom.

However, the urgency of the problems besetting educational institutions, a quickened sense of change blended with hope, and perhaps a suppressed nostalgia for oracles led many to expect too much of theoretically oriented work. The use of social science versions of scholarship in educational administration yielded a variety of theoretical approaches, each with a different focus, each selecting and confronting phenomena in its own terms. Theories were not competitive in the sense that rival predictions were rare. Empirical results were ordinarily very tentative, sometimes hard to interpret, and never final. In manner and style, a tough-minded skepticism was featured that challenged the comfortable convictions of many professors and practitioners alike.

Thus, we got what science commonly confers: some conceptual frameworks that varied in scope and coherence but were at least directed toward explanation, some tentative conclusions that denied the quest for certainty and remained open to correction and revision, and a greater incidence, if not a wide acceptance, of a probing, critical stance devoted to the question, "why?"

Although the field has profited markedly from its initiation into the ways of inquiry, much remains and will remain to be done. A decade or so of effort signals a beginning, not an ending. We should keep alive and strong our visions of as yet uninvented theories and investigations that might add to, or even transform, our knowledge about educational organizations.

During a time when a variety of constraints threaten to constrict and curtail inquiry, it behooves us to contrive counteracting strategies. Here, I wish to make a specific proposal that could be accomplished through a UCEA task force or other appropriate mechanism. A number of research areas should be selected for their significance to educational administration. Then, instruments should be constructed that tap salient aspects of each area. In effect, each instrument would furnish an operational definition for a relevant concept. Careful attention should be given to the technical adequacy of each measure. Finally, these devices should be made available in a coordinated manner for dissertation and other studies conducted through university departments of educational administration.

This course of action is designed to foster programmatic and cumulative investigations on key questions. The prognosis for success is good because of departmental and especially graduate student needs for significant research topics. Past experiences with measures such as those on organizational climate and pupil control orientations demonstrate the potential fruitfulness of the approach. Further, the cost-benefit relationship is favorable.

In proposing the foregoing, I do not intend to imply that investigations that utilize paper and pencil instruments are better than other forms of scholarship. I feel otherwise, and previously have extolled the virtues of field studies done in an anthropological vein. Nevertheless, the plan suggested could add to the vitality and focus of inquiry in educational administration at a time when the dark shadow of decline clouds the future.

Here, I wish to comment on another aspect of the domain of inquiry, synthesis. We all recognize how much talk and what little activity has marked this area. Perhaps an effort should be marshaled simply to clarify what synthesis involves and requires, a complex undertaking in itself. Perhaps this arena properly is the province of the lonely scholar, a type whose obituary has been written prematurely by certain grantsmen and others of a collectivist bent. In any case, whatever the procedures employed, it seems desirable to re-examine and resurrect synthesis.

Crowns of Glory and of Thorns

Although knowledge getting is essential to understanding, and scholarship is a primary aim of the university, educational administration is one of those fields crowned with a concern for the application of its results to that slice of human activity that is its fit topic, life in educational organizations. However, given the inherent pitfalls and tangled webs of complication that mark the effort to integrate theory and practice and use knowledge well, educational administration's crowning glory is also its crown of thorns.

To use knowledge in the service of man is an old ideal that, happily, like old soldiers, never dies. Nor has it faded away, although a history of turbulence, conflict, and unrealized hopes has dampened pretention and eroded confidence. Plato and Aristotle in different ways sought the improvement of mankind's lot through rational means, as did John Dewey centuries later. Social scientists have been haunted by the question, "knowledge for what?" Distinguished school administrators, of whom W. T. Harris is a sterling early example and Marcus Foster a recent martyr, have sought to gain noble ends through knowledge about educational organization and administration.

But the past teaches that the attempt to use knowledge to improve social institutions, including educational ones, will take its toll of fallen banners and bent lances. Rainbows fade and promises wilt. To come to grips with this fundamental reality will do much to temper exaggerated and naïve expectations.

In efforts to abet knowledge utilization, it should be understood by all that neither perfection nor even its faint shadow is likely to be achieved. Cosmetics should be set aside and the lists entered with all warts showing.

Yet, once put in the perspective afforded by a grasp of limitations, inquiry has the potential to make signal contributions to practice. Moreover, the alternatives to inquiry as a foundation for practice such as intuition, faith, lore, and authority, are grim as well as false.

There already exists a substantial amount of knowledge about school organizations, although often not in a readily applicable form, a point I had in mind in suggesting the resurrection of synthesis. We know something about schools as social systems, their character and modes of coping with uncertainty, and the consequences these have for educational change. Obviously, we need to know much more and the opportunities for research as part of the theme of knowledge utilization are legion.

In reality, the boundaries between theory, research, development, and use are hazy. These activities are interwoven, as experience in some research and development centers, educational laboratories, and other settings shows. More than once, programs devoted to instructional improvement have been prematurely launched and it has been necessary to seek knowledge about knowledge utilization itself in order to salvage what remained.

Although investigations of schools as organizations and social systems arch over most of the areas related to the application of knowledge to educational practice, it is possible to study a host of specific topics. To cite one pedestrian example, in-service education could be examined to discover why it sometimes works and often doesn't, and to determine what values, norms, and attitudes impinge upon that activity.

All this may sound as if emphasis is being placed upon cognitive operations. It is. After all, an understanding of affective domains is gained by cognitive methods. Explaining something is not the same as experiencing it, and raw experience lacks the special meaning that conceptually informed experience confers. In any case, the interrelations of knowledge and its uses forewarn that emphasis on knowledge utilization should not signal an attenuation of inquiry. Moreover, theory and research on knowledge utilization itself is clearly appropriate territory for students of educational administration.

Constraints and Conscience

In mounting efforts to use knowledge to improve schools, it is well to take into account the current constraints faced by universities. Reduced budgets and ebbing federal support for research, along with a growing disenchantment with institutions of higher education, are creating a climate of crisis.

Universities, like other organizations, seek stability through adaptation.

But adaptation is essentially reactive and crisis may erode conscience and confound deliberative and purposive action. The siren songs become more difficult to resist. Fads are followed and dubious programs are undertaken in the pursuit of security.

Let me be more specific. Because the notion of competencies has been rediscovered and widely advocated, should universities devote major energies to furthering this doctrine that lacks both theory and wit and is seemingly destined to reproduce those undistinguished laundry lists of "shall be able tos" popular in a less thoughtful time in education? The idea of competency is attractive and there appear to be no spokesmen for incompetency. Yet the past portends a maelstrom of effort that will remain essentially unfocused and unfruitful. I recently saw an inventory of 403 teacher competencies developed as part of a large project. Some of them were genuinely entertaining, even richly humorous, and since the catalog included only competencies general to all teachers and was billed as incomplete, the promise of additional comic interludes waits in the wings. But enough of this potentially endless topic.

Because organizations other than universities and some pseudouniversities advance courses of preparation designed to cater to clients by eliminating worthy as well as merely difficult program features, should universities do the same?

Should not a major aim of university departments of educational administration be the critical examination of educational organization? If these departments commit themselves only to their immediate clients, present and potential administrators, how well will the larger end of disinterested analysis that ultimately abets the public school's own student clients be served?

Inquiry enjoys a cardinal place in the traditional university. There, departments are pressed to cultivate scholarship geared to opening new vistas in their subjects. Unconventional and sometimes unpopular questions can be asked. Such functions are not likely to be performed adequately if adaptation spawns its special brands of fashion and orthodoxy. Nor will they be performed by agencies calling themselves universities but chiefly devoted to profit and the furnishing of advanced credentials or degrees to those willing to pay the price. Although such agencies may be entrepreneurial successes, they will add little or nothing to the storehouse of knowledge.

In spite of the minatory environment facing higher education, I believe that conscience can coexist with constraints. In the long run, we will better serve education and ourselves if we plan rather than pander. Current pressures must be mediated by plans joined to purposes. Otherwise, chameleon-like units will be buffeted by variable winds as the fashions of the moment become discards and today's treasures become tomorrow's junk. Furthermore, the communication of purposes and the means designed to achieve them can have consequences that contribute to adaptation. And gaining stability in this manner is likely to refresh rather than subvert organizational goals.

Although I advocate that kind of response on the part of university departments of educational administration, it would be unfair to condemn in moralistic tones those organizations that exhibit the expedient modes in turbulent circumstances predicted by organization theory. The boundaries that separate responsiveness from prostitution, rationality from rationalization, and flexibility from lack of commitment are sometimes foggy, and tolerance, though not assent, is appropriate.

Quixotic Journeys, Exportable Inventions, and High Horizons

Whatever activities are undertaken to advance knowledge utilization, the generalizable experience or exportable invention should be sought. Although concern with the unique elements of particular situations presents pressures in the opposite direction, those aspects of development or installation endeavors that enhance understanding and furnish lessons for others should be emphasized. In pursuit of the generalizable experience, an integral part of plans for knowledge use should be procedures designed to probe the consequences of intervention and discover why varying degrees of success or failure result. This is easy to say but it has not often been done and it is hard to do well.

Our heritage is mixed, but a recognizable model from the not far distant past is the itinerant preacher. This wandering wizard works first with one school faculty, then another, and yet another. His stock in trade is the sermon that inspires, and although an occasional dramatic conversion occurs, these are quixotic journeys, sometimes traveled with panaceas, but ordinarily ending with the windmills intact.

Generally, our thinking in educational administration has been too person oriented. By this I do not mean that we should not place a high value on individuality, diversity, and uniqueness. We should. Rather, I mean that commonly used analytic categories tend to stress person-type concepts and slight system concepts.

Ubiquitous organizational development approaches of a clinical type that are steeped in gamesmanship that glories in the expression of personal guilt and hostility, and deny the dignity of silence and privacy seem to equate organizational development with individual expurgation. Our longstanding love affair with leadership is a less oppressive focus but it has directed attention away from social and organizational elements toward personal qualities. Charisma is celebrated in more extreme versions of this outlook. Yet, one of the most charismatic leaders of our times was Adolph Hitler.

In education, the field of supervision has foundered because it treats instructional improvement on the basis of a one-to-one teacher-supervisor relationship. In educational administration, efforts to deal with account-ability will falter until accountability is defined in terms of the specifi-cation of organizational and social structures designed to unify means and ends. It is spurious to address student achievement, or even teach-ing, without a prior review of the extent to which structures prevail that are congruous with desired outcomes.

The point of all this is not that frameworks that stress the individual and commonly exhibit a psychological orientation are full of error. They are not. To the contrary, they often furnish important insights. But such modes have dominated the thinking of many educators, a state of affairs reinforced by the tangibility of the person as an object of analysis as contrasted with the misty, abstruse quality of system concepts.

Yet, the most basic problems that arise in connection with knowledge utilization may be those that stem from the social and organizational character of educational institutions.[1] A few university adaptations al-ready have been highlighted. Public schools display a myriad of norma-tive and other regulatory structures that promote internal predictability, as well as a host of adaptive mechanisms that reduce external un-certainties.

Given the defensive postures assumed and pressures for ornamental rather than substantive knowledge utilization, it is important to design programs that address system features and avoid trivial thrusts. Examples of trivial thrusts are activities such as sensitivity training for principals, internships that produce carbon copies of existing administrative styles, and others based on the assumption that the key to organizational change is individuals of good will or certain experience.

Illustrations of system-oriented approaches are efforts to mute organi-zational characteristics such as stimulus overload by routinizing planning opportunities for teachers; rearrangements and regroupings of organiza-tional positions better to serve ends; alignments of role expectations and organizational purposes and gearing of reward and status systems to purposes; interventions intended to reshape teacher norms; the develop-ment of structures that protect the organization and its personnel but have positive consequences for students; confrontation of the problem of variety reduction by searching for ways in which schools can maintain orderly but humane environments that foster individuality; and the scraping of manipulative public relations in favor of organizational de-fenses based on the articulation of the rationality of school programs, or means, in the light of what is desired and sought, or ends. Any one of these could be the basis for a potentially fruitful and instructive knowl-edge use project.

---

[1] This idea and others related to it are developed in "Schools, Values and Educational Inquiry," *Educational Administration Quarterly,* **9** (Spring 1973); and "Educational Change and Functional Equivalents," *Education and Urban Society* **2** (August 1970) and in sources cited therein.

vice-president in charge of good-bundles. He writes the proposals for new projects; he commutes to Washington; he gets "the long green." But he seldom is the man who operates the project and who is responsible for its success. No, he delegates this task. He hires a director, and the director hires a staff.

The proposal itself does have at least a therapeutic value for those men and women who are charged with the responsibility for making the program work. When their spirits flag, when they see that they are not getting results, that in many respects they really do not know what they are doing, they can always read the retoric of the proposal again, and again, until they convince themselves that they are, indeed, doing what the rhetoric says they are doing, and that they are accomplishing what the rhetoric has told them that they would accomplish. These members of the project staff find themselves in the same position as the man who has bought his new Concubine Eight; he seeks his reassurance therapy from the rhetoric of the ads; the members of the project staff seek their reassurance therapy from the rhetoric of the very project proposal that gave birth to their jobs.

Once a program has been funded, the personnel who operate the program immediately acquire a strong vested interest in the perpetuation of the program. Their jobs are at stake. No matter how stupid or pointless the program may be, once a man accepts a job with it, he must proceed to bolster and defend his own personal decision; so he uses rhetoric to tell himself that his decision was, indeed, a wise decision. As he becomes aware of the fact that he has made a stupid decision and that he has joined a stupid organization, the more then must he spin out even more fanciful rhetoric about the success of the program and about the changes that he and the program are so successfully inducing. If he cannot become, in fact, an agent of change, he at least can become an *agent of the rhetoric of change.* He can always attend the various professional meetings where other "agents of the rhetoric of change" foregather to wallow in a common pool of rhetoric, and to inspire each other to return with fresh dedication to their respective projects and to give it one more try. At these meetings, the agents sometimes play musical chairs, and go back to a different project. An agent rarely finds a new project too strange or too uncomfortable; the rhetoric is the same. By substituting a few words or by juggling a few paragraphs, the annual report for one project can often make out as the annual report for another.

The Planner starts with certain convictions, and he must illegitimatize any new or alien information that in any way threatens his convictions. How, therefore, can one expect him to listen to any critic who dares to suggest that many social difficulties at the individual level of behavior can be "explained" with equal plausibility by reversing the line from *West Side Story* to read, "I'm deprived because I'm depraved."

Let me return now to my earlier comments about certain changes in our perception of human behavior that have taken place between the twenties and the sixties. Please note that during this period the behavior of human beings themselves has not changed; the individual has the same kind of nervous system, responds in similar ways to his environment, and learns or does not learn even as he has always learned or has not learned. No, it is not the individual who has changed. What has changed is the way in which we have *chosen* to explain human behavior.

The changes in our "explanation" are not a simple and direct function of changes that have been brought about by new knowledge about human behavior. Actually, insofar as scientific knowledge is concerned, perhaps the area within which the most dramatic advances have taken place in the past decade is the field of genetics. Research on DNA and RNA tends to show that the inexorability of genetic transmission is not *less* coercive than we previously had thought it to be, but rather that it is *more* coercive.

Facts themselves have little to do with current social action. The critical point is that the particular form of new knowledge or the specific form of any new interpretation of knowledge that is accepted and extolled at a given point in time is determined in large measure by the political, the social, and the religious testaments of faith that prevail in the society at that point in time. And in every instance such a testament is an act of rhetoric on the part of a speaker, or a writer—an attempt to persuade others, yes—but also an effort to persuade himself. Yet, what we must always remember is that the rhetoric about change may or may not have anything whatsoever to do with what does take place at the level of individual behavior or at the level of change within the social-political sphere.

In essence, our rhetoric is built upon what we *will to believe*, what we *must* believe because to accept the alternative that a given situation confronts us with may be more than we, as humans, can bear to live with. Thus, in view of the terrifying social problems that beset our big cities, an emphasis—even an extreme overemphasis—upon the cultural deprivation thesis, gives us the illusion of a small ray of hope, the vision of at least a tiny rainbow somewhere at the end of a dark tunnel. The alternative to acting on this hope is so dismal, so shattering, that few of us can live comfortably with the idea. So, most of us now "believe" in the social action programs that are based upon the cultural deprivation assumption not because the validity of this position is objectively demonstrable but only because of the hope, no matter how small it may be, that is promised by such a course of action. It is this *need to believe* that energizes our rhetoric about the social changes we hope to bring about. The rhetoric has a ritualistic, if not indeed a "religious" function. As always, the greater the doubts that we may harbor—concealed, often even from ourselves—the more eloquent and the more fervent must this rhetoric become.

A rhetoric of change is developed for every new social or intellectual movement. Thus, for example, during this century, we in education have moved from the vocabulary of John Dewey through the vocabulary of Kurt Lewin—and his self-proclaimed disciples who zealously sought to make a religion out of group dynamics—to our current end enthralling vocabulary about "social change." We now have "The Great Society," "Planned Change," "Head Start," "Compensatory Education," and the many other slogans conjured up by cohorts of image-makers.

Change is, indeed, the order of the day. Certainly no honest, God-fearing, true American can be opposed to change. And if change is so good for us, then all of us must get right in there and innovate. What's more, you will be funded for innovating. If you learn the right vocabulary, if you insert into your proposals the right magic words and incant them properly, you, too, can get yourself a goodie-bundle. You, too, can live the Funded Life. Step right up. And once you have stepped onto this escalator, how can you any longer be content with being only a humble and willing worker in the vineyard—teaching students, maybe even helping them learn, or perhaps giving a boy or a girl, through your own compassion, fresh insight into the human condition? Would you want to confess to your own children that you are only a worker in the vineyard while all the other fathers and mothers in your neighborhood have already become "agents of change?" That would be worse than not owning a color TV.

Our current mythology says that we—and for the moment, let's not try to define that "we" too precisely—can manipulate human behavior and social events by means of massive, prefabricated programs of planned social change. The term *planned* assumes that the intended change is in a *desirable* direction. Now, obviously, no social change of any kind can be completely or equally desirable for all the parties concerned. Every time a man makes a choice, he loses something; he probably gains something, too, or else he would not make the choice he does.

No matter how omniscient "The Planner" may presume that he is, his decision about a *desirable* direction for change inevitably fails to take into due account countervailing judgments about what change, if any, should be induced. Knowing this, "The Planner" uses a basic ploy indispensable in the rhetoric of change. He declares that his decision about the desirability of a given direction for change has been achieved through consensus. Consensus? Of whom? Even a third-rate administrator knows how easily he can rig consensus into a group, especially if he extrudes dissenters, composes his own committees, and illegitimatizes critics. But because the announced consensus is at best a testament of faith, and at worst a fraud, each new program of planned change starts out with built in self-limitations—with constraints imposed by resistance and dissent from those very sources that "The Planner," or the innovator, has most vehemently declared to have been already illegitimatized. This, of course, is why there always is, and there always must be, a vibrant tension between permanence and change, between stability and disequilibrium. Accordingly, how can a man expect to understand and respect change and the need for change unless he can also understand and respect stability and the need for stability? Both go together.

Of course, those whom Eric Hoffer describes as "The True Believers" have no pricks of conscience on this score. The True Believers disdain the realities of the past and the present, and dedicate their already despoiled and empty lives to a passionate belief in rhetorical promises about the future, a future conceived somehow as disconnected from both the present and the past. Indeed, the psychological dynamics of The True Believer impel him to deny the present, to wreck it if he can, to wipe it out.

I must digress briefly to speak about rhetoric and human motivation. Rhetoric, according to Webster, is defined as "the art or science of using words effectively in speaking or writing, so as to influence and persuade." This definition includes no object for either of the two verbs in that last sentence. The implicit assumption is that the purpose of rhetoric is to influence or persuade *others*. Yet, most of us forget that the more effective and the far more insidious use of rhetoric is to influence and persuade *ourselves*. And this point has especial relevance for one possible interpretation of human motivation.

From day to day, often from hour to hour, every mature man or woman must make dicisions that affect his life and the lives of his loved ones. No personal decision is made in an abstract vacuum; each decision is made at a specific moment and within a specific concrete situation. *Furthermore, the viable options available to the decider are always fewer than the number of theoretically possible choices available, as these choices may be constructed by an outside observer, or even, indeed, as they may be perceived by a "significant other" within the situation itself.* The decider is, metaphorically, locked into a situation, and his decisions must be made within contraints over which he often has little or no control. Then, the decider, having made his decision—no matter how wisely or unwisely—is compelled to account to himself for why he has decided as he has. What he then says about what he has done, and about why he has done what he has done, is his "explanation" of his "motivation." Over the course of many critical decisions, each of which has been made within a concrete situation, the decider—the man, or the actor—attempts to impute self-consistency to his own behavior. To accomplish this, he draws upon the vocabulary of motives that is in greatest currency within his own culture, or within his own subculture, at a particular stage in time. And from this vocabulary, and with whatever rhetoric the actor may command, he builds an image of himself and of his motives that he can live with—without too much pain, without too much anxiety, and without too much distress.

Please note one critical point. This rhetoric comes into play *after* the decider has made his decision—often only after the very exigencies of the situation have coercively defined and delimited the decision for the actor. Few men have the courage to whimper, "There was nothing else I could do. I was only a puppet within the situation." So, the actor must heal the scars to his ego and must protect himself from confronting the existential reality, the frightful degree of his own helplessness within the random flux of life. He heals his scars and he protects himself through the rhetoric that he *invents* to describe his own motives. Here I have deliberately used the word, *invents,* and I use it in the same sense and for the same purpose as do the existentialists.

So the actor invents the rhetoric of his own motivation or, if you will, he invents a "cover story" that he can live with. One "cover story" combines with another, and with another, until in the due course of time the actor succeeds in inventing "a fabricated life." Now, please note one further critical point. The actor's cover story is useful; it minimizes both cognitive and affective dissonance. But the actor can live with his cover story only under the condition that there are no severe discrepancies between "the cover story" and what is "out there," especially when what is "out there" is defined by the fall of blunt physical, biological, economic, and social events. Each one of us usually gives the other a margin of compassion—a tolerance for moderate defections from "reality" if for no other reason than that we each succor a similar margin of compassion for ourselves. If, of course, the discrepancies between the cover story and what is "out there" become too severe, then the actor has become autistic, and hence in the most brutal and most literal sense, he must be declared as alienated. (Please recall that in an earlier day the man whom we now call a psychiatrist was then called an alienist.)

Let me now paraphrase what I have just said and apply it to the rhetoric of politics, and, if you will, to the rhetoric of change. As human beings we are inclined to give each other a margin of compassion provided that—in respect to the discrepancies between the cover story and what is "out there"—the credibility gap is not too great. Stated another way, a man's "cover story" for his own motivation includes a promise to himself and to others about how he will behave in the future; how he does, indeed, behave then becomes a measure of the extent to which this promise has been fulfilled.

To return specifically to the rhetoric of politics, what most savagely turns the credibility gap into a credibility chasm? Simply, the realization by the public that day by day, and month by month, the discrepancies between the promises of planned social change and the actual fulfillment of these promises have not been diminished, but instead have become even more glaring. And as each promise, in turn, is given the lie, "The Planners" and the image-makers discover themselves again locked into a new situation in which the decisions that they must now make must be made under even more exigent constraints. By this time, The Planners dare not declare that their promises have been empty. So, instead, what do they do? They offer fresh promises and projects new. (Or, perhaps, they just send in more troops.)

My purpose is not to indict The Planners, not to ridicule them, not to scoff at them. For I, too, as a human being, must give to the other a margin of compassion. My task, as a scholar, is not to judge, but only to reflect, and hopefully to try to understand what I see "out there." Now this is where the view that I have cited earlier about the relationship between rhetoric and human motivation again seems helpful. "The Planners," the political men, the men of action, are each men locked into their own respective situations in time and in place. They, too, are men in a box, but in a box that has glass walls. Even more than in the case of the individual man making decisions about his own life, yet necessarily making these decisions under constraint, the heads of state, public officials, administrators of corporations, and of institutional programs, must all make fateful decisions about the lives of others, and furthermore, they must make these decisions under constraints far more pressing and far more frightening than those that lock each of us as individuals into our own personal boxes. Consequently, the public official, the administrator, is impelled to reduce the complexity of the events that confronts him to a sufficient level of simplicity that will allow him to live with the situation, and with his own decisions about the situation, without too much pain, without too much anxiety, without too much guilt. Literally, to protect his own sanity, the administrator must *invent* a rhetoric that will provide him with a "cover story" that he can live with.

Sometimes, of course, the sheer force of events shatters the rhetoric. For example, our Treasury Department in 1966 made a solemn and public announcement that there would be no change in the ceiling price of silver, only a week before the ceiling was suddenly and dramatically lifted, and lifted by the Treasury Department itself. In the fall of 1967, Finland devalued its currency by 31 per cent. Yet, less than four days before the act of devaluation, the Finnish government officials had repeatedly denied rumors of devaluation and the governor of the Central Bank, the very man who later announced the devaluation, had gone on record as a staunch opponent of devaluation. And, in the autumn of 1967, each fresh declaration by Harold Wilson that the pound sterling was sound was followed by a new speculative run on the pound. And in each case the Bank of England and the IMF rushed to the pound's support. But eventually, the discrepancy between the cover story, as fabricated by Wilson, and the actual state of affairs became so great that the English government was left with only one course of action: to devalue the pound. However, when the public announcement about devaluation was made, Wilson stated, "We have decided to devalue the pound sterling." What an understatement! The events themselves, including above all else, the disastrous state of England's balance of payments, had forced the devaluation. Indeed, it was a strong recommendation on the part of treasury officials in Washington combined with concurrent and equally forcible recommendations on the part of the continental bankers that had left Britain with absolutely no choice: sterling had to be devalued. Wilson's announcement and his "explanation" to the British people were, therefore, a case of rhetoric *after the fact*. He had to be allowed this face-saving gesture. He had to be allowed the chance to behave *as if* the decision had been made by the British government, and by himself as prime minister. But this was merely a case of window-dressing; the events themselves had already made the decision.

Wilson's behavior during the crisis of devaluation illustrates a point that applies in many other situations within the political milieu. Until the very moment of truth when the force of events shatters the facade of the rhetoric, the administrator, the public official, the man of action, must cling with increasing desperation to the rhetoric that he has invented to protect his own sanity from the slings and arrows of outrageous randomness.

The discrepancies between the promise and the fulfillment pervade our entire society. We read a menu that tells us about crispy, crunchy delicacies while the counterman slops onto our plate a joint of stringy chicken that has been cooked in Southern-fried grease. The TV commercial praises the virtue of Plummet Airlines, "You won't go out with a whimper . . ." Plummet promises us punctual schedules, tasty meals, and service, service, service. But whenever I travel by Plummet, I wait for overdue flights, endure cabins that are overcrowded and underventilated, and find that even the stewardesses have given up to phony effulgence that they have been taught at "smile school."

The men who write the menus are not the men who operate the restaurants. The men who devise Plummet's commercials are not the men who operate the airlines. The men in our schools and our universities who write proposals in request of goodie-bundles are not the men who actually operate the projects. Indeed, the sponsors and the applicants play a delightful game of rhetoric with each other, and any relationship between the rhetoric and what actually goes on in the schools is entirely coincidental. Even as the TV commercials for each new product become increasingly absurd, and as the script-writers search desperately for a gimmick with a new shock-value, so too, in the game of grantsmanship, must each new proposal become increasingly ecstatic about its promise. The writers of the proposals search desperately for "innovations" that will have *impact*. Whether a proposed "innovation" can, or cannot, be made to work is irrelevant; all that counts is whether the proposed action can be made to look *as if* it were working.

Several years ago I knew a handsome young man who, as a sales representative for a publisher, traveled on a liberal expense account and enjoyed a good income. He looked as if he had just stepped out of the pages of *Playboy,* the very image of the successful young executive. I know that girls found him attractive and that he played the field. One night when he was visiting me, he told me that he was thinking seriously about getting married. He described the girl's many charms and then said, "I'm sure that she isn't a virgin, but that's all right; she looks like one." How beautifully his remark epitomizes an attitude widely prevalent in society today: that appearance is of greater importance than actuality. Thus, the sales manager instructs his men, "Above everything else, BE SINCERE—even if you're not!"

As I listen to the noisy rhetoric about planned social change, I find myself continuously surprised that no one ever raises a question, or even a doubt, about the authenticity and the integrity of any program of social reform, or of any "revolution" that is so loudly and brazenly accompanied by the merry jingle of the cash register. Nor are we even affronted by references to The Education Industry, or worse yet, by references to "The Knowledge Industry." The staggering fact is that we as educators— and also as human beings—have become so inured to nonsense that we now take all of this rhetoric in stride. We have lost a sense of outrage, and we have allowed ourselves to be "taken on a trip" by our own rhetoric.

Consider, for example, only one among the many, differentiations that we need to recognize in the vocabulary we used. We speak of "change" and of "innovation." Both words are saturated with value-judgment and with emotion, because our culture venerates "change' 'and regards stability with contempt. Out of the Kurt Lewin school came the expression "agent of change"—or "change-agent." I suspect that this expression is nothing more than a title that it attached to an ambiguous professional role in a vain effort to dignify, in respect to social status, whatever the incumbent of that role may do. But as I have noted earlier, the man who pretends to function as an agent of change, oftentimes is merely an "agent of the rhetoric of change." His function is to use words to convince himself and to convince others that certain specific changes should take place, and furthermore, that because of his efforts or those of his colleagues, these changes are, indeed, being effected.

Within recent years, I have seen yet another professional role emerging. Change itself has become a substantive area for inquiry; a body of literature is being built up that deals with new and different ways of perceiving the nature of change, and of new ways for identifying those conditions under which planned change takes place. Accordingly, we now have on the scene some men and women whom I can describe best as "agents of the rhetoric of change in respect to change itself." I know that such an expression is silly, but I also know that the phenomenon described by this expression is really "out there." And this phenomenon disturbs me because it is so disgustingly narcissistic. As you will recall,

Narcissus was so in love with himself that, infatuated by the face that he saw in the mirror of the lake, he fell in and drowned himself. I suspect that those educators and politicians who insist upon making such a "thing" about change may be doomed to a fate similar to that which befell Narcissus. They may drown themselves in their own rhetoric.

I find myself nagged by one other bleak suspicion. I have a hunch, whether we are dealing with an individual facing complex personal problems or with a nation facing complex social problems, that as the individual (or the nation) becomes, in fact, increasingly impotent in his capacity to actually deal with the problems—because of inexorable juggernaut qualities that inhere in the problems themselves—the individual (or the nation) becomes increasingly reckless and flamboyant in his declarations of what he intends to do, and what he, by God, *will* do. In short, the eloquence of his rhetoric is generated not from strength, but instead, from fear, from weakness, and from the dull, terrifying recognition of his own impotence in the face of a world in which the sheer randomness of events—social, physical, technological—is accelerating at an exponential rate.

Please understand: I am not fighting against change. I know that in the early nineteenth century, when the Luddites wrecked spinning jennies, they fought a hopeless battle. The textile industry flourished for more than another hundred years until it was later brought almost to its knees, not by the successful action of a new set of Luddites, but instead, by the technolocgial discovery of how man could produce synthetic fabrics. Nor can we today wreck the computers and stop them from wiping out thousands of jobs.

Technological change has acquired a staggering momentum all its own. And this momentum mocks the folly of any Planner who gets in its way. And demographic and physiographic changes also introduce consequences in social behavior, and even in individual psychological behavior —consequences with a momentum and an inevitability all their own. Moreover, great ideas and the men who create them, introduce widespread social change. For example, consider Galileo, Charles Darwin, Karl Marx, Sigmund Freud, Jean-Paul Sartre, and Erich Fromm. Each man in turn spoke or wrote, and once he had spoken, whether his ideas were accepted or rejected, the social scene was no longer the same as it had been before he had spoken. In brief, ideas have consequences, and the social consequences of great ideas are seldom clearly predictable. Furthermore, in each instance the author lets his ideas go free from the cage of his own mind, free to fly like birds wither they will. To say this in another way, the creator of a great idea it motivated by intellectual curiosity, not by an intention to control or manipulate human behavior within the social and political sphere. Thus, the impact of technological change, of demographic and physiographic changes, and of the changes stimulated by great ideas is such that the social consequences are let free to develop as they may. No intention in respect to what will ensue enters the picture.

In the case of planned social change, the situation is just the opposite. The planning originates with a declared intention of objectives, it starts with the purpose of altering the free play of those social consequences that have ensued from the three sources that I have just mentioned. And these intentions, for the most part, are determined by *political* factors.

To repeat: I am not fighting against change. I knew that I, too, cannot turn back the shadow of the sundial. But I do feel it necessary to distinguish between the nature of the social changes that happen in consequence of technological discovery, of demographic and physiographic changes, and of great ideas, in contrast to the nature of the social changes that take place as the result of intentional political action. Let us call the one "free change" and the other "planned change." Today the idea of planned social change is part of the *Zeitgeist*. We incant the mythic claims of change almost as if we were reciting a litany.

Here I must state a highly personal bias. I am not convinced that the mythology that we have constructed about the advantages, the feasibility, and the desirability of planned social change is anything more than that—a mythology, a belief-system designed to protect us from the terrifying recognition of our own impotence in the face of "free change" and also—and perhaps more important—in the face of the increased randomness in our world that results as a further consequence of "free change." It is extremely difficult for any human being to live with the amount of randomness that is present in the world today. Consequently, it is no accident that The Planners devise a mythology and a rhetoric that will provide them with an illusion of potency and control in the face of this randomness. I think that it is for this reason that, politically, we presume to believe that we can do much, much more than we can, in fact, do, alter the consequences of free change. And here again I am back to a point I made earlier: In many personal and social situations, we believe because we *must* believe; the alternative to this *will to believe* is too shattering for must human beings to bear.

I know of no one who has analyzed the situation I describe here more brilliantly than Jacques Ellul, Professor of History and Contemporary Sociology at the University of Bordeaux, in France. I enthusiastically recommend two of his books that are both great and exciting: *The Technological Society*, first published in English, by Knopf, in 1964, and *The Political Illusion*, first published in English, by Knopf, in 1966.

No, I am not fighting against change. There is not much that I can do. But I can call attention to the pretentiousness, and perhaps even to the arrogance, of the many men who presume to plan and organize social change. I can suggest that we all should attempt to be less gullible in accepting at face value the rhetoric of the change-makers. I have already discussed the relationship between rhetoric and human motivation and, in passing, I have shown how this view of motivation applies especially to the behavior of men who occupy political roles. Perhaps all that I am now seeking to do is to sensitize each of us to the danger of confusing rhetoric with reality. In short, today, perhaps more than ever before in American history, we need less gullibility and much more probing skepticism. This applies to each of us—in his professional role, in his role as a citizen, and above all else, in his role as a human being.

INDEX OF NAMES